An Introduction to Corporate Environmental Management
Striving for Sustainability

Stefan Schaltegger, Roger Burritt and Holger Petersen

Prof. Dr **Stefan Schaltegger** is a full professor of Corporate Environmental Management and director of the Centre for Sustainability Management (CSM) at the University of Lüneburg, Germany. Between 1996 and 1998 he was an assistant professor of economics leading the chair of public economics and policy at the University of Basel, Switzerland, where he became an associate professor for management in 1998. After his PhD in Environmental Management in 1992 he spent one year as a visiting research fellow at the University of Washington, Seattle, USA.

His research areas include environmental accounting and information management, sustainable finance, sustainable entrepreneurship, stakeholder management and the integration of environmental economics and management.

Stefan Schaltegger is member of the editorial board of the international journals *Business Strategy and the Environment* and *Greener Management International*, and of the editorial advisory board of *Corporate Social Responsibility and Environmental Management*, the steering committee of the European Eco-management and Accounting Network (EMAN-EU), the SustainAbility Faculty, London and the board of the RIO Impulse Management Forum, Switzerland.

Stefan Schaltegger has lectured at various universities, including the Universities of Basel and Bern, the Norwegian School of Management BI, Oslo, the University of Jyväskylä Finland, and the HCMC University of Technology, Ho Chi Minh City, Vietnam.

schaltegger@uni-lueneburg.de

Roger L. Burritt, BA (Jt Hons) (Lancaster, UK), M. Phil (Oxford, UK), FCPA (Australia), CA (Australia), CMA (Australia), ACIB (London), is a Reader in the School of Business and Information Management and member of the National Institutes of the Environment, and Economics and Business, at The Australian National University (ANU) in Canberra, Australia, where the environment, management and accounting are his main areas of research and teaching. He is also the International Co-ordinator of the Asia Pacific Centre for Environmental Accountability (APCEA), a networking group for people with an interest in environmental management, environmental accounting, reporting and accountability. APCEA has branches in Argentina, Australia, China, Japan, New Zealand, and South Korea.

Roger has lectured widely throughout the world, is a member of the Environmental Management Accounting Network–Asia Pacific (EMAN-AP) Steering Committee and the Sustainability Experts Reference Group for the ACT Government in Australia.

roger.burritt@anu.edu.au

Holger Petersen has been working at the UmweltBank AG Nürnberg, since January 2003. The UmweltBank AG Nürnberg is a leading environmentally focused financial institution in Germany. Between 1999 and 2002 he worked as a research assistant to Prof. Stefan Schaltegger at the Centre for Sustainability Management at the University of Lüneburg. His PhD was on the subject of ecopreneurship and strategic management. Holger conducted empirical research and wrote case studies on the competitiveness of leading environmental companies with a special focus on SMEs.

Together with Stefan Schaltegger, Holger Petersen has written more than ten German course books on corporate environmental management and co-ordinated the course materials on environmental management for the leading German distance-learning university in Hagen. At the Centre for Sustainability Management (CSM) he was an initiator of the world's first MBA programme on Sustainability Management and Entrepreneurship which is currently under development.

hpetersen@uni-lueneburg.de.

An Introduction to Corporate Environmental Management
Striving for Sustainability

Stefan Schaltegger, Roger Burritt and Holger Petersen

Greenleaf
PUBLISHING
2 0 0 3

Acknowledgements

Stefan Schaltegger would like to express thanks for their support to Cornelia Fermum, Ana González y Fandiño and Anke Schöndube.

Roger Burritt would like to thank his family in Australia, Patricia and Christopher, and Gary Monroe for ongoing encouragement and support.

Published by Greenleaf Publishing Limited
Aizlewood's Mill
Nursery Street
Sheffield S3 8GG
UK

Produced by Bookchase UK Ltd, London
Printed and bound in the EU
L.D.: SE-3355-2005 European Union

British Library Cataloguing in Publication Data:
    Schaltegger, S. (Stefan), 1964–
        An introduction to corporate environmental management :
        striving for sustainability
        1. Industrial management - Environmental aspects   2. Social
        responsibility of business
        I. Title   II. Petersen, Holger   III. Burritt, Roger
        658.4'08

        Hardback: ISBN 1874719667
        Paperback: ISBN 1874719659

Contents

Part 1
Overview

Part 1
Overview

Part 2	Part 3
Success factors and fields of action	**Strategic environmental management**

Part 4
Concepts and tools of corporate environmental management

1

Overview

Purpose, structure and contents of this textbook

This textbook invites you to join in an exploration of the ways in which companies can engage in environmental management. Companies operate in markets through, for example, their customers, suppliers, managers and employees and these actors help determine whether sustainable business practices aimed at reducing environmental impacts can be successful. The following material and text should prepare you for taking the environment into account in your daily business thinking and decisions in a way that will also help you to improve your financial results.

Knowledge gained from this book will present you with the opportunity to change your thinking and the thinking of your business about environmental issues in a productive way. The book presents a way of creating value for your company, for your friends and family and for you. It does this by teaching about a future where business and individuals co-exist in a world that recognises the environmental impacts of human activities. Such recognition leads to an empathy for reducing these impacts to the absolute minimum while coming to understand that market-based businesses, guided by sound governance structures, are a necessary part of an environmentally harmonious world. Study of the book will reveal new values for your business and for you and will present you with a personal challenge, whether or not you are at present concerned about the interaction between business, individuals and the environment. While completing the book, do engage yourself with the material by:

- Examining whether the contents reflect your own professional experience, take your own experience further or oppose your own views

- Noting which of the ideas presented are especially important for you, add to your own ideas or encourage you to react (positively or negatively)

- Answering questions creatively based on your own perspective of the issues

- Encouraging yourself to be inspired by questions, which can be investigated further through other written sources of information on an issue,

through the Internet by using keywords for searching on a topic, in conversations with acquaintances or by considering comments in the media
(television, press, radio, etc.)

● Relating to others who are studying with this book and to the authors if
there are matters that you would like to see added to this book or information about further sources that you consider useful in developing your
knowledge in this area

● Thinking about and planning the ways in which you can use and implement in your own situation what you have learned

The text makes clear what an environmental orientation is, why it is good for
business management to adopt such an orientation and the range of themes within
such an orientation that are examined here. It makes things clear by using a four-
part structure (see the figures on pages 7, 53, 171 and 205).

The first part of this book briefly but clearly sketches the fundamental ideas and
linkages behind business management, the environment and sustainable development. The second part outlines the criteria against which environmentally oriented
business management can be assessed and the fields of action in which success can
be achieved. After this, the third part presents a discussion and examples of
strategies for environmental management, which are linked, in the fourth part, to
important tools of environmental management, especially eco-marketing, environmental accounting and eco-control. Also, the book is illustrated with a range of case
studies and examples related to the main contents of each chapter.

Although you can begin the book at the first chapter and work through until the
end of the final chapter, you may wish to move about the contents of the book in a
flexible way, especially if you want to follow up on a particular topic at the time it is
introduced. The materials are designed to be used for understanding and reference
rather than to be learned by heart. The main aim is for you to obtain a practical
understanding of the relationship between management and environmental issues.
The text is supplemented with numerous figures, references, Internet site addresses
and boxes. Boxes provide examples, definitions or additional information about
issues explained in the main text. Comments about useful literature are also
included, to help if you wish to read further about a particular issue. Several pieces
of literature are recommended as background to this course on environmental
management and a number of useful websites are also listed to help you get a quick
lead in to the subject.

Recommended reading

Schaltegger, S., and R.L. Burritt (2000) *Contemporary Environmental Accounting: Issues, Concepts
and Practice* (Sheffield, UK: Greenleaf Publishing).
Welford, R., and A. Gouldson (1993) *Environmental Management and Business Strategy* (London:
Pitman).

Recommended websites

The Australian National University, Canberra, Australia
anulib.anu.edu.au/elibrary/search.html

BSR (Business for Social Responsibility)
www.bsr.org

Centre for Sustainability Management, University of Lüneburg, Germany
www.uni-lueneburg.de/csm

Environmental Defense
www.scorecard.org

Environmental News Network
enn.com

Greenbiz: The Resource Center on Business, the Environment and the Bottom Line
greenbiz.com

International Organisation for Standardisation
iso14000.net

Natural Resources Defense Council
www.nrdc.org

OneWorld
www.oneworld.net

Pew Center on Global Climate Change
www.pewclimate.org

Pollution Online
pollutiononline.com

Social Investment Forum
socialinvest.org

Sustainable Development Communications Network
sdgateway.net

WorkingForChange
workingforchange.com

Question for review

1.1 What are the four main sections in this book? Why do you think that each section is important for an understanding of environmental management by business?

2

Overview

Management and business companies

There are numerous definitions of 'management' in a business context—but, most of the time, these are not satisfactory, because they define the concept of management with use of words that also need to be explained. This means that a simple understanding of what management involves is not usually conveyed. Typical would be a definition that management involves 'reduction of uncertainty', 'leadership' or 'motivation', without an explanation of these terms being given (see Neuberger 1994: 5). To avoid this problem in defining management, in this book an analytical path is provided to help with your understanding of the meaning of management (see Fig. 2.1).

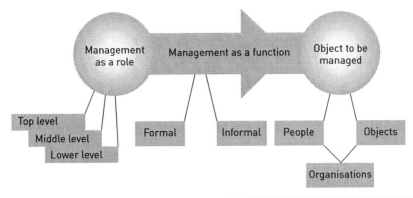

Figure 2.1 Subjects and objects of management

Management presupposes two things: a subject that manages (e.g. a single manager of a small business company) and an 'object' that is to be managed (e.g. the whole business company). 'Management' is often used instead of the word 'manager'. When the word 'management' is used it refers to one of two aspects of the subject that manages. Either it refers to the role of managers—what managers do that is different from what others (e.g. employees) do—or it refers to the function of managers—what the specific activities of managers are.

The **role** of managers is closely related to the powers that are conferred on different levels of management—top-level, middle-level and lower-level management. Even top managers have limited powers and they practise management within the constraints set down for companies by the government within the current political framework. The **function** of managers can be divided into formal and informal aspects. Formal functions are established in contracts and job descriptions (e.g. for a product manager, finance manager or production manager). Informal functions of managers are related to the personal style, influence and charisma of each manager—the way a manager interacts with other people. Distribution of management roles and functions in each company depends on the extent to which each employee is capable of solving problems (see Probst 1993). If an employee has high capabilities and strong personal motivation to work in the interests of the company, then there is less reason for management oversight. The **object** of management can be a person or group of people, including lower-level managers, or objects with which the company is involved (e.g. buildings, machinery, materials, products, services or abstract objects such as company reputation).

Management can relate to many types of organisation such as a business company, a household or a government. In this textbook the focus is on management of a business company—including the formal and informal functions mentioned above. The business company is defined as being a separate legal entity that has, as its main purpose, the creation and distribution of economic wealth. It provides an independent legal basis for transacting in the marketplace and the technical infrastructure for producing and delivering goods and services to consumers. Most business companies involve people and are also, therefore, social entities. As social entities business companies can be viewed as consisting of a network of stakeholders that supply resources to the business and receive services from the business (see Fig. 2.2).

Stakeholders are defined to include every individual, or group, that has a claim on the company (Freeman 1984: 25). Usually, the claim arises through an exchange

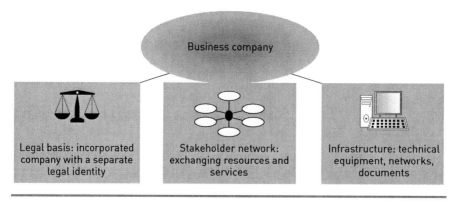

Figure 2.2 **Aspects of the business company**

relationship whereby the stakeholder provides resources, and goods, or services, are received in return. Such exchange most often involves an economic settlement between the parties, but the company is also involved in social exchange and exchange with the physical environment in which it operates. In all cases, stakeholders rely on the company in order to attain their own economic, social or environmental goals. Likewise, in order to achieve its goals and increase its economic wealth the business relies on resources provided by its stakeholders. Interactions between the business and its stakeholders are guided by rules, routines, established procedures, common standards, negotiations, debates and use of power. Each company uses some or all of these mechanisms in different combinations to achieve its purposes. Different combinations of mechanisms distinguish one company from another.

Management, through its interaction with various stakeholders, is responsible for company direction, change and development, for putting in place technical processes and procedures, for securing finance for company investment and operations and for getting people to work with each other towards the company goals—a position of **goal congruency**. Management influence and credibility depends on its ability to balance relationships with each group of stakeholders while focusing attention on specific stakeholder problems as they arise.

Five fundamental ideas are useful for understanding the processes of management. Management implies:

* Dynamics

* Orientation

* Freedom of action

* Power

* Responsibility and accountability

2.1 Dynamics of management and leadership

Management is a dynamic process. The situations that managers face involve constant change. The challenge is for managers to try to ensure that the companies they manage can adapt to changes when these occur. Management determines the direction that companies will take when they need to adapt. Such direction is often summed up with use of the word 'leadership'. In etymological terms, the word 'leader' (conductor) is derived from the word 'lead' (to be in front) and describes the **process** of getting and keeping the company on the right track towards achieving its goals (see Drosdowski 1998). Hence, management is a dynamic process oriented towards adaptation of people (stakeholders) associated with business in order that business, individual and group goals can be achieved. Management leads the business towards its goals and keeps it on course, or 'steers' it towards its goals, as expected and unexpected changes occur. This process is referred to as '**steersmanship**'.

2.2 **Orientation of management**

Management is oriented towards achieving the goals established for the business company. Managers have their own goals, but the main reason for their employment is to achieve the goals of company stakeholders. If a single manager is the owner of a small company, the aims of the manager and the owner will be identical and will determine the business goals. In a large or medium-sized business, owners also maintain a strong claim to establishing the goals of the business, but managers also have to consider satisfying the goals of other stakeholders as well if they are to ensure that the company survives and prospers to benefit all parties. It is a convention that stakeholders may be thought of as being external to the company (e.g. suppliers) or internal to the company (e.g. employees). However, this distinction becomes restrictive and less relevant as, for example, alliances made with suppliers draws them into close co-operation with the business. Similarly, managers themselves can be viewed as internal stakeholders in a business, but where they receive their rewards through shares and options in equity their values and goals become similar to those of shareholders—who are usually classified as external stakeholders. Hence, the distinction between internal and external stakeholders can be less useful than might be thought. One of the formal tasks of managers is to express the general aims of stakeholders in terms of specific goals that can be measured, to establish priorities between these goals and to allocate responsibilities for the achievement of these goals while ensuring that different managers are accountable for actions taken towards the achievement of these goals.

2.3 **Freedom of action for management**

Managers identify and pursue potential opportunities where there is an expectation that this will result in the business achieving the goals that keep stakeholders involved or engaged—for example, where employees are satisfied with their remuneration, customers are satisfied with the prices of products and shareholders are satisfied with their dividends (Emmanuel and Otley 1985: 18; Simon 1947). Managers have close familiarity with business operations and, because of this, they need freedom to take action where they think this will help achieve company goals. With such freedom comes the freedom of managers to innovate in order to meet and beat businesses acting in direct competition. The ability to be creative, or innovative, in the courses of action that managers choose means that they use their **judgement** when selecting potential courses of action and choosing between them.

Management freedom of action is constrained by a range of factors. Economic costs and benefits have to be taken into account, because if they are not then the company may not survive. Legal constraints are also imposed on business; because an incorporated company has a separate legal identity (e.g. a banker may impose a maximum limit on the debts that a company can incur), it must operate in compliance with the law (e.g. it must pay minimum wage rates if these are specified in legislation, and it must not employ child labour if this is not permitted). Finally, management may be granted discretion to take actions that are in the best interests of the business. Given these constraints, within market economies, managers have a wide **scope** for conducting their activity, because they can enter into market transactions on behalf of the company (e.g. to buy and sell the company, parts of the company or the assets of the company, or to hire employees, outsource activities, enter alliances or incur debts).

2.4 Power of management

Management is also concerned with the exercise of power to help achieve the goals that are established for the company. Power is a phenomenon that is based on the relation between two or more stakeholders, or participants in the company. **Power** is defined as the ability to get other participants to change their behaviour so that they act to achieve the goals of the person exercising the power (see Hill 1993; Morgan 1986; Weber 1980). When a manager exercises power it is usually with the intention of getting people to take action that will help achieve the company's goals when they would otherwise be acting against the company's interests. Of course, other stakeholders may also use their power to counter management freedom. This is referred to as 'countervailing power' (Galbraith 1983) or 'negative power'. **Negative power** is used by stakeholders to resist the imposition of power available to other stakeholders (see Crozier and Friedberg 1979). For example, top management has the power to hire or fire employees and can use negative power over employees. Unions have the power to encourage strikes by their members and can use negative power in their negotiations with management. Negative power does not actually have to be used to be effective; the threat of using such power may be sufficient to change behaviour in the desired direction.

Power provides the basis for actions taken in the social network within the business (see Braun and Schreyögg 1989) and is always related to the set of participants involved. Power can be conferred by formal means, through an organisational structure, or can be acquired informally through personal charisma. Power resources include: access to information, availability of informal contacts, recognition as an expert, the ability to provide rewards and incentives and all other ways of forcing dependency on an individual or group (see French and Raven 1959).

2.5 Responsibility and accountability of management

Although managers can exert power and have freedom to choose the actions that they judge to be of benefit to the company, they also have to accept responsibility for their actions and be accountable for the results of actions that they have taken. Management has to ensure that a company meets the needs of different stakeholders. If a company does not satisfy a stakeholder (e.g. if dividends are too low for several years), then the stakeholder will protest and eventually withdraw from the company. As stakeholder interests are sometimes in conflict (e.g. shareholders may prefer larger dividends at the expense of lower wages for employees), managers have to decide how far they can resist the demands of a particular stakeholder before the coalition of interests and the business breaks down. When labour contracts are negotiated, employees, their union representatives and shareholders in the company have their own expectations. These constantly changing expectations are generated by the personal, social, religious, political, economic and cultural backgrounds of the stakeholders. Management has to assess these changing circumstances when negotiating with stakeholders and making choices (e.g. whether pay should rise by a set proportion, or whether dividends should increase when pay has been static for some time).

Managers make such judgements and live by the results of their choices. However, management freedom is constrained. For example, large companies receive close attention from government. Government does not like to see large numbers of employees being made redundant and may criticise managers if they choose to shut down factories that are large employers of labour. Hence, the larger the company becomes the greater is its exposure to government concern and monitoring. Companies that are large and important employers can have a significant impact on the welfare of employees and are thought of as **quasi-public or virtually public institutions** (see Ulrich 1977). Such institutions are closely monitored and their managers are tightly held to account to ensure continuation of the social legitimacy of the business.

Managers **account** for their actions and accept responsibility by regularly gathering and disclosing information about the results of their activities. Top management provides feedback to company members in order to demonstrate the value they add to the business through their management roles and functions. In this way they are held responsible and accountable for actions taken and the impact of those actions on different stakeholders.

2.6 Summary

The potential for conflict between the demands of different stakeholders in a business requires a realistic evaluation of the degrees of freedom that should be given to managers to help them implement the company's political decisions (see Ulrich 1968: 77ff.). Hence, the interaction between the company and its sociopolitical environment is one of the key management fields to be considered. On the one hand, companies aim to secure and expand freedom for their activities (e.g. Schaltegger 1999); on the other hand, companies have to be made to use their degrees of freedom in accordance with acceptable ethical criteria (e.g. Pfriem 1995). From the point of view of the company's management, it is clear that these people have the power and discretion to carry through plans according to their own expectations, irrespective of the wishes of any particular stakeholder group. However, managers have responsibility for outcomes that affect stakeholders. Company management balances the individual judgement associated with management freedom to make decisions with management responsibility. An environmental orientation can be reflected through the way that managers exercise their discretion, judgement and responsibility. This orientation is illustrated in the next chapter.

Questions for review

2.1 What is a stakeholder of a company? Why are stakeholder relationships important? Can stakeholder relationships be managed? Provide an example where the aims of two stakeholders in business differ.

2.2 Briefly describe the five fundamental ideas that are useful for understanding the processes of management. Do you think that one of these ideas is more important than the others? Explain your view.

2.3 How is information related to each of the five fundamental ideas for understanding the processes of management?

Overview
Environmental orientation

The word 'environment' is taken to mean all living conditions, including nature in its pristine state and the habitat generated by human beings (Schaltegger and Sturm 1994: 3). The emphasis in this book is on human living conditions. People often distinguish between a pristine natural environment and an environment created, or affected, by human beings. This is a somewhat artificial distinction, given the history of human intervention in nature over most of the globe. For example, current concern over human influence on the world's climate points to the widespread interaction between human activities and the environment. The need to gain an exact perception of the relationship between humans and the environment encouraged the development of the subject of ecology. In 1866, Ernst Haeckel recorded the relationships between organisms and their surrounding world in a scientific way for the first time (Maunders and Burritt 1991: 9). Ecology is a small part of the discipline of biology—the study of life forms. Today, the word 'ecology' is widely known because of growing concerns about the effects of increased environmental pollution by humans on ecosystems. An ecosystem is the network of interactions between organisms and their environment (see Fig. 3.1). These concerns have led to a greater focus on the need for systematic measurement and recording of interactions between humans and their environment through the development of technical cybernetics (see Wiener 1948) and associated research into ecosystems (see Bick 1998).

Ecosystems include living and non-living components. Taken together, these components make up the **ecosphere**. Living components of an ecosystem include plants and animals. These fit into particular roles, such as producers, consumers and decomposers. Non-living things in an ecosystem include the soil type, weather and shape of the land. The cycling of nutrients is an important aspect of non-living ecosystems because all living components depend on this cycle for life. The cycle is normally considered to be **self-regulating** and self-sustaining. However, concern is expressed about possible human involvement in the ecosphere that is leading to a breakdown in self-regulation, a loss of equilibrium and a threat to the existence of life. Although some of the basic assumptions behind ecology, such as that of ecological equilibrium, still need to be put into perspective, modern ecology owes its expan-

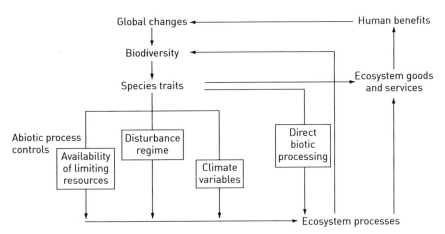

Note: The arrows show cause-and-effect chains illustrating some links between global changes and biodiversity.

Figure 3.1 **Example of an illustration of an ecosystem**

Source: www.nature.com/nature/journal/v405/n6783/fig_tab/405234a0_F4.html

sion to its attempts to explain the reasons for increased environmental damages such as changes in climate, diseases caused by toxic substances and the extension of deserts, called **desertification**. In the study of management 'environmentally oriented business management' considers these comprehensive ecological issues from a business perspective.

Management actions are environmentally oriented when they consider matters related to the ecosphere (Schaltegger and Sturm 1994: 7). This orientation has assumed two forms. First, adoption of an environmental orientation has meant linking social behaviour and cultural developments in organisations with nature through the use of **analogies** by, for example, treating an organisation as an organism and considering the organisation's survival, or viability, as being its major aim (see e.g. Janisch 1992). The second, important, environmental orientation takes into account the observation that ecosystems have a limited capacity that constrains the use and exploitation of natural resources. It is this second interpretation that forms the basis of this text.

In addition to **survival**, society is concerned about the quality of life (see Pfriem 1995: 57). From the perspective of human beings, that is from an **anthropocentric** view, quality of life refers to the lives of human beings. A consideration of the importance of nature also adopts this anthropocentric focus. Furthermore, economic questions are asked about the extent to which goods (or resources) provided by nature contribute to the quality of life of human beings. Possible answers to this question are to be found in models of **sustainable development**. The idea of sustainable development highlights what is meant by adopting an environmental orientation. For this reason, the following chapter casts further light on the notion of sustainable development.

Question for review

3.1 How would an anthropocentric view of business environmental management differ from an ecocentric view?

Overview
Sustainable development

Sustainable development merges three important areas—environmental, social and economic—into an integrated single perspective (see Bebbington 2001; Van Dieren 1995: 105ff.). The integration of groups of two of the three pillars of sustainable development leads to the concepts of eco-efficiency, eco-justice and socio-efficiency, which will be discussed in Part 2 in more detail (see Fig. 4.1). The notion of sustainable development has been inspired by the ongoing need for an assurance throughout the world for individual and group opportunities to improve the quality of life.

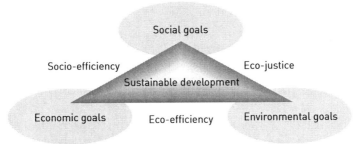

Figure 4.1 **The three main goals of sustainable development**

Expressed simply, sustainable development recognises that the economy and society depend on the biosphere and environmental processes occurring within them (Dunphy *et al.* 2000: 22). In forestry, this principle has attracted interest since the middle ages (see Nutzinger and Radke 1995: 15) through the notion of a sustainable yield, but there is now widespread general interest in the idea largely because of concerns raised by the World Commission on Environment and Development (WCED, also known as the Brundtland Commission; see WCED 1987) about the need for sustainable societies.

According to the general definition provided by the WCED (in the Brundtland Report; WCED 1987) sustainable development is: 'development that meets the needs of the present without compromising the ability of future generations to meet their own needs'.

Sustainability is the goal of the process of sustainable development. Of particular importance to this course is whether actions taken by businesses help human beings towards sustainability or whether they discourage or act against progress towards sustainability. Sustainability, or the ability to sustain life at the highest possible quality, means that every generation has the ability and is responsible for realisation of the highest quality of life by taking all opportunities for improvement.

Of course, quality of life is a subjective notion that depends on the perspective of the person or group answering the question as to whether their environmental situation is the same or better than that available to previous generations. Views will differ within and between business, government and local communities. On some occasions, these views will be in agreement. Where they conflict sustainable development requires concern over equity between the parties and outcomes that are perceived to be just by the parties involved. Sustainable development is a normative ideal. This means that policy-makers consider that sustainable development should be accepted as an objective. The objective is accepted by policy-makers and then the natural and social sciences work together to help policy-makers achieve the goal. However, no specific scientific reason can be deduced supporting the view that sustainability should be an objective. Neither ecology nor economics provide the rationale for sustainable development. Renn (1995: 22) explained this situation as follows:

> Both disciplines can help us better evaluate the effectiveness of our behaviour with respect to the goals of sustainability. However, they do not provide any reason for sustainability. When we postulate sustainability, then, we do this for ethical reasons.

Hence, the idea of sustainable development is open to a wide spectrum of interpretations and is subject to the motives of different actors who themselves have different and sometimes conflicting goals. Fundamental areas of dispute concern, for example, the difference between weak and strong sustainability (see Nutzinger and Radke 1995) and the question of the extent to which ethical requirements for an **intergenerational** equity (i.e. equity between generations) is to be supplemented by the requirement for **intragenerational** equity (i.e. equity between people in a given generation), particularly between the populations of the Earth's poorer and richer countries (see Pfister and Renn 1997). Some of the main points of discussion regarding sustainable development are outlined in Box 4.1.

In spite of these different interpretations, 'sustainable development' does represent a serviceable basis for a dialogue about quality of life and how to improve that quality of life. The strength of the idea lies both in its simplicity and in its fundamental assumption that environmental issues need to be integrated into everyday thinking, decision-making and accountability processes and that, without exception, the principle of sustainable development is to be considered in relation to every environmental problem. For example, the European Union (EU) recognises that a key element for promoting sustainable development is the principle of integrating environmental requirements into other policies. The following problems represent some of the critical issues being addressed:

Weak or strong sustainability?

Adherents of strong sustainability state that the existing stock of natural capital must be maintained and enhanced because the functions it performs cannot be duplicated by manufactured capital. Hence, in their activities humans should use only that natural capital that can be regenerated. Irreversible interference by business in nature's condition is unacceptable. Exploitation of fossil fuels has to stop. Environmental and social crisis is recognised.

Adherents of weak sustainability, in contrast, accept that manufactured capital of equal value can take the place of natural capital. This perspective allows continued use of stocks of natural capital because substitution can be made through investment and technical advances in manufactured capital. Only the total value of natural and manufactured capital combined need correspond to the original value of natural capital for sustainability to be achieved. Those who advocate weak sustainability accept that the natural environment can be mastered through existing economic systems that can be used to help solve environmental problems. Strong and weak sustainability are two extreme views of sustainability—the former idealistic, the latter arbitrary because there is no substitution for some aspects of nature. A third position, adopted by some economists, takes a view of sustainability that is midway between weak and strong sustainability. In this view, the possibility of substitution between natural and real capital is not excluded but is restricted to cases where the underlying functions of nature are not endangered (see Lerch and Nutzinger 1995: 294ff.).

Intergenerational or intragenerational equity?

Sustainable development, as defined by the World Commission on environment and Development (WCED 1987) is closely concerned with intergenerational equity. If such a goal is accepted, then the goal of intragenerational equity becomes equally important. Intragenerational equity suggests that all people should have equal opportunity to access natural capital, whether they inhabit the poorer countries of the world with their less-developed economies, or whether they come from countries with prospering economies. Sometimes this concern is referred to as 'eco-justice'. The question is whether opportunities to exploit natural resources are distributed equally (see BUND and Misereor 1996; Pfister and Renn 1997: 12ff.). Extravagant use of natural resources contingent on wealth acquired by the industrial nations and the consequences of poverty, such as the depletion or erosion of land quality, or an increase in population, lead to a waste of natural resources. Hence the requirement for a global approach to minimum living standards is becoming more important, and the importance of an ethical standard is growing as people with a high standard of living waste resources.

Nevertheless, conflicts between intergenerational and intragenerational equity need to be resolved in a pragmatic way. A rising level of environmental consciousness among business and attempts to reduce the volume of energy and materials used to achieve given output levels means that, from a statistical point of view, the environmental impact (or damage created by each unit of total sales) is less in the wealthy countries than it is in the poorer countries (see Renn 1995: 14ff.)—although the total environmental impact is increasing in the wealthy countries as total output increases and hence more of the world's environmental waste sinks are being dominated by developed countries.

Part of a pluralistic world order or guidelines for a new world order?

Finally, the significance of the idea of sustainability for a global society has been questioned (see Knaus and Renn 1998: 80ff.). Is it to be the main objective of policy, or

Box 4.1 Central points of discussion about sustainable development (continued over)

is it subsidiary to the objectives of peace, improving human welfare, democratisation, emancipation and empowerment? In practice, a balance between these and other objectives is important and necessary for government to survive.

What are the answers?
This book is designed to stimulate thinking; it cannot provide any ready answers to these questions. These are current questions. They are important questions. Awareness of the issues is an important starting point for anyone considering the links between business and the environment. The search for credible and justifiable answers to these questions depends on the application of considered thought, dialogue and teamwork to help develop understanding of the reasons behind these different perspectives and movement towards their practical resolution.

Box 4.1 (continued)

- The vulnerability of life, highlighted by the breakdown of the stratospheric ozone layer and the accumulation of gases that cause, or exacerbate, the greenhouse effect (global warming)

- The destruction and waste of biodiversity through damage to and poisoning of natural living spaces as well as direct eradication by human activities

- The change in the quality of the oceans because of pollution and over-fishing and because of rising temperatures in the seas caused by use of water for energy-generation processes and industrial processes, with consequences for coral reefs and sea currents

- The exhaustion of potable water supplies in the dry zones of the Earth and the ever-increasing expenditure on enhancing the quality of drinking water

- The degradation of soils through overuse, erosion, desertification (the extension of desert boundaries) and the sealing of land surfaces for human habitation, transport and commercial activities

- The clearing of forests, particularly in the humid tropics (Achard *et al.* 1998)

To these can be added social and economic problems between developed and developing countries, which are interrelated with environmental problems:

- Neglect of environmental and social standards in world trade because of different environmental and social regulations which permit lower standards to be followed in developing countries

- The decoupling of financial and commercial markets with the danger, for environmental issues, that worldwide recessions and drastically reduced wealth associated with stock-market crashes will lead decision-makers to ignore critical environmental issues

● The increasing indebtedness of many national economies, particularly in the developing world, with rising interest costs and threats of liquidation that limit the scope for consideration of environmental issues

● The danger of impoverishment because of economic crises induced by increasing interdependency in the global economic structure

● Unequal opportunities for education between people in countries with high and low economic wealth, rural and urban areas, females and males

● The ungovernability of people in mega-cities as represented by the breakdown of infrastructure and corresponding increases in criminality

This book concentrates on the business response to environmental issues. Figure 4.2, while not complete, provides an overview of the company areas relevant to sustainable business and highlights where management has the greatest chance of securing sustainable value for the company and society. For example, production and services both play an important part in reducing the demand for physical materials and increasing the availability of 'green' funding for projects that reduce environmental impacts.

No matter in what area of business environmental management is active, three basic strategies can be distinguished: efficiency, sufficiency and consistency (see Fig. 4.3).

● Strategies of **efficiency** aim to reduce the environmental damage associated with the production of each unit of output (Schaltegger and Sturm 1990). Technical, organisational and marketing innovations help reduce material and energy inputs in such a way that existing consumption patterns and the financial profitability of production remain at least as high as their existing levels. Use of fewer material resources in production, extension of the life of products and production equipment, reduction of waste output and lower rejection rates are common ways of reducing the environmental impacts of business (from von Weizsäcker *et al.* 1997).

● Strategies of **sufficiency** are less of a technical solution to environmental issues and more of a behavioural or psychological solution. Sufficiency means having enough. When an individual has enough of something then demand ceases and unnecessary use of resources is curtailed. A strategy of sufficiency can follow 'reflection about the environmental consequences of personal consumption and way of leading one's own life' (Reisch 1998: 44). Strategies of sufficiency place less emphasis on material values as an important quality of life. Material consumption is not abandoned altogether but is balanced with a greater emphasis on leisure, a sense of community and closeness to nature. One problem is that many aspects of business focus on having more rather than having enough.

● Strategies of **consistency**, like strategies of efficiency, are linked to technical innovations. Strategies of consistency, however, do not reduce energy and material usage but try to harmonise such usage with the underlying environmental purpose. They strive for 'a composition of matter streams

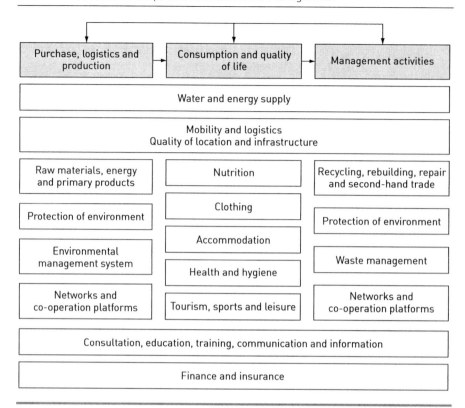

Figure 4.2 **Areas of activity for environmental management and sustainable business**

and energy forms which is able to exist permanently in an industrial ecology' (Huber 1998: 27). For example, in a strategy of consistency, traffic lights may be designed to use the same set of coloured lights in sequence and therefore use a specific amount of electricity. However, in a strategy of efficiency traffic lights could be designed to use photovoltaic energy, thereby saving on the use of fossil fuels as well as on material that would otherwise be required to connect a set of traffic lights to the main electricity transmission system. Although strategies of efficiency and sufficiency have physical and psychological borders, the scope for improved consistency is unlimited.

These three strategies cannot always be clearly distinguished from one another. For example, re-usable systems can save energy and improve efficiency as well as provide more consistency than disposable wrappings. Moreover, depending on whether weight or the collection and return of containers is rated as the key aspect of packaging, the notion of sufficiency is also involved. Figure 4.3 illustrates the common ground between these three individual strategies.

Business management needs to build its own business strategies, based on these three types of strategy. To help understand this process, this book examines in turn

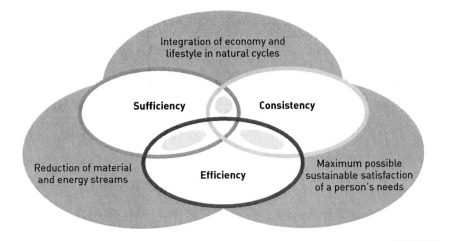

Figure 4.3 Basic environmental strategies behind sustainability

the purpose (Chapter 5), stakeholders (Chapter 6), fields of action and criteria for success (Part 2) of the environmentally oriented business.

Questions for review

4.1 Sustainability is the end and sustainable development the means towards increasing the quality of life both now and for future generations. Do you agree? Provide reasons for your view.

4.2 'Sustainability is an ethical not a scientific ideal.' Discuss this proposition.

4.3 Select an industry from a standard industrial classification. What are the main considerations for establishing a sustainable business in that industry?

4.4 Explain the three business strategies through which business may respond to environmental issues. Are these strategies independent of one another? Provide an example to illustrate your view.

Overview

Business management
on its way to sustainability

In simple terms, to be sustainable is to remain in existence. This is a most appealing notion to business managers. Over recent years a number of environmental problems have threatened the existence of business. The hole in the ozone layer led to a global ban on the production of halons (as used, for example, in fire extinguishers, air-conditioning units and refrigerators). The ban was introduced under an international agreement called the Montreal Protocol (www.unep.org/ozone/Montreal-Protocol/Montreal-protocol2000.shtml). Companies using the banned technology to produce these products went out of business if they failed to adapt to the new circumstances by using acceptable substitute raw materials. Global warming has also threatened to put manufacturing companies out of business when they emit too much carbon dioxide (CO_2) and has led insurance companies into financial failure because of unexpected environmental risks. However, at this point, there is no workable international agreement about the ways in which global warming should be addressed. Until such agreement is reached, global warming will remain an important environmental uncertainty in the strategic thinking of many business managers.

Environmentally oriented business management requires reconsideration of the location and scale of companies (e.g. factories), business areas (e.g. divisions and departments), performance (e.g. individual products and groups of products) and the entire business organisation (see Box 5.1). It is concerned about inanimate resources, such as material and energy flows (see Fig. 5.1), as well as about the protection of species and animals—the flora and fauna in the biosphere.

Environmentally oriented business management aims to reduce the environmental impacts of business. It does this by adapting its products, organisational processes, organisational structure, stakeholder attitudes, business conduct and performance towards environmentally benign activities and away from environmentally damaging activities.

Box 5.1 Reducing environmental impacts

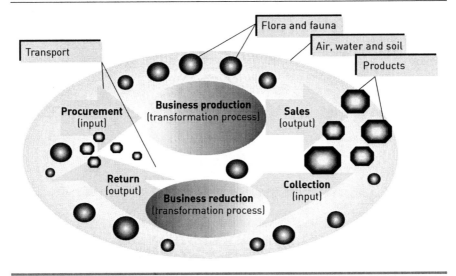

Figure 5.1 Transformation processes taking place during the exchange between business and nature

5.1 Perspectives on corporate environmental management

An engineer's perspective of the business process has a focus on scientific–technological aspects of business. From this perspective, production can usefully be represented through a simplified input–transformation–output model, as shown in Figure 5.2. Business management accepts the task of systematically reducing environmental damage and environmental risk through technological innovation while creating business value by reducing material flows and improving economic flows. Business value can be increased by reducing use of inputs for any given level of output, by improving transformation processes and by removing or reducing outcomes related to environmental damages, effects, impacts and waste associated with business activities.

From a socioeconomic perspective, business management is concerned about the social, legal and commercial impacts on the company and associated business performance. The strategy that a business adopts towards the environment can provide it with a competitive advantage when business management solves environmental problems in commercially acceptable ways, when it resolves conflicts of interests between stakeholders (e.g. by engaging stakeholders in a dialogue) and, thereby, improves business credibility and acceptability in the community. Hence, business management needs to mediate between the scientific–technological perspective and the socioeconomic perspective about the performance of production activities (Box 5.2). Figure 5.3 compares these two perspectives (for a discussion of the links between these views, see Dyllick *et al.* 1997).

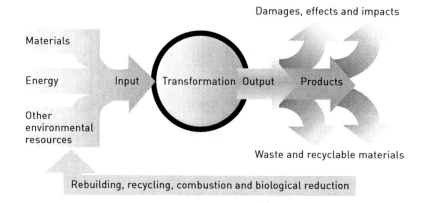

Figure 5.2   **Environmental management: the scientific–technological view of material flows**

> To sum up, the task of environmentally oriented business management is to reduce environmental impacts imposed by existing technology in an economic way, as far as possible. Particular emphasis is placed on reducing or removing unacceptable impacts that lead to socioeconomic damage to the present and future quality of life.

Box 5.2   **The environmental task of business management**

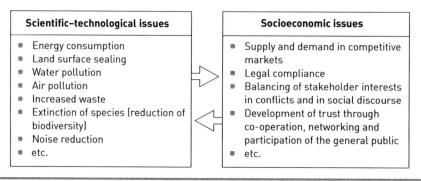

Figure 5.3   **A comparison of scientific–technological and socioeconomic issues in environmental management**

5.2 General business and its functional characteristics

Since all areas of management contribute to business influences on the environment and should have a hand in their reduction, development of an appropriate orientation towards the environment is a generic functional task of business. The functional tasks of business are conventionally referred to as the **value chain**. The environmental impacts of business (see Box 5.3) touch on and draw in all aspects of the **value creation chain** from procurement of goods and services through to sales and after-sales services for customers, including re-use or disposal of products that are no longer wanted. At the same time, all value creation is connected to the creation of harmful substances—no value added without environmental impact added (Box 5.4).

Environmental impact is defined as the influence of a corporation's activities on the physical environment (e.g. the impact on land, water and air quality and on biodiversity). The emphasis is on processes and activities.

Box 5.3 Environmental impact: a definition

Source: Schaltegger and Sturm 1990: 280

Environmental impact added is defined as the sum of all environmental impacts that are:

- Caused directly or indirectly by business activities
- Significant because of the type and quantity of material and mass of energy used by businesses in their activities
- Assessed according to the relative environmental harm they cause

---

Box 5.4 Environmental impact added: a definition

Source: Schaltegger and Sturm 1990: 280

To achieve improved environmental performance it is necessary to reduce environmental impact added. In order to achieve this, environmental management examines production processes and all support functions such as planning and control, human resources, financing and organisation (see Fig. 5.4). Environmentally oriented business management is, therefore, a multifunctional activity.

The environmental orientation of a business also stretches right across the company. Its success often depends on co-operation between different functions. For example, in order to introduce integrated recycling and waste disposal systems, identify and implement solutions to ecological problems or guarantee the development and quality of environmentally benign products over the complete value chain (e.g. from cotton grown in the field to the distribution and recycling of textile goods; see Meffert and Kirchgeorg 1998: 19ff.) co-operation is essential.

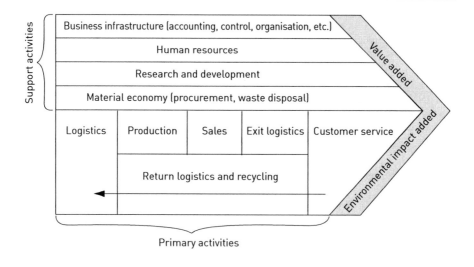

Figure 5.4 **Management functions in the chain of value creation**

Source: Porter 1999b: 66

This general character—the need for solutions based on co-operation—brings business management face to face with the task of institutionalising **environmental management,** so that ecological objectives can become an integral part of management in the individual functional areas. Environmental management, as part of overall business management, is often created as a separate internal group within the business. The environmental manager has authority to seek to implement environmental solutions through co-operation with other managers. Without an environmental manager to lobby other managers there is a danger that environmental interests will not be integrated into business thinking. Environmental management is normally introduced through project groups or permanent multifunctional teams (e.g. production, marketing and waste handling).

In practice, presence of a multitude of ways of institutionalising environmental expertise into business demonstrates that there is no single answer to the question about how to organise environmental management. At worst, environmental management can become an isolated and poorly funded function. At best, organisational structures exist that, with a high level of support and commitment from top management, provide resources to ensure that environmental management practices are integrated throughout the business. Such integration of environmental thinking and activities can be promoted and facilitated by an environmental co-ordinator and should be integrated into all support and primary activities of the value chain (Fig. 5.4). Attention is needed that environmental management is not delegated to a separate support group that is isolated from all other primary and support activities.

5.3 History of corporate environmental management

Corporate environmental management has a long tradition. Farmers have always had to consider risks associated with the vagaries of nature. Anthroposophical businesses following Rudolf Steiner's (b.1861, d.1925) theories[1] focused on overcoming environmental problems long before the science of ecology was conceptually associated with environmental problems. Followers of William Morris (b.1834, d.1896), a socialist working to see the excesses of industrialism replaced with the spirituality of craft industry, established businesses founded on harmony with nature. More recently, environmentally oriented business management was promoted in the 1970s and 1980s. On the one hand, committed people in business followed their personal convictions and, like Georg Winter or Claus Hipp, began to strive for economic success through a combination of ecological and market principles. On the other hand, alternative businesses with a focus on communal property and social visions were founded following student movements in the late 1960s that tried to encourage business to look beyond profit-seeking behaviour and private industry and adopt an environmental character.

The pioneers had an influence on managers of multinational companies exposed to concerns about the environmental impacts of their corporate activities, especially in developing countries. Managers of these multinational companies realised that social acceptance and legitimacy are part of economic success. By the end of the 1980s, environmental issues became an argument in the advertisement of products as being 'clean and green', a motivation for cost reduction and an institutionalised organisational task. The environmental technologies and services industry developed, in reaction to the increasing demand for pollution prevention, clean production and environmental services. Its focus was mainly on the USA, Europe and Japan. In the 1990s, business received further encouragement to be aware of environmental impacts through the introduction of environmental management standards (i.e. the ISO 14000 series, the EU Eco-management and Audit Scheme [EMAS] and BS 7750) and swathes of environmental law backed up by increasing civil and criminal penalties for abuse of the environment by business, such as the 17-year jail sentence for an Idaho businessman who exposed employees to cyanide (see www.usdoj.gov/opa/pr/1999/May/180enr.htm).

Environmental management systems and performance can now be certified and communicated in a standardised way. One of the most recent developments is sustainable entrepreneurship (Box 5.5) and ecopreneurship, where start-up companies specialise in providing products and services aimed at achieving a sustainable society or an ecologically sustainable society. Such companies develop business opportunities through environmental innovations (e.g. in the field of regenerative energy supply, energy contracting and environmentally benign mobility). In contrast, the conventional environmental technology industry emphasises production of end-of-

1 Such businesses include Waldorf schools, biodynamic farms and gardens, and anthroposophically extended medical practices, therapists, artists, scientists, colleges and adult education centres (see the 'Directory of Initiatives', at www.anthroposophy.org/DoI/intro.html).

Sustainable entrepreneurship can roughly be defined as entrepreneurship realising market success with sustainability innovations. Sustainable entrepreneurship companies worldwide are entering a new phase in which integrated responsibilities for people (regarding employment, health, education and human rights), profit (concerning economic and financial continuity) and the planet (providing a clean environment and preserving resource stocks) are becoming a necessity for good entrepreneurship (see Schaltegger and Petersen 2001; Schaltegger 2003; Schaper 2003). A shift from shareholder value maximisation towards stakeholder value maximisation is taking place. Governments, non-governmental organisations (NGOs), customers, labour unions and shareholders demand firms take on this wider array of responsibilities regarding social–ethical and environmental issues. These are in addition to the traditional economic responsibilities of business firms.

National social issues related to provision of employment and healthy and safe work conditions are now being expanded through international issues associated with human rights: businesses are required to contribute to the improvement of human rights in the countries in which they operate.

Environmental issues are also becoming an integrated part of the management of companies. Environmental care of companies has grown beyond reactive compliance with environmental rules and regulations to include eco-efficient production processes and the ecodesign of products and services to contribute to a healthy and sound environment, at the local and national levels. Environmental care of business firms is now growing to become the proactive management of the environment to ensure the availability of nationally and globally sustainable levels of resource stocks of water, energy, biodiversity, minerals, land and nature, for present and future generations.

Box 5.5 Sustainable entrepreneurship

pipe pollution prevention and clean-up technologies such as sewerage and waste-water plants. Sustainable or eco-entrepreneurs concentrate on developing innovative products that do not primarily provide an environmental service but that provide environmental benefit through the products (e.g. organic clothes, organic food). The emphasis has, once again, returned to the integration of environmental, social and economic issues and the responsibilities of business.

Questions for review

5.1 'Environmentally oriented business management aims to reduce the environmental impacts of business.' What factors might stop a business trying to reduce its environmental impacts?

5.2 Does government have a role in balancing scientific–technical and socio-economic factors in environmental management? Explain the reasons for your answer.

5.3 Define the following terms and explain why each of these ideas is important to business environmental management:

- Goal congruence
- Value chain
- Co-operation and collaboration

5.4 How does labour relate to the chain of value creation outlined by Porter (1999b; see also Fig. 5.4)? From an environmental perspective, is labour an important part of the business value chain?

Overview

Business management and its stakeholders

The environment of the business or company can be distinguished by its specific actors (i.e. the stakeholders in the institutional sphere), and the main environmental issues raised (i.e. the general sphere of influence) (Fig. 6.1). The institutional sphere is characterised by various stakeholders with specific socioeconomic interests in the company. These socioeconomic spheres are embedded in the ecosphere. Businesses create value for their different stakeholders. As Hill (1985: 118) puts it, 'businesses do not exist or develop easily as purposeful organisations, but they are created or formed in order to fulfil certain claims'. This draws attention to the fact that individuals and groups have interests in business activities. These individuals and groups are called **stakeholders** (see Freeman 1984). Business tries to fulfil the needs of different stakeholders in order to be successful. For example, **shareholders**—people who give their money to a business in return for dividends and hoped-for capital gains on their ownership share in the business—are one type of stakeholder. The basic reason for the existence of a business from the shareholder's point of view is improvement of the business's monetary value (**shareholder value**), subject to compliance with the law. **Employees** are a second group of stakeholders. They are concerned about the working climate, the economic security of the business that employs them, health and safety in the workplace and personal development. **Suppliers** are another group of stakeholders. Suppliers contract supply goods or services to the business and view it as a paying customer. **Non-governmental organisations** (NGOs) provide another example of a stakeholder group. They are important in environmental issues. NGOs have no contract with the business and no market relationship but they are followers of business behaviour and are drivers of change where unacceptable behaviour is observed (e.g. in the case of excessive pollution from a factory).

The variety of stakeholder perspectives provides a framework for the analysis of social relations between stakeholders and business. The stakeholder perspective describes enterprises as constellations of co-operative and conflicting interests (see e.g. Cyert and March 1963, 1992; Donaldson and Preston 1995; Göbel 1995: 62ff.). The approach makes clear the fact that enterprises not only have to fulfil the

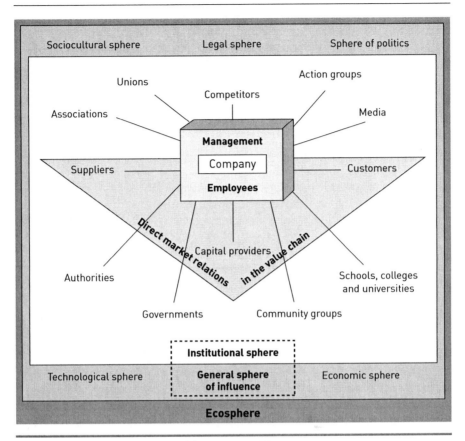

Figure 6.1 **The business as a multi-purpose entity**

Source: based on Schaltegger and Sturm 1994: 9

requirements of their customers and employees but also have to represent the interests of other groups that reach beyond market relationships and into political and social concerns. If important stakeholders are neglected in environmental management, or if their interests and power are not taken into account, there is a danger that the process of value creation will be impaired (see Jones 1995; Näsi 1995).

Stakeholders can be subdivided in accordance with certain criteria: **internal** stakeholders include groups such as management and employees, whereas **external** stakeholders can be classified into trade creditors, external authorities such as regulators, NGOs, or business, industry and professional associations. However, the usefulness of this distinction between internal and external stakeholders is becoming harder to justify as development of the 'virtual' company, project-related employment and the broader availability of information makes a clear demarcation more difficult. A second classification suggests that stakeholders can be distinguished according to their explicit action-relationships (see the inverted triangle in Figure 6.1 for direct market relationships in the value chain). Relationships to the company are viewed as either being founded on implicit obligations, short-term contracts, or are totally open.

6.1 Stakeholders from an environmentally oriented point of view

Stakeholder analysis can be further differentiated on the basis of environmental problems. New stakeholders have emerged whose functions are driven by external considerations (e.g. environment organisations, local community initiatives) and by internal considerations (e.g. environmental representatives within business). Conventional stakeholders are also concerned about environmentally related claims on business—with issues ranging from securing a healthy workplace (e.g. lowering noise pollution) to securing returns from contracts with business (e.g. the examination by credit institutions and insurance companies of possible soil contamination). Hence, a wide spectrum of environmentally related stakeholder positions has emerged. Table 6.1 lists stakeholders according to their functions and provides an indication of the main motivation of each group (see Gröner and Zapf 1998).

Finally, more recently, associations have been established to counter the messages and intentions of associations that are encouraging business to consider environmental issues in their activities (e.g. Waste Watchers, and the PVC Association and Environment). These associations adopt more or less open opposition to existing environmental NGOs (see Dettmer and Niejahr 1995).

Development of countervailing groups of associations makes it harder to regulate stakeholders that have a specific stance on the adverse impacts of business on the environment. Until the mid-1980s environmental associations and action groups tended to conflict with business about environmental protection. Managers and shareholders tended to adopt a defensive position about the environmental impacts of business, whereas other stakeholders were rarely involved in any discussions, or firmly supported one of the two other views—'greens' versus business.

In the 1990s there was a shift towards the establishment of a fundamental agreement about the existence of environmental problems. Various stakeholders, including business, began to recognise the need for a strategic commitment towards environmentally benign behaviour. Pragmatism (or opportunism) and the playing down of ideological standpoints has, in many cases, led to a policy whereby loose networks have been established between stakeholders (see e.g. Brunnengräber and Walk 1997; Murphy and Bendell 1997) to help address environmental problems. As part of this strategy, business management has accepted the need for co-operation rather than conflict on these issues. Many NGOs are looking for co-operative ventures and partnerships with business (e.g. the partnership between Greenpeace and the World Business Council for Sustainable Development [WBCSD] in support of

Stakeholder group	Motivation
Shareholders and investors	To appraise the influence of environmental damage as well as environmentally benign activities, or omitted activities, on business value (shareholder value)
Banks and insurance companies	To avoid credit and liability risks relating to the environment and to seek profitable and secure capital investments for themselves and for their customers
Labour unions and employee committees	To secure better pay and working conditions, improved social and health situations, the enhancement of freedom of expression and security of employment for all dependent employees
Customers	To look for lower-priced, higher-quality goods and services, encouraging or ignoring the adoption of environmental standards by their suppliers through contractual arrangements
Suppliers	To adopt or neglect to adopt environmental quality criteria in relation to the goods and services offered
Managers and executives	To seek to enhance the (short-term) success of the business and minimise environment-based business risks and to strive personally for higher monetary rewards, prestige and a new sense of environmental awareness as encouraged by social and business pressures
Media	To capture the attention of existing and potential audiences
Employees	To secure their position in the business, to pursue personal goals relating to career and position and to obtain environmentally healthy work conditions that promote personal wellbeing
Neighbours and local community residents	To maintain or improve the environmental quality of the areas they live in

Table 6.1 **Motivation of stakeholders in relation to environmental issues** (continued over)

Stakeholder group	Motivation
Non-governmental organisations	To act as advocates for the environment, as watchdogs and as catalysts working towards environmentally benign behaviour by business (see Murphy and Bendell 1997)
Authorities and governments	To pursue protection and conservation of the environment on behalf of society and to use measures related to the environment as a political instrument in the struggle for votes
Technicians and research staff in business	To try to develop or prevent the introduction of environmentally oriented innovations (see Schein 1996)
Business and professional associations	To act on behalf of members and to achieve the goals set by members for the association, including goals related to environmental protection
Competitors	To look for cost advantages, to compare their performance with that of their cohort of competitors and to search for opportunities that may stem from improving environmental quality
Academics	To strive for the application of their research results and to have an effect on the formation of opinion through teaching

Table 6.1   (continued)

the Kyoto Protocol on greenhouse gas emission reductions (archive.greenpeace.org/earthsummit/wbcsd); see also Quote 6.1, by the WWF).

Put simply, on any environmental issue stakeholders tend to cluster into those who support and those who defend 'the environment'. However, the composition of these stakeholder groups varies from case to case, situation to situation and over time in relation to the same issue. Nevertheless, stakeholders continue to operate in different spheres. In Figure 6.1 these are structured as follows:

- Technological sphere
- Economic sphere
- Legal sphere
- Sociocultural sphere
- Sphere of politics

• Changes in corporate practice are essential if there is to be real progress in tackling global warming, moving to renewable energy systems and clean technologies, phasing out toxic chemicals and ensuring the sustainable use of natural resources such as timber, fish and agricultural products.

Although corporations are often part of the problem, they should undoubtedly be part of the solution.

WWF believes that corporate engagement is a key to transforming markets, to changing domestic and international law and to adopting and promoting a sector-wide shift to sustainable development and corporate best practice.

WWF's policy is to enter into business and industry relationships, with the priority to develop programme-led relationships, which deliver conservation on the ground and contribute to the achievement of our mission, while endeavouring to protect and enhance WWF's reputation, independence and integrity. WWF will work with most companies that demonstrate a real commitment to the principles of sustainability and are prepared to adopt challenging targets for change. Although principally we choose corporate partners that represent the very best in CSR (Corporate Social Responsibility) and environmental best practices, we also engage with companies that have a poor or mixed record on the environment where there is a real potential for positive change. The crucial question is: can we effect a positive change for people and the planet?

Three of the most important of WWF's own guiding principles for engagement are mutual respect, transparency and WWF's right to criticise: WWF and the corporate partner will not agree on all things all the time. Agreeing to disagree in the context of a transparent framework has been a key factor in sustaining relationships that are beneficial to both partners.

WWF's approach to working with business is constructive and solutions-oriented. It is both collaborative in its methods and challenging in its objectives. And it is always forward-looking: WWF works with companies to help them change the way they do business.

For more information on WWF and Business, contact Jean-Paul Jeanrenaud (jpjeanrenaud@wwfint.org) or Maria Boulos (mboulos@wwfint.org) at WWF International.

WWF currently works with business on the following levels:

- **Conservation Partner:** major global sponsorship from multinational corporations
- **Corporate Supporter:** substantial financial or in-kind support from medium to large companies
- **Corporate Club:** membership of a Corporate Club of environmentally aware local businesses
- **Product Licensing:** licensing agreements for companies to use WWF's world-renowned trademarks. •

Quote 6.1 **Business with the WWF: an overview of corporate relationships with the WWF**

Source: WWF web page, at www.panda.org/about_wwf/how_we_work/partnerships/index.cfm

In an abbreviated form, such analysis exceeding legal compliance assurance is sometimes referred to as PEST analysis—political, economic, sociocultural and technological analysis. Each sphere is examined in turn below.

6.2 General stakeholder spheres of influence

The general stakeholder spheres of influence are briefly discussed here and dealt with in more detail in Part 2.

6.2.1 Technological sphere

In the technological sphere new discoveries and inventions are regularly generated. Innovations take place, when inventions become useful in practice and, consequently, marketable. They improve the effectiveness of processes and products, enhance safety or promise new and broader possibilities for action. Innovations enhance the effectiveness of trading from the point of view of the user (e.g. suppliers and competitors). Test reports, scientific journals, patent licensing, trade fairs and presentations provide signals or indicators of trends and recent developments. Innovations determine the limits to progress and serve as a catalyst for new fields of action for enterprises. Markets for environmentally benign techniques—for example, in the fields of waste management, water treatment, prevention of air pollution, noise reduction, energy supply or technology for measuring and control (see Meffert and Kirchgeorg 1998)—form an important part of technological development. Estimates of the size of the market for environmental technology vary, but the Organisation for Economic Co-operation and Development (OECD 2000), using a fairly narrow definition of the industry, estimated that in 2000 it was worth US$300 billion.

Apart from the expansion of technical possibilities, the natural sciences and engineering help to establish new insights into environmental problems through the development of improved measuring instruments. Their importance lies in the exploration of correlations between causes of problems and effects on the natural environment. Because of these advances, environmental risks and the potential for identifying environmental impact added can be linked to the business value creation process. Environmental **side-effects** become transparent. Ability to assess the technical efficiency (strength of performance, and rate) along additional dimensions (toxicity, volume of waste and degree of incineration) is improved (see Schaltegger and Sturm 1994, 2000). Analysis of damage to the environment and of risk and publication of results can encourage new claims from, or the perception of new opportunities by, new and existing stakeholders (see Section 7.2). The result can be additional pressure on and market opportunities for business and the search for innovations to overcome the environmental problems revealed. Increased research and development (R&D) activity in many countries and a rising level of education mean that technological change is accelerating throughout the world in many fields.

Economic incentives are needed to ensure that innovations do actually become a commercial reality. The economic sphere is considered in the next section.

6.2.2 Economic sphere

In a narrow sense, the economic sphere brings together potential market participants—a business, its suppliers and customers (see inverted triangle in Fig. 6.1). Competitors, inflation and price stability, and the trend in interest and exchange rates in the financial markets and in selling and buying activities, form the core of the economic sphere.

In order to continue in existence the business must operate in a profitable way, so that it can provide a normal return on its capital. In the first place this requires **sales turnover**—to meet demand for products. Consumer consciousness about the environment and the resultant consumer behaviour can contribute to increased turnover in some cases (e.g. for products with an eco-label or thought to be environmentally benign) and reduced turnover in other cases (e.g. the reduction in petrol sales made by Shell in Germany when it experienced opposition to the sinking of the *Brent Spar* loading platform in the North Atlantic in 1995). Other factors implicitly drive the demand for environmentally benign products, such as thrift, product life or health issues, without directly involving the perceived need for environmental protection. Hence, turnover can be increased or reduced because of increasing consumer awareness about the environmental impact of products and a range of other factors that may not be related to environmental awareness (e.g. the importance of price, as most consumers do not have an unlimited amount to spend).

Increased sales turnover can be achieved at a loss or a cost: for example, by spending increasing amounts on marketing (Baumol 1959). Turnover leads to economic success only when the desired level of **profitability** is achieved. Therefore, in the second place, **efficiency** must be sought in the amount of resources used. Efficiency means that to achieve a given output fewer resources (inputs) are used or that greater output is obtained from a given resource. Whereas turnover is usually seen as the concern of businesses selling in markets, efficiency is regarded as a central goal of the entire economic system. In general, efficiency expressed in monetary terms measures expenditures on **inputs** that are purchased in order to produce and sell a given **output**. This relationship has an important influence on **net income** (defined as revenue from sales minus expenditure on inputs purchased to produce those sales). The fewer resources used, the lower the expenditure and the higher the net income. Hence, the greater the efficiency the higher the business income. For example, increased productivity from labour, or a reduction in the use of resources for environmental reasons, both contribute to increased efficiency. The monetary gain to the business can also be compared with environmental damage caused by business activities. This provides a measure of **eco-efficiency** (see Section 8.1).

Since eco-efficiency is produced by a favourable input–output relationship involving the environment and financial gains to a business, conditions in the economic sphere must also be considered. According to Porter (1999a), competition and competitiveness are affected by five factors (see Fig. 6.2).

Suppliers may negotiate higher prices. New competitors may enter the market, thereby making it more competitive and strengthening the need for innovations.

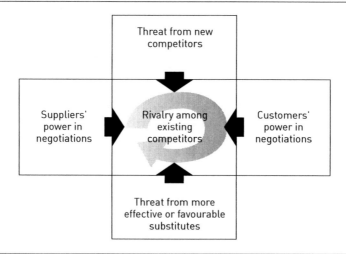

Figure 6.2 **Factors affecting competition**

Source: Porter 1999b: 66

Customers may have varying powers to negotiate discounts and to impose their wishes on product designers. Substitutes may be available for many products, thereby restricting prices that could have been charged. All these factors act together to drive the business towards greater efficiency in its activities. Imitations and the entry of entirely new products can lead a business to reduced output and a lower turnover when competitors satisfy customer needs more efficiently.

6.2.3 Legal sphere

Businesses can prosper only when the basic economic conditions are favourable. At the same time, laws are introduced to guarantee that businesses increase social **welfare**. The central question for a business considering the legal sphere is, therefore, which fundamental legal requirements affect it. From one perspective, businesses are confronted with laws, regulations, taxation and additional requirements that constrain their activities (e.g. minimum pay legislation, occupational health and safety legislation). However, businesses exist only because, if incorporated, they obtain a separate legal existence, can sue and be sued and can gain legal protection that limits the money lost if business ventures turn bad. For example, they can make contracting partners legally responsible under civil law or prosecute any offences against their ownership rights in accordance with criminal law.

When considering the legal sphere, authorities, administrations, professional associations, the police, courts, ministries and representatives of the people in parliament need to be added to the list of stakeholders. These groups are directly or indirectly authorised to use their **sovereign influence** to ensure that businesses comply with the law. At the same time, the legal framework establishes the regulatory framework for market participants under civil law. Through regulation of their rights in sovereign nations, rules are established for market trading by market participants that possess the monetary or physical means to conduct transactions.

Change in legal requirements has, so far, been the strategy that has dominated changes in attitude and behaviour towards the environment by business. The rising tide of environmental laws has added considerable complexity to the conduct of business. Violation of these environmental laws can lead not only to sanctions, such as prison, fines and other penalties, but also to a loss of credibility. Lost credibility is becoming an important driver of improved behaviour towards the environment, especially for organisations in environmentally sensitive industries and those that rely on maintaining a sound environmental reputation. Environmental law also opens up opportunities for organisations, as new markets are created or old markets go into decline because unacceptable environmental behaviour is outlawed. For example, the banning of halon production, because of its damaging effect on the ozone layer, led to an increase in the demand for substitutes. Likewise, if the cost of a resource is increased through the imposition of an eco-tax, there is a stronger incentive to economise on resource use. New legal requirements can, therefore, encourage product and process innovations as organisations follow up new market growth opportunities to foster environmentally benign activities.

Market opportunities, driven by changes in legislation relating to environmental protection, do also present dangers for business. When environmentally friendly technologies—such as filters used for improving air quality, or electricity generated by wind farms—maintain their share of the market only because they are subsidised by government, the danger of relying on government subsidies for survival and on the results of political lobbying become all too real. As governments change over time, there is a political risk that legislation to protect the environment will change, and anticipation of such change needs to be factored into decision-making by business. For example, export opportunities for environmental technologies will be created and destroyed by changes in subsidies provided by different sovereign nations. If there is an international agreement about a particular environmental problem, then greater certainty and less political risk will encourage business into international trade. Hence, the international alignment of standards associated with environmental regulation will encourage trade in environmentally benign technologies by reducing risk from changes in government (see Jänicke 1998).

6.2.4 Sociocultural sphere

Customs, norms and traditions usually precede and operate in parallel with the current legal structure. Claims related to the sociocultural sphere can still dominate or drive events in the legal sphere. The fundamental purpose of business, and its acceptance in the community, are affected by sociocultural factors. In particular, the **legitimacy** of business depends on its social acceptance. Purchasing boycotts, protests and loss of credibility demonstrate the power of **public opinion** in affecting corporate behaviour towards the environment. Where problems become evident, it is often the case that well-known personalities, organisations with a credible environmental record, citizen groups, scientists and the media take up critical themes and make them public. When organisations, products and personalities are highly regarded by the public, the sociocultural sphere is at its most powerful as a driver of change in business behaviour. Community 'trust' in organisations is not easy to achieve and is easily lost. Achievement of such trust requires an organisation to be transparent about its approach to the environment and environmental issues. Cover-ups and cosmetic reporting lead to a loss of trust.

Each country has a different sociocultural composition and associated with this are different views about the importance of environmental issues and the usefulness of specific measures to protect the environment. For example, the planned sinking of the loading platform *Brent Spar* by Shell was considered to be of relatively low significance in the United Kingdom, whereas opposition to disposal of the platform in this way generated an almost hysterical atmosphere in Germany (see Hecker 1997). It should be remembered that different views also exist within a specific society as well, with different sub-regions and sub-groups holding diverse perspectives on a given issue. Nevertheless, the idea of sustainable development and, within this, the need for environmental protection is one concept that seems to have found broad acceptance throughout the world—even though its meaning remains somewhat ambiguous at this point.

6.2.5 *Political sphere*

Public discourse and moral bans are only one possible way of supporting claims about bad environmental behaviour by business. As mentioned in Section 6.2.4, in discussion of the sociocultural sphere, politics can play an important part in determining the success or failure of a business. Stakeholders have different degrees of **political power. Negative** power can be demonstrated through strikes by employees and through manipulation and bribery of officials (which is usually frowned on). In contrast, **lobbying** is a recognised and accepted part of the use of power in pluralist democracies. Lobbying involves the exertion of power by interested parties on politicians who can vote about a particular issue—such as whether a tax on CO_2 emissions should be introduced. Lobbying in parliaments, political parties and associations is particularly important. The word 'lobby' originally referred to an area in parliament (or some other legislative building) where people waited to discuss an issue with their representatives. The sphere of politics is used as a way of solving conflicts between stakeholders (see Crozier and Friedberg 1979), especially where market solutions in the economic sphere do not work because of inequities, lack of resources to enter a market and market failure, such as the complete absence of markets for certain commodities. In the business context, the sphere of politics is related mostly to struggles over distribution of the value that has been created by corporate activity.

The struggle is related to the fact that goods are scarce and economic resources limited. Hence, absolute satisfaction of the desires of every stakeholder is not possible. Management must therefore decide on how to allocate value that has been created by business activity relative to the claims of certain groups on the business (see Schaltegger 1999). If stakeholders disagree with the allocations or the allocation process, conflicts arise. Stakeholders can exert economic pressure by interrupting the supply of resources to the business that they control, or they can disrupt the business by making it difficult to operate: for example, by working strictly in accordance with formal rules of behaviour laid down by the organisation (see Schaltegger and Sturm 1994).

Requirements placed on businesses to ensure environmental protection can also lead to the involvement of **pressure groups** and **associations** that seek to achieve their own environmental goals. For example, if there is concern about noise and emissions from local factories, or about waste emissions from all sites belonging to the company, groups of local or national members may form to bring pressure on the business to reform its behaviour. Pressure groups or local community associations may not seek the closure of factories, because these provide local employment to residents. However, pressure groups may succeed in getting temporary closure of a factory until environmental problems are resolved. This could lead to a loss of income—one that could have been avoided if management had prevented the problem occurring in the first place. In all these cases there is a trade-off between the rewards to different stakeholders. Political solutions that use or lose business value compete with other uses such as safety in the workplace or dividends for shareholders. This means that conflict can exist between management and the other stakeholders and also between individual groups of stakeholders in the political sphere. Through coalitions and alliances various groups of stakeholders tend to form on a given issue. For example, manufacturers of polyvinyl chloride (PVC), their industry association, politicians and worker associations and employees demonstrated against environmental associations and 'green' politicians after use of the material was restricted (see Huber 1998).

6.2.6 Interdependencies among the spheres

Each sphere examined in the above sections stands for a particular perspective that management can use to address environmental issues. In practice, the different spheres are interrelated. The sociocultural sphere flows into the sphere of politics which in turn links up with legislation and the legal sphere through the politics of sovereign nations. Individual stakeholders, such as environmental associations, can be viewed from a political perspective as parties in conflict or partnership with business, from a sociocultural perspective as guardians of moral standards, or through the economic sphere as influencers of consumer behaviour. It should also be remembered that an individual person can be a member of different stakeholder groups at the same time.

Since businesses tend to act primarily in the economic sphere, with management keeping a keen eye on the monetary bottom line, they are concerned about influences on competition in the markets in which they operate (Fig. 6.3). Competitive advantages can be gained from technological developments that are not available to competitors. However, technological innovations for relieving environmental problems can often only be applied and a **competitive advantage** obtained when the underlying problem is highlighted and kept alive by pressure from the general public. The process of **public opinion formation** is thus important to business.

First comes setting the agenda, through which critical business issues are promoted in the public arena. The process of **agenda-setting** involves journalists and editors who present certain themes in their publications (see Eichhorn 1996: 51ff.). The question is: how are those themes chosen? Matters drawn to the attention of edi-

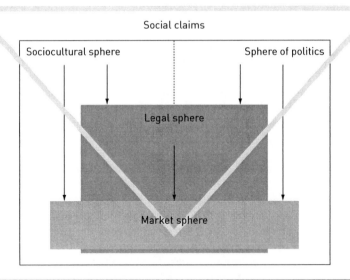

Figure 6.3 **Influence of social claims on the market sphere**

tors and journalists affect the themes chosen. From a business perspective what editors and journalists think about can be influenced through communication (see McCombs and Shaw 1972: 177). Rumours, information leaked by different stakeholders, and press procedure all influence the agenda. Hence, public relations has become important as a means of initiating stories for the media to adopt if they feel that their readers will be interested. In agenda-setting, business has as much chance as campaigners or activists to influence the agenda and of reaching *their* target groups with *their* stories and concerns. Engagement in influencing the agendas of editors of, for example, *Time* magazine, *The Economist, Wall Street Journal* and *Tomorrow* becomes critical. International media, such as CNN News or the BBC World News try to reach out beyond the interests of a limited stakeholder group. They try to give balanced coverage of issues, but often do not succeed, because, for example, some parties are unwilling to be interviewed. Public relations personnel are responsible for moving the agenda forward when called on as well as for setting down issues for the agenda of media personnel.

In the development of public concern certain themes, events or perceptions emerge based on the social claims of different groups. Environmental problems are no exception. Attention can be drawn to accidents, catastrophes or research results about particular environmental issues. For example, once the problem of water pollution is on the agenda, even small incidents strengthen the impression that it is a significant problem and provide evidence that water conservation and protection will remain an important issue into the future. Stakeholders become aware that issues can be amplified and that they pass through a cycle that begins with vague problem awareness and develops into concrete claims made in the political sphere, suggestions for problem solving and suggested solutions being implemented (see Steger 1988: 189). Involvement of business in this process can bring about the solution that business desires. Non-engagement in this process means that other stakeholders are more likely to have their solutions accepted. Businesses, through the media, can publicise particular solutions that they favour, or they can show how they are affected by solutions proposed by other stakeholders.

When issues are raised in public by business, representatives of business or their industry associations, the mere presence of public discussion allows business and its representatives to generate intense political interest. By making the financial implications of issues of concern to society transparent, discussion of various solutions expressed in normative terms (we *should* do this, or we *should* do that) tend to surface. Discussion involving perspectives from the political sphere, the legal sphere and sociocultural sphere coalesce and lead to the eventual outcome that provides a guide to business activity in the market or economic sphere—an outcome that may be quite distinct from the scientific–technological ramifications. A classic case in point relates to the disposal of toxic waste at Love Canal in the USA (see Box 6.2).

Accordingly, public disputes and their influence on the market sphere in which business operates can be viewed from two perspectives. On the one hand, businesses are bound by social bonds to respect the public interest and operate within it. Such bonds are often implicit and, if violated, can lead to social sanctions being generated and penalties implemented. On the other hand, control of public opinion through the media can be used to justify the actions of business in certain situations. Businesses can take early action to secure the 'power of interpretation' in relation to themes considered important (see Liebl 1997: 19). In this way they seek to preserve their social legitimacy.

Lindblom (1994) argues that businesses can adopt a number of legitimation strategies when faced with threats to their legitimacy (e.g. a major pollution leak). These include attempts to:

The Love Canal disaster in New York State had a particularly sobering impact on the US public and the chemical industry. Its impact through time on the technological, economic, sociocultural, legal and political spheres was as follows:

- Chemical waste was dumped in a canal between 1942 and 1953 and covered over: legal sphere

- Later, the area was excavated and redeveloped: economic sphere

- By 1976 residents were complaining about seepage of waste and about health problems: technological and sociocultural spheres

- The media took over and by 1980 a State emergency and a federal emergency declared by President Carter were linked to mob outrage: political sphere

- Permanent relocation of 700 residents cost US$30 million in compensation: sociocultural, political, economic and legal spheres

- A tax on the chemical industry was used to source a Superfund, created to clean up toxic waste sites: economic, legal and political spheres

- Between 1980 and 1995 approximately US$30 billion was committed to cleaning up Superfund sites: economic sphere

---

Box 6.2 Spheres of influence in waste disposal at Love Canal in the USA

Source: Schaltegger and Burritt 2000: 33

- Educate stakeholders about the business's intention to improve performance

- Change stakeholder perceptions of the event that led to the problem, but without changing the organisation's performance

- Manipulate attention away from the issues of concern (e.g. by concentrating on an alternative positive issue)

- Change external expectations about the business's performance

These legitimacy strategies can be used to close any legitimacy gap that exists between stakeholders and the business. Each strategy can be used to address problems raised within any of the different spheres of interest. Education may take place through lobbying in order to ensure that the market's legal framework is protected. Disclosure and increased transparency can be used to try to change stakeholder perceptions in the sociocultural sphere. Stakeholder participation can be used to guide attention towards issues that businesses see as important while giving the impression of pluralist democratic solutions. External expectations can also be changed through appropriate disclosures. However, each of these strategies implies manipulation by business.

Many businesses will not wish to be associated with these strategies and will instead look towards the development of voluntary solutions to environmental problems conducted in an open, transparent way, backed up with independent verification of the statements and claims made by business in relation to the issues of concern. They will seek to involve stakeholders in a dialogue that encourages stakeholders to adopt ownership of problems and hence ownership of solutions to problems (but see Quote 6.2).

In summary, environmental problems can promote consensual views between stakeholders, conflicting views, or both. Basic consensus normally exists about the worth of environmental protection for goods and services that are environmentally

---

• Public participation in a wide range of environmental management and risk policy decisions has increased substantially over recent decades, creating new ground rules and new expectations for a host of federal and state-funded actions. Many of these efforts to democratise the development of policies—including opinion polls, focus groups, town-hall meetings, open houses, advisory committees and a variety of economic surveys—have proven useful. However, too often decision-makers cast a wide net for hearing citizens' views but then disappear behind closed doors to interpret what they have heard and to work out the tough conflicts that inevitably arise across disparate points of view. A charitable interpretation is that decision-makers' access to tools for deeply understanding the concerns of community residents, technical experts or interest groups and for incorporating objectives and trade-offs effectively as part of policies or legislation has not kept pace with the rhetoric of public involvement. It is therefore not surprising that there remains a widespread dissatisfaction with the quality and meaningfulness of stakeholder input to many environmental risk-management decisions. •

Quote 6.2 Use of stakeholder values to make smarter environmental decisions

Source: Gregory 2000: 2

benign, but disputes remain about the way this protection can be achieved and about who should bear the cost of protection. Coalitions and conflicts also arise that resolve issues against the business and in favour of environmental protection. When there is an environmental problem, whether consensus, conflict or both occur, in each case there is an interrelationship between the sociocultural sphere and the economic sphere (e.g. demand preferences, environmental costs, environmental liabilities). Often, the sphere of politics is invoked and this provides the basis for resolution through the introduction of changes to regulations (the legal sphere; see Fig. 6.3).

6.3 From the general stakeholder spheres of influence to the fields of management action

Different spheres represent possible sources of influence that can be considered by business as the basis for resolving environmental issues with which they are involved. However, it is not sufficient merely to observe the spheres, for business management spheres have to become **fields of action**. It is not enough for business to react to external pressure when claims are made by stakeholders. Management must be proactive and have a strategy to address issues and problems before they arise. If accidents do happen, management must also have contingency plans to ensure effective, efficient and equitable resolution of problems. One way to encourage this is to involve stakeholders in discussions about potential problems. Such a strategy provides the chance of following the path of sustainable development towards sustainability, through environmentally oriented business management.

Successful businesses are distinguished today by their ability to learn and develop innovative solutions. They are in a position to face the environmental challenge in a creative way. 'Personal mastery' is, according to Senge (1996), one of the basic disciplines for the construction of a business that is capable of learning. For managers to succeed in personal mastery, one basic condition needs to be established: '[The manager must hold] a creative as opposed to a reactive view of life' (Senge 1996: 173). Such a view is said to be founded on the creative tension between a clear personal vision of goals and a precise sense of the present reality. The person that establishes this tension considers reality to be an ally not an enemy and learns 'to identify powers of change and to use instead of fight them' (Senge 1996: 175). The contrast between this **creative orientation** to life compared with a **reactive orientation** to life is summed up in Table 6.2 (see Roberts 1996).

Personal mastery is not an inherent property but a life-long learning process. Creativity in professional life does not exclude a reactive stance in private life, and vice versa, and so the manager normally moves somewhere between the two polar extremes of creation and reaction. To take personal mastery seriously means the manager has to accept the reactive side of their personality as well as the creative side.

Finally, Roberts (1996: 264) also points to the reverse of an exclusively creative orientation. By way of synthesis an **interdependent orientation** is suggested. Whereas the reactive orientation tries to bring the environment under control and

Creative orientation	*Reactive orientation*
The environment presents:	
Possibilities to intervene in its formation	External forces beyond control that influence people
The basic questions are:	
What do I want to create? What can I do to match the environment with my wishes?	What do other people want from me? Who is responsible for my problems?
Motivation exists in:	
Following a hope and going along with others	Coming out of the 'mess' and being left in peace
The strategy is centred on:	
Discovering those chances and allies that are available in the present	Locating and blaming hostile forces responsible for one's own problems

Table 6.2 Creative compared with reactive orientations to life

Source: based on Roberts 1996

the creative orientation simply seizes the opportunity to be proactive, an interdependent orientation identifies the **networking** possibilities in relation to the environment, which engages them as well as encourages them to participate creatively in its protection.

Questions for review

6.1 'Enterprises not only have to fulfil the requirements of their customers and employees, but also they have to represent the interests of other groups—interests which reach beyond market relationships and into political and social concerns.' Are market concerns or political and social concerns, or all of these, of importance to business environmental management? Why? Explain the reasons for your view.

6.2 Is it true to say that 'virtual' companies have no environmental impacts?

6.3 Select one of the spheres of influence. Describe the main characteristics of that sphere. How is the sphere related to the eco-efficiency of business?

6.4 Why is agenda-setting an important tool for business in environmental management?

6.5 How are spheres of influence and fields of action related in environmental management? Is networking the best way to bring the two together?

Part 2
Success factors and fields of action

Part 1
Overview

Part 2	Part 3
Success factors and fields of action	**Strategic environmental management**

Part 4
Concepts and tools of corporate environmental management

Corporate environmental management, if it is to serve as a guide to deliberative action, must be more than an *ex post* explanation of what has happened in the past, more than an accidental reading of the signs and data about the environmental impacts of business. Instead, it must guide management towards achieving the strategic and operational environmental goals of the business. Corporate environmental management needs to be based on criteria that are useful for assessing the success or failure of the business in meeting these goals. A range of spheres of influence have a bearing on what these goals might be. Legal, economic, political, technological and sociocultural spheres may all play a part. Company success will depend on the perceptions of different stakeholders as to whether and how their expectations about environmental impacts of the business are being addressed. Part 2 of this book provides a normative, heuristic framework based on the spheres of influence as the foundation for a deliberative management approach by business to environmental issues.

7

Success factors and fields of action

Balanced socioeconomic management of the environmental challenge

People introduce business management in order to improve the prospects of success for their business and for themselves. They develop **goals**, use certain **means** and try to influence the course of projects entered into. In practice, this means–goals process is experienced as part of daily life so that individual activities are often not well defined. Certain actions become routine and occur almost subconsciously. Nevertheless, it is expected that managers, when asked to, will be able to justify their actions (see Giddens 1997: 53ff.) and to explain why and how they contribute to business success.

7.1 Balanced management and criteria of balanced business success

Actions lead to results and, depending on the manager's intentions, these indicate the level of success or failure. If the manager's actions are judged to be successful, rules and methods that led to the result can be devised. These rules provide a guide to future actions, which lead to further results, which lead to possible changes in the rules and so on in a continual process. **Balanced management**, however, is more than using means to achieve financial goals. Goals have many dimensions—there may be monetary and non-monetary goals for the business. However, one thing is common to all goal achievement—the means to achieve them are scarce. Balanced management, therefore, is also concerned with having clear priorities when goals are set. Goal conflicts have to be resolved and goal complementarities encouraged, as these can produce synergies (i.e. when two things work together to produce something that is greater than if the two were working independently of each other, given limited resources).

Balanced management includes goals related to all spheres of influence, including considerations of legitimacy, morality, legality and empathy in addition to efficacy, efficiency and freedom of action. It requires the application of ethical principles and understanding of what motivates people because they are affected by their own actions. Hence, an understanding of **norms** and **communication** are important in effective balanced management. The fact that means and goals cannot always be separated from each other must also be considered. For example, if the means (e.g. human capital) are given an **intrinsic value** (e.g. a trustworthy relationship is valued), means also acquire the characteristics of goals. Hence, in this case, the attainment of trust is a goal which, when achieved, becomes the means for attaining other goals (Chambers 1966: 42).

Finally, balanced management is also important for individual understanding of personal boundaries and for encouraging personal growth and the readiness to learn. When the results of actions are compared with previously established goals, in order for any learning to occur the goals and actual results must be **measurable** in similar terms, and the ability of the manager to **influence** future goal-setting and results must be taken into account. Hence, criteria must be defined, according to which the extent of success in achieving goals can be made apparent—that is, measures are needed to assess the effectiveness of management (where effectiveness is seen in the broad sense of nearness to achievement of goals). The next chapter examines such **success criteria** for management. Such criteria form the basis of balanced business management. Balanced management is different from one-sided financial management, and aims at considering all factors of success according to their relevance for a successful business company. In the German literature this approach has been discussed under the notion of 'socioeconomic rational' management as a contrast to conventional economic rationality (Hill 1991; Schaltegger 2000; Schaltegger and Sturm 1994).

Goals provide the benchmark that defines the condition that is sought—whether social, environmental or monetary. Success criteria provide indicators for assessing whether and how (e.g. efficiently, or equitably) goals have been achieved. In order to describe this use of success criteria with greater clarity, individual symptoms need to be recorded and indicators of success identified. For example, if the criterion is called 'fun', symptoms such as 'laughter' point to the degree of success. If a 'day's duration of laughter' is measured by using a stopwatch and is compared with the extent of laughter the day before, an indicator exists that shows whether the 'fun' has increased.

One basic task of management is to select indicators that reflect the goals that the business, or manager, is trying to achieve (see Bea and Göbel 1999: 15ff.). Success criteria must have clear, unequivocal **indicators** that are relevant to assessment of the particular goals. The number of criteria should be as small as possible, in order to facilitate decision-making under conditions of uncertainty, but large enough to demonstrate balanced success across all the goals being sought—to provide a **balanced scorecard** about performance.

As mentioned above, management needs to select indicators that reflect the strategic goals that the business, or manager, is trying to achieve. Where these goals relate to the environment, then indicators need to be developed as part of the overall measures of performance of the business. The balanced scorecard is one tool of analysis that has been designed to provide information about performance at a strategic level (Kaplan and Norton 1996).

Short- and long-term goals of management are both considered in the balanced scorecard; hence, the socrecard concept is ideal for combining information about long-term environmental impacts with economic measures of success. To support strategic goal-setting and achievement, a set of lead and lag indicators is produced as the basis for decision, action and management accountability. Goal-setting and goal achievement are measured in similar terms, thereby facilitating comparability over time and between different parts of the business. Cross-comparisons between, say, economic and environmental performance are built into the general management processes. Debate continues about the appropriate small set of relevant environmental and social indicators that business could adopt, with the Global Reporting Initiative providing one of the most recent perspectives (GRI 2002).

Kaplan and Norton's (1996) balanced scorecard provides measures of performance relating to four aspects of the business: financial, customer, operational processes and organisational learning. Balanced scorecard indicators could be extended to include each of the spheres of influence relevant to the business—technological, economic, legal, sociocultural and political—with environmental indicators being fully integrated within each of these aspects of the business. A current tendency is to focus on three areas of a business—environment, social responsibility and economic performance—the result being a sustainability balanced scorecard that provides a strategic guide to action related to these three separate, or 'triple', bottom lines. One problem is that the three areas may not be distinct as they can be interrelated. For example, are increased emissions of noxious gases into the atmosphere in a local community an issue for the environmental or social bottom line of a business, or both? Which indicator or indicators should reflect this, and in which section of a triple-bottom-line report should these appear?

Each manager may be able to determine his or her own success criteria; however, in many cases **structure** and **function** are imposed on lower-level managers from above. In business, managers are dependent on the balance of resources provided by other stakeholders. Stakeholders use their own criteria and indicators to assess the success of managers. Each stakeholder, including management itself, has a different perspective and a different set of indicators of business success. Cyert and March (1992) recognise that a constant series of sequential, bilateral negotiations between management and different stakeholder groups tend to reflect the reality of managing a business. Mintzberg (1973) emphasised 30 years ago the fact that management is confronted with various socialising activities, networking and representation in order to create a productive basis for company operations. Management balances the demands placed on business by all stakeholders and takes the particular goals of any stakeholder group into account when negotiating any matters of substance and when reporting on the success of business performance.

In Chapter 6 five spheres were introduced in which business operates. Specific success criteria differ in each sphere (see Table 7.1).

In general, success criteria reveal the effectiveness of business management when dealing with stakeholder claims. In the narrow sense, **effectiveness** is considered to

Scientific– technological	Economic	Legal	Sociocultural	Political
Main focus:				
Degree of influence Accuracy	Proportion of output to input	Regulations Norms Laws Standards Benchmarks	Values Morality Reliability Notification	Achievement of political interests
Question to be answered:				
To what extent is technical influence achieved?	What is the relationship between profits (yield) and costs (expenditure)?	What is the extent of non-compliance with laws?	Which social purposes should be pursued by business?	How do relative powers of stakeholders limit the field of business action?
Criterion for success:				
Effectiveness	Efficiency	Compliance/ legality	Legitimacy	Freedom of action
Type of rationality:				
Technical	Economic	Legal	Normative (communi-cative)	Political interests

Note: In order to achieve the desired style of management all these indicators need to be balanced.

Table 7.1 **The concept of balanced management**

Sources: based on Hill 1991; see also Schaltegger 2000; Schaltegger and Sturm 1994

be a rule related to the successful introduction, development and use of **technical** processes. Expenditure on and use of technology, and the benefits of such use, can be measured in terms of capital productivity. Assuming that the technical measuring devices are **accurate**, then an increase in the measure indicates an increase in productivity. Health and safety legislation forms a backup to ensure that measures related to technical processes do indeed provide accurate readings. Technical measurement infrastructure is critical to the success of commerce and business environmental management.

In the socioeconomic field of business management action, results are always subject to uncertainty. Human reactions are not entirely predictable, unless humans are made to be completely subservient. Although natural sciences and technology presuppose constant laws of nature, culture, economy, social relationships and people react on the basis of their historical, social and cultural development. If humans are considered by management as technocratic cyborgs or robots this will, inevitably, lead to disquiet, upset, demotivation, eventual exit and loss of corporate learning and intellectual capital.

Increased productivity caused by the introduction of new techniques, or better use of existing technology, is called **technical progress**. Of course, technical progress can improve the performance of a business, but it can also affect the other spheres of influence. For example, the quality of life may deteriorate when new technology is introduced, because the technology stops employees talking to each other at work. In other words, there is often a trade-off between the benefits that accrue in some spheres and the impacts that are imposed on other spheres. Technical innovations rarely have a one-dimensional effect. Technical progress can lead to adverse **side-effects** through undesirable environmental impacts of business activities (see Knaus and Renn 1998: 127ff.). Balanced management must recognise that gains from science and technology are linked to the social and environmental context of problems. In consequence, solutions sought by business must examine the balance between technical progress and environmental regress, or degradation. If indicators of both are available, then management will be able to demonstrate when improvements in both occur in parallel (e.g. through the introduction of new cleaner technology).

Technical data reveals whether a technical goal is successfully achieved. However, the goal originates from management balancing the desires of different stakeholders and the decision of that management to be involved with the business organisation and its activities. Stakeholders provide information about which natural state is considered to be desirable and which environmental influences are more or less harmful and relevant. Effectiveness must therefore be balanced with further success criteria, which, as indicated in Table 7.1, include **efficiency, legality, legitimacy** (including **equity**) and **freedom of action**. Balanced business management has the role of making sure that an acceptable balance between all these goals and the means towards achieving these goals is maintained. Included in this balance is sound environmental management.

7.2 Technical effectiveness and its socioeconomic reference

In the environmental context, effectiveness describes the physical influence of rules on nature. A central question here is the extent to which a particular goal is achieved (see Schaltegger and Sturm 1994). If, for example, the emission of a harmful substance can be reduced through technical innovation by 50% annually in relative terms, or 100 tonnes annually in absolute terms, the effectiveness of the innovation can be indicated in either of these ways. Effectiveness is influenced by the type of technology constructed and installed, its size and its anticipated technical duration. Technical readings can be made in relation to expected goals and past performance, independent of the economic cost of the technology. Expressed in physical units, such items of data can act as indicators of environmental impact added, or saved, by the new technology through measures of input (e.g. energy consumption) or output (e.g. the amount of waste produced). (For definitions of environmental impact and environmental impact added, see Boxes 5.3 and 5.4 on page 31.)

Environmental management that is undertaken within a balanced management framework looks for reduction of the environmental impact added by its business. One way of reducing the environmental impact added is to examine each and every action undertaken within the business, find out whether it leads to adverse environmental impacts, rank these findings in terms of unacceptability and then methodically try to reduce the impacts of each activity, beginning with the most serious. This would be a technical approach to reducing environmental impact added. However, other spheres of influence must also be taken into account because of the interdependencies discussed in Chapter 6, particularly Section 6.2.6. For example, if environmental impact added could be reduced through the introduction of new technology which also assists management in improving its economic results, at least two groups of stakeholders will be satisfied by this course of action. This is commonly known as a **win–win situation**, where stakeholders concerned about the environment are satisfied and investors are also satisfied.

Assessment of whether technological improvements can be delivered rests largely in the hands of natural scientists, in discussion with executive officers. Technicians in most cases stand out from others in the workforce because of their technical terminology, their expert knowledge and their technical enthusiasm (see Schein 1996). However, environmental technologies must not only satisfy the technical requirements of experts but also match the needs of users and the routine of the business if all their gains are to be captured. In addition, outside the business, environmental dialogues, or rather dialogues about environmental risks, can be entered into to establish the extent of acceptability of the new technology (e.g. whether a new high-temperature incinerator is acceptable to a local community, even though it performs the destruction of waste in a technically efficient manner).

At the socioeconomic level, four fields of action associated with distinct modes of action can be distinguished:

- Markets (economic)
- The legal regulation system (legal)
- Partnerships (communicative)
- The political arena (political)

In these fields of action, social co-ordination with stakeholders takes place. Such co-ordination includes bringing the actions within each of the above fields into line with each other (Fig. 7.1).

The chapters that follow in Part 2 (Chapters 8–11) illuminate relationships between businesses and their stakeholders in each of these four fields of action. Division of the analysis in this way should stimulate students to take the following into account when thinking about and implementing balanced management:

- Markets
- Rules and guidelines

- The importance of individual trust
- Personal interests and perspectives

Levels of natural sciences and technology (scientific-technological)	Fields of action at the socioeconomic level			
	Market (economic)	Legal regulation system (legal)	Partnership (sociocultural)	Arena (political)
Degree of influence, accuracy *To what extent is technical influence achieved?*	**Related to claim** Proportion of output to input *What is the relationship between profits (yield) and costs (expenditure)?*	Regulations, norms, laws, standards, benchmarks *What is the extent of non-compliance with laws?*	Values, morality, reliability, notification *Which social purposes should be pursued by business?*	Achievement of political interests *How do relative powers of stakeholders limit the field of business action?*
Trying and measuring	**Basis for action** Exchange and competition	Order and obedience	Trust and commitment	Exertion of influence and dispute
Effectiveness	**Criterion of success** Efficiency	Compliance	Legitimacy	Freedom of action
Technical	**Type of rationality** Economic	Legal	Normative (communicative)	Political interests

Balanced business management

Figure 7.1 **The concept of balanced management indicators**

Source: based on Hill 1991; similar to Schaltegger and Sturm 1994; Schaltegger 2000

Questions for review

7.1 What are the main characteristics of balanced environmental management? How are they related to success criteria (indicators of success)? Is a balanced scorecard a necessary or sufficient condition for assessing the success of balanced management?

7.2 How does the balanced management approach address the link between socioeconomic and science/technology fields of action?

8

Success factors and fields of action

Markets, efficiency and eco-efficiency

Businesspeople primarily focus their actions on **market activity**. Market participants voluntarily contract to exchange their resources in a way that is beneficial to all participants. Markets operate on the basis of competition between producers and consumers. Consumer demand determines whether products and services can be sold by the producers of goods or by the suppliers of services. For example, consumer preferences determine whether sales are made, whether a limousine uses green fuel or whether a detergent 'washes whiter than white'. Costs of supply help determine whether producers will offer a good or service for sale. Prices and costs of goods and services determine the quantity demanded and supplied at a given level of quality. Hence, the economic activities of consumers and producers are determined by market price. The relationship between price and costs provides an indication of the **economic efficiency** of the producer or service provider and of the success of socioeconomic management.

Field of action	*Market*
Main focus	Proportion of output to input
Question to be answered	What is the relationship between profits (yield) and costs (expenditure)?
Basis for action	Exchange and competition
Criterion for success	Efficiency
Focus	Economic

Table 8.1 Markets and efficiency

8.1 Efficiency and eco-efficiency as criteria of market success

Markets contribute to value creation by increasing the volume of goods and services available at prices that reflect efficient operations. Markets provide a decentralised and impersonal (in an 'apolitical' sense) way of making decisions about the allocation of goods and services, provided that potential participants have sufficient monetary wealth to transact in the marketplace. In turn, competition takes care of the need for participants to be efficient in the management of their organisational activities and processes. Of course, where a market has an **oligopolistic** (a few key suppliers) or a **monopolistic** (a single supplier) structure, market pricing can be less effective and consumers can pay more than they would in a more competitive situation. Likewise, if there is a single customer (a condition of **monopsony**), suppliers to the market may be disadvantaged and be unable to survive.

Since inputs to production are in limited supply, efficiency is a key consideration for businesses. Improved efficiency provides one means whereby a supplier of goods or services to a market can gain an advantage over the competition. Corporate efficiency is measured through productivity and profitability. **Productivity** refers to the technical relationship between inputs and outputs, whereas **profitability** refers to the monetary relationship (Schaltegger and Burritt 2000, 2001a). Profitability measures economic efficiency, whereas environmental efficiency is a specific example of technical efficiency that examines the relationship between environmental inputs and outputs.

Since the use of environmental resources is often based on situations where resources are being obtained at too low a price, or at a zero price (e.g. waste disposal in the ocean), and where those who cause environmental damages frequently do not pay the total costs associated with these environmental impacts, the value of the natural environment is only partially captured by the financial aspects of market activity. Therefore, integration of technical environmental efficiency and economic environmental efficiency (eco-efficiency) is required if environmental effects on productivity and profitability are each to be taken into account in the decisions made by business.

If efficiency is interpreted in a specific environmental way as being the ratio of desired output to input, business can talk about environmental efficiency. This specifies the relationship between desired environmental performance and environmental impact added by business activities:

$$\text{Environmental efficiency} = \frac{\text{desired output}}{\text{environmental impact added}} \qquad [8.1]$$

Environmental impact added is defined as the total environmental effects or influences of corporate activities. These can be weighted with regard to their relative harm on the environment (Schaltegger and Sturm 1990: 280; see also Box 5.4 on page 31). Measurement of environmental impact added is based on calculations of material flows linked to methods for environmental accounting and environmental performance evaluation by business.

Every time that a business activity occurs there is an increase in environmental impact added—there is no value creation without environmental impact being added. Value and environmental impact added can be linked to each other either through consideration of products or through consideration of functions:

- Ecological product efficiency is a measure of the ratio between provision of a unit of product and the environmental impact added by that product (see Schaltegger and Burritt 2000; Schaltegger and Sturm 1992, 1994, 2000) over the whole, or over a part, of the product's life-cycle (e.g. the number of cars produced per unit of energy consumed). Product efficiency can be improved by implementing pollution prevention techniques or by introducing end-of-pipe devices, reduced use of inputs per unit or through substitution of resources. However, some products will never be as ecologically efficient as others in providing a certain service (e.g. a car will always be less ecologically efficient than a bicycle).

- Ecological function efficiency measures how much environmental impact is associated with the provision of a specific function in each period of time (see Schaltegger and Burritt 2000; Schaltegger and Sturm 1992, 1994, 2000). Ecological function efficiency is defined as the ratio between the provision of a function (e.g. painting a square metre of metal) and the associated environmental impact added (e.g. use of chemicals and metal resources). It can be improved by substituting functions that have a low efficiency with highly efficient functions (e.g. by using a bicycle instead of a car), by reducing the amount used to fulfil the function (e.g. use of car pools leads to a decreased demand for cars), by prolonging the life-span of products (e.g. by giving longer guarantees against corrosion on cars) and by improving product efficiency.

These are two relative measures of performance—they compare two factors as a proportion or ratio. Note that it is also important to consider the total output and the absolute environmental impact: a large number of ecologically efficient products can be more harmful than a small number of ecologically inefficient items.

Although an improvement in environmental product efficiency is desirable in principle, in most cases it can be less beneficial to the environment than improvements in function efficiency. Even the most economical car needs wider roads and parking space in comparison with a tram running on tracks or in comparison with a bicycle. Products can be seen as groups of functions; for example, a lipstick needs to deliver the product to the mouth, to allow the user to apply it cleanly, to be smooth rather than brittle, to be safe for human use and to be retractable when the lipstick has been applied. Each of these functions of the product can be improved by reducing its environmental impact added. Usually, the environmental impact added by a number of functions is changed at any one time during redesign (see Bredemeier *et al.* 1997).

The environmental view of efficiency is enlightening. For corporate decisions about environmental impacts, however, this non-economic view is necessary but not sufficient. In order to solve business problems in an environmentally and economically efficient way, the measures with the greatest environmental net income per unit of capital expenditure (profitability) have to be determined. Therefore, to business, the relevant measure of performance is economic ecological efficiency or, in brief, **eco-efficiency** (Schaltegger and Sturm 1994: 283):

$$\text{Eco-efficiency} = \frac{\text{economic value creation}}{\text{environmental impact added}} \qquad [8.2]$$

Eco-efficiency can be determined for all business actions and activities, even when they do not directly focus on environmental protection. The ratio of economic value created to ecological environmental impact added can be improved over time. For example, greater eco-efficiency occurs when environmental impact added is reduced as much as possible given a specific level of expenditure (e.g. the budget for the environmental protection department). Likewise, eco-efficiency can be improved when, for a given use of natural resources (environmental impact added), the lowest level of expenditure is incurred (net economic value is created). Hence, improved competition can also produce improved eco-efficiency.

To sum up, economically successful business management is marked by an improvement in eco-efficiency in business activities. Eco-efficiency is considered to be an important basis for decisions that are made in many businesses today,[3] the idea becoming popular primarily through the activities of the World Business Council for Sustainable Development (WBCSD; see www.wbcsd.org) and the businessman Schmidheiny (1992).[4]

8.2 A market orientation, efficiency and market failure

Eco-efficient actions undertaken through choices made in markets means that business needs to work with market forces to achieve its environmental goals. **Market forces** are demand- and supply-oriented and rest on the ideas and ideals of competition. Actions arising through markets are **voluntary** because no business is required to be a participant in a market. Instead, willing buyers and sellers come together to form a market through the completion of mutually advantageous contracts. Markets can vary in the degree of efficiency present. Some markets are inefficient if the underlying premises of efficient markets do not hold; for example, if there are insufficient numbers of buyers and sellers, markets may be inefficient. Transactions in markets take place in a decentralised way, as individual buyers and sellers seek their own advantage through market transactions. Price, quantity, quality and required performance of the goods and services being bought and sold can be matched between buyers and sellers in a flexible and direct way (see Streit 1991). Markets can operate beyond sovereign nations and thereby overcome spatial bound-

2   For an example of a manufacturer, see www.basf.de; for the full range of industries involved, see www.environment.gov.au/epg/environet/eecp/examples.html.
3   A description of best practice in eco-efficiency can be found at www.eco-efficiency.net/ edizione2001/eco_uk_best.htm.

aries. In this way, they contribute to cultural networking and globalisation of trade and commerce. This is particularly evident with the advent of electronic commerce, or e-commerce, instantly transacted through computers.

Despite these advantages from the perspective of efficiency in the conduct of business transactions, social and environmental problems demonstrate the market's inability to provide solutions to all problems. Efficiency is often supplemented with **equity** issues; where potential participants have no general purchasing power to enter markets, then inequity and social problems arise. Markets sometimes do not take all costs and benefits into their pricing of transactions in goods and services. Harmful consequences for the environment are caused by such examples of **market failure**. Economists talk of **external costs** (i.e. **externalities**) that are not paid for either by the businesses that cause the costs or by the beneficiaries that buy business products and services. People who benefit in this way are called '**free riders**'. External costs and free-riders lead to overuse of free **public goods**, such as air or water, that are available at no specific cost to the individual (Barton 1999). Market failure to take all, or full, costs into account when transactions take place is a prime reason why much environmental degradation is caused by business (see Fritsch *et al.* 1999; Pearce and Turner 1990).

Business can pass on to consumers only those additional costs for protection of the environment that either have to be passed on because of regulation or that provide the business with an **advantage** (and greater revenue) over its competitors. Environmental protection measures that do not save costs or establish any additional value for business customers are introduced only because of a **moral obligation** to society and the environment.

When establishing the general market conditions that affect commerce and trade, avoidance of market failure is primarily a task for the sphere of politics. If the government permits market failures, then this can be seen as a defect of the sphere of politics in avoiding environmental problems, thereby reflecting **government failure**.

Businesses can also influence the market framework within which they operate (see Schneidewind 1998), but once the market framework is established corporate decision-makers work closely to the rules established. If environmental goods are free, then competitive forces will not encourage business to reduce usage, because to do so might lead to bankruptcy, the inability to pay economic debts as they fall due or liquidation: the life of the business is brought to an end.

Market conditions constantly change. Technological innovation, new organisational structures, new laws and rules laid down by professional associations, media pressure, cyclical changes in the prosperity of a country (e.g. the recent crises in Asia and Japan) that affect income available to consumers, new working conditions—all these contribute to the dynamic of business management. In these circumstances, market or government failure exacerbates any problems that exist, such as those related to environmental problems. This can lead to fluidity in the strategies adopted by business towards the environment.

A market orientation implies the constant pursuit of possibilities for production and sale of goods that are more environmentally benign in order to capture the right moment for entry into and exit from the market. It encourages the introduction of new products and processes into the market through technological innovation where an economic gain might be available.

This chapter:

- Invites readers to identify how the scope of existing markets can be transformed into markets that encourage the survival of sustainable business activity—through the introduction of new solutions, the elimination of waste, improved quality of life and promotion of the need for achievement in this area

- Prepares readers to co-operate in the development of markets that reflect environmental considerations—in other words, to participate in the removal of existing market failures through development of new markets, through the internalisation of environmental costs that at present fall outside the boundaries of the business, by encouraging pricing that incorporates environmental preservation and by supporting the introduction of environmental accounting systems that measure environmental impacts and provide relevant information, and by promoting the consideration by managers of environmental protection in all aspects of business activity

Readers will need to engage the socioeconomic sphere when striving to understand how markets and market mechanisms might be improved, but they will also become aware of limitations that can be resolved only through the sphere of politics and through the technological and legal spheres of action. Actors determine what happens in the market field through their interaction with the other spheres.

8.3 Competitive relationships

Actors transact in markets by making and accepting **agreements**, or **contracts**. From a business perspective, direct agreements are made for the development and design of processes and products, for purchases from suppliers, for the provision of economic capital, for the hiring of employees and for the provision of sales and after-sales services to customers. Apart from these direct relationships between the contracting parties to an agreement, a number of indirect relationships with competitors exist.

The dominant task of competitors is to capture demand for products that are offered to the market. In order to achieve this, competitors compete with each other by **underbidding** each other in terms of price, or **overbidding** in terms of the quality of goods and services provided. Quality is defined here as being represented by **value** of the product or its functions to the customer. **Information** available to the various parties is a critical aspect of these market relationships. Available information portrays the product's or service's **image** to consumers and can enhance credibility in the eyes of the consumer (see Fig. 8.1).

Information is always distributed to the markets in an uneven way (see Picot *et al.* 1998: 20ff.). Therefore, especially in markets where there are too many goods rela-

Note: The inner (unshaded) zone refers to the product; the outer (shaded) zone refers to information on the product.

Figure 8.1 **Determinants of demand for products**

tive to total market demand, the need to **direct** the **attention** of customers towards product features and functions is important to company success. Some information about production will always remain confidential, but information about characteristics and functions of products needs to be disclosed (made transparent) if customers are being asked for payment to purchase such products. Consequently, competition takes place at the different levels indicated in Figure 8.1.

A particular challenge for environmentally oriented business management lies in communicating the benefit of environmentally beneficial or benign aspects of a product or service in a **transparent** and **believable** manner. This is necessary in order to increase sales turnover or to justify a higher price where sales turnover is not being encouraged because of the need to conserve physical resources and to reduce waste-streams related to production.

The environmental characteristics of products are only rarely considered as 'inner qualities' of the goods offered for sale in the search for goods. **Experience goods** permit the buyer to use or taste the product before a final commitment to purchase has to be made. For businesses selling experience goods, return policies usually allow consumers to defer their final purchasing decisions until after they have gained some experience with the goods. **Trust goods** are very similar. If a product is claimed to be energy-efficient and it turns out not to be then return would be allowed within a specified period in order that the customer retain complete trust in the environmental claims or in the chemical composition of the product. Analysis and assessment of independent research institutes may be available in reports to help build trust or to demonstrate independent experience in relation to the product. With **potemkin goods** such evaluation procedures are not possible. Environmental qualities cannot be determined for these products. Hence, in the cases of experience, trust and potemkin goods information asymmetries exist between suppliers and consumers. In these circumstances opportunistic competitors may take advantage of the information asymmetry by providing false statements or distorted pictures about their own products (Fig. 8.2).

In order to overcome these hurdles related to information asymmetry, environmentally oriented business management is dependent on presenting an honest,

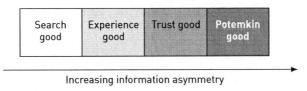

Increasing information asymmetry

Figure 8.2 **Information asymmetry in eco-marketing**

Source: Tietzel and Weber 1991: 117

credible image. To promote honest environmental communication different instruments can be used. Evaluations from neutral institutes such as the magazines *Öko-Test* (www.oekotest.de) in Germany or *Choice* in Australia (www.choice.com.au), or certificates and labels such as the Japanese 'Eco-mark' (www.jeas.or.jp/ecomark/english) or the German 'Blue Angel' (*Blauer Umweltengel*; www.blauer-engel.de), document the product's environmental benefits. In addition, business integrity combined with provision of transparent information on the product lend support to the development of trust and a possible competitive advantage (see Fichter 1998).

Continual improvement forms an important part of the ability to compete in a dynamic marketplace. This is required because as one competitor gains an advantage from a new environmental insight then another competitor strives to improve that achievement and regain the competitive advantage through **price reductions** or non-price means such as **innovations**. Porter (1999a) distinguishes strategies of competition related to cost advantage from strategies of competition related to differentiation of products. Environmental characteristics contribute to **differentiation** when they match effective demand for products (i.e. demand backed up by purchasing power or money). The process of differentiation flowing from one competitor to another presents an ideal picture of the market forces in action. The interaction of innovation and imitation enhances the dynamic of the market economy. In the ideal case, successful innovators pull the performance of the whole market upwards and in this way increase the movement towards sustainable development while at the same time satisfying consumer preferences for 'greener' goods.

So, through a process of general competition companies develop their own fields of business. These fields of business can be ranked in terms of the environmental problems associated with each field. Some fields of business are environmentally sensitive, whereas others are less sensitive. According to Dyllick *et al.* (1997: 60ff.) environmental fields of competition occur in three possible stages of development:

- Actual fields of competition mark existing opportunities for competition inside an existing branch of mass production. Additional environmental benefits are an important factor in customer purchasing decisions and lead to the replacement of conventional product varieties with improved products (e.g. energy-saving household appliances) (see www.aeg.de and www.eastaway.com.au/solutions_hm_2a.html).

- Latent fields of competition are available in market niches and are occupied by new companies that build up their businesses over time. Products survive in the market, but they take time to break into the mass market (e.g. solar panels and wind turbines).[4]

● Potential fields of competition are highlighted by prototypes, methods and new product ideas that are at the research or development stage and attempt to solve a particular environmental problem (e.g. fuel cells and environmentally friendly vehicles).[5]

The transition of an environmentally benign product through its potential status, to the latent and, finally, actual fields of competition does not happen automatically or through coercion. Many new ideas simply do not get beyond the prototype stage because existing products currently appear to be more effective or because these new ideas are not pursued energetically enough in a business context. Even products that prove their worth in niche markets make their way into mass markets only when they have the support of business leaders that have sensed a market opportunity and have decided to take advantage of that opportunity.

8.4 Relationships between customers and suppliers

Only an indirect link exists between suppliers and consumers of products. As shown in Figure 8.3, relationships between customers and suppliers can be classified in a number of different ways, depending on the type of the market and the nature of the product.

Exchange of goods and services takes place in markets only when the price is agreed between a willing buyer and a willing seller. Two types of goods market are important—the consumer goods market (called the final goods market) and the goods market for commercial organisations, business-to-business transactions (called the industrial goods market). The industrial goods market has two parts— the capital goods market and the intermediate goods market (i.e. relating to goods that will be transformed into final products to be sold in the consumer goods market). Note that the purchase and sale of goods has a close association with the financial markets. Money flows in the opposite direction from products and services in the goods markets. Hence, interaction with the financial markets is an integral part of successful business. Insurance of business activities, availability of credit, foreign exchange for overseas sales and purchases, equity, long-term debt and investment markets are all related to the financial markets and, for each type of finance, concerns can be raised about the impact of business activities on the environment. These environmental concerns might lead to difficulties in finance repayment to lenders. Detailed explanation of these markets and their connection with business environ-

4   On solar panels, see www.rueschsolar.ch; on wind turbines, see www.windpower.dk/core.htm.
5   On fuel cells, see www.innovation-brennstoffzelle.de; on environmentally friendly vehicles, see www.ford.com/en/vehicles/specialtyvehicles/environmental/default.htm.

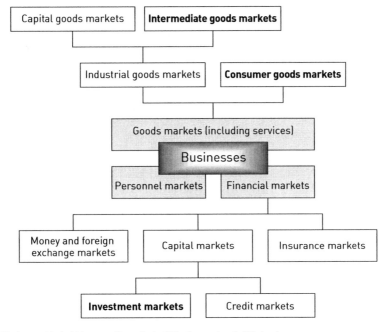

Note: Markets set in bold type are those that will be focused on in this book.

Figure 8.3 **Major types of market faced by a business**

mental issues is beyond the scope of this book. Here, concentration is on the intermediate goods market, consumer goods market and the investment market (set in bold type in Fig. 8.3). Descriptions of these are given in Box 8.1. In the remaining sections of this chapter attention is drawn to relationships between stakeholders. The rest of the chapter is structured as follows:

- Section 8.4.1 looks at relationships between suppliers and consumers.

- Section 8.4.2 looks at relationships between manufacturers and wholesale traders.

- Section 8.4.3 looks at relationships in the intermediate goods market chain.

- Section 8.4.4 looks at relationships between capital providers and businesses.

8.4.1 Relationships between suppliers and consumers

The amount and variety of consumers and their needs is infinite. Consumer goods are designed to meet these needs. Present consumption provides individual enjoyment or wellbeing to consumers. Future consumption patterns and consumer needs are what drives competition in the private sphere. It is easier to secure economic gains from supplying intermediate goods to industry than to capture the market for

Consumer goods markets

Consumer goods markets are characterised by various institutions—for example, a large number of private households, retail businesses, tourist organisations and suppliers of services and food products. Between manufacturers and consumers there is a flow of **trade** from the **wholesale** to the **retail** level. Moreover, advertising agencies and forwarding agencies support or provide the logistics for **promoting sales**. Mass production and distribution through a range of distribution channels, including Internet sales, has been encouraged by the cost advantages that stem from specialisation and has promoted the development of a gap between manufacturers and consumers. Consumers often appear as abstract 'groups' or 'market segments'. Market and consumer research encourage an analytical approach towards targeting customers. However, whether goods really reach the customers they are aimed at is, in the end, determined by the extent and type of communication conducted through wholesale traders.

Intermediate goods markets

Intermediate goods markets represent initial inputs to production, such as raw materials, as well as semi-manufactured products that will be passed on to other producers for completion and sale in the final goods market. The market relationships between businesses involved in the intermediate goods chain are, in most cases, direct and are often long-term.

Investment markets

Corporate finance can be obtained through investment capital (e.g. by means of share or bond issues). In their investment decisions investors seek the least possible risk and the highest possible yield. The yield of an investment is related to dividends and interest payments and also to gains in market value (capital gains). Since capital gains and dividends are uncertain *ex ante*, profitability has to be assessed on the basis of expectations. **Analysts** of banks and superannuation fund groups have an enormous influence on expectations in the market. They estimate the value of the business and make recommendations based on comparisons with share prices quoted on the stock exchange. Institutional **fund groups** act as large investors and often cultivate a long-term interest in a particular business.

Box 8.1 Markets of environmental interest

consumer goods. Final consumers are not passive receptors; their wants and needs can be changed by marketing, advertising and various forms of communication about the quality, function and value of the product. From an environmental perspective, this malleability of consumer demand is an important aspect that can be used to help promote a transition towards the sale of environmentally benign products.

Consumption is satisfied through the procurement of final consumer goods. Procurement is an active part of the value creation process for business. Consumers pay particular attention to the function, aesthetics and symbolism of the goods they acquire (see Liebl 1999: 132). Products acquired must be serviceable for the purposes of the consumer and so information about serviceability and functionality needs to be provided to consumers by business. Business has to provide a serviceable product to the consumer, but through the skilful use of marketing it may also try to convince the consumer that the product on offer has all the functionality desired (see Kritzmöller 1999: 25) even when this is not the case. Often acquisitions do not meet all the needs of the consumer and a compromise has to be reached when a purchase is made. Once a product is perceived to be serviceable, then the chance of repeat buying is increased because of the certainty associated with actual experience gained about the functionality of a product—something that a product made by an alternative supplier may not be able to provide.

Procurement is not a discrete process (see Selle 1993). Consumers change their perception of the functions and uses of goods according to the stage reached in their lives and according to the memories (good and bad) associated with particular products. To some extent, therefore, consumers invent new functions for products (e.g. when a customer uses an antique household appliance as an ornament, or an ornament as a paper weight). Suppliers are not aware of all the functions for which their products will be used and so they provide guidance about the **functional**, **symbolic** and **aesthetic aspects** of a product. For example, an electric hairdryer is designed to dry hair, and a supplier will provide instructions about how to use the dryer to dry hair, such as the distance to hold the dryer from the head and so on; however, instructions will not be given about how to use a hairdryer as a makeshift blowtorch. The hairdryer is not serviceable for this purpose. Hence, consumption and communication are closely interrelated. There are a number of aspects to this link between consumption and communication (see Fig. 8.4).

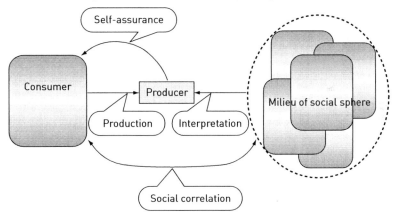

Figure 8.4 **Self-assurance and social correlation during consumption**

Source: Bredemeier *et al.* 1997

In the process of experiencing goods, consumers assure themselves about the qualities and functions of the products they have acquired. They look for **self-assurance**. This means that they seek to develop confidence that the products reflect the functions and purposes that have been communicated by the supplier and the functions that they themselves desire from the product. Purchase of a product links consumers to their social milieu. Actual purchase, when it occurs, discloses the consumer's tastes, income and ethical standards. The product acts as a link, or a social correlation, between the consumer and the social **scene** in which the consumers find themselves. This scene can be represented as a local network of similar people in similar places and with similar lifestyles (Schulze 1996: 747). Examples include being part of an advanced civilisation, a group in a pub, people at work or people at a concert. Social correlation is a two-way relationship between the consumer and the social group that interprets the functions, serviceability and ethics of the consumer (see Brüggemann 1998). Thus, a fur coat is considered by some to be a luxury to be envied, whereas for others it is a symbol of animal torture and the person wearing it is rejected (see Kritzmöller 1999).

Milieus have a special significance in this social correlation. Schulze (1996: 463) defines milieus as 'groups of people, who stand out from each other because of group-specific existence forms and because of enhanced inner communication'. Customers imitate one another because they assimilate characteristics of lifestyles and consumption traits that are marketed, including conscious avoidance of some unacceptable consumption patterns. Consumers learn their consumption patterns from family, friends, neighbours (see Brock 1995) and from the general culture and standard of living in their country. They learn indirectly through their observations of the social sphere.

In the process of value creation consumers and suppliers cross-reference each other. Consumers express their needs by making offers in the marketplace, and suppliers undertake market research about consumer likes and dislikes. Individual consumers and suppliers are invisible market partners in terms of the quantity demanded, the value of goods and services received and environmental impact added in the production-to-consumption process (see Fig. 8.5).

Suppliers create and supply consumer goods in the form of products and services that add corporate value and have an environmental impact—termed 'environ-

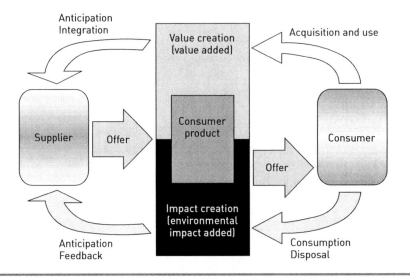

Figure 8.5 **Processes of supplier and consumer value and environmental impact added**

mental impact added'. The consumer confirms the value of the products through **acquisition** and **use**. In parallel with this, environmental impacts are added through **consumption** and **disposal**, which lead to emissions into the environment and eventual waste. In order to create more value for the customer the supplier **antici-pates** the possible desires of consumers. By obtaining feedback from marketing questionnaires and by encouraging customer participation in the design of products and services, consumers are **integrated** into the research, development and design processes associated with new and improved products or services. For example, when a customer visits a hairdresser the supplier and customer interact in the initial decision about cutting, colouring and styling and also throughout the hairdressing experience.

In **eco-marketing**, in order to make the choice easier for the consumers, suppliers also anticipate the environmental impact added by consumption. Hence, the supplier directly influences the product or service and indirectly influences consumer behaviour where environmental issues are considered. This encourages the possibility of 'closing the loop' by taking waste from the final product or service and linking it back to the production process. Closure of the loop may occur directly by re-use of material inputs or components from the final product (e.g. re-use of computer parts in new computers) or indirectly by a transformation process that permits re-use for other purposes (e.g. as in paper or glass recycling).

An essential difference between consumers and suppliers is that suppliers carefully analyse consumer behaviour through market research in order to establish that they can identify and then market their goods or services to selected target groups; in contrast, consumers are not compelled to consider the behaviour of suppliers. Instead, it is assumed that suppliers will be keen to market their products by making consumers aware of all the benefits on offer (Schulze 1996: 444). Consumers are generally concerned about receiving functional and serviceable products and the availability of after-sales service.

Suppliers aim to differentiate their products from those of their competitors. Use of brand names is one way of keeping consumer demand tied to a particular product or supplier. Some suppliers deliberately do not use brand names—in fact, they sell their products as unbranded, or 'no-name', and tend to concentrate on having a lower price relative to those charged by competitors. However, sale of unbranded products becomes a branding of its own (e.g. with the sale of no-frills flights by airlines). Image is constructed in a similar way to that used by suppliers with brand names, through market relations designed to enhance communications between suppliers and customers (see Box 8.2).

8.4.2 *Relationships between manufacturers and wholesale traders*

Manufacturers compete to obtain the custom of people in the final goods market who have the economic resources to buy products on offer. They also have to compete with other manufacturers to get their products listed in trade catalogues, displayed on shelves or publicised by wholesale trading businesses. There may be a small number of wholesalers in an industry, such as food, and a large number of

The image of a supplier can be directed in different ways to different target audiences. For example, the image conveyed to a tax office collecting value added tax (VAT) or goods and services tax has a focus on the provision of accurate and correct statements. In contrast, the image presented to consumers needs to emphasise the quality and functionality of a product for a particular price. A desired image is developed and presented to each specific target group (see Faulstich 1992: 72ff.). For consumers, image is linked to **brands**. These represent the symbolic value of services and products and can be established through the goods themselves or through a **corporate image**.

Corporate image is designed to help promote sales of all products and services supplied. Consumers may not believe in the image being generated by a corporation, because other factors also have a bearing. For example, Shell petroleum may be associated with freedom, uninhibited driving and open-space lifestyles, or it could be seen as typified by the threat of Brent Spar being sunk in the North Atlantic, or social and political involvement with the Ogoni tribe in Nigeria. To some extent, consumers receive independent information about corporations, irrespective of the image generated by market relations (Avenarius 1995: 159).

Avenarius (1995) defines the construction of an image as a process involving reciprocal influences between the image supplier, the audience of that image and other people that may affect the audience's perception. Baskin and Aronoff (1988: 62) sum up the situation as follows:

> An organisation's image is a composite of people's attitudes and beliefs about the organisation. Images cannot be communicated directly. They are built over time, developed through the cumulative effect of many messages. Such messages, which take many forms, are frequently not transmitted intentionally.

According to Faulstich (1992), by taking care of its image the corporation should create a background of trust that encourages sympathy for it, in its role as a supplier, and for the products it offers. If image does create credibility, barriers to the success of products that do have an environmental impact can be addressed and overcome. Target groups decide what aspects of image will be relevant. Of course, the supplier can find out whether an image is authentic only when the products are actually purchased and when feedback is available from the group of purchasers. Development of a dialogue with consumers does, then, help promote assessment of the reality of a particular image. With recent heightened concern about security from terrorist attacks, the background of trust becomes a critical consideration in supplier relationships.

Box 8.2 Image construction

manufacturers or agribusinesses that wish to sell their products to final consumers through wholesalers that 'break up the bulk' of the products they purchase. In 1995 in the German food trade the 10 biggest wholesale enterprises accounted for 79% of the final consumption market, and the 50 biggest enterprises accounted for 98% of total turnover (Kull 1998: 37). Trading groups such as Completefoodservices, Karstadt or Quelle provide a narrow gate for manufacturers to pass through on the way to the mass market. This can be described as a **gatekeeper function** of wholesalers (Hansen 1995: 349ff.). As gatekeepers, wholesalers have a special market power linking manufacturers and consumers, because they can choose the **assortment** of goods they will trade in and the form in which the goods will be presented to retailers. Wholesale trade also has a key function as an assembly point for packaging and disposal of old products (see Meffert and Kirchgeorg 1998: 206ff.). With this background it can be seen that environmental innovations can succeed or fail because of the actions of wholesalers.

As 'middlemen', traders are in a position to apply their influence on the environmental quality of products from both the supply side and the demand side of the market. On the one hand, they have the power to promote the products of environmentally progressive manufacturers, and they can choose to promote 'green' products to consumers (or retailers, who will then sell them on to final consumers) through sales promotions, advertisements and support for environmental brands such as organic food supplies (e.g. Naturkind; The Good Life Store Ltd). On the other hand, they can choose not to pursue 'green' product lines. Wholesaler power to choose can result in fundamental conflicts of interest between manufacturers and traders (see Berekoven 1995: 60ff.; Ceyp 1996: 32).

The wholesaler's gatekeeper role involves the exercise of power over manufacturers through the restriction of trade in products that are unacceptable to the wholesaler's image. Wholesalers are contracted to replace goods on the shelves of retailers and, if the product is not seen to have rapid turnover, even though it is 'green', the products will not be supported unless the margin is high enough. Space is at a premium on the shelves of retailers and needs constant replenishment in an efficient way—something the wholesaler is particularly well equipped to do, especially where just-in-time (JIT) purchasing is used, and which manufacturers of single product lines would find uneconomic in many cases because, as mentioned above, the wholesaler breaks up bulk supplies and then distributes them along with other supplies. Wholesalers can experiment with products. In this process, they examine how the retailer (and final consumer) react to changes on offer and whether demand is increased. Hence, they can test the attractiveness of new environmentally benign products and can remove them from sale if demand does not increase. If a recommended new product disappoints the quality expectations of consumers, the wholesaler also faces the risk of losing the customers for its complete range of goods. Furthermore, the success of environmental products can be problematic for the trade when alternative products to conventional articles in the range are provided and customers become aware of the disadvantages of those conventional articles.

In summary, wholesale trade supports consumption of environmentally benign goods (see Fig. 8.6):

● Through the flow of goods and materials provided in the range

● Through the flow of information, including consultation about the environmental advantages and disadvantages of products

● Through the flow of values and payments associated with economic added value gained from products that exhibit better environmental performance (i.e. having lower environmental impacts)

8.4.3 Relationships in the intermediate product market chain

Before goods reach the wholesale trade and consumers, materials and intermediate products go through multiple transformation processes to emerge as goods that can be sold for final consumption. Organisations often rely on purchases of raw materials from other organisations, or they may be vertically integrated such that they produce their own raw materials as well as transforming these into intermediate or

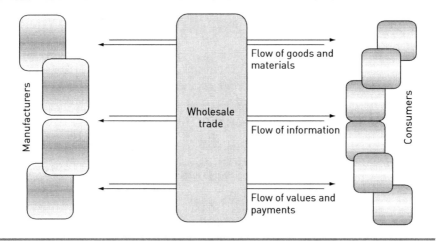

Figure 8.6 **Three flows of wholesale trade**

Source: Kull 1998

finished products. For example, in agriculture the food produced may be sold to a processor, or value may be added in the agribusiness itself by processing the food further (e.g. by canning or bottling it).

The reduction of environmental impact added all along these supply chains is an essential task for environmentally oriented business management. In addition, **closing the chain** is an important aspect in value creation for the business (see Kirchgeorg 1998). This can be illustrated through a model of the chain of value creation for textiles (see Fig. 8.7). Key positions in the intermediate product markets are generally occupied by agriculture, forestry, the chemical industry, transport, companies involved in the recovery and extraction of mineral resources, and the biotechnology sector. Organisations producing intermediate products and consumers of final products need information about the environmental impacts created in the earlier stages of production if they are to take environmentally benign decisions about the stage of product development, production and re-use for which they are responsible (i.e. the aspects of production that they can control). As Spiller (1999: 25) argues:

> In the cultivation of cotton, transparency during all stages in the value chain, from the production of chemicals for application in the field to manufacturing, transport and trade is complex. Often the producers themselves do not know anything about the environmental effects of the production process in the intermediate product stages.

Therefore, for the enhancement of eco-efficiency, corporate supply-chain management adopts the task of improving the recording of information about sources of environmental impact throughout all stages of the value chain. Relationships with suppliers and receivers into storage are included in general business substance chain management. Suppliers of raw materials are included in environmental networking, because raw materials such as cereals, cotton, wood and metal are produced as homogeneous products in tough competitive conditions at global market prices.

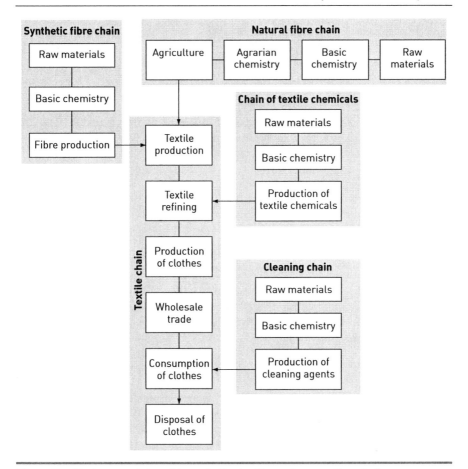

Figure 8.7 Environmental problems in the textiles value creation chain

Source: Spiller 1999: 26, with reference to Hummel 1997

Environmental differentiation is a useful strategy for suppliers to follow when advantageous environmental performance is maintained or built up and communicated to the final purchasers. Substance chain management aims towards the introduction of voluntary standards for self-regulation and co-operation between participants in order to guarantee the truthfulness of the environmental claims that are made.

8.4.3.1 Tasks of substance chain management

Integrated substance chain management is a decision-support tool in which the life-cycle approach is combined with economic considerations in order to analyse and reduce the overall environmental impacts of substance chains (VNCI 1991). The method focuses on (potential) actions but questions such as 'What is the total effect of substance A on the environment?' are not answered within the framework. Instead the 80/20 rule is applied ('What 20% of elements account for 80% of the total?') in order to answer action-oriented questions such as 'What would be the environmental and economic impact of installing a recycling system for substance A?' In conceptual terms, the environmental part of the method is thus very similar to a simplified life-cycle assessment (see www.dk-teknik.dk/ydelser/miljo/LCA%20guide/3rd_ed/loop2212.htm).

The aim is to obtain a clearly defined use for a product with the lowest price possible through co-operation with other companies involved in the value chain. For example, a sports centre, such as the Australian Institute of Sport, arranges fitness programmes and associated experiences that require a combination of services and products—from floor polish for the centre to the muesli (or cereals) eaten by health-conscious participants. Manufacturers (suppliers) of these products have clear preferences about the constituents of their products. Intermediate products for sports centres, such as bulk purchases of muesli, can be identical to final consumer goods. Muesli is offered in intermediate and final product markets and, in terms of its ingredients from one supplier to another, is fairly homogeneous. However, in the field of gastronomy and leisure, muesli may be packaged in larger quantities for the **convenience** of bulk usage. Hence, business-to-business trade can clearly be distinguished from sale to consumers. With business, fewer buyers acquire far larger volumes and consequently relationships between suppliers and customers are much closer. In the supply business—for example, for automobile parts—business-to-business trade is very important in many countries. Businesses buying intermediate products directly influence the price, quality and functionality of the product supplied and expect customer-specific products and services to be supplied through long-term business relationships (see Backhaus 1997: 641ff.).

Formation of these business-to-business relationships leads to two important questions (see Fig. 8.8). These are: 'What is the substance of the business-to-business transaction?' and 'How will the transactions be co-ordinated?'

Specification of the products being traded is identified through a set of **performance requirements**. This set includes related activities such as installation, financing, insurance and, where necessary, arrangements for product return. Suppliers may agree to lease out their products rather than sell them. For example, intermediate metal-based products, such as aircraft, can be leased to business, with the supplier taking over responsibility for disposal (e.g. through dismantling of the aircraft) by building such costs into the lease rentals. Also, carpet leasing has been introduced by Interface (www.peopleandplanet.net). **Business integration** addresses the functions that are associated with business-to-business trade. These might include the information system, agreements, transport and logistics, pre-sales and after-sales customer care and management of the co-operative relationship.

When several enterprises enter into mutual relationships (e.g. alliances) with each other, management of the interrelationship between that larger number of parties is more complicated. Expansion of parties may occur because more businesses are involved at different stages of the value chain or because more businesses get together at each stage of the chain, perhaps encouraged by an industry association. The impacts of such arrangements on the environment can be directly addressed in substance chain management. For example, before a piece of clothing is cut and sewn in a textile factory considerable environmental impacts occur. In cotton

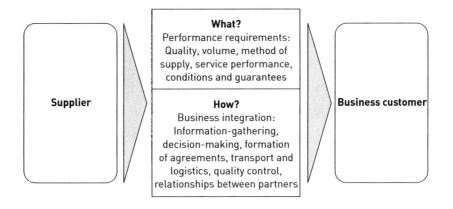

Figure 8.8 **The 'What?' and the 'How?' of business-to-business relationships**

Source: based on Schneidewind 2000

growing, fertilisers may be used, polluting water supplies. In the dyeing process, chemical dyes may be used for colouring and protection, again leading to water pollution; and in the transportation of the textiles there may be a resultant reduction in air quality. Substance chain management, with its focus on life-cycle assessment, encourages an holistic approach to the resolution and continual improvement of environmental problems. It is an ideal mechanism for addressing environmental problems throughout the value chain while maintaining competition between the different parties. An alternative is for the environmental problems to be internalised in a single business, through **vertical integration**. However, vertical integration reduces the extent of competition as each stage of the business tends to get locked in to producing for the next stage.

Substance chain management facilitates the inclusion of environmental considerations and the production of environmentally benign products (see Schneidewind and Petersen 2000). In the following section the co-ordination tasks associated with environmental performance chains are examined.

8.4.3.2 Intermediate product markets as environmental performance chains

For the best environmental results businesses will introduce substance-chain management when considering demand for intermediate products from suppliers. Critical to this development is the inclusion of a suitable flow of information that complements the material flow of goods and the flow of funds in the value creation chain. The environmental quality of materials used in the previous and following performance stages needs to be enhanced and a reduction in usage encouraged. Apart from this, values, information and materials need to be transported through a **counter-flow** in order to channel them back into the value creation cycle.

The importance of, as well as the problems associated with, development of an integrated environmental information system for substance-chain management has increased in recent years. Difficulties arise with (see Schneidewind and Petersen 2000):

- An increase in the variety of materials
- The need to balance the environmental effects
- Concentration on core competences
- Missing communication structures

Variety of materials

The variety of materials available for incorporation into new products has increased considerably. Numerous innovations have occurred in the development of materials, with the addition of new synthetic materials, composite materials, colours and pigments, additives and so on. This additional variety increases the complexity of information stored and the need for electronic recording of data.

Balancing the environmental effects

Apart from factoring in the direct environmental impacts created by the production of intermediate products, different environmental consequences of these impacts have also to be weighed against each other. For example, a composite material may make recycling difficult when the product is finished with, but it can make a considerable contribution to the reduction of environmental discharges while the product is being used (e.g. entailing lower energy consumption, better durability and lower servicing requirements). The same argument holds for a protective coating that contains an environmentally questionable chemical but which also prolongs the life of the product that has been protected.

Concentration on core competences

Businesses increasingly concentrate on their **core competences**. A growing number of peripheral activities are contracted out to suppliers of intermediate goods and services through **outsourcing**. This leads to further division of work associated with various stages in the value chain. With the introduction of outsourcing, control of the flow of information is shifted from internal departments to external businesses. Also, internal payments to departmental and divisional heads are replaced by contractual arrangements with external parties. Although this process imposes a greater distance between each link in the value chain, as the costs and benefits of contractual relationships need to be more clearly spelled out, the flow of information can be improved to compensate. When environmental issues are involved (e.g. in green purchasing contracts with suppliers), process and product specifications are included in the contractual arrangements. Of course, outsourcing leads to less direct control and greater indirect control through the law courts if things go wrong with operations.

In order to limit the costs of co-ordinating outsourcing activities, businesses increasingly are limiting themselves to working with as few suppliers as possible. These suppliers consider their basic competence to be the effective and efficient co-ordination and supply of intermediate product flows. For example, suppliers to the automobile industry supply completed electronic modules with recyclable parts, and the agrichemical industry has begun to exclude active substances from products provided to intermediate businesses. In this way suppliers, as important sources of information, can play a key role in resolving critical environmental problems through business-to-business trade.

Missing communication structures

The supplier communication structures necessary for weighing up the environmental impacts tend to be limited. Only rarely are suppliers in a position to weigh up the full environmental impacts of their intermediate products. In many cases, structures that allow the evaluation of environmental impacts over the whole environmental impact added chain are completely missing. The presence of a supportive communications structure depends on whether business-to-business trade is conducted in industrial, newly industrialising or developing countries. Where business-to-business transactions occur between these three types of country, the need to develop a strategy for global sourcing and to consider environmental impacts assumes greater significance. Modern information technologies enable networking between countries, but they give no real insight into the ecological and social production conditions of the supplier; hence the need to develop and enforce environmentally oriented communication structures is important.

Three focal points provide the basis for a solution to the problem (see Fig. 8.9):

- **Downstreaming.** In parallel with the development of co-operation with suppliers, pressure can be placed on suppliers in order to get them to introduce and maintain improving environmental standards in relation to material flows between suppliers and producers.

- **Upstreaming.** Environmentally benign intermediate products can be used to gain a competitive advantage for the producer by generating an aura of improved legitimacy and transparency in the eyes of direct consumers at the end of the value chain (e.g. in the case of clean waste-disposal systems).

- **Development of information.** By holding contracting parties in the value chain to agreed environmental standards, one can increase the importance given to the introduction of systems for gathering and classifying environmental information and to making that information transparent.

Downstreaming and upstreaming refer to 'what' is going to be co-ordinated, whereas development of information addresses the question of 'how' co-ordination is to take place. Co-ordination between parties involved in intermediate product markets encourages **integrated solutions** to environmental problems. From this perspective, products supplied are viewed as sets of functions that customers value rather than as material products. Emphasis on the functions provided by products helps with the development of a focus on components and services that lead to a resolution of environmental concerns.

To improve communication structures with suppliers, businesses fall back on co-ordination methods such as partnerships and strategic alliances. Both of these co-ordination methods take commerce well beyond the simple transfer of goods and services in the marketplace. Sometimes, an obligatory **standard** for these relationships is determined by government beforehand; alternatively, a **platform for co-operation** between the parties may be constructed in order to make it easier for environmental information about products to be transferred.

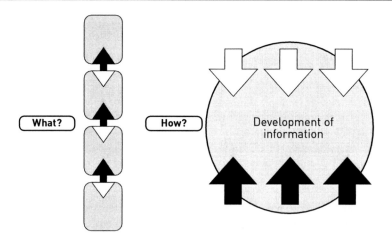

White arrows = downstreaming; black arrows = upstreaming

Figure 8.9 **Focal points for ecological attention in the environmental impact added chain**

The introduction of standards presupposes a willingness to comply, or an incentive system that encourages compliance, by business. For example, one incentive is that the product may receive a **product passport** that describes where materials relating to the product have come from, the processes through which it has been transformed and the criteria with which the product complies. These are sometimes used as a basis for obtaining **eco-labels** that certify the truthfulness of a product's claim to be environmentally benign. Another consideration is the **audit** of all production sites through the whole value chain. This can be part of the eco-labelling, or **certification**, process. Labelling or certification organisations also have to be audited. The effectiveness of these instruments—for example, the product passport—depends on whether businesses at the very end of the value chain (e.g. mail-order firms) demand the application of appropriate standards when dealing with their suppliers. The absence of such standards and certification organisations has stirred some businesses to get together to develop their own standards. For example, the certification norm SA 8000 (CEP 1997; www.bsdglobal.com/tools/systems_sa.asp), addressing social accountability aspects of production standards, is promoted by a number of companies and organisations from a range of industry sectors. It has its own certification agency—Social Accountability International (www.cepaa.org). The ' "Better" & "Best" ' label for natural textiles (www.naturtextil.com/indexblau. ssi) and the Forest Stewardship Council (FSC) certificate for wood products (www. fscoax.org) arose from projects developed by committed businesses. For example, the FSC consists of an association between members from a diverse range of environmental and social groups, the timber trade and the forestry profession, indigenous peoples' organisations, community forestry groups and forest product certification organisations.

Co-operation platforms established in the chain of intermediate products have additional roles. For example, in the TexWeb project[6] an intra-corporate and inter-corporate information network is constructed along the textile chain. The network is designed to create transparency in material flows (thus addressing accountability) and to motivate innovation to reduce the use of materials (addressing eco-efficiency concerns). In the USA, co-operation between power companies and service providers is growing. For example, H Power Corporation installed a 4.5 kW fuel cell system at Yellowstone National Park. The propane-fuelled system provides power to ticket kiosks and to an office at the west entrance to the park; the waste heat from the system will be used for space heating. Downstream mail-order firms such as Hess Natur (www.hess-natur.com) and Otto (www.neu.otto.de) co-operate with enterprises in the textile industry as well as with plantation owners in order to secure the purchase of cotton for their own eco-collections. Remei AG Switzerland (www.remei.ch) has found solutions in both directions, upstream and downstream. As a cotton trader in India it constructed a network of co-operation with spinning mills and it meets demand for high-environmental-quality, low-cost cotton (www.umwelt.de).

The integration of electronic data interchange (EDI) between the partners through the value chain is an important part of the network of co-operation. In particular, data exchange over efficient consumer response (ECR) concepts[7] and business-to-business platforms is representative of the networking of technical information through co-operation platforms. In the following two subsections, greater detail on these concepts is provided.

8.4.3.3 End-of-pipe and integrated environmental technologies

Two considerations are worth observing about the environmental context of intermediate goods supplies—the development of end-of-pipe solutions and integrated environmental technologies. The market for environmental technology developed strongly during the 1970s because of the introduction of environmental laws to protect against the **output** of emissions, noise, sewerage and soil degradation. New environmental laws served as a catalyst for the modernisation of existing production processes and facilities so that environmental impacts could be reduced. Additional methods such as filters, sewerage plants and barriers to exclude noise have the advantage of being able to reduce environmental impacts with relatively low investment expenditure. These methods are called **end-of-pipe** environmental protection measures. Retention of existing corporate production processes is not possible in these circumstances if the company wishes to survive. End-of-pipe investment costs must be incurred in order to comply with legislation. Hence, legal constraints cause investment expenditure that does not necessarily lead either to cost savings or to improved product quality. On the contrary, let us take the example of electric filters. These require additional energy use and disposal of filter dust, thereby increasing business costs and reducing business profitability. Business then needs to consider whether costs could be reduced if production facilities were moved to different legal

---

6   To which, among others, the button manufacturer Günther (www.guentherbuttons.de) and the printer Mülforter (www.mulforter.com) are connected.

7   For background information on the ECR concept, see www.fmi.org/media/bg/ecr1.htm.

jurisdictions with looser technical specifications for addressing environmental pollution.

Since the 1980s end-of-pipe methods have been replaced with or supplemented by integrated environmental protection methods of production. Environmental impacts are taken into account before the construction of new facilities and processes. Integrated technologies encourage the use of reduced quantities of **inputs** in the production process. Likewise, improved profitability is combined with reduced environmental impacts. Hence, reduced consumption of resources, waste emissions and physical depreciation of plant and equipment mean that integrated technologies for environmental protection also lead to economic advantages and an improved competitive situation. The need for expensive disposal of waste and harmful materials is avoided because they do not exist if environmentally benign integrated technologies are introduced with a 'zero-waste' frame of reference (see Holzbaur *et al.* 1996: 269; Schaltegger and Figge 1997). The market for integrated environmental methods is encouraged through legalistic and economic means. With use of these initiatives, innovation through research, development and design for environment is encouraged. From this perspective, the government's role is no longer to establish laws for imposing minimum environmental standards; instead, it is to define clear, ambitious goals for environmental protection so that businesses can determine for themselves the most innovative solutions to environmental problems while improving their profitability and seeking a competitive advantage.

8.4.3.4 Leasing

For an owner, each time production is changed through the introduction of innovative processes additional risks (e.g. technical and economic obsolescence) are incurred and capital is tied up. In order to minimise such risks and to tie up less capital, machines, vehicles and facilities are often leased by businesses. Leasing decouples use of the product from ownership of the product. It passes the risks of ownership to the lessor, who leases the asset out to the lessee. From an environmental point of view, there can be advantages to leasing: for example, with the leasing of intermediate products. The leasing of computers (e.g. by Peacock, www.peacock.de) or of photocopiers (e.g. by Xerox, www.xerox.com) becomes much more attractive to the lessor when the equipment can be leased for long periods of time, does not require much maintenance, is easily repaired and can be dissected in modules when repairs are required or if parts can be re-used when the equipment reaches the end of its useful life. Leasing encourages innovations in these directions. Innovations that reduce the consumption of materials are also encouraged as a reduction in the variable costs of leasing make the leased products more competitive. If the lease rental is related to the function rather than the ownership of the appliance there is a stronger incentive to provide innovations that improve the function for customers. For example, in the case of photocopiers, the need to increase the number of pages copied per minute may lead to improved toner processes being developed. Responsibility for the actual product, including reduce, re-use and recycle decisions, remains with the manufacturer, whereas the services (or functions) generated by the leased equipment are provided to the lessee (the user). The strength of leasing, in encouraging environmentally benign value creation, tends to be through the focus of the lessor on improving the provision of services such as maintenance, up-to-date technology, rebuilding and so on, to gain an advantage over the competition.

8.4.4 Relationships between capital providers and businesses

Banks, insurance companies and superannuation (pension) funds create value for their members by financing the permanent and working capital of their customers. Great interest is being expressed by financiers—the providers of capital to business—in the environmental impacts of business activities for which funds are provided. Financial markets regulate the availability and the price of these scarce sources of funds. The focus is predominantly on expected future opportunities rather than on past performance. In the investment markets in particular the success of environmentally oriented business management is measured less in relation to work already performed than in relation to expectations of good future performance. To compete for finance, businesses need to persuade potential providers of capital about the economic **prospects of success** and the **security** associated with any financial commitment to be made.

In the investment markets negotiations take place over future expectations and over future risks. Access to financial flows determines the production processes, regions and products that capital can be invested in and the conditions under which investments will be made. In this sense, financial actors control the future formation of the economy (see Schaltegger and Figge 1999a; Schmidheiny and Zorraquín 1996). Business management can influence this future and move capital towards projects that have sustainable outcomes, when they can demonstrate attractive monetary yields and calculable risks. Consideration of yields is very much to the fore in the investment market, although market for credit is suppressed by risk considerations, including environmental risks and liabilities associated with these risks (see Fig. 8.10).

However, investment and credit markets cannot be considered in isolation. Together they comprise the capital market and provide external financing through private and foreign capital. When private capital is increased the creditworthiness of the business is also enhanced because of the strengthened capital base. Banks presuppose that private capital will comprise a set proportion, say 40%, of the total capital base. As an alternative to external financing, internal financing is also available to businesses through periodic income being retained and through net cash inflows, which are related to yields, withdrawals and depreciations. The expectation of an increasing cash flow enhances the attraction of the enterprise to new issues of capital.

8.4.4.1 The attraction of environmental protection to the capital market

The value of the enterprise in the capital market is called **shareholder value**. Low risk of business failure and increasing profitability attract capital providers. In addition, positive net cash inflows from investments and satisfactory liquidity also enhance shareholder value.

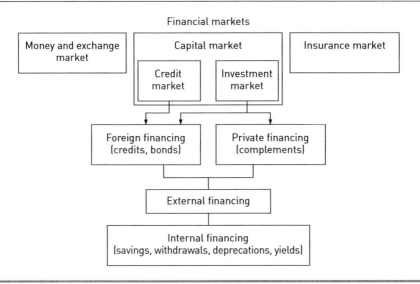

Figure 8.10 Financial markets and forms of financing

Measures to protect the environment can enhance shareholder value only when they contribute to net cash inflows: for example, by reducing the risk of cash outflows or by improving yields (see Schaltegger and Figge 1997). Eco-efficient improvements increase the worth of the business to shareholders because such improvements require monetary gains to be realised from environmental investments. The environmental performance of a business is of interest to financial analysts in banks and insurance companies when it is linked with economic success.

Financial institutions are beginning to realise that they need to assess the environmental performance of the companies they plan to invest in (e.g. to ensure that there are no surprise environmental risks that could ruin the cash inflows of their customers if fines or environmental penalties were imposed). In these circumstances, financial institutions and the analysts working for them are beginning to assume an increasingly important role in the promotion of environmental performance evaluation and in the associated accounting information and reporting systems. In Germany, for example, oekom AG (www.oekom.de) evaluates the potential environmental performance of businesses from a financial economics perspective and makes investment recommendations based on these evaluations. This is equally important in the services sector. For example, in Australia, investment products can be sold to customers only if a product disclosure statement is made—one that must state the extent that environmental considerations are taken into account in the selection, retention or realisation of the investment (Burritt 2002b). Encouraged by the United Nations Environment Programme (UNEP) finance initiatives, bankers and insurance companies are beginning to familiarise themselves with the risks and rewards from environmental performance evaluations.

8.4.4.2 Environmental shareholder value

The link between environmental performance and financial performance has been heavily discussed for many years (EIRIS 1989; Feldman *et al.* 1997; Klassen and McLaughlin 1996; Li and McConomy 1999; McGuire *et al.* 1981; Schaltegger and Figge 1997; Schaltegger and Synnestvedt 2002; Spicer 1978; Wagner *et al.* 2002). Likewise, in recent years, the concept of shareholder value has become increasingly popular as a basis for valuation of companies and financial assets (see Box 8.3). With the growing importance of environmental costs and with many companies earning money from environmental products and services, the question arises as to whether environmental management geared towards eco-efficiency is in conflict or in harmony with the philosophy of shareholder value (see Schaltegger and Figge 1997).

Shareholder value is a conventional investment calculation used to assess financial assets (particularly shares in companies). In technical terms, shareholder value, *SHV*, is the discounted net current value of a company's future free cash flows (Copeland *et al.* 1993, 72ff.; Rappaport 1986):

$$SHV = \sum_{n=1}^{\infty} \left[\frac{F_n^{\text{cash}}}{(1+i)^n} \right] - V^{\text{bcap}} \qquad [8.3]$$

where F_n^{cash} is the free cash flow for period n, i is the discount rate and V^{bcap} is the market value of borrowed capital.

The concept of shareholder value depends on expected free cash flow (F^{cash}), since only this can be used to pay investors. Corporate value, *CV*, is determined by discounting the expected free cash flow:

$$CV = \sum_{n=1}^{\infty} \frac{F_n^{\text{cash}}}{(1+i)^n} \qquad [8.4]$$

To arrive at the shareholder value, the value that is of benefit to shareholders (i.e. increased share prices plus dividends), borrowed capital has to be subtracted from corporate value. Unlike free cash flow, a simple income figure does not take into account the fact that a part of a company's income has to be used for paying interest on borrowed capital, thereby reducing the amount that is available to pay shareholders.

Box 8.3 Basics of the shareholder value approach

In this section, a short assessment of the shareholder value approach to environmental management is given (for an in-depth discussion, see Schaltegger and Burritt 2000). The impact of corporate environmental protection measures on the drivers of shareholder value will be analysed and conflicting effects will be weighed against each other. It should be emphasised that investigation of the effects of environmental management on shareholder value is just one element in a corporate shareholder value analysis.

Among the main advantages of the shareholder value approach is the fact that cash flow figures reflect basic inflows and outflows of cash and thus cannot be manipulated as easily by accounting practices and standards as income based on accrual accounting figures (Copeland *et al.* 1993). Compared with income figures used in financial accounting, shareholder value has a major advantage when it comes to environmental management: it is future-oriented and focused on long-term increases in company value. Like most environmental protection measures, shareholder value is concerned with investment now in order to derive future benefits.

The shareholder value approach does not explicitly embrace environmental objectives but, with its focus on economic variables, it has a strong, direct influence on business activities and thus an indirect influence on corporate environmental impact. The anticipatory nature of the shareholder value philosophy—particularly its orientation towards the future and its emphasis on sustainable value increases—has more in common with the principles behind eco-efficiency than those behind conventional financial accounting, which is based on past transactions, events and standards, looking at historical costs rather than market values.

However, the philosophy behind the shareholder value concept also faces major problems. For example, the expectations of investors and management play a significant role in determining applicable discount rates and estimated future cash flows. If these expectations are poor predictors of the future (e.g. because of the neglect of future financial impacts resulting from existing environmental contamination), calculations will not correspond to the ideal shareholder value. Furthermore, values created in the distant future will often not be considered. This is because analysis of future trends is restricted to a period of 5–10 years ahead, because of the reductionary effects caused by discounting cash flows. In these circumstances, there is a danger of inappropriate management and investment decisions being made. Thus, given the inherent problems related to the shareholder value concept, the quality of the assessment of company value will depend more on the skills and expertise of the assessor than on the choice of assessment method. Nevertheless, in modern business practice, the concept of shareholder value has gained a great deal of support (see e.g. Volkart 1995).

Environmental management has various influences on shareholder value. To answer the question of how far a corporate environmental management system is in conflict or harmony with the shareholder value philosophy, a brief look at the underlying philosophy will be necessary. One way to approach the issue is to discuss the conclusions that can be drawn about corporate environmental management from a shareholder value approach. This can be undertaken by considering the drivers of shareholder value. With its strict emphasis on efficiency, the shareholder value concept is basically more conducive to economically efficient environmental protection, characterised by the fact that desired protection of the environment is achieved at minimum cost, or with cost savings or additional profits. This is in line with the purpose of improving eco-efficiency.

According to Rappaport's thesis (1986), management measures can be assessed on the basis of value drivers and management decisions related to investment, operational management and financing (see Fig. 8.11). The value drivers behind changes in shareholder value include:

- Investments in fixed assets
- Investments in current assets

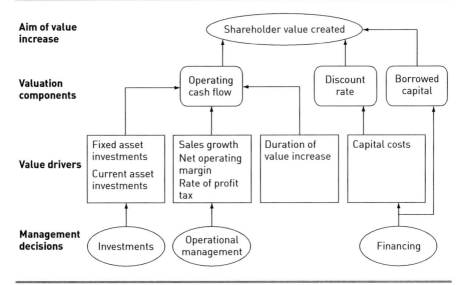

Figure 8.11 Drivers of shareholder value

Source: based on Rappaport 1986: 79

- Sales revenue growth

- Net operating margin and rate of tax on income

- Capital costs

- Duration of value increase

Value drivers are affected by environmental interventions to differing degrees, depending on the nature and size of the company. Environment-related investments include effluent treatment plants (fixed assets) as well as necessary working supplies such as chemicals used to neutralise acids (current assets).

Sales revenue growth and net operating margins may be affected, for example, by 'green' product lines. Duration of any increase in value is determined by asking how long a return that is better than the market average can be sustained (Rappaport 1986). In contrast to these value drivers, capital costs do not affect the valuation of cash flows but do affect the discount rate.

Obviously, the shareholder value approach does not take a positive view of every act of environmental management, only of measures enhancing enterprise value in the long run. Thus measures to improve eco-efficiency (Schaltegger and Figge 1997):

- Are capital-extensive, relating to software rather than hardware (involving 'smarter', smaller, cheaper installations)

- Consume low amounts of material, reducing throughput (through lower purchase, storage and depreciation costs)

- Are sales-boosting, increasing the benefit and attraction to customers (through the provision of more desirable products and services for more customers)

- Are margin-widening, increasing the benefit to customers and reducing the costs of producing products and services (fetching higher prices because of the greater benefit and involving lower operating costs through improved operating efficiency)

- Safeguard the flow of finance, gaining the confidence of the capital market (involving lower and more unsystematic risks and 'winning' a 'green bonus')

- Enhance value over the long term in anticipation of future costs and earnings potential

By incorporating the shareholder value concept into the formulation of corporate environmental management, it is possible to integrate the relevant parameters on which an economic decision is based into a single measure.

When assessing the cash inflow and cash outflow generated by alternative proposals, it is necessary to take account of the impact on different value drivers: that is, on three parameters (see Fig. 8.12):

- Expected additional cash outflow caused by the net investment

- Necessary additional net cash inflow from operational activity

- Expected additional risk

If, for example, management bases its decisions solely on expected income, it risks making an investment that may promise the highest return in absolute terms but

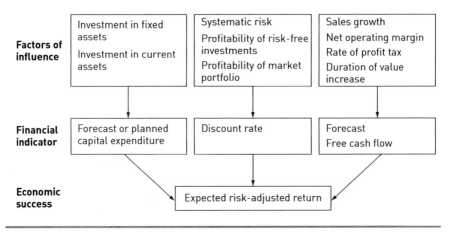

Figure 8.12 Integrated financial evaluation of environmental management

Source: Schaltegger and Figge 1998: 19

only a low return relative to the required capital investment, thus delivering only a poor return. In addition, it is possible that an investment will involve not only a high return but also a high risk that may not be adequately compensated by the return.

Additional enterprise value is determined not so much by the absolute additional income but by the relative additional return after adjustment is made to take into account anticipated risk. In this way, the shareholder value concept offers an *ex ante* valuation method for the implicit integration of the relevant parameters on which economic decisions are based.

To sum up, it may be said that a system of environmental management geared to increasing shareholder value provides a way in which the financial impact of environmental management can be assessed on the basis of the value drivers. At the same time, it provides a way of quantitatively assessing conflicting financial effects on an *ex ante* basis and weighing them against each other. In conclusion, a system of environmental management that enhances shareholder value is essentially in harmony with a market-oriented environmental policy and the concept of eco-efficiency. However, it is constrained by what the legal, political and market circumstances will allow and by what other stakeholders demand.

Within the context of corporate environmental management, the shareholder value concept faces certain economic and social hurdles. In addition to the fact that financial liquidity is not explicitly included in the calculation of shareholder value, problems may also arise wherever and whenever a company is unable to avoid certain risks through diversification—because of its size, perhaps. As investors can diversify their investments, unsystematic environment-related risks are not considered in the calculation of the discount factor. Nevertheless, these risks can be relevant for management if they cannot be balanced internally and if they influence the economic success of the company or perceived environmental credibility of environmental management.

The shareholder value concept takes only market risks into account. However, companies are also exposed to the risks of a possible loss of social acceptance and of legitimacy (Cowe 1994; Gray *et al.* 1996; O'Donovan 1999; Schaltegger and Sturm 1994; Schaltegger 2000). In this regard, the fact that the concept does not support any explicit analysis of the social aspects of corporate environmental protection and of corporate learning processes can be regarded as a significant shortcoming. In particular, the shareholder value approach stands in the way of the concept of sustainable development if it is used to argue for a redistribution of resources between social and environmental interests on the one hand and the interests of capital providers on the other.

If company management wishes to succeed in the marketplace and in society, it must safeguard its legitimacy. This may mean refraining from courses of action that, according to a purely arithmetic analysis, would lead to the biggest increase in shareholder value. Even from a strictly economic viewpoint it is necessary, therefore, not only to consider the net present value of free cash flows but also any option value of being able to remain in business (see Brealey and Meyers 1991; Dixit and Pindyck 1993; Figge 2001; Schaltegger and Burritt 2000: 143).

Questions for review

8.1 'Products can be seen as groups of functions; for example, a lipstick needs to deliver the product to the mouth, to keep the user clean, to be smooth rather than brittle, to be safe for human use and to retract when the lipstick has been applied. Each of these functions of the product can be improved by reducing its environmental impact added.' Based on the notion of a value chain, suggest ways for improving on the environmental impact added of a lipstick. Is there a better, alternative design? Can waste be eliminated?

8.2 Comment on the view that an improvement in eco-efficiency represents economically successful business management.

8.3 'If market failures are permitted in a society, then this is the fault of government.' What is market failure? What is an externality? Provide an example. Is the government responsible for removing externalities? How do you think this might be done?

8.4 Under what conditions might business include the costs of externalities caused by its products in the market price of those products? In your answer identify the spheres of influence involved.

8.5 What is information asymmetry? Why is information asymmetry important for a customer trying to find out about the environmental credibility of experience goods, trust goods and potemkin goods, but not trying to find out about search goods? How might eco-labels help? Provide an example.

8.6 Explain the difference between capital goods, intermediate goods, consumer goods and investment goods. Provide one example of each.

8.7 Why are wholesalers an important link in the process of 'greening' products?

8.8 What are supply-chain management and substance-chain management? Do they differ? Do they give rise to different information needs?

8.9 What are the main difficulties in providing an integrated environmental information system as the basis for substance-chain management?

8.10 'The leasing of intermediate products separates use from ownership and provides an incentive for manufacturers to reduce environmental risks associated with their products.' Comment on this view.

8.11 What is shareholder value? Explain whether—and, if so, why—shareholders might be interested in the environmental management of business. What is the connection between shareholder value and eco-efficiency?

9

Success factors and fields of action

Systems of legal regulation, environmental norms and standards

As seen in the previous chapter, the market presents one way of co-ordinating actors in an economy. A second sphere of influence on business is contemporary and anticipated legislation and regulation (see Table 9.1). These represent the legal sphere of influence. Legislation can direct the behaviour of business. Environmental laws are established to change the behaviour of businesses towards their environmental impacts. Monitoring is the process used to establish whether laws are complied with. Enforcement of the laws is through penalties for non-compliance. In addition, if a business establishes a good record on compliance with environmental laws, or going beyond the requirements of law, there may be less tight scrutiny of that business by

Field of action	*Legal regulation system*
Main focus	Regulations Norms Laws Standards Benchmarks
Question to be answered	What is the extent of (non-)compliance with laws?
Basis for action	Order and obedience
Criteria for success	Compliance
Type of rationality	Legal

Table 9.1 Legal regulation (see also Table 7.1 on page 58)

the regulator, as trust is built up. Hence, regulators have at their disposal a **regulatory mix** of instruments designed to encourage businesses to 'do the right thing' for themselves and society. Regulators may penalise poor behaviour, including sending company directors to prison, or they may reward behaviour that goes beyond compliance. In this chapter, aspects of the regulatory mix and their implications for environmental management are examined.

9.1 Costs of environmental regulation

Business is subject to strong legal influence over its external relations with its stakeholders (e.g. employees, consumers and suppliers). These are particularly important in the environmental context because of the imposition of environmental law and regulations that implement the law. The governments of sovereign nations (e.g. Australia, Germany, Guatemala, Nigeria, China and the USA) and, increasingly, supranational governmental institutions (e.g. the European Union [EU]) establish laws and regulate market activities as well as the internal hierarchical activities of business. They achieve this through the threat of imposing penalties for non-compliance with legislation. It may be expensive to comply with the law, but non-compliance may cost the business even more once non-compliance is discovered.

There are many and diverse costs of complying with environmental law (US EPA 1995: 9). These touch on all aspects of the value chain of a business, from research and development (R&D), through production and marketing, to disposal of the product once a consumer has finished using it. Costs affected by environmental law have been referred to as **upfront, operational** and **back-end** environmental costs (US EPA 1995: 10).

- Upfront regulatory costs include those of:
  - Environmental impact analysis required by local or federal government
  - Obtaining permission to operate in a particular area, or industry
  - Installing environmental monitoring equipment or engineering production facilities to comply with legal requirements

- Operational costs of compliance include those resulting from:
  - Notification to regulatory agencies
  - Internal and external reporting on compliance with environmental laws and regulations
  - Ongoing monitoring and testing
  - Continual remediation of sites that are being disturbed (e.g. by a mining company)
  - Record-keeping
  - Training and education of employees in relation to legal requirements
  - Inspection of operations to ensure the company is not breaching the law

- Insurance against environmental risk where required by the government
- End-of-pipe pollution control, as set down in regulations
- Contingency plans to respond to an environmental emergency (ongoing)

■ Back-end costs of compliance with environmental laws include:
- Costs or fees of waste disposal
- Decommissioning costs for a plant and other costs of clean-up
- Costs for disposal of unused inventory (e.g. chemicals that are no longer to be used)
- Costs for post-closure care of sites
- The cost of surveying sites on a regular basis once operations have ceased

Often these costs are not separately identified by business and so their importance may be hidden from management.

Where regulation costs are seen as part of normal business activity, they may be passed on to the consumer as higher prices, to employees as lower wages, to suppliers as lower prices, or in various forms and ways to other stakeholders of the business, if competition permits this to occur. Businesses in one country where there are no subsidies for pollution control will exhibit considerable resistance to the imposed costs of environmental regulation if another country does provide such subsidies (e.g. tax relief for expenditure to clean up the environmental impacts of business), as they are then at a cost disadvantage.

For all businesses, especially those engaged in environmentally sensitive industries or activities, the alternative to incurring upfront, operational and back-end costs is the imposition of **penalties** when environmental laws are breached.

■ Costs of non-compliance include:
- Lost time when directors are sent to prison if they break the law in a criminally irresponsible way
- Fines imposed on directors or business for breaking the law
- Costs incurred through lost reputation when non-compliance with environmental law is made public

Where a business is a **laggard** and breaks the law, the costs imposed are expected to be higher than those of a proactive **leader** that deals with potential environmental impacts of business before they occur.

When laws direct the business to act in a certain way, as indicated above, this is referred to as regulation through **command and control**. Command and control represents a social system of regulation backed up by sanctions or negative incentives for non-compliance with the law. This system of command and control must be followed by the business, otherwise civil or criminal penalties may be imposed. In order for the law to be effective from an environmental perspective, facilities, processes, procedures and products must comply with agreed minimum technological requirements established by the law (see Section 9.2.1). Compliance with the law by those in authority within business means that penalties for breaking the law will not be enforced. In these circumstances legal continuation of the business is secured, and contracts can be entered into by the business in its own name without fear of prosecution for non-compliance (see e.g. Kissler 1984: 92ff.).

However, the law is not necessarily prescriptive. For example, in the case of the EU Eco-management and Audit Scheme (EMAS), EU law offers a **voluntary** system for standardisation of environmental management procedures and practices. Participation in standardised systems of environmental management is voluntary, but, once a business seeks certification of the quality of its environmental management system, the criteria are binding on the business (see Section 9.2.2). Likewise, self-regulation may occur: for example, when an industry association establishes rules for environmental management for its members (see Section 9.2.3). Auditors are specialists that can be asked to attest as to whether a business meets the requirements laid down in a voluntary, self-regulated or legislated system of regulation (see Section 9.2.4).

9.2 Regulation and environmental management

Command-and-control regulation is, today, supplemented in many countries and situations, thereby facing business with a range of other strategies put together by the regulator in order to encourage business to behave in a way that helps achieve the outcomes desired by government.

9.2.1 End-of-pipe regulation and environmental management

Regulation can produce indirect benefits to business as it encourages desirable environmental changes. For example, the international decision to stop production of halons and change to hydrochlorofluorocarbons (HCFCs) because of their lesser impact on the stratospheric ozone layer was of benefit to companies that had access to HCFC production technology (Burritt 1995). As noted in Section 8.4.3.3, end-of-pipe environmental laws enabled the market for environmental technology to develop strongly during the 1970s. Modernisation of existing production processes and facilities so that environmental impacts could be reduced was encouraged by an expanding range of new environmental laws.

Royston (1982: 2) puts the view that dated technology is both inefficient and leads to low profitability. He suggests that investment in low-pollution technology should encourage several interrelated aspects of cleaner business: adoption of higher technology with integrated environmental protection methods, the development of greater skills in employees, lower energy and resource use, and higher value added and profitability. Porter (1990) also argues that command-and-control regulations can encourage technological innovation in pollution prevention through the emergence of new pollution-prevention industries that have developed from the competitive advantage in international export markets gained from tight government-imposed technology standards (as in the case of Germany). Evidence suggests that command-and-control regulation has been relatively successful in curbing pollution where the exact source of a specific medium can be identified (e.g. air pollution emitted from a specific factory stack)—that is, where there is **point source pollution** (see Gunningham and Grabosky 1998: 42).

An alternative view is that highly prescribed regulation designed to impose a technological standard on business does not encourage investment in technology that goes beyond the minimum standard required by environmental law. End-of-pipe command-and-control legislation is suggested not to encourage innovative responses from business to address environmental impact reduction. Instead, where an approved technology is prescribed for dealing with a specific environmental problem in a specific industrial process, business is thought to adopt this as the best practice as well as the minimum standard.

Evidence accepts that command-and-control technological standards are less effective in dealing with (Gunningham and Grabosky 1998: 44):

- Transitory, mobile sources of pollution involving remote businesses that are difficult to keep track of

- Diffuse, non-point sources of pollution

- Pollution that can be transferred from one medium to another

- Situations where technologies are rapidly changing (the law just cannot keep up with the change)

Problems faced by government in imposing on business standards based on command-and-control technology include (Gunningham and Grabosky 1998: 45):

- The need for government to have up-to-date knowledge of the available technologies and a comprehensive and accurate knowledge of industry workings and the capacity that this implies

- The absence of incentives for business to go beyond the minimum standards established, which means that government is always in the position of having to increase standards as it sees necessary

- The fact that the cost of enforcement is high and is often inadequate because insufficient resources are committed

Finally, interaction with other spheres is important in the decision to impose a legal standard. The political sphere interacts with the legal sphere because there is a temptation for political decisions to be made about whether and when new environmental technology should be imposed on business. A complex web of environmental and other regulations on business means that votes may be lost or that it may be considered inappropriate for tighter standards of technology to be introduced. The economic sphere interacts with the legal sphere because development of market incentives is seen by some as a more efficient way of addressing environmental protection. For example, a market in pollution rights could be introduced by government as a way of favouring business that adopts cleaner technology. The cleaner businesses would need fewer rights to pollute and would gain a competitive advantage at the expense of environmental laggards.

Through regulation, the legal frame for conducting business is provided by individual sovereign nations. In the context of environmental law, administration of justice by sovereign nations is increasingly being supplemented by agreements made under international law and governed by international institutions. Among others, organisations such as the World Trade Organisation (WTO, www.wto.org), the United Nations (UN, www.un.org) and the EU (europa.eu.int) represent the global or regional networking of nations. This has led to a supranational layer of governance and to appeal systems of regulation at the international level (e.g. the International Court of Justice, www.icj-cij.org).

In order to encourage business value creation to consider the long term, laws regulate exploitation of the environment in the short term. As administrators of public goods, governments of sovereign nations have assumed the task of protecting land, air and water from over-exploitation by individual economic interests, to treat biological diversity and the health of the population as welfare goals and to protect the global climate through ratification of international agreements. Government actors in many countries have pursued a national environmental and, more recently, a sustainability strategy (e.g. Australia, from 1992, www.ea.gov.au/esd/national/nsesd/index.html; and Germany, from 1971, www.dialog-nachhaltigkeit.de). As the number of countries introducing environmental strategies increases, there is a move towards global convergence and an increase in the standards required by environmental law (see Jänicke and Weidner 1997; Urbani *et al.* 1994). Sustainable development—the process of moving towards sustainability—cannot be considered in the absence of the introduction of international 'green' product standards and the introduction of rules to restrict transfers of capital to countries where environmental laws are less strict, thereby leading to exploitation of the environment.

Businesses operating across national boundaries have for many decades had to consider whether to impose common environmental process, product and procedural standards on their international operations. For example, companies operating across developing and developed countries have to address this issue on a daily basis. Environmental requirements are often less strict in developing countries because of the lack of capacity (technical, financial, political and organisational) to encourage the implementation of higher standards. Today, over 4,000 laws and regulations in Germany and over 1,000 in Australia (Bates 1995) are fairly representative of the complexity and density of legal environmental requirements. As new environmental problems are discovered, these laws are supplemented and amended on a regular basis, thereby adding to existing complexity and making the need for global standards that much more urgent.

9.2.2 *Voluntarism and environmental management*

Voluntary agreements are entered into by a business without pressure from the government, the regulator, or an industry association of which the business is a member. Environmental management systems provide a case in point. At the international level, the International Organisation for Standardisation (ISO) has introduced the ISO 14000 series of generic environmental management system standards. As mentioned in Section 9.1, the EU has its own scheme, EMAS. ISO 14001 is a system of environmental management that can be used for internal or external purposes. When used for external purposes, an independent third-party certification process may be used to demonstrate that the requirements of the standard have been met. ISO 14001 incorporates a feedback loop to environmental management whereby a business plans, implements, controls and takes corrective action to ensure continual improvement in the environmental management process. One of the key differences between the ISO 14000 series and EMAS is that external reporting is not a requirement in EMAS.

Other voluntary schemes are encouraged by government. For example, biodiversity conservation by farmers is encouraged in Australia through management agreements between government and the farmer (www.ea.gov.au/land/bushcare/publications/motivating/pubs/motivating.pdf). A monetary reimbursement is provided to enable the farmer to recover certain capital and operating expenditure associated with Landcare (see www.landcareaustralia.com.au). Farmers enter into contracts to undertake activities such as fencing and the protection of habitat for native fauna in exchange for funding support. Other voluntary agreements involve government encouragement of environmental protection by business. For example, the Greenhouse Challenge, another voluntary scheme in Australia (www.greenhouse.gov.au/challenge), links government and business through a contract to take action to reduce greenhouse gas emissions and to report on progress towards established targets. Similar arrangements are commonplace throughout the world. Energy efficiency is one area where schemes abound. For instance, the USA has instituted a Green Lights programme designed to encourage business to adopt energy-efficient lighting (208.254.22.6/ia/business/pk_manual.pdf).

Voluntary schemes are often started by government, but such schemes do have some problems, especially where the interests of the volunteer are not congruent with the government's interests. A co-operative approach to environmental protection by business works well where there is trust between business and government. However, business exposes itself to monitoring and periodic audit where contracts are voluntarily entered into in exchange for funding or other support, such as favoured involvement in other government programmes as a *quid pro quo*. Where industry associations are involved, the term 'self-regulation' is used, as explained in the next subsection.

9.2.3 *Self-regulation and environmental management*

The notion that command-and-control regulation is neither effective nor efficient in certain situations leads to the adoption of a broader set of considerations when government considers the design of a regulatory system. Five main principles can be identified for designing a regulatory system that can encourage 'good' environmental behaviour by business (Gunningham and Grabosky 1998):

- Principle 1: prefer policy mixes incorporating a broader range of instruments and institutions.

- Principle 2: start with the least interventionist measure that works.

- Principle 3: ascend a dynamic instrument pyramid to the extent necessary to achieve policy goals.

- Principle 4: empower participants who are in the best position to act as surrogate regulators.

- Principle 5: maximise opportunities for win–win outcomes.

Self-regulation is one of the instruments included in design principle 1. Self-regulation can refer to internal regulation of a business. Systems of legal regulations provide mutual support for the behaviour of people in organisations and for the public administration of justice. For example, an employee's rights and obligations are regulated by employment legislation, pay and work agreements as well as by instructions and in-house rules provided about expected employee behaviour inside the business. Organisational hierarchy represents an alternative method of co-ordination to market regulation (see e.g. Williamson 1985).

In general, hierarchies can be described as command-based systems designed to organise transactions, with information passing up and down a chain of command between superiors and subordinates. The hierarchy has the power to get people to do things, not because they have preferences for the goods and appropriate purchasing power, as occurs with a market transaction, but because it provides an explicit and stable relationship between people (e.g. a manager and a worker). It establishes acceptable norms of behaviour (i.e. acceptable ways of doing things). Therefore, hierarchy creates security in the relationships between parties, based on the principle of order and obedience, rights and responsibilities (see e.g. Frey and Kirchgässner 1994: 173ff.; Kreitner and Kinicki 1992: 452ff.).

When such command systems are used regularly, they represent **routines**. If the norms are open and transparent, then it is clear what the result of following a particular course of action will be. Constraints imposed by the command system help decision-makers recognise the limit of their authority to take decisions. Such systems also indicate when decision-makers are expected to react quickly to expected events that are under their control and for which authority has been delegated.

Markets and hierarchies are often seen as different ways of co-ordinating activities (see Jost 2000: 52ff.; von Hayek 1986). Foundations of hierarchical organisation go back to Weber's (1980) model of bureaucracy. An ideal bureaucracy has four main characteristics: specialised groups of workers undertaking well-defined jobs; a hierarchy of authority that distinguishes between the administrators (with different ranks, from high to low) and the people being administered; a well-defined system of rules; and impersonal decision-making, as the aim of the rules is to provide the basis for consistent decisions no matter who makes those decisions. Authority is exercised in accordance with the rules, so that it is not arbitrary. Privileges are also allocated in accordance with the rules on rank and seniority, so that people in favour with an individual are not rewarded more than people out of favour. Impersonality is the characteristic that distinguishes bureaucracy most clearly from other types of organisation, such as kinship, which is common in less-industrial societies. It is also a characteristic that is cited as an advantage of market relationships.

Self-regulation is also seen as a way for industry associations to establish norms of behaviour or codes of conduct for their members. Good environmental management may be imposed not by government but by an industry association acting on behalf of its members. This form of self-regulation is often encouraged by government or is overseen by government. If self-regulation does not work, then government may well impose tighter, prescribed regulations on business. Responsible Care in the chemical industry provides one example of self-regulation in action; the Australian Minerals Industry Code for Environmental Management provides another.

The chemical industry developed a poor public image following a number of disasters at chemical plants worldwide (e.g. Bhopal, Sandoz, Seveso), with the threat of government involvement. Responsible Care was launched in 1988 by the American Chemistry Council to respond to public concerns about the manufacture and use of chemicals. Member companies of the Council are committed to supporting a continuing effort to improve the chemical industry's responsible management of chemicals. Responsible Care imposes a number of requirements on members:

- To improve their health, safety and environmental performance on a continual basis

- To listen and respond to public concerns

- To assist each other to achieve optimum performance

- To report their goals and progress to the public

One of the codes of conduct of Responsible Care relates to pollution prevention (see www.americanchemistry.com). This code is designed to encourage members to achieve ongoing reductions in the amount of all contaminants and pollutants released to air, water and land from their facilities. Responsible Care is now adopted by the chemical industry in over 40 countries.

The Australian Minerals Industry Code for Environmental Management was introduced in 1996 (MCA 2000); once again, this was in order to reverse the declining image of the industry in the eyes of the public and the implicit threat of government involvement. The Code addresses environmental management and public accountability. The Code requires signatories to report within two years to the public on their environmental management activities. Completion by the company of an annual Code implementation survey is required to assess progress against implementation of Code principles. Furthermore, the results of the annual survey have to be verified by an accredited auditor at least once every three years. Energy Resources of Australia, one of the signatories, commits itself to (see www.energyres.com.au/environment/code.shtml#intro):

- Integration of environmental, social and economic considerations into decision-making and management, consistent with the objectives of sustainable development

- Openness, transparency and improved accountability through public environmental reporting and engagement with the community

- Compliance with all statutory requirements as a minimum

- A continually improving standard of environmental performance and, through leadership, the pursuit of environmental excellence throughout the Australian minerals industry

These two examples of self-regulation codes illustrate that environmentally sensitive industries are willing to address environmental improvement issues without the actual presence of penalties being imposed from a government regulator. In each case, the need to improve public image was paramount.

Self-regulation does have certain strengths and weaknesses associated with it as a means of social control. It is claimed to be flexible in comparison with command-and-control regulation, it readily responds to market situations and should lead to standards that are based on direct knowledge of technology and management practices in the industry. Continual improvement, as one of the characteristics of the code, should lead to an even higher standard of environmental behaviour.

However, self-regulation codes often do not deliver the promised increase in standards and are seen as a way of improving image without improving environmental performance and as a means of providing government with a way of avoiding its responsibility to society to impose obligations on industry for a minimum standard of behaviour. Enforcement of code requirements is often weak, standards set are low and punishment of members that do not comply often takes place behind closed doors. When the business can make an economic gain at the same time as improving environmental performance, self-regulation is likely to be successful because the interests of society and of business converge. For example, new technology that reduces the amount of material inputs, waste and electricity used is of benefit to the environment and to the financial results of the company.

Gunningham and Grabosky (1998: 54) suggest that the situations where self-regulation is more likely to be successful are as follows:

● Where the fate of all participants in the industry is determined by the worst member (e.g. when the *Exxon Valdez* ran aground in Prince William Sound, it affected the environmental risk insurance premiums of all petroleum tankers in the industry [www.oilspill.state.ak.us])

● Where enterprises are aware of one another's behaviour and can detect non-compliance—the larger the numbers, the more opportunity there is to cheat (i.e. not comply with self-regulation) in order to gain an advantage

● Where industries have a history of effective co-operation (e.g. members of an industry association, such as the Australian Minerals Industry)

● Where there is a means of punishing non-compliant behaviour (e.g. where dismissal from an industry association would lead to too heavy a penalty on the business)

● Where consumers, employees and suppliers value compliant behaviour and can identify compliant businesses

9.2.4 *Government monitoring, auditing and environmental management*

Whatever type of environmental regulation is used from the regulatory mix—command and control, self-regulation or voluntary initiatives—monitoring provides a basis for confirmation that the business has achieved what it set out to do, whether this be simple compliance with the law or moving beyond compliance as a means of gaining a competitive advantage.

An environmental audit is a verification process whereby experts confirm whether claims made by a business about its environmental management procedures, processes and actions to protect the environment are justified. On the one hand, regulators may insist that an environmental audit take place in line with the law; on the other hand, an environmental audit may be undertaken as a foundation to understanding the environmental issues that a business needs to address. Environmental monitoring through auditing or verification provides a basis for enforcing environmental laws and regulations as well as contracts between parties or for confirming to a business that it has taken actions that continually improve environmental protection. If regulators are to allow leaders to benefit through looser regulatory control, or to exert tighter control over laggards, then it is necessary for the environmental impacts of business to be monitored, checked against expectations or targets and an assessment of performance made.

Questions for review

9.1 What is the legal sphere of influence? Is it linked to any of the other spheres?

9.2 Explain the meaning of the term 'regulatory mix'. What is being mixed, and why?

9.3 'Command-and-control environmental regulation comes at a cost.' Outline the main costs and the potential costs of environmental regulation to business, to government and to society.

9.4 Examine the proposal that the costs of non-compliance with the law are greater than the costs of compliance. Provide an example to support your view.

9.5 Upfront, operational and back-end costs of regulation differ from each other. How do they differ? Provide an example of each.

9.6 All parts of the value chain are said to be affected by the costs of complying with environmental law. Outline the different functions in a typical value chain for a manufacturing company and identify the costs associated with environmental laws in relation to each function. Is one part of the value chain affected by environmental law more than other parts?

9.7 Why does it matter to business if the costs of regulation increase? Can it not pass these costs on to customers?

9.8 Why in many countries is command-and-control regulation the most dominant way of influencing business behaviour towards the environment?

9.9 Why are objections made to end-of-pipe regulation? Does this type of regulation have any advantages over self-regulation or voluntary regulation? Explain.

9.10 If environmental regulations are less strict in a developing country, will business move to capture this advantage? Give reasons for your view, citing a recent example with which you are familiar.

9.11 Is government regulation related to voluntary environmental management systems in any way? Discuss the reasons for your answer.

9.12 Markets and hierarchies are seen as different ways of co-ordinating business activities. How do they differ? Why are markets used to promote environmental protection on some occasions and in-house co-ordinating devices used on other occasions?

9.13 'Responsible Care and the Australian Minerals Industry Code for Environmental Management were introduced to avoid government regulation.' Do you agree with this comment? Explain why you do or do not believe this to be the case.

9.14 Discuss the reasons why voluntary or self-regulation are considered to be part of the legal sphere of influence over the environmental actions and impacts of business.

9.15 Are there any mechanisms available for sovereign nations to control the environmental impacts of multinational companies? Explain the advantages and disadvantages of any mechanisms that you identify.

9.16 Critically comment on the view that 'Environmental monitoring is an unnecessary encumbrance on business.'

10

Success factors and fields of action
Partnerships and legitimacy

Partnerships come into being because of the development of social relationships through mutual trust and commitment (see Table 10.1). Commitment means that partners are motivated to act in accordance with their common intentions (see e.g. Sprenger 1995). A committed partner agrees to do something and then does it. For example, if partners agree to recycle more natural resources, they should do it, and be seen to do it. The implication is that partners have a good understanding of what it is they are committed to—they have reached a good **understanding** through their dialogue with other partners. Partners are usually considered to have **equal power** and hence one partner can control another to only a limited extent. Partnerships require high **trust relationships** in order to succeed. When a high level of trust exists between partners and there is agreement that one another's actions might be constrained through rules, roles and relationships, in the interest of the partnership, the parties willingly accept these constraints as legitimate (Fox 1974: 14).

Field of action	*Partnership*
Main focus	Values Morality Reliability Notification
Question to be answered	Which social purposes should be pursued by business?
Basis for action	Trust and commitment
Criterion for success	Legitimacy
Type of rationality	Normative (communicative)

Table 10.1 **Partnerships (see also Table 7.1 on page 58)**

10.1 **Legitimacy as a criterion of success**

Partnerships legitimise their own actions through social confirmation of their credibility. All stakeholders in the partnership (parties affected by the partnership in some way) need to legitimise partnership activities. Only businesses whose existence and work is accepted by the stakeholders can build high-trust relationships and thereby operate successfully, taking the long term into account, secure in the knowledge that they have the support of their stakeholders. If public trust in the **social benefits** of the enterprise and the **credibility of information** provided about its activities is missing, resistance and conflict will result.

Members of society are typically concerned about security of employment, economic stability and environmental protection. Stakeholders expect their values and cultures to be considered and seek policy stability rather than constantly changing policy, as this reduces insecurity and uncertainty. Trust in a partnership is based on the availability of expert information, public opinion (e.g. whether there is an environmental crisis, irrespective of what the scientific evidence reveals), media reports and leaders of opinion in society, such as politicians and church leaders. To safeguard their **legitimacy**, in order that they are allowed to continue with their activities in the face of a failure in organisational performance, businesses may adopt a number of **normative strategies** (Dyllick *et al.* 1997; Gray *et al.* 1996: 47; Schaltegger 2000: 113ff.). First, an organisation may seek to 'educate' its stakeholders about its intentions to improve performance. Second, it may seek to change the stakeholders' perceptions, but without actually changing its performance. Third, it may seek to distract attention away from the issue of concern, by emphasising good performance in some other, often related, area of activity. Finally, the partnership may seek to change external expectations about general performance. Reactions to these strategies will help determine whether societal acceptance is confirmed.

Apart from following strategies to secure acceptance of the partnership within society, the corporation may attempt to develop networks or bilateral relations. **Co-operation** is encouraged in order to solve problems that reach outside the legal boundary of the corporation. For example, **networking** may assist with the introduction of innovations (e.g. new, cleaner technology), development of green products may lead to co-operation with non-governmental organisations (NGOs) and certification of green credentials through eco-labels may require co-operation with several stakeholder groups. For these and other purposes, close bilateral partnerships between individual parties may be arranged: for example, as part of intermediate product chains or the development of innovative processes by suppliers.

To sum up, successful partnerships are based on high-trust, co-operative relationships, where information is shared and issues of confidentially are overcome. In addition, networking between stakeholders and mutual acceptance between businesses, community groups and society are further important characteristics of successful partnership arrangements.

10.2 **The meaning of trust**

Every social exchange is based on trust that has been formed in one way or another (see Fox 1974: 66; Hellmer *et al.* 1999: 60ff.). The degree of trust is based on relative power relationships between the parties. People higher up in the organisation's hierarchy have greater authority. Trust is assumed to reside with such authority as is the associated responsibility. In contrast, people lower down in the hierarchy are trusted to follow rules laid down and to be accountable to the senior personnel who establish the rules for others to follow. Trust in a bureaucracy is related to the need for a lack of discrimination in the distribution of favours and in consistency of treatment authorised by establishing a clear set of rules to be followed. In other words, trust is present because of the impersonality of decision-making. In the marketplace, trust relates to the fact that if purchasing power is handed over by a customer the goods or services received are what they are claimed they will be—that is, serviceable for the intended purpose. In partnerships, however, trust relates to agreement between partners to work together for a common purpose, with all partners committing resources to achieve the desired outcomes.

Trust provides the foundation for partnership activities. Empirical evidence examines trust in the context of the practices of a particular business (see World Bank 2001; see also Apelt 1999; Bierhoff 1995; Fontanari 1995). Partnerships have to be negotiated, with an open dialogue and agreement being reached on the mutual rights and obligations of each partner. Key elements include mutual benefit, clearly defined expectations, rights, responsibilities and accountability. Such elements of balance and mutuality are seldom found in the initial stages of a relationship. Hence, partnerships generally develop over a period of time with a sense of longer-term commitment, because trust is of paramount importance (World Bank 2001).

Many sociologists, economists and psychologists talk today about the expanded meaning of trust for social co-ordination in the economy and society (see Bachmann and Lane 1999; Frey 1997; Loose and Sydow 1994; Luhmann 1973; Rotter 1980). Box 10.1 lists seven factors that are decisive in the success of such co-ordination.

Although it is misleading to consider trust as a purely altruistic attitude, trust is accompanied by a moral commitment. Trust is not only given but also invested (see Junge 1998: 27; Osterloh *et al.* 1999) as the expression of trust is reciprocal—a two-way relationship. Partners can respond to a demonstration of trust by exhibiting their own trust which, in a situation of high trust, can promote an open dialogue and exchange of information. These high-trust situations presuppose:

- Elimination of anonymity. Strangers are not normally trusted until some familiarity and opportunity for reciprocation arises.

- Repeat meetings. Trust can be reciprocated only when communication between the partners is repeated. A one-off meeting does not form the basis for building a strong, trusting relationship.

- Possibility of sanctions. Trust can partly substitute for conventional control and punishment mechanisms, but where trust is abused sanctions are imposed based on the reduced level of trust that is perceived to exist

The increasingly intangible character of output

Value creation and business values are increasingly based on intangible factors. Knowledge, image, continued existence of customers and efficient organisational structures are today, most of the time, more important for economic success than favourable access to raw materials and processing capacities. Since intangible values can be neither seen nor touched, stakeholders must often simply trust their quality and, occasionally, even their existence (e.g. brand values).

An increase in calculable risks

Added complexity in the interrelationships between environmental consequences and economic risks means that risk situations are rarely directly understandable. The formation of opinions about these areas presupposes a trust in expert judgements and moral authorities (see Beck 1986).

Substitution for social controls

Giddens (1997: 161ff.) believes that the meaning of trust lies in the ability to organise relationships flexibly over space and time. In virtual networks and e-business, trust substitutes for the loss of social controls (see e.g. Fuderholz 1998; Krystek 1999; Stengel 1998).

Transportation of creativity

If mistrust comes to dominate, the main focus in relationships is quickly drawn to the need to avoid mistakes (negative consequences of actions) because of the fear that outside controls may be imposed (see Nieder 1997: 61).

Long-term advantages of efficiency

Trust facilitates long-term efforts to solve problems rather than placing a focus on fixing short-term problems.

Expansion of the organisation's boundaries

Trust encourages the contracting-out of non-core business activities rather than maintaining them in-house (Greve 2001). Increased security risks act in the other direction by reducing trust in 'outsiders'.

Partial loss of values

Trust increases in importance where traditions, social values and customs are being eroded (see Dederichs 1997). To express this in an economic way, trust becomes a scarce resource when values are eroded; or, in a business sense, when low-trust relationships become the norm, high-trust relationships have a high value.

Box 10.1 Expanded meaning of trust in value creation: decisive factors for social co-ordination in the economy and society between the parties. Such sanctions represent a return to stronger conventional controls on the relationship.

Trust and mistrust often become self-fulfilling prophecies—they escalate on the basis of the reciprocal behaviour of each partner and perceptions of trustworthiness (see Fig. 10.1).

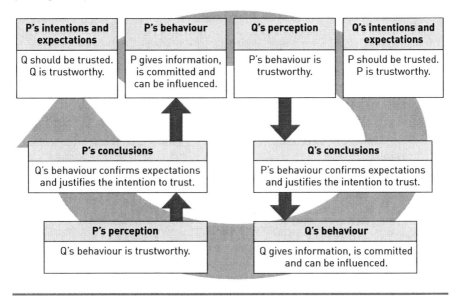

Figure 10.1 High-trust spiral between partners P and Q, based on reciprocal reinforcement of positive expectations

Sources: Fox 1974; Krystek and Zumbrock 1993: 10

In partnerships both **personal trust** as well as **institutional trust** (e.g. trust in a company) can exist. Personal trust tends to precede institutional trust. Empirical surveys show that trust between organisations depends heavily on personal relationships between individuals, such as managers or project researchers. Trust can be transmitted from individuals to the organisation when individual expectations are in accord with the intentions of the organisation. In these circumstances the individual exerts sufficient influence to secure the link between his or her organisation and individual trust. The development of partnerships does not eliminate the need for rules. Certain rules precede the formation of a partnership, in order to enhance reliability (see Sydow 1993: 186). Rules are tailored to provide a stable base for the shared needs of partners. Partners face the task of seeking out appropriate forms, reasons and procedures to help consolidate their partnerships. These are based on criteria or rules of partnership:

- There must be an open exchange of information and discretion must be used in relation to confidential information.

- There must be an openness towards alternative opinions, standpoints and ideas.

- There must be participatory decision-making and unified action.

- Mutual help and support must be given in the event that problems arise.

- Partners must keep their promises and engagements and give notification when unforeseen circumstances lead to broken promises and engagements.

- Consistent behaviour and calmness must be shown in response to the unexpected actions of partners.

- Common successes must be celebrated and all involved must share in the joy of the successes of other partners.

In order to stabilise business partnerships, it is necessary to develop rules in advance for handling potential conflicts and failures in order that unnecessary escalation of conflict can be avoided (see Burgheim 1996: 61). Hence, partnerships can include limited and mutually accepted sanctions as well as mechanisms for making confessions, providing forgiveness and repairing damage (see Krystek and Zumbrock 1993: 9).

10.3 Co-operation and networks

In concrete terms, business partnerships are fostered through co-operation and networking. When dealing with customers, suppliers or regulatory authorities, it is necessary and an everyday occurrence for people in business to behave in a co-operative way. However, **co-operation** clearly reaches well beyond **co-operative behaviour** (see Balling 1998: 12ff.; Picot *et al.* 1998: 279ff.). A number of characteristics can be identified regarding co-operation:

- Co-operation is created during long-term team activities, especially during project work.

- Co-operation results from a conscious suggestion; hence, it does not automatically come into being through increases in routine interaction. Instead, it requires agreement of the actors involved.

- Co-operation can exist between organisations. Information exchange between partners (e.g. between the environmental managers of two companies) represents co-operation only when the need for teamwork between participating organisations is recognised, introduced and sustained.

- Co-operation resides with a well-defined number of organisations. Hence, mostly bilateral or trilateral relationships are established. If several organisations are involved, it makes more sense to talk about a network or a combination.

- Co-operation does not remove the economic or legal autonomy of participating organisations. Co-operation is voluntarily entered into by a partner and can be terminated unilaterally.

■ Although co-operation can be initiated and terminated voluntarily by a partner, costs of entry into and exit from co-operative arrangements exist. Entry costs exist, for example, because of initiation processes, investments or unilateral outlays that have to be made in order to attract potential partners. Exit costs exist, for example, through the possible loss of image when a co-operative arrangement is terminated or if sanctions are imposed by ex-partners.

■ Co-operative arrangements do not, of course, limit the general autonomy of the actors, but they do create dependencies in relation to issues that are subject to collective decision-making.

For business management, the success of co-operation depends on whether interaction is based on common interests and on whether the partners remain unconstrained to follow their own interests. Wurche (1994: 47) describes this process in terms of the integration of goals and means. The choice of means and associated actions must be made in such a way that the needs of each partner are appreciated and included in the calculation of mutual benefits resulting from co-operation (see Fig. 10.2).

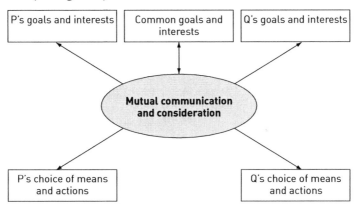

Figure 10.2 **The integration of goals and means by partners P and Q within a co-operative arrangement**

Source: Wurche 1994: 48

Less tightly coupled businesses co-operate mostly through networks. **Networks** are used to bring together a number of additional actors. Not everybody is constantly engaged in a network or always has contact with other parties. When, why and how firms engage in different forms of inter-organisational networking—such as strategic alliances, joint ventures and long-term accords for collaboration between competitors as well as with suppliers and customers—is a key aspect of networking (Ebers 1999). Through networking, businesses open themselves up to a larger number of options for teamwork with different partners (see Boos *et al.* 1994). Networks tend to come into being either before or after engagement in co-operative arrangements (see Fig. 10.3).

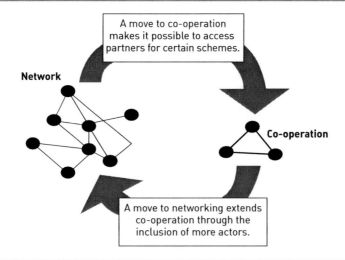

Figure 10.3 **Mutual interrelationships between networks and co-operation**

In the corporate context, until the beginning of the 1990s the term 'network' was normally associated with electronic data processing (EDP). A network was seen as a collection of terminals, computers, servers and components that facilitates the easy flow of data and use of resources between computers. Although the need for efficient EDP networks has retained its importance, more recently the meaning of the term 'network' has been dominated by discussion about efficient forms of organisation and how these evolve (see e.g. Bea and Göbel 1999; Hope and Fraser 1997; Picot *et al.* 1998; Probst *et al.* 1999; Sydow and van Well 1996; see also Box 10.2).

Networks are unbounded structures that, contrary to the notion of a group, cannot be precisely defined at any given time. In network organisations:

- Lateral relations are more important than vertical relations.
- Hierarchies are either very flat or disappear altogether.
- There needs to be a common intention in order to allow the network to develop and become effective.

Box 10.2 **Networks: a definition**

Kantner (1994: 2) argues that the traditional hierarchical organisation can no longer keep pace with constant technological change in a dynamic global market. The inability of conventional organisations to adapt and be flexible has led to the emergence of new network organisational forms (see Box 10.3). The process of change is referred to as 'debureaucratisation' (Mintzberg and Quinn 1996: 350). In debureaucratised organisations technical and social networks use a web of lateral associations (hyperlinks, project groups, etc.) as an alternative to conventional hierarchical organisational structures (e.g. by using organigrams and hierarchical organisation charts).

In **network organisations** there tends to be less focus on technical issues and a greater focus on cultural aspects of the organisation, such as (Drucker *et al.* 1997: 18):

- How to lead organisations that create and nurture knowledge

- How to live in a world in which companies have ever-increasing visibility

- How to gain and maintain the ability to learn, both as individuals and as organisations

Box 10.3 Network organisations

Hope and Fraser (1997) identified the importance of network organisations for organisations that rely on the intellectual capacity and knowledge of their staff as their main asset rather than relying on physical assets such as plant and machinery. They suggested that Asea Brown Boveri (ABB), voted from 1994–97 by its peers as Europe's most admired company, had adopted many of the essential features of the 'N-form' (i.e. network form). ABB is a multinational company involved in power and automation technologies that enable utility and industry customers to improve performance while lowering environmental impact (www.abb.com). The ABB Group of companies operates in more than 100 countries and employs around 140,000 people. It has created a federation of some 1,300 distinctive and separate businesses, each with multiple profit centres. It has a very lean headquarters (employing about 150 people) and is highly decentralised. Research and development (R&D), for example, is devolved to operating units. Each unit manages its own finances as if it were an independent company, but information across and up and down the group is open and fast. By adopting this N-form model, ABB has created a widely distributed network of entrepreneurs, thus improving responsiveness while retaining the benefits of scale through the introduction of mechanisms for horizontal integration of the operating units (Hope and Fraser 1997).

In the N-form organisation, front-line managers are the entrepreneurs, strategists and decision-makers, constantly creating and responding to new opportunities for the business; middle managers are the horizontal integrators, building competences across the organisation (and with external partners); and top managers provide inspiration and a sense of purpose while frequently challenging the status quo.

Hope and Fraser (1997: 2) suggest that, whether they recognise it or not, many businesses have already adopted many of the elements of the new N-form organisational model. Total quality management (TQM), business process re-engineering, decentralisation, empowerment, economic value added and the balanced scorecard are all said to be pieces in this new jigsaw (Hope and Fraser 1997).

A second example of an organisation with a network structure, from Austria, is the Neuwaldegg Group. For more than ten years this Group, which is experienced in the management of networks of social and cultural organisations, has favoured the idea of a network as an entrepreneurial growth strategy. Together with 50 network partners, it has introduced a systematic approach to consultancy based on networks (see www.neuwaldegg.at/ueberuns/index.html). A further example, based in London, is Michaelides & Bednash, a media entertainment and advertising company. The company illustrates the variety of network forms. Elements of a network culture are embedded in the organisation: total participation in decision-making, an absence of work procedures and job descriptions, a flat structure and open communication (Williamson and Boyle 2000). The Michaelides & Bednash example illustrates how networks are linked less with offices, posts, roles and job descriptions than with personal contacts, agreements and interpersonal trust.

Investment in personal relationship 'capital', perceived as knowledge, authority or empathy in relationships, creates the **relationship potential** of a network. In such relationships there is a need for a common intention, idea or purpose to which the actors involved can direct their relationship capital. This common intention ranges from development of competitive advantage from strategic networks (see Sydow 1993) to the growth of self-help in poor Mexican districts (see Esteva 1992). The relationship potential is initiated and made visible through a range of possible current causes cemented together at gatherings, campaigns or workshops. Once the cause has been met, the relationship becomes dormant, but it retains its potential to be ignited as future causes become apparent (see Boos *et al.* 1994).

In a network, boundaries remain blurred, actors are loosely coupled, their connection is local and dynamic and relationships inside the network can be dormant or active. Of course, actors in a network are not always equally important. Some actors have active relationships and operate in the core areas of interest whereas others may operate in marginal zones and be only sporadically called on. Hierarchical structures and networks are distinguished with use of constructs such as the pyramid and circle. The head of a hierarchy stands alone at the top of the organisation, whereas the **focal** actors of a network are 'pulsating' central points on the circle, spider's web, cluster or starburst organisational structure.

10.4 Partnerships in an ecological context

In the 1990s, co-operation and network forms of organisation were developed into a key aspect of ecologically oriented business management (see Schneidewind 1995). They play an important role both in the development of corporate environmental policy (e.g. Freimann and Hildebrandt 1995; Hellenbrandt and Rubik 1994; Oikos 1994) and in special environmental situations where contingency planning is being developed.

Apart from works developing the theory of partnerships in environmental management (Aulinger 1996; Brockhaus 1996; Götzelmann 1992; Schneidewind 1998), some contributions simply illustrate instances of co-operation that are used in practice. In particular, co-operation with environmental associations has become important (see Murphy and Bendell 1997; Schneidewind and Petersen 1998; Zhang 2001; see also Box 10.4).

Environmental organisations have come to realise that partnerships in social networks can help promote sustainable development by intensifying the pressure brought to bear on governments. The importance of these networks became apparent to the public for the first time at the 1992 Rio 'Earth Charter' conference. This meeting enhanced to a great extent the reputation of the environmental associations (see Klein 1997; Walk 1997). More recently, co-operation in opposition to the

- Corporate intervention in nature and its effects on the affluence of species, health and the chance of survival of future generations has an impact on the core values of all the company stakeholders.

- Implementation of effective, efficient and equitable agreements about production and waste systems presupposes open flows of material and information between stakeholders along the corporate value-creation chain. Co-operation and networking facilitate the development of mutual arrangements and standardised agreements.

- Information for consumers referring, for example, to the origin and processing of raw materials is increasingly being requested. Therefore, co-operation with raw material suppliers (e.g. in the cotton industry) aims towards guaranteed compliance with ecological or social standards established in the extraction of raw materials.

- Product development partnerships serve to build up funding for research budgets and common technical competences in organisations (e.g. as a basis for developing an eco-label scheme such as those of the Forest Stewardship Council [FSC] network (www.fscoax.org/principal.htm) and of the Marine Stewardship Council network (www.msc.org) which started through the co-operation of the World Wide Fund for Nature (WWF) and Unilever). The interdisciplinary foundations of environmental management enhance the attractiveness of co-operation with research institutions, environmental associations and universities.

- Comparability of environmental performance between businesses presupposes that certain standards (e.g. about eco-balancing or product quality) have been agreed. These standards are partly arrived at through mutual agreement by companies, but they may also require collaboration with external regulatory, professional or industry authorities and other non-governmental associations.

- Partnerships can be directed towards initiating public discussions or intensifying the exchange of opinions, or dialogue, with stakeholders. This can occur through jointly organised conferences, exhibitions or discussion forums. Co-operation with environmental associations helps avoid unnecessary confrontation and serves the process of harmonising different points of view.

- Partnerships are used to promote certain political interests; for example, in order to lobby in favour of environmental positions being adopted when monetary considerations tend to dominate.

Box 10.4 **Reasons encouraging the adoption of partnerships in the practice of environmental management**

environmental credentials of the World Trade Organisation (WTO) and the World Economic Forum (WEF) has led to conflict rather than partnership. In 2002, partnerships were encouraged at the World Summit on Sustainable Development (WSSD), held in Johannesburg. These partnerships are described as type 2 outcomes from the Summit (see www.johannesburgsummit.org/html/sustainable_dev/questanswtype2.doc). Type 2 outcomes are voluntary partnerships between any combination of business, communities, governments and NGOs that are not negotiated by governments. Type 2 outcomes have been criticised by some NGOs (e.g. Friends of the Earth [www.foe.co.uk]) as a way of encouraging 'greenwash' from polluting companies that wish to divert attention.

Businesses that advocate sustainable development also network with each other. Prominent examples with regard to the above are the proactive ecological business associations such as:

● The World Business Council for Sustainable Development (WBCSD, www.wbcsd.org), a coalition of 150 international companies united by a shared commitment to sustainable development via the three pillars of economic growth, ecological balance and social progress (see also Box 10.5)

● Environment Business Australia (www.emiaa.org.au), the peak body representing and helping organisations in the business of providing goods, systems, services, technology, infrastructure, financing, R&D and education that improve environmental outcomes

● Bundesdeutscher Arbeitskreis für umweltbewusstes Management (BAUM, www.baumev.de), founded in 1985 by a group of German entrepreneurs who wanted to support each other in the implementation of environmental management in their companies

The World Business Council for Sustainable Development (WBCSD) was initiated by Stephan Schmidheiny as a communication and research platform following on from the UN conference on environment and development in Rio de Janeiro in 1992. It had the purpose of enlisting companies in moves to implement sustainable development. One of its research groups is the Scenario Unit. In order to foreshadow possible ways in which a sustainable economy could be arrived at, the group drew up three underlying scenarios (www.wbcsd.org/newscenter/reports/1997/exploringscenarios.pdf):

● Frog ('first raise our growth')

● Geopolity

● Jazz

With the help of the scenario technique the effects of these three alternatives are examined. In the case of Frog, governments and companies recognise the importance of sustainable development but accept that economic growth is of primary importance, even though the outcome is unsustainable. This may be the perspective adopted by some developing countries. Economic growth through the Frog scenario may, of course, be opposed by environmental organisations.

Geopolity and Jazz offer two entirely different scenarios. They begin with a succession of signals—some real, some imagined—that an environmental and social crisis is looming. Governments seem ineffective and businesses unwilling to respond. Governments are rejuvenated as focal points in a civil society, and markets are used to try to achieve sustainable outcomes.

The third scenario, Jazz, is based on self-organisation in networks and is marked by the open interaction of different actors in competition and co-operation. In the world of Jazz environmental organisations, governments, informed users and companies co-operate in order to sustain the general ecological and social framework in which a global market economy is possible (Sonntag 1998: 36). This is a world of social and technological innovations, experimentation, rapid adaptation, much voluntary interconnectedness and a powerful and ever-changing global market. Through Western notions of value, autonomy and personal responsibility the WBCSD is trying to realise as much as possible of the Jazz scenario in order that it does not have to retreat to Geopolity more than necessary.

Box 10.5 Networks in the scenarios of the World Business Council for Sustainable Development

- The Buy Recycled Business Alliance (BRBA, www.brba.com.au), a business-based, non-profit organisation in Australia that promotes the purchase and use of recycled content products (RCPs) and materials utilising a model of leadership by example, education and information, R&D and partnerships

- The International Network for Environmental Management (INEM, www.inem.org), an international non-governmental, non-partisan, not-for-profit organisation founded in 1991 by BAUM Germany, BAUM Austria and Svenska BAUM, with members consisting mainly of businesses and industries; it is dedicated to environmental management and conservation

Business Action for Sustainable Development (BASD), representing business at the WSSD, provides on its website (www.basd-action.net/initiatives/index.php) information about partnership initiatives, giving examples of business working openly with others to promote sustainable development in the areas of water and sanitation, energy, health, agriculture and biodiversity. For example, under the WBCSD Cement Sustainability Initiative, the WBCSD is working with ten cement industry participants to identify key sustainability issues for the cement industry.

An interesting recent convergence of views was between WBCSD and Greenpeace (archive.greenpeace.org/earthsummit/wbcsd). They share the same belief that the threat of human-induced climate change requires strong efforts and innovation by all sectors in a common international framework. They have agreed to convene a dialogue to urge governments to act more forcefully to provide an international political framework that enables, stimulates and rewards innovation and implementation. Together, Greenpeace and WBCSD also call on others in the public and private sectors to step up action to combat climate change risks. This could be the first step towards development of partnerships in the area.

The importance of developing partnerships in the context of solving environmental problems and improving environmental performance is examined below through consideration of three possible ways of building up trust:

- Section 10.4.1 looks at how co-operation between companies and environmental organisations is seen to be enjoying increasing popularity.

- Section 10.4.2 takes networks in the value chain as a central theme.

- Section 10.4.3 examines the assumption of social responsibility under the banner of corporate citizenship.

10.4.1 Co-operation between companies and environmental associations

Co-operation between companies is facilitated by the fact that they have similar motives (e.g. increasing yield, turnover and profitability). Co-operation is normally easier with other businesses than with organisations, such as non-profit organisations, that have a different goal orientation. However, even where organisations have different goals, there can be complementarities between them that encourage the exchange of viewpoints, mutual learning, the sharing of power over certain issues and attention-directing in relation to certain issues of mutual concern. These stimuli are of particular importance when companies and environmental associations consider co-operating with each other. Table 10.2 provides an overview of the most important environmental NGOs, and Box 10.6 quotes the views these NGOs have of themselves, as evidenced on their websites.

The notion of co-operating with business remains fairly new and reflects a considerable change in the attitude of decision-makers both in companies and in environmental organisations. Murphy and Bendell (1997) talk about the transformation

Name	Website	Year founded	Sponsors	Other comments
Australian Conservation Foundation	www.acfonline. org.au	1966	Strategic alliances with a range of organisations and corporations	Australia-specific
Bund für Umwelt und Naturschutz eV (BUND)	www.bund.net	1995	230,000 members	Worldwide, associated with Friends of the Earth
Earth First!	www.earthfirst. org	1979	Autonomous	Active in 13 countries of the first and second world
Earth Island Institute	www. earthisland. org	1982	Projects manage own fundraising with foundations and general public	More than 30 projects worldwide; results achieved through education and activist campaigns
Earthwatch Institute	www. earthwatch. org	1972	Private, corporate donations and volunteers	Projects in over 50 countries, with offices in the USA, Europe, Australia and Japan; formerly known as the Centre for Field Research

Table 10.2 **Examples of important environmental non-governmental organisations (NGOs)** (continued opposite)

Name	Website	Year founded	Sponsors	Other comments
Friends of the Earth	www.foei.org	1971	Federation of 66 groups; a million members, 5,000 local activist groups; 1,000 employees	Worldwide, associated with 69 countries
Green Cross	www.greencrossinternational.net	1993	Well-known personalities from around the world have accepted to be members of the honorary board	Active in 21 countries
Greenpeace	www.greenpeace.org	1971	2.8 million supporters worldwide	Represented in 40 countries
Natur-schutzbund Deutschland eV (NABU)	www.nabu.de	1899	260,000 members	Formerly the Deutscher Bund für Vogelschutz
National Audubon Society	www.audubon.org	1905	600,000 members, 500 chapters	State offices in 27 states of the USA
Sierra Club	www.sierraclub.org	1892	Over 700,000 members	USA-based
Natural Step	www.naturalstep.org	1989	Founded in Sweden; in 2001 57% of funds were derived from foundation grants, 18% from individual contributions and 25% from earned income	Operates in nine countries
WWF	www.panda.org	1961	Almost 5 million members worldwide	Represented in 100 countries; formerly the World Wide Fund for Nature

Table 10.2 (continued)

Australian Conservation Foundation (ACF)

ACF is a non-profit, membership-based environment group. We take a solution-oriented approach to environmental issues, and seek to form partnerships with community groups, governments and business to achieve ecologically sustainable outcomes. Our work includes natural heritage protection, water resource management and global warming, endangered species, uranium mining and sustainable cities. We lobby governments and work to raise the level of awareness of environmental issues within Australia.

Bund für Umwelt und Naturschutz Deutschland eV (BUND)

We, the members of BUND, offer the chance to draw away once and for all from the role of the defenceless victim and the helpless accomplice. We fight insistently and obstinately for the protection of our home planet, the Earth, in its whole beauty. And also more and more often—successfully.

Earth First! (EF!)

EF! is a network of autonomous local groups. It has no central office or paid officers and no decision-making boards.

Earth First! means putting life first. Ecology and the teachings of pre-civilised societies tell us that the Earth is one living organism, and that humanity is as much a part of it as any other species. EF!ers believe that the situation we face is so serious, and the changes demanded by it so massive, that the only solution is for people to take their future in their hands and physically halt further destruction of nature, while creating a classless ecological society which will transcend the present one.

Earth Island Institute

Our Mission: Life on earth is imperilled by human degradation of the biosphere. Earth Island Institute develops and supports projects that counteract threats to the biological and cultural diversity that sustain the environment. Through education and activism, these projects promote the conservation, presentation, and restoration of the Earth.

Earthwatch Institute

The mission of Earthwatch Institute is to promote the sustainable conservation of our natural resources and cultural heritage by creating partnerships among scientists, the general public, educators and businesses. We believe that decision-making involving these issues not only requires objective scientific data from the field but must engage the general public through active participation in the scientific process if it is to become widely accepted and effective.

Friends of the Earth International

Friends of the Earth International is a federation of autonomous environmental organisations from all over the world. Our members, in 69 countries, campaign on the most

Box 10.6 Self-representation of some of the environmental non-governmental organisations (NGOs) listed in Table 10.2 (continued opposite)

Sources: www.acfonline.org.au; www.bund.net; www.earthfirst.org;
www.earthisland.org/abouteii/abouteii.html; www.earthwatch.org/aboutew/mission.html;
www.foei.org; www.greencrossinternational.net; www.greenpeace.org;
www.nabu.de

urgent environmental and social issues of our day, while simultaneously catalysing a shift toward sustainable societies.

Green Cross

Green Cross International was founded by Mikhail Gorbachev in 1993, building on the 1992 Earth Summit in Rio de Janeiro and Agenda 21. Green Cross is a non-governmental, non-profit organisation. Our mission is to help create a sustainable future by cultivating harmonious relationships between humans and the environment. Green Cross concentrates its efforts on five programmes whose common theme is to promote a significant change in human value and address the environmental causes and (significant) consequences of conflicts.

Greenpeace

Greenpeace is an independent, campaigning organisation that uses non-violent, creative confrontation to expose global environmental problems, and force solutions for a green and peaceful future. Greenpeace's goal is to ensure the ability of the Earth to nurture life in all its diversity.

Naturschutzbund Deutschland eV (NABU)

The preservation of nature and the security of the future cannot be achieved by one person alone. Therefore, members and sponsors of the Naturschutzbund Deutschland eV try to jointly accomplish this goal through various commitments. This includes practical nature protection activities as well as scientific research. Political commitment, innovative environmental education and public relations work are likewise part of our work. Furthermore, we are engaged in various discussions about economic policies.

Box 10.6 (continued)

from a 'blame culture' into a 'solutions culture' that is expressed through critical dialogues and limited co-operation to help achieve the goals of both parties. Tighter environmental legislation and NGO involvement in decision-making at international discussions about sustainable development (e.g. at the WSSD in 2002) have changed the perspective of business towards a more pragmatic view of NGOs. Companies seek to participate in the formation of sustainable society where this accords with their own goals: for example, through improved public relations with NGOs.

Environmental associations not only want to be able to address issues in an open way with business but also wish to seek solutions. For this, constructive exchange is necessary. Although the conventional attitude of environmental associations towards companies has been expressed in neutral or aggressive tones (see Fig. 10.4), modern co-operation through attempts to gain wins for the environment and business together is now the mainstream way of changing business attitudes (see Box 10.7).

Among the conventional neutral associations for the protection of nature established many years ago are organisations such as the German federation for the protection of birds (Deutsche Bund für Vogelschutz; founded in 1899, and today called Naturschutzbund Deutschland [NABU]; see Table 10.2). In contrast, organisations established in the 1970s and 1980s, such as Greenpeace, which arose from the more recent ecological movement, have shown their readiness to be aggressive

Figure 10.4 Greenpeace activists in the 1970s

Source: *Der Spiegel* 11 (1995): 47. Photo credit: © Keziere/Greenpeace

In 1989 Protection of Nature in Germany (Bund für Umwelt und Naturschutz Deutschland, BUND) started its first co-operative venture through business with the Hertie Waren- und Kaufhaus GmbH (Hertie) department store. Agreed co-operation requires continual business consultation in relation to ecological issues, such as the redesign of certain varieties of goods in accordance with ecological criteria and the removal of products that are particularly harmful to the environment (such as banning pesticides in the garden maintenance product range). The plan is of benefit to both partners in two ways. First, agreed actions formed the basis for good external publicity and increased credibility for both parties. Second, apart from favourable external effects, co-operation between the actors provides a basic framework for association between and communication with new partners. These provide the foundation for the mutual transfer of ecological and economic knowledge (see Bassfeld 1997; Dittmann 1994).

A gradual building-up of trust between the two parties is based on common learning processes and external disclosures about reduced environmental impacts. Both parties had to overcome significant reservations over whether to engage in formal co-operation, because of the potential for misuse by Hertie of BUND's reputation as a non-governmental organisation searching for a better environment, and Hertie's concern that the costs of changing its products would be too great. BUND's 'capital' is prestige, reliability and contacts with media on environmental issues, and this is something not to be lightly shared. Environmental organisations normally attach great importance to not having links or dependencies with the companies that they see as the cause of environmental problems.

Box 10.7 An example that became the standard: Bund für Umwelt und Naturschutz Deutschland, and Hertie Waren- und Kaufhaus GmbH and to start a conflict (see Box 10.6), but, as noted above, it has recently taken joint action with the WBCSD in support of initiatives on climate change.

The common concern over the need for sustainable development first provided the incentive to encourage shared goals and responsibilities between companies and environmental associations. Furthermore, with their increasing size and professionalism, environmental organisations are beginning to recruit managers from business to help them understand business. Also, companies recruit environmental activists to learn about the perspectives of environmental associations. In this way, some viewpoints are being blended. Nevertheless, there remains a wide spectrum of controversial issues.

From a business point of view, co-operation with environmental associations is linked with an ecologically proactive business strategy. The examples listed in Box 10.8, taken from current co-operative practices, give some indication of the variety of different intentions and goals of the partners.

Systematic examination of these examples—their purpose, specific goals and instruments used for co-operation—is outlined in the following subsections (see Table 10.3). Sections 10.4.1.1–10.4.1.3 look, respectively, at:

* Normative levels of management

* Strategic levels of management

* Operative levels of management

10.4.1.1 Purpose of co-operation

The common **purpose** outlines the way that sustainable development can be promoted (see Fig. 10.5). A distinction can be made between market-related, normestablishing, political and sociocultural co-operation. The main question concerns which of these to adopt as a way of demonstrating the benefits of co-operation to the outside world. Possible purposes include:

* **Competition**: strengthening the ability to compete

* **Norm establishment**: developing and establishing new norms and standards

* **Conflict resolution**: establishing coalitions

* **Publicity**: consciously undertaking public relations work

Ability to compete
In market-related co-operation, environmental organisations support the development and marketing of product and process innovations in order to demonstrate the feasibility of environmentally benign techniques (e.g. the three-litre 'Smile' car; see Stafford *et al.* 1999; see also Box 10.8), to intervene in the design of products in a deliberate way (e.g. the goods variety of Hertie) or to support the introduction of new products to the market by increasing their reliability (e.g. the PVC-free computer keyboard from Cherry Mikroschalter GmbH; see www.cherry.de). Through the creation of better products and processes that are less environmentally damaging, individual companies obtain a competitive advantage.

Some examples of co-operation between companies and environmental organisations are as follows:

■ The collaboration of the World Wide Fund for Nature (WWF) and the Accor Asia Pacific Lend Lease Consortium when constructing the Novotel Ibis Olympic Hotel prior to the Olympic Games held in Sydney in 2000 (www.greenpeace.org.au/archives/olympics/reports/1000_days./pdf)

■ The joining-together in public of the AEG Hausgeräte GmbH and the Bund für Umwelt und Naturschutz Deutschland (BUND) for economic–political reforms, especially for the implementation of ecological tax reform (see AEG 1997: 59)

■ The co-operation between Greenpeace and a network of innovative companies for the construction and exhibition of the three-litre car 'Smile' (see Stafford *et al.* 1999)

■ The co-operation between BUND and Cherry Mikroschalter GmbH for the development and marketing of a PVC-free computer keyboard (see www.cherry.de)

■ The co-operation of Verein zur Förderung des Fairen Handels mit der 'Dritten Welt' eV (the Union for the Promotion of Fair Trade with the 'Third World' [TransFair, www.transfair.org]) with different importers, firms and coffee-roasting shops through eco-labelling products received from the developing countries (see TransFair 1998)

■ The establishment of Gruppe 98, a co-operation platform of the WWF and several wood-manufacturing and wood-trading companies (e.g. Otto-Versand, Kinnarps-Büromöbel, Baufritz-Fertighäuser, OBI-Baumärkte) for the promotion of sustainable forestry in tropical forests; the 'FSC-Gütesiegel' (Forest Stewardship Council seal of approval; see www.fscoax.org) was the most important instrument that resulted from the group's work

■ The 'liability community' between Tengelmann and the Naturschutzbund Deutschland eV (NABU) for the exchange of know-how and for the implementation of common environmental projects

■ The co-operation of the Rheinland Versicherungen with COOL eV to offer automobile insurance that included participation in a reforestation programme as an offset to its own carbon dioxide emissions (see www.rheinland-versicherungen.de)

■ Co-operation between BUND and Alpirsbacher Klosterbräu for the establishment of a new recycling system for beverage containers

■ A joint project of the Marine Stewardship Council, Unilever (as a seller of fish products) and the WWF to explore the ability of different fish in the oceans to reproduce, undertaken as part of the development of a sustainable fisheries economy (see www.msc.org)

Box 10.8 **Examples of co-operation between companies and environmental organisations**

Establishment of coalitions

Alliances, like those for the implementation of environmental tax reform, come together as political interests to promote common ideas by lobbying parliamentarians, by involving international bodies or by mobilising voters when other parties are preventing the implementation of ecologically oriented reforms.

Management level	Question for investigation	Focus of question
Normative	What should the actors want?	Purpose of co-operation
Strategic	What do the actors want from each other?	Motives that relate to the strategic choice made by partners in the co-operative arrangement
Operative	How do the actors get what they want?	Instruments and operational structure of the co-operative arrangement

Table 10.3 Management levels and questions in relation to co-operative arrangements

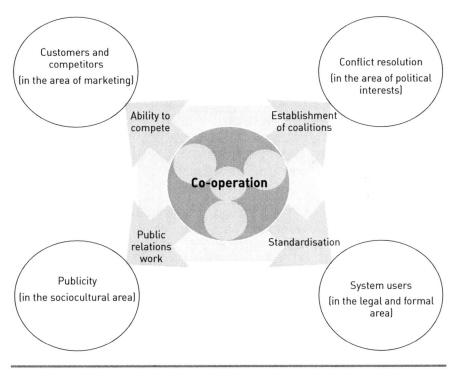

Figure 10.5 Purpose and goal orientation of co-operation in different fields of activity

Standardisation

Co-operation based on norm establishment develops environmental standards and voluntary or self-regulation for a section of the corporate value chain (e.g. design). Co-operation schemes taken up by system designers encourage the acceptance of new norms and standards (such as recycling systems, product labels and certification norms) on a wide basis. The norms become embedded when other companies, as system users, formally commit themselves to the standards. Such norms and standards supplement legal requirements and take companies beyond compliance with the law.

Public relations work

Socioculturally oriented co-operation aims to arouse public awareness to environmental solutions in relation to suspect consumer behaviour or transportation issues. It achieves this through activities such as exhibitions, open forums and public events (see Brockhaus 1996). Apart from these outwardly focused functions, co-operation helps in the promotion of internal organisational learning (e.g. through the exchange of information about environmental protection or management) or in the exertion of pressure to influence company or association environmental policy.

10.4.1.2 Strategic choice of the co-operation partner

From a business perspective, all forms of co-operation with environmental associations are related to promoting business know-how and capital by drawing attention to and generating sympathy for actions undertaken. The strategic goals of the partners that are co-operating relate to the exchange of know-how and capital resources.

Companies do not have the same environmental credentials and public goodwill enjoyed by environmental associations. A partnership allows the environmental organisations to exert influence on company decisions about production processes, products and the range of goods on offer and product marketing; in turn, the business, through its association with the environmental organisation, will gain a better public image and competence in environmental matters. Hence, co-operative partners bundle their individual expertise, and the company's environmental performance should improve as a result. Choice of a particular environmental organisation as a partner depends on that organisation's technical and professional competence, its public importance or on both of these factors (see Table 10.4).

From a business point of view, the following indicators demonstrate the potential importance of an environmental organisation:

- Number of members
- Volume of donations and contributions
- Successes in dealings with other corporate stakeholders
- Surveys that give a high ranking to name recognition
- Regional and international networking capacities and abilities
- Quantity and qualification of professional employees

Competence	*Area of application*
Dealing with the news media Media contacts	Agenda-setting Press relations Public presentation of events
Networking	Exchange of information Mobilisation Lobby work
Environmentally related specialised knowledge	Research Consultation Discourse Agitation
Education	Child and youth labour Educational advertising Attitude changing
Construction of meaning	Personal identification Motivation Mobilisation
Acquisition of experience	Actions Events Understanding of natural phenomena

Table 10.4 Competences of environmental organisations relevant to business partners

● Inclusion in the deliberations of international bodies (e.g. by means of UN bodies and sovereign governments)

Importance is reflected especially in the readiness of people to identify with the environmental organisation. In a questionnaire addressed to young people (*Der Spiegel* 28 [1999]: 96ff.), in answer to the question 'Who is an idol for you?', environmental groups such as Greenpeace were chosen by 40%, ahead of sporting personalities (36%) and religious leaders (14%). Pop stars and politicians were chosen by only 12% combined. According to Kriener (1999) donations are constant or increasing for all associations. In some countries (e.g. Germany) Greenpeace lost donations and members, but these losses have been more than compensated for at the international level, especially because of increased activity in China (see Bode 2000).

In turn, environmental associations are aware of their relative attractiveness and are sometimes able to place high demands on companies in exchange for a formal association. Greenpeace appears to prefer medium-sized companies as partners rather than multinational companies. The Bund für Umwelt und Naturschutz Deutschland(BUND), during its conference of delegates in 1995, formulated the following conditions for a co-operative partnership:

- Co-operation with small and medium-sized companies has priority. The larger the company, the higher the requirements from the expected environmental success.

- Protection of nature and the environment must be codified as business goals in the company's principles and be represented through the establishment of clear responsibilities by business management.

- Adequate financial resources must be provided for completion of planned environmental protection tasks, and competent bodies must exist for implementing the company's environmental orientation.

- Co-operation occurs, basically, only in relation to projects.

- The ability to withstand criticism by the partner must be sustained.

- The number of co-operative partnerships is to be limited to high-profile projects.

10.4.1.3 Operation of the co-operative arrangements

This subsection looks at the formation and operation of co-operative agreements (for a summary, see Box 10.9; for some tips on forming such an agreement, see Box 10.10). A practical guide for the implementation of advocacy organisation–business partnerships has been published through the Alliance for Environmental Innovation project of the Environmental Defense and Pew Charitable Trust in the USA.[8]

Before choosing the appropriate partner the actors first define their **claims**. Companies are required to recognise their own **strengths** that might make them attractive for link formation with environmental organisations. In order to make contacts, companies must know how to win the **interest** and **sympathy** of the environmental organisation. For a successful partnership, it is critical that representatives of both organisations have empathy, trust and respect for each other through their contacts at the personal level.

Operation of the partnership is expressed formally in writing in a co-operation agreement. Evaluation of the co-operative agreement is possible through well-defined measures of goals and programme schedules. Organisations learn from the process of evaluating the success of co-operation. In this process, people can be held to account if the expected benefits do not materialise, expectations of both parties can be reviewed and goals and actions can be amended for the future.

The co-operation agreement and each step in the co-operation process must take the integration of goals and means into account (see Fig. 10.6). Goals, and their level

8   See www.environmentaldefense.org/Alliance. This Internet site, together with its links, is exemplary for the excellent networking it provides with most environmental organisations. For example, at www.environmentaldefense.org/Alliance/modelagreement.html it records a model environmental agreement for potential partners (reproduced in the Appendix of this book). The one additional characteristic to which attention is drawn is the emphasis on confidentiality agreed to by both partners when information has been obtained from the business. However, there is some provision for transparency as information will be made available to the public on completion of the project.

1 Arouse interest and arrange contacts prior to arrangement of the formal agreement.

2 Offer reasons for getting to know each other and for communication.

3 Agree on the form of the communication (workshops, discussions by the fireside, business dinners, the agenda, number of participants, duration, ambience and so on).

4 Clarify general goals, expectations and claims on the co-operation partners during discussions; search for opportunities and common points of view.

5 Find consensus or compromise on disputed issues or, if this is not possible, define areas of disagreement as precisely as possible and at least reach an agreement about the meaning of the disputed points and expectations about what will be discussed at future meetings.

6 Define and roughly schedule the orientation of the business and the environmental association as well as specific goals.

7 Plan, co-ordinate and schedule as precisely as possible measures, instruments and the sequence of activities.

8 Arrange the input of resources to be supplied by the different participants.

9 Specify the exact responsibilities and people involved and agree on the incentives, disincentives and controls over the partners.

10 Organise methods for co-ordination and communication.

11 Implement and evaluate measures of performance.

12 Initiate a learning process (e.g. education and training) from feedback of evaluation results and have arrangements for termination of co-operation.

Box 10.9 **Twelve steps in the operation of a co-operative agreement**

- Consult those involved in similar initiatives in order to assess the practicality of the proposed goals.

- Find out the levels of expertise held by the proposed partner, assess its campaigns and identify the benefits it could offer.

- Involve those departmental managers who will be substantively affected by the partnership.

- Communicate the vision, successes and limitations of the partnership to key stakeholders.

- Prepare research reports to ensure that lessons may be learned.

- See the initiative as a pilot project with potential implications for the future.

- Attempt an assessment of the costs and benefits.

Box 10.10 **Tips for the formation of co-operation agreements**

Source: Murphy and Bendell 1997: 249ff.

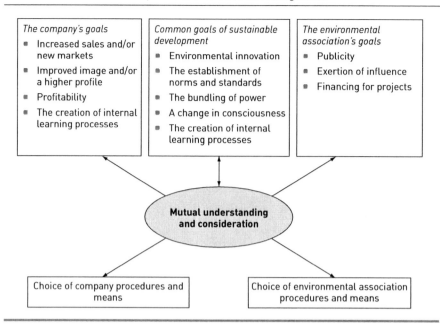

Figure 10.6 Integration of goals and means in business co-operation with environmental non-governmental organisations (NGOs)

of achievement, need to be made transparent to learn about possible future development of relationships between the partners. Both parties must also agree on the procedures or means to help achieve the goals and the necessary information requirements so that the reliability of the environmental organisation and the company's image are safeguarded in the co-operation process.

10.4.2 *Networks in the environmental performance chain*

The importance of networks and co-operation platforms in the environmental performance chain has already been discussed in Section 8.4.3. In particular, examples in textile and food production were discussed. Attention was directed primarily towards the environmentally benign development of raw materials such as wool or crops and the banning of harmful chemicals in the processing of raw materials. Pressure for the establishment of networks is especially strong at the two ends of the environmental performance chain. At one end, sellers of final products, such as mail-order firms or food chains, want to develop for themselves the potential means of success by environmentally differentiating their products. At the other end, lack of supply of environmentally sound raw materials is a perpetual problem.

Until recently, in agriculture, at the beginning of the chain most organic farmers (also known as bio-farmers) could compete only in a niche market, selling their products in health or wholefood shops, through self-marketing or through regional co-operation with local restaurants (see Muntwyler 1994: 77ff.). In consequence, such farmers have tended to operate as small organisations incapable of supplying the large amounts that bulk purchasers require. In contrast, wholesalers in agricultural produce, especially supplies from overseas (e.g. wool, citrus and tropical fruit, cut flowers) trade large volumes of low-cost homogeneous products at competitively determined world prices. The conventional, anonymous structures of wholesale trade do not assist in environmental control or in obtaining proof of quality of the environmental fitness of products.

Within this structure of niche markets for organic products and wholesale trade, the challenge is for purchasers of intermediate products to organise new strategic chains of supply that will offer environmentally sound raw materials that, at the same time, remain attractive and stylish. In the construction of these **strategic networks** a typical model is evident. The companies, or co-operating partners, assume the **focal position**, plan the whole process, choose suitable partners for the network and control the value-creation process. They also take on the business risk associated with investments in network construction. Through close collaboration with individual companies along the environmental performance chain it is possible to achieve environmental improvement in competitive conditions as well as to position products at an acceptable price to compete in mainstream markets (see Box 10.11).

Strategic networks

Strategic networks, such as those undertaken by the Swiss trading enterprise Coop in its textile segment, called Natura Line, delves even deeper into the value chain than attempted by simple co-operation partnerships (see Caldas 1995; see also www.coop. ch). Natura Line features an 'eco-collection' of textiles with biologically cultivated wool—no use of synthetic plant protective agents or fertilisers is permitted. The manufacturing processes at all other stages of value creation are also environmentally sustainable. Nevertheless, the textiles can be offered at prices in the market that are similar to those of conventional products. How can this be? The answer is that, although manufacturing costs are about 20% more than conventional costs, these are compensated for by costs being spread across a higher turnover. The Coop Natura Line represents one of the first examples of a successful eco-collection in the mass market.

Coop overcame most of the obstacles during the implementation of its project through co-operation with partners along the value chain. The company:

- Developed close co-operation with the thread trader Remei AG (www.remei.ch), which functions as an intermediary in the chain

- Involved selected textile refineries and Konfektionäre, such as the Sidema AG

- Promoted an environmental wool project in the Indian Maikaal

It set out to (Schneidewind 1998):

- Establish environmental know-how in the chain

- Secure volume quantities, high qualities and competitive prices

- Provide the farmers involved with the incentive to convert their cultivation process by introducing a secure demand for their product

Through their activities Coop and Remei AG made a significant contribution to the development of the growing market in environmentally benign textiles. In addition, the infrastructure established for 'organic' wool, and further processing stages in India, have enabled other companies to produce environmentally benign textile collections.

Box 10.11 Networks in the textile industry (continued over)

One pioneering effort was the construction of a spinning mill in Maikaal by Remei AG through co-operations with an Indian plantation owner. The spinning mill disposes of the seeds and carries out the harvest. Farmers receive a premium of 20% above the world market price for their bio-quality (organic) produce. The spinning mill also controls a net of agricultural advisers that disseminates information about the various biological pest-control methods. Moreover, through its integrated network, the spinning mill cuts the average transport distance of a T-shirt by thousands of kilometres (see Faltin and Ohlendorf 1997; see also www.umwelt.de).

Since September 1995 the wool and cotton acquired have been used by Coop in the vast majority of its range of underwear. Hence, the Swiss company is now one of the first mass producers to be active in the environmentally benign fabrics market segment. Its market share in textile retailing in Switzerland is approximately 10%. The long-term-oriented co-operation between the partners helped to reduce the high economic risks resulting from the environmental changes required. Finally, the arrangement has allowed partners to produce at levels that have enabled them to charge competitive prices in the mass market (see Schneidewind 1998).

Accounting for network benefits

A study by the Michell Group in Australia, sponsored by the Institute of Chartered Accountants, of the internal networking of activities associated with processing wool revealed further environmental benefits (Environmental Protection Authority of Victoria 2003: 55). The study documented the physical flow of resources through the carbonising process, a process used for wool with higher amounts of vegetable and other foreign matter. Attention was on how the accounting system allocated costs within the process. Suggestions were made to show how the accounting process could be modified to make sure that the different classes of wool were allocated appropriate amounts of energy, water, detergent and transportation costs in order to ensure that cleaner classes of wool did not subsidise dirtier classes of wool (www.icaa.org.au/events/index.cfm?menu =275&id=A105292878).

Box 10.11 (continued)

10.4.3 *Corporate citizenship*

For corporations to act as citizens in society means that that they must respect the social, cultural and political contexts in which they operate. Corporate citizenship is emerging as an important issue for business. The concept addresses the engagement of a business with social, environmental and economic issues in order to solve social problems (see Westebbe and Logan 1995). Engagement with social problems may be undertaken in order to defend a company's reputation and avoid potential financial loss, to achieve cost benefits for strategic business reasons and to help manage risks and promote innovation in learning in a dynamic and complex environment (Zadek 2000). It is a way of encouraging legitimacy for the continuation of business operations, but it is more than altruism, where personal motives of businesspeople 'to do good' is expressed through, for example, donations to and patronage of various causes (see Bruhn 1990: 3). Such patrons often employ private means (e.g. trusts) that operate independently of the means of their businesses and can be seen as mere paternalism. In contrast, corporate citizenship is seen as a core business activity. Corporate citizenship involves acceptance of and accountability for the total impact of the business on society at all levels of operation. This means, for example, that business may adopt particular social goals, or assume responsibility for external costs that it has caused.

One essential use of corporate citizenship lies in the long-term preservation of the business, its geographical distribution of sites and activities and its products. Internal and external communication of the substance and form of business engagement with social issues provides a way of maintaining the goodwill of certain stakeholders (see Bruhn 1998: 275). It also helps promote the view that corporations have rights as well as responsibilities (Logan 1998).

Acceptance of the corporate citizenship culture by business will have an impact on the type of personnel it employs. For example, if the image of being a good corporate citizen is conveyed through the media and actions are taken to back this up, then the pool and quality of employees available to the company will increase. Novartis comments (www.novartis.com):

> We embrace the idea of 'corporate citizenship'. Today, concern for health, safety and environment is no longer sufficient to achieve sustainable development for our planet. Novartis accepts the responsibility of taking a broader, holistic view of its role in society . . . We believe in our people. Our people are the key to who we are today and what we aspire to be tomorrow.

Acceptance of **social responsibility** distinguishes business management because its knowledge that social, cultural and environmental issues such as security, quality of workplace and democracy partially assist value creation and profit generation. Manipulation of views through public relations is not enough to secure the trust and respect of broad groups of stakeholders. The basis of communication has to be through substantial commitments and actions that are open to public scrutiny. Responsible environmental behaviour is not easy to demonstrate, as many stakeholders are sceptical of claims made and may even see awards achieved as diversionary tactics when environmental damage often continues unabated. Commitment must be full and holistic, and engagement with environmental goals must be extensively documented and integrated with basic activities (see Bruhn 1998). Isolated partnerships, such as with environmental associations such as BUND, are not enough to demonstrate full commitment.

In general, social engagement can take two forms (see Fig. 10.7). One form is for businesses to provide additional social functions, thereby enhancing their **social usefulness**. Another form is to recognise, make transparent, openly discuss and then take action to reduce the external costs they impose on society (e.g. through the reduction of environmental damages).

The provision of compensation is associated with both forms of social engagement. For example, where a company voluntarily acknowledges that its environmental impacts have social consequences (e.g. the local construction of a high-temperature incinerator), it could offer to compensate the local community by establishing community facilities (e.g. a local entertainment complex). Such offers of compensation, however, are easy for stakeholders to see as bribes and help resolve problems in only a few cases. Ideally, greater transparency of information and better stakeholder understanding should be achieved before any measures are introduced

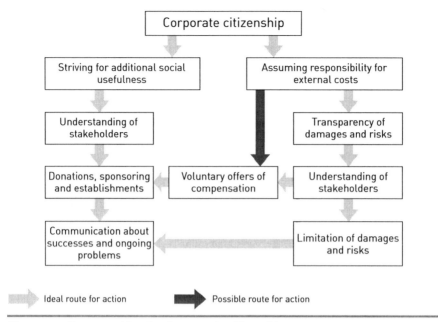

Figure 10.7 **Forms and levels of corporate citizenship**

to soften possible damages. In practice, though, the ideal route (indicated by the light arrow in Fig. 10.7) may not be followed.

To elucidate the processes illustrated in Figure 10.7, the remainder of this section is structured as follows:

- Section 10.4.3.1 discusses social engagement in terms of striving for additional social usefulness (see also Fig. 10.7).

- Section 10.4.3.2 discusses social engagement in terms of the assumption of responsibility for external costs and risks.

- Section 10.4.3.3 looks at environmental reporting, including:
  - Transparency of damages and risks
  - Communication about successes and ongoing problems

- Section 10.4.3.4 examines dialogue about the environment, including gaining an understanding of stakeholders.

10.4.3.1 Striving for additional social usefulness

To help improve common welfare, businesses make **resources** available (e.g. premises, other assets or their products), offer **services** at no charge to other organisations (e.g. through their own accounting, legal or information specialists) or make **funds** available. The funds can be associated with the purchase of property, with projects to be undertaken or may be spent at the discretion of the recipient. Provision of resources, services and funding for environmental projects can be effectively integrated when stakeholder support is agreed. For example, the planting of trees to help stop water tables rising where such a rise will make the soil saline and destroy local community livelihood on the land can be helped by the provision of funds for tree purchasing, a vehicle for tree planting and the services of a local specialist in native forestry. Involvement of the community in this process has the advantage of producing **results** and also **experiences** for those participating during implementation. This supports a positive association between the business, the employees and the project partners (e.g. environmental organisations and neighbourhood groups).

Such useful projects for the local population can turn a hope into reality by means of donations and sponsorship or by direct management or involvement in the project. Common to the making of donations and sponsoring is the fact that businesses provide direct support to an external party. There are differences in the reasons for and effects of adopting these two forms of help (see Bruhn 1990: 4):

- One special **motive** for making donations is that the business obtains tax advantages as well as the recipient's goodwill. In contrast, sponsorships aim more at enhancing the image of the sponsor by lending support to a community project that might otherwise not succeed,[9] rather than looking for tax advantages from government.

- Donors generally remain anonymous, whereas sponsors aim to maximise **media exposure** through announcements, press conferences, logos and slogans. Sponsors may allow use or interchange of logos (e.g. the WWF's Panda, or NABU's Stork) for certain occasions or on certain products.

- Sponsorship requires **co-operation** between the business and recipient during implementation of the activity being sponsored. However, donations imply no co-operation and do not obligate the receiver to perform in a particular way (e.g. through an event).

If there is an ethical dimension to the relationship, such as occurs in environmental or charitable fields, the conventional reasons for choosing between being a donor or a sponsor are not as clear-cut. Where the environmental or charitable issue is the main focus, sponsoring partners, such as environmental associations, do not want to have the performance constraints of sponsorship placed on them; in addition, the moral value of an environmental association declines with its 'purchasability', and so the use of donations also prevents problems. Consequently, sponsorship that does not accept broad image-building is encouraged (Bruhn 1998: 277). Business accepts that it will be advantageous if it makes its support known in a discreet way (e.g. through environmental reports rather than media communication). Three types of voluntary corporate contributions to society with their outcomes to business are summarised in Table 10.5.

With community investment, long-term benefits from an ongoing sponsorship are seen to be important. Continuity in the relationship is often the function of a business foundation. Foundations can be distinguished from conventional donating and sponsoring organisations because of the special fields to which they contribute. Foundations have a clearly defined, special purpose and criteria for making invest-

9   For example, see WhaleNet at whale.wheelock.edu/Welcome.html.

Type of activity	Motive	Example	Outcome for the business
Charitable gifts	To promote the common good	Corporate philanthropic donations Support for employee volunteering and giving	Measurable benefits to the business are rarely sought, but a reputation is established for being a 'caring company'.
Community investment, from community budgets, aimed at a few areas of interest to the company	To protect and promote the long-term interests of the company	Support by retail businesses for local anti-crime initiatives Work to improve education and training Local health provision to benefit employees, their families and the wider community	The returns to the business are measurable in some degree by an improved physical or social environment in which to do business and a better pool of potential employees.
Commercial initiatives, supported by business budgets such as marketing, human resources and research	To achieve a wide range of business goals and to promote brands	Cause-related marketing Support for research in universities Supplier development	Returns to the business are measurable in terms of increased sales and market share or access to new ideas and the best-qualified employees and suppliers.

Table 10.5 **Three forms of voluntary corporate contributions to society: charitable gifts, community investment and commercial initiatives**

Source: www.corporate-citizenship.co.uk/publications/download1.doc

ments, for sponsoring, for making donations or for awarding grants (for an example, see Box 10.12).

Funding is sought on a long-term basis with different donors coming together to keep the special purpose of the foundation operating in perpetuity. Foundations that provide benefits to the public do receive tax advantages, because they allow for the deduction of one-off or annual contributions on their transfer. Furthermore, dealings with a foundation are private and confidential between the foundation and the donor.

The distinction can be drawn between **special foundations** (providing scholarships, grants and so on; see the example of the Sonora Area Foundation in Box

The Sonora Area Foundation, a community foundation in California, explains how it offers significant advantages for individuals and organisations looking to meet charitable goals:

- **Flexibility.** Gifts of all sizes are welcome, and donors may advise where their gift goes; whether it will:
  - Benefit a specific need or an existing charity
  - Establish a start–up fund that will grow
  - Add to the Foundation's unrestricted funds, which provide grants to a range of community groups
  - Establish a fund with a cash contribution, with closely held stock, insurance proceeds or other assets
  - Create a fund through a will or trust

- **Privacy.** All dealings with the Foundation are confidential and donors may choose to keep gifts anonymous.

- **Permanence and security.** The Foundation's skilled financial administrators place charitable funds in secure, carefully managed long-term investments.

- **Convenience.** Donors can achieve several charitable goals through one organisation. The Foundation takes care of all paperwork, and can make it simpler and less costly for the donor company than handling the details on its own or setting up a private foundation.

- **Experience.** The management and directors of the Foundation have extensive experience in helping donors meet their wishes and address community concerns. It is happy to work directly with donors and their attorney, trust officer, accountant or other financial advisors.

***Box 10.12* The Sonora Area Foundation**

Source: paraphrased from www.sonora-area.org/about-3.html

10.12), **institutional foundations** (e.g. hospitals and asylums) and **project foundations** (see Anheier 1999). Project foundations are particularly important in the environmental context. Examine, for instance, two German foundations, the Allianz-Stiftung for the protection of the environment (www.allianz-umweltstiftung. de) and the Michael Otto Stiftung foundation for environmental protection (www.stiftungsindex.de). The Allianz-Stiftung supports large ambitious projects for the protection of nature and landscape (e.g. for the protection of the eagle, the heraldic animal of Allianz Insurance plc [donor/founder of Allianz-Stiftung]) or in the construction of new areas in Berlin. In particular, Michael Otto Stiftung für Umweltschutz has supported preservation of the landscape around the Elbe (see Brickwedde 1999). Within a framework of corporate citizenship, companies do not wait to be asked to contribute; instead, they are proactive and systematically pursue strategic ideas that they feel will benefit the public.

10.4.3.2 Assumption of responsibility for external costs and risks

The concept of corporate citizenship is also applied in the context of corporations assuming responsibility for external costs and risks that they impose on others. Once they have permission to set up and trade, businesses are free to enter markets and trade voluntarily. Some effects of business trading have an impact on stakeholders not directly involved in the market transactions conducted by business. These impacts are called **external costs**, or **externalities**. Businesses may be required to take external costs into account by government regulation. However, many external costs not regulated by government are caused by business. In these circumstances, business is not required to bear those external costs but may voluntarily choose to do so.

Where environmental issues are important to a critical group of stakeholders a business may take voluntary action to curb environmental costs. An important part of this action is to engage stakeholders in dialogue, adopt meaningful agreements and to monitor progress towards shared aims. Without this approach, the importance of stakeholder engagement can be reduced to farcical levels and agreements be seen to be cosmetic rather than substantive. For example, early work by the United Nations Environment Programme (UNEP) to establish a link between banks and the environment and sustainable development proposed three ways to integrate the environment with the business of banking (unepfi.net/fii/tor.htm). The first way is through internal operations by looking at issues such as energy usage, resource throughput and waste output. These issues are relevant as a first step everywhere in the world and are frequently useful in gaining the support of management within the organisation and turning the culture of the organisation towards environmental responsibility because they almost always can show short-term or medium-term gains through cost reduction. The second way is by signing the UNEP Statements by Banks on the Environment and Sustainable Development (unepfi.net/fii/tor. htm), which emphasise recognition that identifying and quantifying environmental risk should be part of the normal process of risk assessment and management. The third way is to promote the development of products and services that will actively encourage environmental protection—particularly in relation to asset management tools. However, lack of resources and monitoring has meant that progress has initially been very lacklustre in spite of outward appearances.

An extensive and relatively demanding initiative for the common assumption of responsibility is the Responsible Care programme of the chemical industry, which is supported by associations from 46 countries (see www.americanchemistry.com/ rc.nsf/secondaryprofilesid/lsgs-4dnmdz?opendocument). Over 80% of all chemical enterprises worldwide are asked to join the programme. The programme requires member companies to:

- Improve their health, safety and environmental performance on a continual basis

- Listen and respond to public concerns

- Assist each other to achieve optimum performance

- Report their goals and progress to the public

Hence, the success of Responsible Care depends on the willingness of the businesses and industry associations to allow their performance to be measured according to the established continual improvement criteria, to evaluate progress towards environmental goals, to include stakeholders in the process of performance improvement and to report on progress.

There are three particular tasks to be undertaken by individual businesses. These tasks are also mentioned in the guidelines of the chemical industry (www. americanchemistry.com):

● Public dissemination of information about corporate goals and extensive information for the stakeholders about the harmful effects of the business and risks to the environment: to ensure **transparency**

● Gaining an understanding with stakeholders about the assessment and evaluation of the existing environmental problems caused by the company and to discuss conflicts and how these might be resolved: to promote **dialogue**

● Implementation of technical and organisational measures in accordance with the wishes of stakeholders, to solve environmental problems or provide compensation where a solution is not possible: to take **action**

Group programmes such as Responsible Care rely on the development of best practice through interaction between other businesses involved in the programme. As the image of the whole chemical industry depends on progress made with Responsible Care, mutual support from individual companies for their competitors that have weaker environmental performance provides a necessary incentive for improvement across the whole industry. In parallel with this, collective industry pressure is brought to bear on all companies to continually improve their performance (see Meister and Banthien 1998: 117).

10.4.3.3 Environmental reporting

Corporate citizenship is subject to two important principles: measures must be communicated to stakeholders, and communications between stakeholders must be reflected in measures of established goals. **Information** and **dialogue** form part of environmental communication. Communication involves representation of the reality associated with the need for corporate environmental protection and meets the demands of the stakeholders in relation to these needs (see also www. globalreporting.org).

Environmental reporting provides the information that is fed into the communication process. Environmental reports disclose the environmental damage and risks imposed by the business as well as the successes it has had in its strategy to achieve environmental protection. Businesses can fulfil the demand for information by stakeholders through several media by using different instruments (see www. kohtesklewes.de/start.html). Choice of these media and instruments depends on the specific interests of the stakeholders. Some information is provided in a specific form for direct transmission to stakeholders. For example, information about environmental expenditures, including fines for non-compliance with environmental legislation, can be provided directly to a bank that seeks environmental information prior to granting a business loan. Regulatory authorities also obtain specific environmental information provided directly by companies in relation to the environmental issue being regulated. Further direct and specific corporate environmental information is transferred in interviews with journalists, in the course of insurance premium negotiations or through suppliers when managing material flows. Separate from this is the provision of general information to stakeholders in a standardised format, with the environmental interests of a wider public being taken into account (see Fig. 10.8).

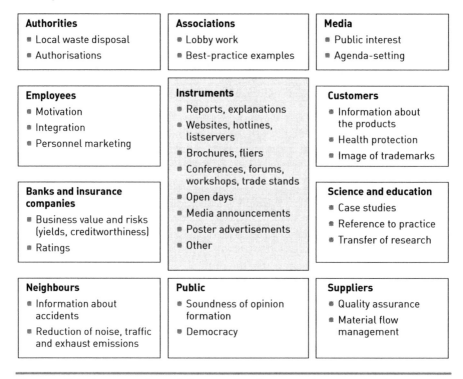

Figure 10.8 **Instruments for and themes of environmental communication**

Source: Clausen and Fichter 1995

Environmental reports and environmental explanations are essential aspects of environmental communication about stakeholder goals and the extent to which they have been achieved. Environmental reporting has traditionally been a voluntary method of communicating environmental performance to an organisation's stakeholders (see cei.sunderland.ac.uk/envrep/reports.htm). Environmental explanations and reports offer a basis for gaining insight into data on the interaction between business and the environment, being typically between 20 and 100 pages long. These sources of information cover an introductory comment from the chief executive followed by the corporate structure for environmental protection—including environmental policy, the environmental goals of the business, actions planned by the business to achieve these goals and possible new targets for future environmental performance. Websites provide extracts and summaries of environmental reports and, sometimes, references to websites are included in annual financial reports. The Association of Chartered Certified Accountants (ACCA) in the United Kingdom provides a useful guide to best-practice environmental reporting on the World Wide

Web (ACCA 2001). Views of small business about reporting on the Internet have also been canvassed (Gowthorpe and Flynn 2001). The Global Reporting Initiative (GRI) is currently evolving as the main guideline organisation for sustainability reporting (www.globalreporting.org).

General corporate environmental reporting tends to be based on the heterogeneous information needs of the various target groups: for example (Skillius and Wennberg 1998), legislators; NGOs and standard-setting institutions; government departments; ranking and rating companies; management and business partners, such as investors and financial analysts; the general public; and mass media. In their general form, environmental reports and explanations have the problem that they address the different goals of many groups, but they reach only a few of these target groups. Many business representatives express their disappointment that universities and business consultants are the first to ask for environmental reports when the opportunity for a dialogue is started. More important stakeholders, such as customers, employees, shareholders and suppliers, seem to show only moderate interest in such reports (see UBA 1999: 41ff.). The combination of all environmental information in a single environmental report can be confusing from the addressee's point of view and cannot do justice to the different interests of individual stakeholders. Nonetheless, the environmental report can be seen as a channel of communication that can open up a dialogue between the business and stakeholders regarding the goals, content, form and channels of delivery of the business report (see Schaltegger 1997).

Another possible cause of the lack of interest is the euphemistic presentation contained in many environmental reports. Seen as a conventional source of advertising, problems and negative aspects of business environmental management are left out of the report or disguised by the inclusion of agreeable, positive or inoffensive expressions, such as a list of environmental awards recently received. This is understandable to a certain extent because environmental reports are used to convey the business image; however, such an approach ignores the importance of maintaining credibility and trust.

Presentation of information about unsolved conflicts or problem areas would present stakeholders with the catalyst for meaningful involvement in the process of resolving business problems concerning the environment (see Fischer *et al.* 1995: 57). If these aspects of business interaction with the environment are played down, scepticism and lack of interest are the inevitable result.

Associated with the asymmetrical presentation of information, whereby only positive events and processes are reported, is the problem of interpretation. Such figures do not permit meaningful comparison and reduce the relevancy to decision-making of the information disclosed. The danger of an increasing lack of interest among important stakeholders can only be addressed through *standardisation of the content, indicators and measurement* presented in the reports (Schaltegger 1997; Schaltegger and Burritt 2000). A further problem with most environmental reports is the lack, or at best the cursory mention, of economic data. Without such data it is not easy to assess business performance through the combination of environmental and economic measures, as is required for assessing eco-efficiency. Internet-based information does frequently provide separate access to the annual financial reports, but this does not mean that monetary environmental information is separately identified, reported or linked to environmental activities or impacts. This means that the monetary consequences for a business with an environmentally oriented mission that addresses business development, market opportunities, cost and liability reduction and asset development are rarely apparent. Environmental management seems less attractive as a result.

Contemporary environmental reporting takes the goals of business and major stakeholders into account, includes statements about environmentally friendly products produced and services offered, classifies the main environmental themes (e.g. transport, energy use), encourages external stakeholders to express themselves through guest contributions and replies and, apart from disclosing environmental data, also makes transparent the methods of calculation (see Clausen and Fichter 1995; Fischer *et al.* 1995). It also communicates the information on which accountability relationships with external stakeholders are founded.

10.4.3.4 Dialogue about the environment

Stakeholder understanding about business environmental performance is based on information such as that contained in the various forms of environmental report. However, to be held accountable for that performance business has to answer to stakeholders for good and bad performance. Dialogue with stakeholders is one way of finding out what they feel about the reported performance and what main issues should be addressed in the future. Dialogue is a conversation about a common subject between two or more persons with differing views, the primary purpose of which is for each participant to learn from the other so that each can change and grow. Dialogue, a key part of stakeholder democracy, has unfortunately become a 'buzzword' in corporate public relations. It is called for, or announced, everywhere, often without indicating the method that will be used to make any such dialogue meaningful and effective. Provision of a hotline number is 'smart thinking' but is not a real invitation to participate in a dialogue (see Hansen *et al.* 1995).

Dialogues about the environment first presuppose that stakeholders are interested in being involved in decision-making about the environmental impacts of business. This implies stakeholders are following a cause. Stakeholders may seek to be involved in a dialogue because they are personally affected (e.g. through noise, risks from accidents, or health issues) or because they consider themselves as representatives of an environmental interest group, such as a government authority or an environmental association. Bilateral dialogues are the least complicated. These involve a meeting between representatives from the stakeholder group and the business. This can take place in the business or at a place chosen by the stakeholder. Where local citizens are involved in a dialogue with business, a range of methods are available. Conferences, open days, workshops, learning circles or forums can be used. The purpose of these meetings is: to establish common goals or to highlight the reason for conflicting views; to share ideas and suggestions; and, if possible, to find possible solutions to existing problems. A number of general rules can encourage successful dialogue (Hansen *et al.* 1995):

- Respect for and attentiveness to the other person

- Equal and open opportunity to be involved in the conversation, enabling all participants to put their questions, to be critical or to make their position clear

- A search for mutual understanding based on the examination or consideration of free-flowing ideas arising during discussion about reasons for conflicting opinions

- Openness of results, established in the framework of a shared learning experience, from which the outcome cannot be planned in advance

These general rules provide a framework for successful dialogue. In addition, if understanding is to be improved and possible solutions arrived at, dialogues will sometimes need to provide a stimulus for innovative thinking and the finding of creative solutions to problems. Such a stimulus is often attained through brainstorming, *charrettes*, visioning or small-group techniques (USDT 1996). A focus on the central theme is one way of directing attention to the major issues at hand. This focus can be chosen by business, the stakeholders or in combination prior to commencement of the dialogue proper. In complex stakeholder dialogues the principle of **representation** is adopted because it is not physically possible for every person affected to be involved in the dialogue. In these circumstances, representatives acting on behalf of the stakeholder group get their chance to bring the business decision-makers face to face with the perceived problems. Hence, dialogues between business and stakeholder representatives in practice move between strategic negotiations and development of understanding (see Saretzki 1996).

One problem with dialogues is the dilemma as to how best to contact and involve members of the general public. If dialogues are dealt with in a full public meeting, perhaps in the presence of journalists or through a panel discussion between experts and an audience made up of members of the public, the participants generally tend to behave in a 'politically correct way' and changes in views are less likely to occur. Indeed, the majority of the representatives can be completely excluded through their inability, or unwillingness, to articulate their views at large public meetings.

Solutions to problems addressed through dialogues can be achieved when the risks associated with future projects are addressed early in the decision-making process and when dialogues take place repeatedly, in order to build the confidence of participants over time. Instead of the business organising and running the agenda, location and duration, the stakeholder groups can begin to own the problems and be influential in choice of solutions. The presence of an independent **moderator** (**facilitator**) or a **mediator** is also helpful. Moderators direct the conversion but are neither allied with the business nor allied with the stakeholder groups. Moderators raise questions of interest, clarify issues when necessary and make sure that all participants are included in the dialogue as it moves towards the conclusion, thereby encouraging empowerment and consensus. Mediators are also neutral parties. However, whereas the moderator attempts to facilitate understanding by parties to the discourse, the mediator tends to be a negotiator seeking resolution of conflict through the encouragement of compromise yet protecting the characters of the participants (Zillessen 1998: 17ff.). The process:

- Helps participants resolve differences without resorting to court cases

- Facilitates agreement and addresses the primary concerns of all participants

- Helps business work with stakeholders to ease the implementation of its
  plan or project

- Helps participants reach agreement without the need for government to
  impose an unpopular or polarising decision

- Allows stakeholders to deal directly with the business as equal participants
  in cases where views are in conflict and where power is shared unequally

As the outcome of environmental dialogues is associated with the distribution of
economic resources between parties, such dialogues can be heated and unproduc-
tive. As can be seen above, dialogues do not just happen. An overall strategy is
necessary if the result is to be of any use in decision-making. Methods to orchestrate
ways to contact people, give them the needed information, hear their views, respond
to their comments and incorporate their concerns into plans and decisions must be
carefully chosen. Business needs to establish a systematic, planned approach to
working with stakeholders so that they get the kind of information they need when
they need it. At the same time, good organisation encourages flexibility, openness
and transparency in communications.

Questions for review

10.1 What is corporate legitimacy? How many and what types of strategies are
available to businesses in order to manage their legitimacy in the eyes of
stakeholders?

10.2 Is there a difference between trust between partners and trust in the market
for goods and services? Explain.

10.3 How do the expanded meanings of trust (Section 10.2) encourage informa-
tion-sharing among stakeholders about the environmental impacts of business?

10.4 Partnerships for environmental management may be encouraged in a number
of different circumstances. Explain these circumstances. Provide an example
of a partnership resulting from the World Summit on Sustainable Development 2002 in Johannesburg and analyse the circumstances that led to its
creation.

10.5 Outline the four main purposes of co-operation between business and
environmental non-governmental organisations. Provide an example of
co-operation relating to each purpose.

10.6 How important to business are the methods used by environmental non-
governmental organisations (NGOs) to achieve their aims? In your answer,

refer to the set of criteria that determine whether or not businesses and NGOs will enter a co-operative venture together.

10.7 Can corporate legitimacy and public trust be maintained through public relations and isolated partnerships? Provide reasons for your view.

10.8 Can additional advantages accrue to a business from environmental sponsorship, compared with donations to environmental projects of NGOs, to help fund the reduction of environmental impacts?

10.9 Growth of the Internet and the World Wide Web has increased the publication of corporate environmental reports in electronic form. Identify the main advantages and disadvantages of Internet reporting for each of the stakeholder groups outlined in Section 10.4.3.3.

10.10 Why might stakeholders wish to engage in a dialogue with business about its environmental impacts? Is a hard copy of an environmental report a good basis for establishing a dialogue? Is an Internet-based report better? Does your view change if you consider stakeholders located in developing countries?

11

Success factors and fields of action
Political arenas

Stakeholders make direct and indirect claims on business. A wide range of stakeholders with a broad range of claims exists. However, the means available to settle the claims of stakeholders is limited and, in practice, not all claims can be met. Where stakeholders meet resistance from management in relation to specific claims made, conflict can occur.

11.1 Management in the political arena

Determination of whether stakeholder claims can be enforced against business is made in the political **arena** (see Table 11.1). This arena is a field of management activity where disputes between different political interest groups are contested. Diverse interests are involved and, where these interests diverge, latent or open conflict can arise. When interaction between external stakeholders does not lead to attainment of all goals, then the goals of individual stakeholders can be achieved only at the cost of the goals of other stakeholders. The outcome of any dispute between stakeholders is determined by the relative attractiveness of claims made by the different political interests, by the relative power of the different actors and by the actions contemplated or taken by actors in support of their own goals. The process behind these conflicts can be described as stakeholder politics—the politics of political interest groups. In stakeholder politics, decisions are made and actions taken to ensure that goals of individual stakeholder groups are realised.

The concept of politics referred to here does not involve government institutions; instead, it relates to processes and strategies that are designed to achieve implementation, a specific stakeholder group's goals in social disputes (see Frooman 1999; Schaltegger 1999). To achieve this, the exercise of **power** is necessary. Power signifies the capability to influence others to act contrary to their original intention (see Hill 1993; Weber 1980) or to resist the influence of others (see Crozier and Friedberg 1979). From this perspective, power is seen not as either an instinctive or as a

Field of action	*Political arena*
Main focus	Transformation of interests and achievement of political interests
Question to be answered	Who holds the balance of power?
Basis for action	Influence and resistance
Criterion for success	Freedom of action
Type of rationality	Political interests

Table 11.1 Management in the political arena

moral phenomenon but as an everyday, ongoing 'raw material' of politics that helps actors in the social network of organisational activities to try to achieve their own independent goals (see Becker and Langosch 1995; Ortmann 1998). Power is a relative phenomenon. It is assessed relative to the power of the other actors involved. Consequently, the exercise of power—stakeholder politics—occurs everywhere, throughout all levels of society (for sources of power, see Box 11.1).

The following are the most important sources and types of power:

- Formal, conferred authority (e.g. the formal authority of superiors)
- Control of scarce resources (e.g. market power)
- Control of decision processes (e.g. as in majority decision-making)
- Control of knowledge and information (e.g. the power of experts)
- Control of boundary conditions (e.g. of barriers to entry and exit)
- Ability to deal with insecurity (e.g. power by controlling insecurity and risks)
- Control of technologies (e.g. power over large-scale technologies)
- Formation of alliances, networks and informal structures (e.g. informal power)
- Symbolism and charisma (e.g. personal authority)
- Discrimination structures and attitudes to value (e.g. dominant male behaviour)
- Existing organisational structures (e.g. power of the status quo)
- Acquired power (e.g. power of hierarchy)
- Negative power (e.g. power to disrupt)

Box 11.1 Sources and types of power

Sources: French and Raven 1959; Morgan 1986: 171

Power relationships are process-based. As power is the characteristic of interaction between parties, at least two actors have to be involved. The behaviour of other actors can be influenced, but not in a deterministic way, because power relationships change over time and from issue to issue as the involvement and strength of different stakeholders changes.

Analysis of political interests pays little attention to whether stakeholder demands are legitimate. Of greater concern is whether and how stakeholders can enforce their claims. In extreme cases, stakeholders are 'blackmailers' (Liebl 1997: 18). In a less extreme case, stakeholders may threaten to use, and may actually use, negative power if their demands are not met, acting against the interests of all other stakeholders. Some groups with an interest in the impacts of business cannot directly form stakeholder groups—for example, working children and non-human living species (e.g. endangered species). Instead, mediators intercede on their behalf.

The **arena model** was originally introduced by Lowi (1967) into US literature to explain the process of political interests. According to Renn and Webler (1994), the arena, perceived as representing the external world of business, is composed of four groups (see Fig. 11.1):

- Reporting media

- Political institutions (e.g. the judiciary)

- Institutions affected by the result of conflicts being dealt with (e.g. the interest of local communities and churches in disputes relating to tax policy)

- The general public

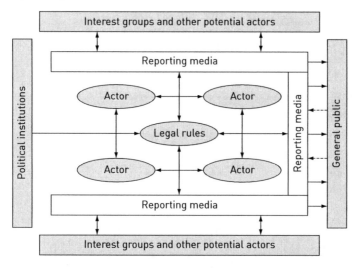

Note: Solid arrows indicate the primary sources of power; broken arrows indicate a secondary source of power; shaded ovals are core areas of the arena; shaded rectangles are areas defining the framework and structure of the arena; unshaded rectangles are reporting media.

Figure 11.1 The arena model

Source: Renn and Webler 1994

In the core arena, representatives of interested stakeholders (described as 'actors' in Fig. 11.1) compete against each other for business resources. The state political institutions (in particular, the judiciary) provide the legal rules that are designed to safeguard actors and, if necessary, allow them to enforce their claims against business. However, the state can also be an interest group that takes sides on an issue. Power resources are gathered together or mobilised by the core and peripheral areas (shaded grey in Fig. 11.1) of the arena through the reporting media.

11.2 Political interests based on concern for the environment

To perform in an environmentally benign way businesses use the resources stakeholders have provided. These resources include natural resources, such as air, water, land and fuel. Active stakeholder support for the use of natural resources is acquired by a duty to be accountable for such use. Passive support is also forthcoming when stakeholders silently tolerate business use of certain media, such as air or water. As long as business use of natural resources is seen to provide an overall benefit to society, passive support is likely to continue. Or, to put this another way, as long as the benefits associated with the loss of resource use exceed the damages caused to stakeholders, support will continue (see the discussion in Emmanuel *et al.* 1990: 22).

Benefits to stakeholders from business use of natural resources may be commercial or political. Stakeholders can obtain commercial advantages from business and personal involvement in markets through income generation, distribution and use arising from corporate activities. Market transactions are entered into freely, to the advantage of both sides participating in the exchange. In addition to involvement in market activities, stakeholders seek to obtain a share of the actual value created and the estimated value expected to be created by business through the exercise of political power. Each stakeholder group makes claims for business resources to be distributed in their favour. Conflicts over the distribution of resources can be interpreted as compensation for market failure to take all costs into account in pricing. For example, environmentally motivated stakeholders would seek compensation for external costs imposed on stakeholders by business. They look for compensation over and above any economic calculation of their losses, such as lost income that could have been generated in perpetuity (a constant amount received periodically forever) or an economic annuity (a constant amount received periodically) over the remaining life of the natural resource degraded by the business. Independent of whether an economic annuity or additional compensation is sought, political institutions impose laws and penalties that restrict the exercise of political power over other actors in conflict.

Stakeholders can also be involuntarily involved in conflicts. The key aspect of market processes thus lies in the restricted set of political activities that are engaged in that might affect the freedom of action of other stakeholders (Dlugos 1981; Morgan 1986). Strikes, lobbying and segmentation of markets to restrict competitive pressure are all based on the use of political power to achieve their ends. Business management can respond either in a passive, neutral way to the use of power by stakeholders or they can actively pursue their own political interests. Conflicts of interests have an impact on the economics of business, especially as there is only a limited amount of monetary resources available to fulfil the needs of all stakeholders.

Business management, in agreement with other stakeholders, has to try to balance the competing interests by indicating through negotiation that certain claims are not viable.

Concern of business management about political interests is particularly evident when addressing environmental issues. Since the 1970s, demonstrations, blockades, media campaigns and action by environmental associations, community action groups and other parties have had a large part to play in environmental disputes. Recent examples include the *Brent Spar* affair (see www.greenpeace.org), prohibition of building materials containing PVC (polyvinyl chloride), the castor blockade (see www.oneworldweb.de) and diverse campaigns against intensive livestock farming, especially battery chickens (see worldanimal.net/henlegislation.html). In principle, with each environmental impact added, business constantly draws on its public approval and thereby opens itself up to potential claims from different stakeholders.

Claims related to protection of the environment are different from the conventional claims of interest groups because of the altruistic background. There is a sense of responsibility exhibited when claims are made on behalf of future generations and different species that are unable to represent themselves. In consequence, it is not unusual even for the illegal actions of environmental groups to be endorsed by large parts of the population. If businesses come under fire from such political interest groups, their legitimacy is threatened. From a business perspective, this complicates the process of reaching agreement and solving environmental problems related to business activities. On most occasions, environmental claims do not directly aim for monetary compensation. Instead, they aim to get business to stop the environmental practice regarded as being unacceptable (e.g. noise pollution or the odours from the factory). However, these effects do indirectly change the costs of business relative to the competition.

Consequently, there is a high incentive for businesses to adopt environmental improvements through eco-efficiency and also to take up environmental market opportunities, especially in the field of technology. When the cost of environmental goods (e.g. raw materials) increases, improvements in eco-efficiency lead to changes in competition and a competitive advantage for the business. When potential advantages are seen, the business can become a political actor (e.g. when advocating environmental tax reform).

Stakeholders face a conflict of interests when they simultaneously represent two opposing views. For example, all stakeholders are interested in receiving part of any increase in value created by the business, but they may have opposing views about the kinds of values to be created, the meaning of environmental impact added, amounts of compensation payments and how business income should be used.

Environmental claims can present conflicts for people who work in businesses under threat. Rural employment may depend on logging operations that are opposed by local communities in favour of promoting sustainable tourism as an alternative. Efforts will be made by both groups to secure the benefits of community taxes or subsidies for their industries. Regional Forest Agreements, in Australia (see www.rfa.gov.au), provide an environmental management system that is designed to create jobs and protect forests at the same time, based on comprehensive regional assessments of forest resources. The agreements have given support to the construction of the first new pulp mill to be built in Australia for two decades—Visy's Tumut Mill, in New South Wales. The near-zero effluent and odourless mill will produce 240,000 tonnes per year of kraftliner using 800,000 tonnes per year of plantation pine and sawmill residues and 50,000 tonnes per year of recovered paper. However, the mill is not without its political opponents, such as stakeholders concerned that tree felling will increase salinity in the region—a major environmental problem for agriculture in the Murray–Darling Basin ecosystem. Other examples with the potential for regional turmoil are: the choice to use the Ems River by Meyer Wharf, which has the largest, roofed dry docks in the world; the construction of a leisure centre in the Lüneburger Heide (the Lüneburg heath) by the CenterParcs business. Today, the foundation of a citizens' action committee for the protection of the environment is often soon met with the countervailing power of another committee with conflicting interests.

Stakeholders can also disagree about the best course of action to take to help the environment. For instance, some environmental goals compete with each other (e.g. use of wind power and the protection of pristine landscape), different evaluations of environmental effects may be made (e.g. to reduce emissions of carbon dioxide by drawing on nuclear power, which adds to radioactivity) or there may be differences in relation to how radical are the environmental visions of the future. Furthermore, environmental organisations compete with each other for scarce resources provided by the communications media and contributions from members and potential sympathisers (Mutz 1995). Within business management itself, the extent of commitment to environmental goals is often controversial. Personal motives play a key role, independent of economic considerations. However, in the politico-economic analysis that follows, it is assumed that consistent positions are taken by different 'representative' stakeholders (Schaltegger 1999).

11.3 Politico-economic analysis of stakeholder behaviour

Politico-economic analysis is based on the fundamental assumption that actors act in order to maximise their benefits. Alternative courses of action are chosen on the basis of individual preferences and external constraints. Decisions depend on the balance between the benefits and costs of an action. In the following sections politico-economic analysis is used to clarify: the conditions under which stakeholders have the **incentive** to establish a political interest group (Section 11.3.2), the conditions under which stakeholders can **organise** themselves in an effective way (Section 11.3.3) and, finally, the situations in which stakeholder groups can **enforce** their interests in preference to those of other stakeholders (Section 11.3.4). Subsequently, some conclusions are drawn for business management. First, Section 11.3.1 brings to light the reasons for pursuing political interests (for an overview of the subjects considered in Section 11.3, see Fig. 11.2).

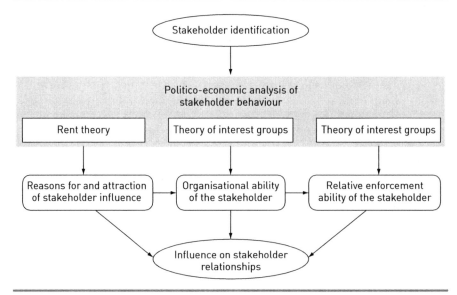

Figure 11.2 **Politico-economic analysis of stakeholder behaviour**

Source: Schaltegger 1999: 7

11.3.1 *Reasons for the pursuit of claims through political interests*

Different reasons encourage stakeholders to pursue environmentally related claims through political interests rather than through the market. This approach can be used to:

- Substitute missing markets and adjust for market failures (Section 11.3.1.1)

- Change market framework conditions (Section 11.3.1.2)

- Abolish market processes (Section 11.3.1.3)

- Distribute environmental risks (Section 11.3.1.4)

- Reduce information asymmetries (Section 5.3.1.5)

- Reduce asymmetries in negotiations (Section 5.3.1.6)

11.3.1.1 Substitution for missing markets and adjustment for market failures

For contractual exchange to take place, there is a presupposition that the parties to the market transaction have the exclusive right to contract with each other (the exclusion principle), and that the benefits accruing from a contract accrue exclusively to the buyer and no one else. If more than one person can obtain benefit from property, they are referred to as public goods (Barton 1999; Frey *et al.* 1993; Fritsch *et al.* 1999). With public goods the same benefits are available to all. Nobody is excluded from use. This is a case of externalities where consumption benefits can be shared.

Many natural resources have the distinct characteristics of public goods (e.g. rivers, or the atmosphere). Some goods that can be bought and sold in the market (e.g. trees to a woodyard, trees in a game reserve) also have public good functions (e.g. as carbon dioxide sinks, regulators of the water supply to households). For public goods it is inefficient to exclude any one consumer from partaking in the benefits as that person's consumption of the good does not reduce consumption by anyone else (Barton 1999: 210). For this reason, the market value of public goods is less than the overall value to all potential consumers. Finally, another case of externalities is where social costs exceed private costs, and some interference in the pricing mechanism can be justified because of market failure to take all social costs into account. In these circumstances, political regulations can be justified as a way of increasing the private costs up to the level of social costs.

Internalisation of external environmental costs usually depends on recognition of the need to reduce the environmental impact added by business (e.g. the polluter-pays principle). Alternatively, the costs associated with excess use of a public good can be avoided if the precautionary principle is adopted in the absence of scientific evidence to indicate what these costs might be. In spite of these additional costs being imposed on business, if production processes that better protect the environment are introduced, the relative competitive position of the business can still be improved. Therefore, redistribution of wealth creation (called 'rent-seeking' behaviour) is sought not only by environmental organisations, scientists or other stakeholders but also by the business itself, from other businesses. Business-to-business transfers of wealth are part of the political landscape and are not simply limited to market transactions (Marggraf and Streb 1997; Staehlin-Witt 1993). The chance of being able to use public environmental goods for private commercial use can turn business into environmentally protective stakeholders, especially when there are strong economic incentives for conserving the natural goods. Examples are sustainable tourism, bio-prospecting (i.e. the protection of species for their genetic resources; see CoA 2001) and regulated game shooting.

11.3.1.2 Changing the market framework conditions

Even when markets function efficiently, there are incentives for stakeholders to become politically active in order to obtain a more favourable starting point when seeking increased profits or wealth. One way of achieving this is to change the framework conditions of the market system. Framework conditions define the basic issues that must be addressed by a system. Stakeholders can try to increase the sales of the goods they place on sale, or which they prefer to buy, and to reduce the costs of the resources needed by them by changing the basic issues the market framework must address. The Natural Step outlines framework conditions that could be prerequisites for markets in a sustainable society (see www.naturalstep.org/framework/framework_strategy.html):

- Nature should not be subjected to systematically increasing:
  - Rates of extraction of substances from the Earth's crust
  - Rates of production of substances by society
  - Degradation by physical means

- In sustainable society human needs should be met worldwide.

For example, a state tax may be used to discriminate in favour of the introduction of environmental production methods and products to help meet these conditions. Competitive advantages or disadvantages arise, depending on whether conventional or organic agriculture, coal mining or solar energy receive relatively stronger support. Conflicts of interest between businesses arise here, as different levels of eco-efficiency will become the decisive influence on competition through the framework conditions behind the market. In Western culture, business associations can lobby parliamentary representatives either to try to penalise environmentally inefficient processes and practices or to maintain the unsustainable status quo. Organic agriculture provides a case in point. The Biological Farmers of Australia Co-operative, Australia's largest certification agency for organic and dynamic production, prides itself on the high quality and greenness of Australian products, as does Organic Beef Exporters, a consortium of 30 farmers covering seven million hectares.[10] In contrast, Meat and Livestock Australia first and foremost provides services to its owners—Australia's livestock producers—to increase the consumption of meat, rather than serving suppliers of organic meat.[11] These business associations can oppose each other in the political sphere.

11.3.1.3 Abolition of market processes

An extreme form of the politics of interest groups is oriented towards the complete abolition of markets. Abolition can occur by means of the introduction of a planned economy, the sanctioning of monopolies or the approval of cartels. Political power and monopoly profits provide the drivers for this form of restriction on markets. 'Deep green' theoreticians and critical theorists often support this solution to market failures to protect the environment. State utility monopolies, such as those that existed in the electricity industry over many decades, in the USA, Europe and Australia, stopped the development of markets for renewable electricity by failing to support development of the technology through the provision of sufficient funds.

A further possible reason for eliminating markets is to end trade in certain goods (e.g. endangered species, drugs, ivory). As a consequence, black markets are introduced to take the place of normal markets. In black markets, where supply is illegal and thus limited, prices are very high for potential purchasers. The effects of black markets can be devastating; for example, in the case of species protection, poachers seeking large financial rewards are an ever-present threat to the survival of species. Market elimination by regulators and the associated presence of black markets constrain the progress of commercial hunters of endangered species but may not lead

---

10 On the Biological Farmers of Australia Co-operative, see www.bfa.com.au; on Organic Beef Exporters, see www.abc.net.au/landline/stories/s138110.htm.
11 On Meat and Livestock Australia, see www.mla.com.au.

to the sustainable survival of species that the regulation of trade is designed to protect.

11.3.1.4 Distribution of environmental risks

Environmental risks associated with production may be caused by, among other things, accidents, poisoning, the release of radioactive substances or genetic engineering. Regulation of these risks is made difficult because the size of the risk can be much larger than the ability of the perpetrator to compensate for it, even where damages are reversible. In addition, environmentally related risks are often unexpectedly large (e.g. as in the case of spills at nuclear energy production facilities). This reduces the possibility of marketability, as production cannot be insured, or can be insured only at an exorbitant price (Leggett 1996). In other cases (e.g. contamination of public water with chemicals), establishing who is responsible for environmental damages is often a very difficult and drawn-out process (see Marggraf and Streb 1997).[12]

Harmful incidents directly affect local communities of people, public institutions, insurance companies and banks; for example, banks can suffer because borrowers may become bankrupt and default on loan repayments because of fines and penalties or having to pay compensation or because the value of security is reduced as a result of new environmental liabilities (e.g. related to dumping of dangerous waste in the past). Finally, all other claimants, with legally subordinated claims when environmental damage occurs, are also interested in the distribution of environmental risks between stakeholders, from a political point of view.

11.3.1.5 Reduction of information asymmetries

There is a link between the desire to reduce the unequal distribution of information and the take-up of limited environmental risks through the publication or inspection of the business's register of environmental data. Information asymmetries (Akerlof 1970) are discussed in economic theory as part of the 'principal agent problem' (Eisenhardt 1989). Management acts as the agent of shareholders who, as principals, provide risk capital to the business. Managers normally have better information about corporate activities than do shareholders, and so there are economic incentives for managers to take advantage of these information asymmetries. For example, if toxic waste has been dumped on a business site, managers responsible can conceal this information until they move on or retire from the organisation. In the meantime, managers gain a higher level of rewards than they would do if information about the toxic waste and its potential monetary impact on the business were known.

Providers of capital will wish to limit their risks associated with such information asymmetries. In some countries supervisory boards (or 'administrative boards') of

12 Marggraf and Streb (1997) looked at the case portrayed in the film *Erin Brockovich* (Columbia Tristar, 2000). Based on a true story, *Erin Brockovich* is a film that details the struggle the title character endures while trying to juggle her role as mother of a family of three young children, a new job as a lawyer's assistant and handling a large civil action suit against a water utility for poisoning a small town's water. The utility uses its large financial resources to fight the case, and loses.

joint-stock companies fulfil the function of obtaining critical information for shareholders and of calling management to account for their actions. To limit environmental risks, provision of an environmental account can be required (Schaltegger and Burritt 2000). Some Swiss and German financial businesses (e.g. Sarasin Sustainability Research, www.sarasin.ch; Umweltbank AG, www.umweltbank.de) go so far as to set up an environmental advisory council that operates in parallel to the supervisory board. The former observes business activities from an environmental perspective and is responsible for whether management meets its environmental obligations (e.g. the emissions of sulphur dioxide established for a particular plant).

To a business, the need for improved environmental transparency means that additional costs will be generated. First, environmental data may not be gathered because of this cost and because its collection involves the use of technical experts. Environmental information gathered can reveal the need for management to take action to improve certain environmental impacts. At the same time, if disclosed, the new information will make environmental problems evident to other stakeholders, who then will be in a position to support their claims against the business. In consequence, management may be inclined not to promote transparency in environmental issues.

Increased transparency does, however, help environmentally oriented businesses to enhance their legitimacy, because voluntary environmental reporting can build confidence in business management. Such disclosure signals readiness to engage with environmental problems and a conciliatory approach to environmental stakeholders.

Introduction of a mandated legal requirement for supervised environmental reporting, as occurs, for example, in Denmark, the Netherlands, Korea, France and New Zealand, leads to a loss of business autonomy. It also reduces the power of business management to use information asymmetry to its own advantage. Other examples where information asymmetry is reduced by government action include the duty to submit environmental reports within the framework of the Toxics Release Inventory (TRI; see www.epa.gov) in the USA (Aucott 1998), mirrored by the National Pollutant Inventory (NPI; see www.npi.gov.au) in Australia.

11.3.1.6 Reduction of asymmetries in negotiations

In principle, market processes are based on voluntary negotiations between equal contracting partners. In practice, however, the preferences of the market participants and also the relative negotiating power influence the exchange relationship between parties. Power imbalances can sometimes be overcome if these are essential to negotiating an acceptable outcome to all parties where asymmetries exist. For example, protection of the interests of private consumers (consumer protection) and employees (employee protection) is embodied in legislation because of the perceived imbalance in the power bases involved. However, business-to-business trading tends to be conducted on the basis of equal power relationships, although this clearly is often not the case.

Consumer associations, unions and works councils are able to introduce constructive environmental claims on business through political lobbying and supporting legislation. For example, consumer protection can be improved through information on food packaging. Labelling for genetically modified (GM) food illustrates the situation. Political persuasion results in the position in Australia where, in 2000, the Australian Consumer Association found, according to an ABC television report, that around 75% of foods were derived from GM sources or contain a GM ingredient. But the food industry estimates that only about 5% of supermarket products will require the GM label under new legislation because of exemptions and a few manufacturers seeking GM-free food sources (see old.smh.com.au/news/0111/19/national/national14.html). Research results can prompt unions and consumer watchdogs to encourage tighter regulations for health protection (see www.choice.com.au/articles/a100255p1.htm). Environmental labels can be used to reduce the information asymmetries in negotiations and exchange relationships, but their success depends on the relative power of the different stakeholders to obtain meaningful labels.

11.3.2 *The attraction of focusing on political power*

From an economic perspective the attraction of focusing on political power depends on two considerations: the amount of the expected benefits to the stakeholder and the size of the costs. On this basis, rent-seeking theory examines the incentives that exist for individual stakeholders to use their political power to achieve the results they seek (Hahn 1989; Krueger 1974; Tollison 1982; Tullock *et al.* 1988). Entry into the political arena is worthwhile for a stakeholder when the value created by a political activity is higher than the cost of it. Thus, the attraction of using political power is increased where:

- Business has few alternatives to the services of the stakeholder concerned (Section 11.3.2.1).

- Dependency of stakeholders on management is low (Section 11.3.2.2).

- Exchangeability of goals is low (Section 11.3.2.3).

- There is clear identification of outcomes (Section 11.3.2.4).

- Allocation of responsibility for moral costs is unclear (Section 11.3.2.5).

- There are prospects of a favourable media response (Section 11.3.2.6).

- The size of the potential benefit is significant (Section 11.3.2.7).

11.3.2.1 Low ability of business to find alternatives to the stakeholder's services

The stakeholder can rely on receiving high payment for supplying services only when few substitutes are available. Political claims on business are effective only when a competitive source of supply exists. Business encourages alternative sources of supply, thereby increasing competition in the market for services (e.g. education, training and professional development of employees). The absence of such alternatives reduces the ability of a business to find a substitute if it needs to and increases the chance of rent-seeking behaviour by stakeholders. Business can use its political power to avoid competition in the supply of its own goods and services by establishing barriers to the entry of competitors (e.g. by lobbying government for increased tariffs on imports from overseas).

In the environmental context, business seeks to gain access to and use natural resources. Natural resources are often available for use at no cost to the business (e.g. solar energy), at a cost imposed by government (e.g. for the clean-up of degraded land), through public toleration (e.g. of noise pollution) or through the market (e.g. for fruit and vegetables). If a natural resource is unavailable in one country and technical substitution is impossible, then supply might only be obtained by changing location to another country. For example, if a free natural resource such as a sink for waste is removed through government charges, business could move its operations to another country where no charges are imposed. International standardisation of approaches to environmental problems helps to reduce this undesirable outcome.

11.3.2.2 Low dependency on management

The more independent of management that stakeholders are, the more extreme can political claims be. Dependent stakeholders (e.g. employees) are hesitant to make extreme demands on management because the costs of their political activity work through the market process and consequently have an impact on them (Frooman 1999; Schaltegger 1999). The significance of low dependency was seen in 1996, for example, in the conflict between Greenpeace and Shell about the *Brent Spar* oil platform. As long as the members of Greenpeace approved the actions being taken to stop the sinking of *Brent Spar* in the North Sea, the non-government organisation (NGO) could be uncompromising in its opposition to Shell's proposal, because Greenpeace is not dependent on Shell. In contrast, where an NGO is in partnership with a business it has common goals, a higher level of dependency and is less likely to make extreme political claims on the business.

11.3.2.3 Low exchangeability of goals

Stakeholders, such as employees, who are closely linked to the business have a range of methods available to achieve their goals through negotiation with management. This provides flexibility, as they may have a range of claims that, to a certain extent, substitute for each other (e.g. improved working conditions may be accepted in place of salary increases). However, wide scope in the fields of activity can sidetrack representatives of stakeholder interests from the pursuit of their original goals, leading them to accept side-payments in order to maintain the image that they are successful negotiators. Where goals are mutually exclusive and cannot be exchanged for each other, compensation by trading off one goal for another is not acceptable. Environmental organisations, having a narrow focus, can, as a consequence, negotiate on an 'all or nothing' basis (Krüssel 1997). When personal goals (e.g. status, prestige) are substituted for stakeholder goals, a lack of goal congruency may exist and the potential for resolving negotiations through the exchange of one stakeholder goal for another may be wasted.

11.3.2.4 Clear identification of outcomes

Use of political power by stakeholders is easier when a clear link can be made between the actions that business management can take and their ability to control those actions in order to achieve the desired outcome (Frey and Kirchgässner 1994). *Brent Spar* illustrates a situation where the action being discussed was Shell's practice of disposing of an oil platform by sinking it in the sea. Shell management could clearly comprehend the outcome of such an action, and it had complete control over any decision to reverse such an action. Outcomes were also clearly established and under the control of the management of Coca-Cola when it was challenged by Greenpeace to adopt a new refrigeration policy before the world's first Green (Olympic) Games in Sydney to reduce the company's impact on global climate change—a challenge that was met (see www.greenpeace.org.au/archives/coke/index. html). However, Greenpeace's opposition to an upgrade of the nuclear reactor site in Sydney—the Lucas Heights plant, accepting imported medical isotopes from overseas countries where accelerators rather than reactors are used—is more difficult to judge (see www.greenpeace.org.au/nuclear/pdfs/nonsense.pdf). Identification of the outcomes can depend on the following factors:

● The clarity of stakeholder preferences about the available alternatives

● The number of parties using their political power (e.g. a single antagonist, or many antagonists)

● The clarity of the definition of the problem and the geographical limits over which political influence will be exerted

● The length of time for the campaign

In the case of *Brent Spar*, Shell explicitly preferred to sink the oil platform in the sea. Greenpeace was the first to raise the issue of dissembling the platform and the only stakeholder to suggest this course of action. Other stakeholders merely reinforced their support for the idea. The campaign was totally concentrated on Shell. The political power play took place over several weeks, after which the energy producer gave in to Greenpeace's demand. In contrast, the debate over the Lucas Heights plant in Sydney has been simmering for many years and, with increased concerns over security for goods transported from overseas, the idea of total reliance on outside suppliers of isotopes that could be wanted urgently for medical purposes needs revision. Whether isotopes are imported or made domestically does not address the separate issue of waste disposal, which Greenpeace recommends be kept in improved facilities at the Sydney Lucas Heights site, and appears to smack of a 'not in my back yard' (NIMBY) approach to resolution of the issue while simultaneously recommending the complete cessation of the production of nuclear waste (see www.greenpeace.org.au/nuclear/whatawaste/solutions_spentfuel.html).

11.3.2.5 Unclear allocation of responsibility for moral costs

Ethical issues can arise from a stakeholder's claims on a business (Schaltegger 1999). For example, an environmental group may bring about the bankruptcy of a business that is known to be a 'dirty' producer. If the business is small and people become unemployed, a moral cost is imposed on the business if it could have become a 'green producer' and retained jobs; if people are unable to find alternative employment, they may feel their lives have been destroyed by the redundancies and a moral cost may be attributed to the environmental group. Moral costs increase in relation to clarity in the correlation between the requirement for improving the environment and the occurrence of harmful effects (see Frey 1997). If the business is a large multinational, the illusion may be created that nobody will personally suffer as people can be transferred within the business, or redundancy could be seen as part of natural turnover. In these circumstances, the link between the action required to achieve environmental goals and the effect on employees becomes obscure and moral responsibility is harder to force home.

11.3.2.6 Prospects of a favourable media response

If claims are communicated—a possibility that would be seen as being more important if public pressure can be exerted on business—the communications media can act to reinforce the claims. Media reporting would need to be ongoing and favourable for the most successful form of reinforcement to occur. Media personnel look for issues that will help sell their programmes or products. They concentrate on news content, explosive themes, flamboyant personalities, public interest and spectacles (Buner 1996). Voluntary reporting of news and other issues is covered by the sales, advertising and mobilisation of support.

11.3.2.7 Extent of the potential benefit

Finally, the size of the potential benefit influences the attraction of political power play (Schaltegger 1999). The greatest effect on environmental protection can be achieved through businesses that are heavy users of environmental resources and have strong financial backing. Higher standards can be applied to large, prosperous businesses that are in the public eye in comparison with small, anonymous, financially less well-resourced businesses. Moreover, the larger the size of the business, the more apparent is rivalry between the various stakeholders in the distribution of corporate value created.

11.3.3 Organisation of stakeholders

In order to increase their political influence, stakeholders organise themselves into groups and, in many cases, create alliances and networks with other groups that have claims on the business. The ability of stakeholders to organise depends on the costs and benefits of the organisational process (Becker 1983; Mitchell and Munger 1991).

11.3.3.1 Organisational costs

Costs of stakeholder organisation are, to a great extent, a function of the number of members and the homogeneity of their interests. If the coalition of stakeholders has only a small membership and partners with homogeneous interests, lower organisational costs accrue. It is easier for small interest groups to safeguard their coherence with use of simple social controls such as face-to-face contact, which ensures members feel as though they belong. Once induced to the group, the social costs of leaving a small group are high. Large, anonymous groups with loose coupling and heterogeneous interests (e.g. those consisting of 'taxpayers' or the 'environmentally conscious') are harder to organise and may rely on arm's-length communications.

Members of environmental organisations tend to be one of two types: passive (financial contributions only) or active. With a clear strategic plan for active members, co-ordination is made easier. At the same time, basic contact with members and ability to secure donations are linked with credible representation of goals and means to achieve these as well as the adoption of democratic principles, such as participation in strategic decisions. Representatives from the active membership implement decisions made, sometimes at great personal risk (e.g. by sailing in rubber dinghies in protests about whaling or about the undisclosed carriage of nuclear weapons by ship). Hence, precision, timing and spontaneous backing from all members with possible help from an unlimited number of sympathisers is necessary (e.g. the castor blockades of nuclear waste in Germany, and the blockade of logging and bulldozing of old-growth forests in Australia).[13] Organisational control over peaceful picketing by members is needed but gets harder as size of the organisation increases.

Finally, the size of costs to individual members influences the ability of organisations to achieve their goals. If costs are low, even large groups can be encouraged to engage in actions that favour perceived ethically correct environmental behaviour, even where interests are heterogeneous. Mass protests at the World Economic Forum against business involved a diverse range of stakeholders: 50,000 in Seattle; 300,000 in Genoa. Symbols are used by these protesters as a metaphor for change. Klein (1999), in her critique of brand bullies, observes that, when the USA launched a trade war against France for banning beef containing artificially added hormones, Jose, Bove and the French Farmers' Confederation did not get the world's attention by drawing a comparison with import duties on Roquefort cheese; they did it by 'strategically dismantling' a McDonald's (Klein 1999). Nike, ExxonMobil, Monsanto, Shell, Chevron, Pfizer, Sodexho Marriott, Kellogg's, Starbucks, The Gap, Rio Tinto, BP, General Electric, Wal-Mart, Home Depot, Citigroup and Taco Bell have all found their gleaming brands used to shine light on everything, from bovine growth hormone in milk to human rights in the Niger Delta; from labour abuses of Mexican tomato farm workers in Florida to war-financing of oil pipelines in Chad and Cameroon; from global warming to sweatshops (see Klein 1999 and www.nologo.org/article.pl?sid=01/10/05/1317201&mode=thread&threshold=). For example, the Coca-Cola brand has been parodied to highlight the importance of climate change issues and Coca-Cola's suggested involvement (see Fig. 11.3 and www.cokespotlight.org/html/indexflash.html).

13   On the castor blockades, see www.anawa.org.au/news/castor.html; on the blockade of logging and bulldozing of old-growth forests, see www.wilderness.org.au/projects/Forests/intro.html.

Figure 11.3 Parody of a Coca-Cola advertisement, designed to highlight the company's alleged contribution to climate change

Source: www.cokespotlight.org/html/indexflash.html. Photo credit: www.adbusters.org

11.3.3.2 Benefits of the organisation

The benefit of engagement in an organisation that is using political power to achieve its aims increases with the level of homogeneity of claims made by the group. It also increases with visibility of the group. When members have homogeneous aims, interest groups can be well organised and the individual benefits from membership accrue to each person every time an action is taken. The focus is narrow and the benefits do not have to be spread across a range of issues. In these circumstances, the incentive for individuals to participate is enhanced. When they pursue public goods, such as the pursuit of international environmental protection to enhance environmental quality, groups can be affected by the free-rider problem, where control of the benefits to each participant is not possible (Frey and Kirchgässner 1994; Jänicke *et al.* 1999). Free-riders are not part of the organised group. They obtain benefits from the action of others but incur no costs because individuals have no incentive to stop them as costs are too high, even though collective action would be beneficial to the group.

The personal environmental benefit for the member of an organised group is very low in heterogeneous groupings. However, involvement in local issues, such as the prohibition of a thoroughfare along a member's own front garden, can be beneficial. Neighbourhood relationships create social incentives to attend meetings on issues of common interest. National impacts of political interest groups (e.g. the state, trying to increase environmental protection) must either be organised through compulsion (e.g. as happens with the enactment of environmental law) or by offering members personal benefits (e.g. magazines, social contacts, group experiences and recognition) and an intrinsic satisfaction from the outcome that is denied to others.

11.3.4 *Relative enforcement ability*

Stakeholders can enforce claims against business management and other groups only when they have power and use it effectively or demonstrate their readiness to do so in a credible way (see the discussion of latent power in Pfeffer 1992). The power of a political interest group is based on its ability to attract resources and keep them in reserve as a bargaining instrument. Hence, a stakeholder has a strong ability to enforce its claims, when:

- There is no substitute for the controlled resource, except at a high cost to the business (e.g. time and money required to develop an alternative).

- There is no alternative to the stakeholder as the supplier of the resource to business, except at very high cost (e.g. there is a natural monopoly and it would take considerable resources to arrange for a new competitor to be developed).

In the environmental context the term 'interest' refers primarily to the use of natural resources, which in the case of public goods can be related to market prices to only a limited extent. Stakeholders such as environmental associations, political parties and media do not have access to the desired natural resource. Instead, their performance consists mainly of securing social acceptance, which the business needs to gain continued access to the resource.

Acceptance is expressed through social legitimisation of the right to use natural resources—through favourable public opinion as well as through legislated permission to conduct business activities. The critical resource for an environmentally protective stakeholder consists of its moral, political or scientific competence and its credibility, all of which can be used in attempts to secure changes to legislation.

With this power, environmental organisations can be distinguished from other stakeholders in two ways:

- For most stakeholders, the substitution of critical resources is perceived as a threat (e.g. substitution of employees by robots, substitution of a petroleum company's products by wind power produced by a rival company). However, substitution is desired by environmental organisations (e.g. replacement of use of fossil fuels with use of solar energy). Environmental organisations identify the crisis and aspire to resolve the crisis by using political means.

- Environmental organisations with similar interests compete with each other to see who can accomplish the greatest improvement in environmental quality. Competition can be strong for donors, helpers and media contacts, as knowledge-based and communications resources are limited in supply.

The network of political interest groups can increase their ability to enforce their claims by pooling complementary resources. Public agencies, parliamentarians, private associations and media representatives are all considered as partners in the environmental coalition. Alliances with business can also be used to mobilise market forces in favour of preferable environmental outcomes—but all of these organisational forms increase dependency on others to secure results, and this is a prime weakness as the coalition increases its number of members.

11.4 Consequences from the perspective of business management

Politico-economic analysis of stakeholder behaviour adopts a certain viewpoint—through the cost and benefit analysis of political activities rather than through moral discourse. Ethical issues are treated as constraints that can give rise to costs. The analysis does expose opportunistic behaviour, but it also points to the fact facing business that pursuit of almost every personal or public goal intentionally or unintentionally causes costs. From a business perspective, only those goals that produce value to the business for its stakeholders can be sustained.

If claims on the business are unrestricted, too many resources (natural and financial) are used and business capital is eroded. Business management strives for survival of the business and needs to secure its field of activity, physically and financially, for economic success. In some circumstances it must be assertive, to achieve its political aims in relation to claims that would otherwise lead the business to failure. It may also form alliances or associations with stakeholders to secure their constructive participation. However, the primary emphasis is on survival and legitimisation by means of the creation of market value. Therefore, the involvement of environmentally oriented business management in politics is a means to the end of improving the market structure for products that protect the environment and lead to the internalisation of external environmental costs for all. In this way, market forces are strengthened through the pursuit of environmental issues by business management.

11.4.1 A focus on critical stakeholders

Critical stakeholders for the business depend on how well they can organise and how well they can enforce claims (Fig. 11.4). A critical stakeholder group can directly affect the market value creation process in either a negative way (e.g. through strike action by employees) or a positive way (e.g. through the maintenance of intellectual capital). It takes time and other resources for managers to address stakeholder claims made on the business. These considerations mean that claims of critical stakeholders have to be addressed in sequence (Biesecker 1998; Cyert and March 1963; Donaldson and Preston 1995; Janisch 1992). Figure 11.4 outlines the main factors that make stakeholders critical in any given situation.

Business management, providers of capital and employees control vital business resources and find it easier to enforce their interests than do local community

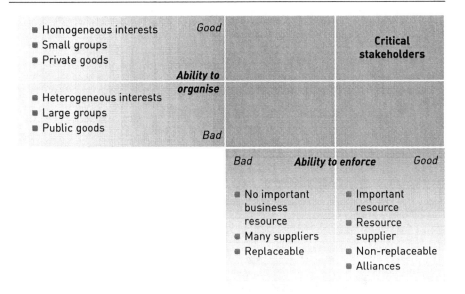

Figure 11.4 **Stakeholders: analysis of organisational ability and ability to enforce claims**

Source: Schaltegger 1999: 15

groups, taxpayers or environmental organisations. However, stakeholders with vital business resources but with poor organisation can quickly develop into critical stakeholders if they improve their organisational abilities. Likewise, well-organised groups that have no critical resource can become more effective in their pursuit of political claims if they form alliances with other stakeholders that do control critical resources. Interest groups can improve their ability to enforce claims by alternating coalitions with media, other environmental associations, businesses or political representatives, even when they themselves have no critical resources in the business where a change in practices is being canvassed. These ever-changing relationships mean that dynamic analysis is necessary if the criticality of stakeholder groups is to be understood.

One further consideration relates to the unpredictability of stakeholder behaviour (Crozier and Friedberg 1979). Whereas the behaviour of employee representatives or of shareholders can be relatively easy to predict, environmental organisations gain power from their ability to change strategy from co-operation to conflict in unpredictable ways. Such unpredictability depends on the internal empathy an environmental organisation has for a particular environmental issue and on media perceptions of the importance of the issue. Scenario analysis is important as a management tool in these circumstances (WBCSD 1997a: 4), as it provides a means of anticipating weak and strong signals from stakeholders (Ansoff 1966). However, open communication between business management and stakeholders is more important in a dynamic setting where recognition of new constellations of power and 'hot issues' are important.

11.4.2 *Common presentation of stakeholder relationships*

Once relevant stakeholders have been identified, business management has to develop appropriate relationships with these stakeholders (see Hill 1993; Mintzberg 1973; Pfeffer 1992). The following considerations can be used as a guide to managing stakeholder relationships (Schaltegger 1999: 16ff.):

- Consideration of claims according to importance. By addressing the requirements of stakeholders in a sequential way the mutual needs of business and each stakeholder group can be pursued.

- Reduction of dependency on a particular group. By developing substitutes, or alternatives such as additional suppliers, within a stakeholder group, dependency on the resources of an individual claimant will be reduced.

- Creation of transparency. If business management discloses relevant information to critical stakeholders early on in negotiations, its credibility can be established in relation to views taken, readiness for discussion of views is promoted and pressure is brought to bear on other stakeholders to be transparent.

- Involvement of stakeholders. Involvement in process and product decision-making can be offered to individual stakeholders (e.g. through co-operation with environmental organisations). Overt co-operation does require a basic amount of trust between parties. On occasion, some stakeholders (e.g. local community organisations, environmental organisations) have an interest in not establishing close relationships with business management as this will result in the loss of their own credibility in the eyes of members.

- Build mutual trust. Trust reduces the transaction costs in economic processes, as fewer external controls need to be imposed in any formal arrangements between the parties. In politico-economic relationships trust can be fragile and easily destroyed, especially where confidentiality or secrecy prevail rather than transparency in information exchange. Mistrust, tighter controls and associated higher costs are the result.

- Signal resistance to manipulation. Business management can show its resistance to manipulation where additional unnecessary costs will be imposed on the business. Resistance to manipulation by business management will increase the costs to other stakeholders when they pursue their partial political interests. In an environmental context, manipulation by environmental lobby groups may be resisted on the basis of other considerations (e.g. social, economic, organisational or ethical outcomes) that other stakeholders are pursuing.

- Contractual restriction on maximum requirements. The maximum requirements of single stakeholders can be restricted through contractual arrangements voted on by the population of a country (e.g. regarding the phasing-out of nuclear power stations).[14]

14 This tool for stakeholder management is useful in negotiations between electricity pro-

● Exertion of influence. Business, like other stakeholders, can exert influence to obtain the political outcome it desires, or it can form alliances to secure the same end (e.g. to secure the introduction of eco-taxes or carbon trading regimes).

In general, it is not possible to say in advance which strategy is appropriate for any given situation. In most situations a mixture of measures for achieving political goals is needed. Observation of stakeholder moves to obtain changes in business actions that have an impact on the environment should not be regarded with paranoia. After all, many changes in environmental behaviour can lead to other (e.g. economic) goals being achieved as well (Senge *et al.* 1996: 262ff.). However, concentration on the economic task of value creation will be facilitated by the threat, or use, of political power to channel political interest groups (or stakeholder groups) in the direction of goals aspired to by business on behalf of all stakeholders.

Questions for review

11.1 Provide examples of the most important sources of power.

11.2 Comment on the view that 'only mediators can form stakeholder groups that act on behalf of other species, minors and future generations'. Does this mean that future generations are powerless to influence the present environmental impacts of business?

11.3 In what circumstances would stakeholders pursue environmentally related claims through political interests rather than through the market? Provide an example to illustrate your argument.

11.4 Should market processes be abolished where irreparable environmental damage is shown to occur through their use? Do practical alternatives to the abolition of markets exist for stakeholders concerned to pursue their environmental claims? Justify your view.

11.5 Why might two businesses oppose each other over environmental protection? How could such differences be overcome? Would the power of a non-governmental organisation in a partnership ever be used to support one business against another business in relation to the reduction of environmental impacts added?

ducers and government about the period over which the phasing-out of nuclear power facilities must occur. In 1990, four years after the Chernobyl accident, Swiss voters elected to impose a ten-year moratorium on nuclear power plant construction (www. parliament.ch/Poly/Suchen_amtl_Bulletin/ce97/automne/453.htm?servlet=get_content). In October 2000, the Swiss government decided to extend the moratorium to 2010 but did not place time limits on the lives of currently operating units, in light of the difficulties foreseen by Swiss policy-makers in finding replacement power while meeting the need to reduce carbon dioxide emissions.

11.6 Can all stakeholders organise successfully against business if business does not improve its environmental protection activities and try to reduce its environmental impacts? Examine the main characteristics of one successful organisation in your answer.

11.7 Choose an environmental problem with which you are familiar. Identify the critical stakeholder(s) by considering the characteristics of one of the critical stakeholders identified in this chapter. Discuss whether the management of the critical stakeholder(s) was successful from the point of view of:

 – The business
 – The stakeholder
 – The environmental problem that needed to be resolved
 – Future generations

11.8 Draw up a matrix of the interconnections that you can identify between the different spheres of influence identified so far in the text. Identify interactions between (i) two spheres of influence and (ii) between more than two spheres of influence. How many spheres of influence does a business face in a typical environmental issue? What does this mean for successful environmental management of the issue?

Part 3
Strategic environmental management

Part 1
Overview

Part 2
Success factors and fields of action

Part 3
Strategic environmental management

Part 4
Concepts and tools of corporate environmental management

Strategic environmental management is 'the positioning of a business to take advantage of environmental challenges. It is the attempt to make these challenges into profit-making opportunities rather than threats that curtail business operations and prospects' (Marcus 1998: 5).

The term 'strategy' has a military origin. In Greek it describes the 'art of commanding the army' (*stratós*, army; *agein*, commander). Strategy defines conditions related to entry into the fray, conditions relating to sustaining the position in the dispute and conditions as to when to leave, or exit. It is dependent on the expected strategy of opponents or competitors and anticipates long-term possibilities in a dispute (Kreikebaum 1993: 25). Strategy contrasts with tactical or operational procedures—which are followed when a given strategy is determined.

In the middle of the last century the term 'strategy', like many other military metaphors, entered the vocabulary of management. Strategic command of a business is also based on anticipation. It is centred on the strategies of competitors, on trends in demand for products and services and development of markets. To evaluate market development in a comprehensive way, strategic command considers additional stakeholders with a claim on the business (e.g. shareholders and non-governmental organisations [NGOs] as well as competitors and customers). Moreover, it highlights the various spheres of the business—political, legal, economic, technological and so on. Nearly every management decision has long-term implications—research, the building of new capacity, the development of new marketing organisations—and managers have to be skilled in making decisions for the long term on a systematic basis (Drucker 1973: 121).

Strategic procedure aims at building the potential for success. Potentialities for success are enhanced through early acquisition of competences (inimitable, rare and non-substitutable) and technologies as a basis for grasping future market opportunities (Gälweiler 1990: 24ff.; Marcus 1998: 1). The long-term strategic perspective is evident: for instance, in the case of petroleum companies that are anticipating technological and legal changes in support of the development of the future mass market for regenerative energy products. If environmentally oriented goals are integrated into strategic processes, the potential for successful environmental management increases. Successful environmental management leads to reduced environmental impacts from the activities of a business associated with entry, maintenance and exit from markets. For this reason, the strategic process is scrutinised more closely in Chapter 12. Basic strategies for handling environmental claims from stakeholders arise from this process (see Chapter 13). In Chapter 14 the competitive market strategies for dealing with these claims are examined. Management of environmental risk is a critical component in strategy; risk strategies are considered in Chapter 15.

Strategic environmental management
Strategic process
and strategic options

Strategic planning defines the longer-term goals of the business. It identifies the business fields in which the company wants to be active, the competences it needs to acquire and the resources needed in order to enter the market and compete successfully. A **business field** describes the combination of potential demand in target markets and the performance required (e.g. competitiveness at the international level and a high-technology orientation), which in total become the focus of the business goals (Steinmann and Schreyögg 1997: 152; see also Quote 12.1). **Strate-**

---

*The chemical business of LG, which started in 1947, has played a key role as a pioneer for the development of Korea's chemical industry for 50 years and has grown up to be a representative enterprise of the domestic chemical industry, which can compete with world-renowned enterprises on an equal footing in the technology, products, and other business areas.

By establishing a vertical systematisation of petrochemical affiliates from petrochemical materials to processed products, LG has secured international-level competitiveness and a variety of high technologies in the advanced chemical field.

LG has recently exerted all-out efforts for active investment in up-to-date fields, including life science, information and electronic materials, and research and developments, while engaging in the study and reform of production capacity in the advanced new material sectors, such as engineering plastics and silicon wafers.

Since its start as Korea's first private refining company in 1967, LG has led the nation's oil-refining and petrochemical industries for 30 years, growing up to be an international-level enterprise dealing with LPG [liquid petroleum gas], city gas and electric power generation businesses. In addition, LG has played a role as a comprehensive energy enterprise, which deals with alternative energy as well as electricity and natural gas.*

Quote 12.1 **The business field of chemicals and energy for LG, a conglomerate business based in South Korea**

Source: www.lg.co.kr/english/about/overview/field/chemical/index.jsp

gies show how a business builds and uses its potential in order to cope with ongoing changes in environmental conditions on the way to goal achievement (Kreikebaum 1993: 25; Staehle 1992: 563).

Agreement about the **business purpose** sets the strategic process in motion (see Fig. 12.1). This may be based on a formal model of the business in which assumptions are made about the intentions of management. Management provides the momentum for developing the business **form** and **substance** that will lead the business towards achievement of its purpose.

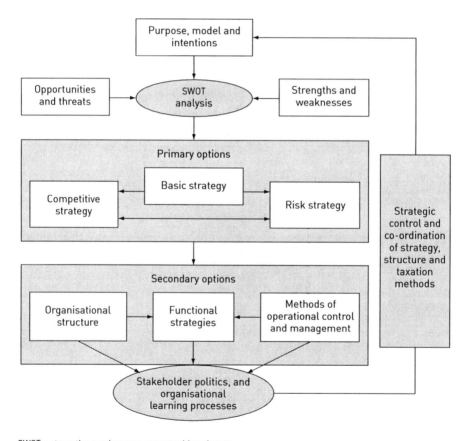

SWOT = strengths–weaknesses–opportunities–threats

Figure 12.1 **Process and components of strategic environmental management**

Source: Schaltegger and Petersen 2002: 25

12.1 Business purpose

Determination of the purpose of the business is influenced by internal and external stakeholders and has historical foundations. Personal, financial and economic claims on the business provide a starting point for understanding business purpose (see Fig. 12.2).

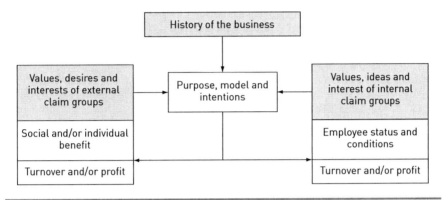

Figure 12.2 **Factors influencing business purpose and business model**

The **purpose** identifies the basic fields in which a business wants to operate—to supply goods or services that meet demand from consumers in the market. In trying to achieve its purpose the business performs social functions by obtaining public sanction for its operations (legitimising itself) and paying taxes to the government to use on behalf of society, providing a working place for employees who receive rewards for their work and undertaking production of 'green products' by means of clean processes. From a financial point of view, plans to achieve certain levels of profit and turnover for external and internal shareholders is an important part of strategy formation. In addition, the personal views of executives also help determine the focus of strategy (Ulrich 1987: 21ff.).

The strategic process rarely begins from a zero base because the intentions of decision-makers and expectations of other stakeholders are founded in **social expectations** (e.g. employees expect to work during their association with the business, and capital providers expect to receive financial reward). As time passes, strategies reflect the strengths, insights and abilities that have been developed in the course of the history of the business and are embedded in the minds of stakeholders and executives who set the business goals (Burgheim 1996).

The word **model** is used to represent the generic principles and purposes of the business. The model provides a guide for employees in their dealings with the business and an image for external stakeholders. Models, guidelines or business principles contain general explanations of the intentions and ideals of the business. These often relate to environmental protection or sustainable development. Strategic

intentions and **ideals** provide no detailed information about the specific **goals** of the business. Most of the time, not too much attention is attached to the general model of the business because models are often constructed by external public relations and consultancy agencies in ways that invoke sympathy and identity with the expressed intentions.

12.2 SWOT analysis and strategic choice

In the process of developing the strategy (see Fig. 12.1) the current external and internal position of the business is determined by means of SWOT (strengths–weaknesses–opportunities–threats) analysis. Information from the different business **spheres** provides the basis for analysis. SWOT analysis (see Fig. 12.3) can be used to highlight opportunities for the business as well as the vulnerability of the business. Once these opportunities and vulnerabilities are understood and a strategy agreed, the strategy has to be implemented; **strategic control** is necessary to ensure that strategies are implemented, are not distorted and do not cost more in time and other resources than planned. Whereas analysis of the different spheres examines external influences on the business and identifies opportunities and threats, the internal business analysis assesses the internal competences and resources available for, and constraints on, achieving strategic intentions. The strengths and weaknesses of the business are identified and then compared with those of competitors, highlighting any competitive advantage or disadvantage of the business relative to its competitors (Smith 1997: 104; Steinmann and Schreyögg 1997: 155ff.). In essence, strategic management is the ongoing organisational process that aligns opportunities and threats from external stakeholders with the strengths and weaknesses of the business, in pursuit of the goals of that business.

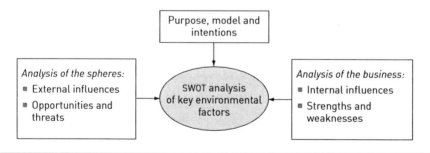

Figure 12.3 Environmental SWOT (strengths–weaknesses–opportunities–threats) analysis

As decisions are rarely made only on the basis of economic criteria, it also makes sense for business management to make personal positions, beliefs and intentions transparent to all stakeholders in the planning process. The same consideration applies to environmental dimensions with which management identifies. Such exposure of personal views does imply a high degree of trust—something that takes time to develop and often leads to disappointment in the lack of trust demonstrated by others.

A **SWOT matrix** (see Table 12.1) is used to merge the analysis of the different spheres of influence over business and key internal considerations. Strategic options can be deduced and selected from the SWOT matrix. Business seeks a competitive advantage in the marketplace in order to achieve its goals. The SWOT matrix reveals that competitive advantage can be built on the strengths of the business, which will be reflected in its financial performance, competitiveness and market impact and through the influence of external factors on the business.

	External factors	
Internal factors	**Opportunities**	**Threats**
Strengths	■ New sales potential ■ Higher market value *Conclusion: increase turnover*	■ New insights ■ Increased knowledge *Conclusion: change production*
Weaknesses	■ Higher claims ■ Missing resources *Conclusion: missed opportunity*	■ Offers by competition ■ Lack of innovation *Conclusion: lower turnover*

Table 12.1 SWOT (strengths–weaknesses–opportunities–threats) matrix for choice of an environmental management strategy

From an environmental point of view, increased sales of environmentally friendly products and services (the goal) can be achieved only when financial performance, competitiveness, market impact and external influences are favourable. Thus, sales must be profitable, knowledge about production must be greater than that of competitors, the image of the business must support the marketing of ecological qualities and the providers of capital must approve of the projected financial position of the business. If the business does not portray an environmentally supportive image (witness the 'transformation' of Shell from its *Brent Spar* and Ogoni image to its current image [archive.greenpeace.org/~comms/brent/brent.html]), then competitiveness will be marred, financial performance fall short and negative outside influences increased.

In the next step **strategic alternatives** can be consolidated, based on the strategic analysis. The basic, competitive and risk strategies of the business are specified, taking an environmental perspective. **Basic strategy** specifies the general orientation—defensive or offensive—when dealing with environmental claims on the business. **Competitive strategy** shows the extent to which competitive advantage can be gained by making environmentally oriented offers to consumers. **Risk strategy** specifies how environmental risks are to be addressed in production and product development and in relation to stakeholders, who often are 'outraged' when they discover that environmental problems caused by business affect them.

Normally, several strategic options are available for achieving business goals; hence the decision-maker's intentions and beliefs are particularly important in the final choice of strategy. Political interests can be aroused when choice of an offensive or a defensive strategy is adopted as the basic strategy. This makes it hard to assess whether one strategy will be more liable to succeed than another. Where controversy is associated with an option, or if the options have different personal consequences for groups of employees, departments or managers, strategic choice involves internal politics whereby decision-makers with power try to influence the strategy by using their own power base, interests and beliefs (Ortmann 1998).

Once the business strategy and business fields are determined, existing organisational structure is adjusted to fit. Given primary strategies and organisational structure, **functional strategies** are specified in the context of environmental goals (Fig. 12.1). If environmental know-how is required in the new functional setting, further education, training and acquisition of personnel versed in appropriate environmental issues are necessary. Functional strategies also include the organisation and equipping of the field of environmental management. Depending on the strategy adopted, environmental management can be integrated with general business management or be represented by a separate department operating alongside the existing functional fields (e.g. the planning and control, marketing, and legal departments). Even decentralised solutions are possible, where there are environmental co-ordinators in different fields forming a network with each other and working in parallel on similar problems.

Taxation methods are also an important secondary option in need of strategic commitment. For example, should external eco-taxes be supported or be imposed internally on lower-level managers to encourage improved environmental performance (Burritt 1998)? The impact on negotiations with employees, financial structure and related performance ratios and the operational planning-and-control cycle can also be high. Operational goals need to be prepared, supervised and communicated based on strategic goals. **Eco-control** (sometimes referred to as eco-controlling) is a function and systematic process of managing and achieving environmental goals. The eco-control process thus includes setting targets, allocating the resources dedicated to achieving the environmental goals, and the processes that lead to environmental impacts, including incentive systems. Where environmental goals are not achieved, repeated examination is made of the strategy. Strategic eco-control provides early recognition of new opportunities and threats and periodic checks on the achievement of strategic goals (Schaltegger and Burritt 2000: 384; see also Chapter 18).

12.3 Strategic planning and strategic reality

The ideal relationship between planned and realised strategies, represented in Figure 12.4, assumes that the specification of environmental goals and strategies is integrated into the overall process of strategy formulation. Without doubt this is desirable—but in practice such an ideal linkage is rarely seen. Often, environmental

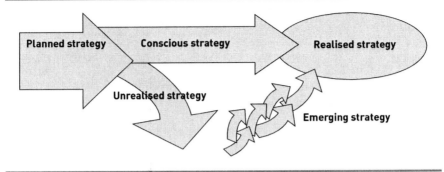

Figure 12.4 **Strategic developments between the plan and reality**

Source: Mintzberg *et al.* 1999: 26

goals are formulated as 'add-ons' to the main business strategy and made to fit in. In some cases, environmental goals that have been established through the business strategy are only loosely coupled; that is to say, the co-ordination between long-term business goals and environmental activities remains totally separate, as the two are regarded as being separate to each other, so that changes in one are not perceived to effect changes in the other. Some businesses have no explicit strategy for achieving environmental goals at all. So, in practice, environmental goals enter strategic goal development in the following ways. They:

- Result from explicit legal requirements
- Are implicit within the personal procedures and the intentions of individual executives and are not open to examination
- Are considered as a cost-reduction factor
- Are explicitly stated in voluntary guidelines to help demonstrate environmental responsibility to society
- Are formulated by chance as part of the business performance profile

The aim is to integrate environmental goals within the strategic planning process in order to link them to possible low-cost leader or differentiation strategies that can produce a competitive advantage for the business while maintaining or improving credibility in the eyes of stakeholders. However, realised strategies not only reflect strategic planning but are also affected by emerging strategies (see Fig. 12.4). Emerging strategies echo ideas that change through continuing research and data collection.

Whereas some goals and projects are quietly forgotten, other procedures emerge and drive strategic development, often before they are officially integrated in the strategic planning process. 'Grass-roots' activities and suggestions for improvement made by committed employees (e.g. through quality circles) can be included here. Environmental managers seize on these and apply them in different fields until they reach the strategic planning process. For example, a chance conversation at the helpdesk may lead the salesperson to discover a previously unrecognised but desirable environmental characteristic of the product. This can help increase turn-over, through explanation to another salesperson. Management of the sales department may be informed about it and, finally, marketing specifically recognises the environmental characteristic and includes it in its marketing strategy. Business managers thus need to consider environmental goals from a top-down strategic planning perspective and through bottom-up procedures designed to effect organisational change. These change the business profile and can therefore be taken directly into account in SWOT analysis.

SWOT analysis leads to the determination of three classes of primary strategies:

- Basic strategies

- Competitive strategies

- Risk strategies

These will be examined in turn in the remainder of this part of the book, in Chapters 13–15.

Questions for review

12.1 What is a business field? Choose a company and establish the fields of business in which it operates.

12.2 The SWOT matrix has four main elements. What are these and how are they related to external and internal factors influencing business strategy?

12.3 How do spheres of influence analysis (Section 6.2 and Table 7.1) and SWOT analysis differ? Use an example drawn from the telecommunications industry to make the comparison.

12.4 Using SWOT analysis, appraise the future of Shell or BP's environmental protection activities. Provide some recommendations for improvement.

12.5 How do environmental goals relate to strategic goal development? In practice, how can you find out about this potential link for a particular business?

Strategic environmental management
Basic corporate environmental strategies

Basic strategies related to the environment reflect the significance a business attaches to environmental problems in the course of production and marketing. Planned, realised and emerging strategies need to be considered (see Fig. 12.4 on page 179). No business is able to operate without causing environmental impacts (Pfriem and Schwarzer 1996). Even when the environment and sustainability are deliberately ignored in planning (*ex ante*), this leads to the realisation (*ex post*) of environmental impacts during production and marketing, and the associated inertia represents an environmentally related strategy (James 1992).

13.1 Environmentally related threats and opportunities

Irrespective of whether managers are conscious of it, every business activity produces environmental effects (e.g. pollution or environmental discharges) that can induce reactions and influence business development (Schaltegger and Sturm 1994). This gives rise to potential threats to and opportunities for the business (Steger 1988).

13.1.1 Potential threats

Potential threats indicate how strongly the business is affected tacitly or overtly by public, media, customer and government expectations about the environment. Operators of large plants and producers in environmentally sensitive industries (e.g. nuclear power plants and chemical companies) are subject to greater exposure. However, conflicts can arise in unexpected fields because managers adopt an insensitive attitude to stakeholders or engage in unacceptable conduct. Public pressure exposes the business and can force management to ensure that its legitimacy is maintained and permission to operate is not removed.

13.1.2 Potential opportunities

Whereas public exposure can lead to the rejection or banning of environmentally harmful products, potential opportunities arise from demonstrable solutions to environmental problems and customer preference for environmentally friendly goods. Potential opportunities arise where investments, competences and the power for innovation are unified in business fields that provide the promise of competitive advantage through new market opportunities (Gälweiler 1990: 24ff.; Pfriem 1995: 74ff.). In addition, competitive advantages can be established related to enhanced environmental credibility, technical competence in green issues, or strategic partnerships. Potential environmental opportunities are not presented to the business as a right (although some businesses feel it is a right, such as when they pressure for 'grandfathering' rather than tendering of rights to pollute just because they have been polluting in the past) but are developed through the use of business strengths and anticipation of growth in new and existing business fields.

13.2 Basic strategy options

Assessment of strategies related to environmental threats and opportunities result from an analysis of the various spheres (external) and the business itself (internal). The combination of opportunities and threats establishes different options (see Table 13.1).

	Potential opportunity	
Potential threat	**Low**	**High**
High	*Defensive strategy* ▪ Resistance ▪ Case-specific PR ▪ Retreat	*Innovative strategy* ▪ Anticipation ▪ Differentiation ▪ Acceptance of change
Low	*Indifferent strategy* ▪ Ignore impacts ▪ Re-evaluation ▪ Cost reduction	*Offensive strategy* ▪ Personal distinction ▪ Market penetration ▪ Market enlargement

PR = public relations

Table 13.1 **A matrix to define basic strategies**

Source: adapted from Steger 1988

If the management of a business is exposed to environmental threats or opportunities it can react to public and political pressure in different ways:

- **Defensive strategy.** The first strategy is to go on the defensive.
    - **Resistance.** If the threats seem unjustified, resistance can be actively encouraged through the development of countervailing campaigns (e.g. publication of scientific surveys that provide contrary views to those of environmentalists) using lobbying, expert legal advice or even passive resistance (by taking no action and just waiting for the issues to decline in importance).
    - **Case-specific public relations.** In such circumstances, case-specific public relations (PR) can be used to try to limit any decline in image. If countervailing campaigns are seen to be specious, then business credibility will be lost.
    - **Retreat.** A final option is for the business to close its operations and move to another region where resistance is thought to be weaker. Such strategic thinking requires closure or departure before stakeholder pressure is escalated or the business's customer base and associated goodwill are lost.
    - **Example of strategy.** The defensive strategy has been used by the automobile and mineral oil industry to react to suggestions that climate change is being caused by carbon dioxide emissions from the burning of fossil fuels (see Box 13.1).

- **Indifferent strategy.** As long as public attention is not aroused, businesses that have undistinguished environmental records can hope to remain out of the limelight.
    - **Ignore impacts.** They can continue to conduct their activities and ignore associated environmental impacts.
    - **Re-evaluation.** Re-evaluation of traditional business fields is undertaken when new environmental laws require such action.
    - **Cost reduction.** Cost savings, the benefit of which can be obtained through reduced resource consumption and by lowering the volume of waste without any additional expenditure on investment, are also available as part of this strategy of indifference to environmental issues.

- **Innovative strategy.** A third strategy is the innovative strategy.
    - **Anticipation.** If business is confronted with public outrage about environmental problems, such attention can be anticipated and used, in order to emphasise the development of innovative solutions to perceived problems, conversion of the goods on offer or the effective awakening of management consciousness in the media.
    - **Differentiation** and **acceptance of change.** The need for change is accepted. If consumers consider environmental problems to be serious, business can benefit from the marketing of environmentally differentiated products, provided that any strategic conversion towards the environment is presented in a believable way.

Representatives of the automobile and mineral oil industry were affiliated to the so-called Global Climate Coalition (GCC) alliance in the mid-1990s. In August 1997, a few months before the United Nations Kyoto Conference on Climate Change, the GCC helped launch a massive advertising campaign designed to prevent the USA from endorsing any meaningful agreement to reduce global carbon emissions (www.globalclimate.org). This group, including in its ranks some of the world's most powerful corporations and trade associations involved with fossil fuels, concentrated its efforts on a series of television advertisements that attempted to confuse and frighten the people of the USA.

Companies such as General Motors, Exxon, Shell, Ford and Texaco used this alliance to pursue a defensive basic strategy to protect their interests against proponents of various measures for climate protection (www.globalclimate.org). These large businesses recognised the direct risk to their competitive positions through reduced turnover, profitability and share prices stemming from attempts to reduce global warming.

The coalition combined public relations and lobbying and emphasised the uncertainty associated with scientific evidence about global warming, which was portrayed as being 'a natural phenomenon'. The coalition played on conflicting scientific evidence and the lack of involvement of developing countries in the reduction of carbon dioxide (CO_2) emissions. The United Nations climate strategy and the political pressure from environmental associations were portrayed to be premature.

However, the public did not view global warming in this way. As the coalition's views elicited less and less sympathy from the public, from politicians and from business, it lost its most powerful members one by one after the end of the 1990s. Membership of the association was putting a strain on the credibility of members. After BP, Shell and Dow Chemical withdrew, Ford, DaimlerChrysler and General Motors followed at the turn of the millennium.

The alliance has now been 'deactivated', with the claim that the coalition has served its purpose by changing government policy against setting targets for CO_2 reduction. Some of the exiting companies, such as BP Amoco, Shell and DuPont, moved to a progressive new group, the Business Environmental Leadership Council, now an organisation of some 21 corporations, founded by the Pew Center on Global Climate Change. Membership of the Council requires individual companies to have their own programmes for reducing carbon emissions (www.pewclimate.org).

Box 13.1 **Opposition to climate protection by the Global Climate Coalition**

- **Offensive strategy.** Last, the business may take an offensive strategy.
  - **Personal distinction.** An offensive basic strategy strengthens the profile of the business and of its products.
  - **Market penetration.** Provision of additional benefits to the environment in products on offer can lead to a positive market response when impacts on the environment can justifiably be claimed to be reduced.
  - **Market enlargement.** The business enlarges the market by cultivating the latent needs of consumers to be close to nature, to take care of their health, welfare or longevity and to create self-esteem and esteem from others.

Basic strategies related to the environment can be examined in greater depth (see Table 13.2, based on Meffert and Kirchgeorg 1998: 202):

Characteristic	Justification
Level of income	Internal ◄——► External
Time element	Reactive ◄——► Proactive
Implementation	Isolated ◄——► Integrated
Level of co-ordination	Individual ◄——► Co-operative
Location element	Regional ◄——► Global

Table 13.2 Classification of basic strategies related to the environment

Source: Meffert and Kirchgeorg 1998: 202

- Internal compared with external justification of level of income. Internal basic strategies focus on obtaining the best production procedures for environmental protection while reducing cost, obtaining technical security and motivating employees. External basic strategies are oriented towards effective consumer demand, the authorities and the public. They are supported by marketing and PR activities.

- Reactive compared with proactive strategies over time. Reactive and proactive strategies are distinguished by the point in time when they are adopted. In proactive strategies the 'first mover' tries new approaches without any previous examples or practical experience. In reactive strategies, the 'second best' mover responds to well-established legal requirements and conventional standards and does not suffer any of the uncertainty faced by the first mover.

- Isolated compared with integrated implementation strategies. Where strategies related to the environment are not formulated as part of the general business strategy but are separately planned and prepared, the strategy is termed 'isolated'. One consequence of an isolated strategy is that conflicts can occur between various goals of the business. For example, should income or the environment dominate in a particular situation? If environmental expectations are included in the formulation of the general business strategy, in the management control process, in job descriptions and in operational control of tasks the strategy is termed 'integrated'.

- Individual compared with co-operative levels of co-ordination. The level of co-ordination adopted indicates whether the strategy is limited to the individual field of activity or whether co-operation is envisaged in order to achieve environmental aims. Co-operation in addressing environmental problems can be through the whole industry (horizontal co-operation) or over the whole 'life-cycle' of a product (vertical co-operation).

- Regional, local, global and 'glocal' strategies. Basic strategy can be fixed in relation to the geographical location. It can be regionally specific, for the local business only or be global. A mixture between global standards and local projects is colloquially defined as 'glocalisation'.

Questions for review

13.1 Basic corporate environmental strategies include planned, realised and emerging strategies. Are the three different? How are these related to the four basic strategy options mentioned in Section 13.2?

13.2 Are the basic environmental strategies used by Shell, BP and Exxon similar or different?

13.3 Is it possible to establish whether Meffert and Kirchgeorg's (1998) classification of basic strategies is used by a particular business? Explain the reason for your view.

14

Strategic environmental management
Competitive strategies

While the basic environmental strategy addresses relationships with the entire sphere of stakeholders, competitive strategies are focused on the market, or economic sphere. Competitors' goals, strengths and weaknesses are assessed in the search for competitive advantage (Section 14.1). Several environmental strategies exist to establish a competitive advantage. Four separate categories of strategy are discussed in this chapter, although they may be adopted in combination:

- Cost strategy (Section 14.2)

- Differentiation strategy (Section 14.3)

- Mass market strategy (Section 14.4)

- Market development strategy (Section 14.5)

14.1 The search for competitive advantage

Competitive advantages result from **market opportunities**. According to Simon (1996), a competitive advantage is achieved when performance or price:

- Are important to the customer (e.g. improving health by means of a reduction in toxic emissions)

- Are made apparent to customers (e.g. by means of an eco-label, or a survey)

- Can be made permanently available (e.g. through know-how that is difficult to copy or through trust built up over time with the customers)

Market opportunities, however, are turned into a potential successes for the business only when they capitalise on the strengths of the business—strengths that are built up over time and provide a market advantage over the competition. Such strengths can be, for instance, in technical know-how, in the provision of a high-quality service or in existing reputation and credibility established with customers. The identification of opportunities, based on strengths, is analysed by means of SWOT (strengths–weaknesses–opportunities–threats) analysis. Porter (1999b) suggests that competitive advantages are based either on cost leadership or on a quality of goods and/or services that allows differentiation of goods and services offered by competitors. Cost and quality advantages can refer to all products on offer or to market niches.

According to Porter (1999a), three main strategies exist for securing a competitive advantage—cost leadership, differentiation and concentration strategies (see Table 14.1). Competitive environmental strategies can emphasise the reduction of production costs and resource savings. They can also emphasise differentiation of products from those of competitors by building in and marketing environmentally friendly aspects of products (Meffert and Kirchgeorg 1998). Concentration on market niches allows business to provide tailor-made services to a narrow group of customers. Concentration creates advantages in relation to suppliers that have a broad range of goods on offer and are unable to satisfy special customer desires in a focused way. Many new entrants to the market choose this type of strategy by offering environmental innovations to an exclusive group of customers (e.g. through organic shops or specialised exhibitions). Suppliers to environmental niche markets draw attention to themselves through market differentiation and the provision of small amounts of quality products. If a business produces high quantities of a very special product, any scale advantage can be used to develop cost leadership. Hence, with a concentration strategy, costs and quality can both be kept in the foreground.

Business field	Competitive advantage	
	Lower costs	Higher quality
Broad	Cost leadership	Differentiation
Narrow	Concentration by emphasis on costs	Concentration by emphasis on quality

Table 14.1 Competitive strategies

Source: Porter 1999a: 38

The decision as to whether to choose a cost leadership or differentiation strategy should be clear, according to Porter (1999a: 31ff.). Experience shows that many businesses cannot easily adopt both strategies. A concentration strategy whereby the parallel pursuit of cost and quality advantages can be secured will work only when the goods on offer are very specialised.

14.2 **Environmentally oriented cost strategies**

Environmentally oriented cost strategies aim to achieve the most efficient use of natural resources in production and logistics. Efficiency occurs by reducing the inputs of materials and energy for a given level of output. Ecobalance and flow cost reports reflect the level of efficiencies expected and achieved.

Environmental costs are defined as the total costs caused through excess use of material flows that do not produce useful products. For example, costs of purchasing resources (energy, water and raw materials), costs of waste treatment and disposal, costs incurred to overcome the risk of accidents and environmentally induced costs of storage or depreciation are all included.

The environmental cost leadership strategy is more important when prices of primary resources, building land, emissions and the volume of waste disposal increase. This presupposes that businesses recognise and react to these changes in cost relations when considering the value added by production and sale to consumers. Environmental cost accounting draws attention to potential areas for cost reduction (Fichter *et al.* 1997; Fischer *et al.* 1997; Schaltegger and Burritt 2000), the assumption being that environmental costs can be classified, recorded and measured as an input to cost reduction decisions related to environmental factors. Only some environmental costs can be measured; others are calculated by means of quite complex allocation procedures.

Some environmental costs cannot be measured at all as they are the common costs of operating a business and can be treated as the commercial costs of operation. For instance, waste disposal charges and the costs of incineration plants are calculated as a normal part of operations. They are clearly environmental costs and are easy to identify as they are defined by the amount invoiced. At the other extreme, the monetary evaluation of environmentally induced risks (e.g. the chance of an oil spill by a shipping company) is more difficult, because probabilities have to be derived and the maximum extent of loss has to be estimated.

Further difficulties with measuring environmental cost occur when investments are made that meet commercial and environmental goals. The environmental component of costs of integrated production technology can be calculated in only an arbitrary way (i.e. by rule of thumb), unlike the costs of installing end-of-pipe pollution technology, which clearly represents environmental cost. For example, if a scrubber is installed on a high chimney to reduce particulates being emitted to the air, the costs can be clearly identified and accounted for as an environmental investment. Integrated production technology reduces emissions into the environment at source, but may also lead to a more efficient use of materials, less waste, lower wages or lower expenditure on control operations (Schaltegger and Burritt 2000).

From the broader perspective, environmental costs are not only incurred during waste disposal activities but are also associated with the purchase of materials that enter into production but do not end up in saleable products. A cost strategy designed to reduce the volume of faulty or reworked products would lead to fewer materials entering production in the first place and to a saving in the volume of materials used. The emphasis here is on improving the efficiency of production. If efficiency improvements can be documented, it can be shown that environmental protection (by acquiring and using fewer natural resources) also reduces the commercial operating costs of the business. If the records first reveal the environmental costs of waste disposal, environmental protection is viewed in a negative way as a cost factor to be avoided (e.g. through illegal dumping). The quality of environmental cost strategies can be viewed in an appropriate way only if the business is able to identify and reveal environmental costs and associated savings in environmental costs in a systematic way.

Competition strategies will still be considered to be defensive as long as ecologically oriented measures continue to be justified exclusively through arguments about cost. Normally, the measures with the greatest cost reduction effect, as well as measures with the lowest investment expenditure, are implemented first. Hence, if business management uses cost arguments at the strategic level, the outcome is unsatisfactory because the savings achieved tend to be seen as self-evident, one-off and not repeatable. Later, cost savings are harder to achieve, as the gains are smaller and the investment tends to be larger. So, whereas in the beginning cost strategies often most clearly reflect the benefits of corporate environmental management, their effect generally is reduced over time because the potential cost savings become harder and harder to find—although competition should drive business to continue the search and implementation of environmental cost-based reductions. The implication is that, for financial success, strategies must shift from an emphasis on costs to an emphasis on yields, and this requires consideration of the customer and of demand for products and services. Thus, successful cost strategies provide the chance for business to adopt an environmentally oriented differentiation strategy.

14.3 Environmentally oriented differentiation strategies

Whereas a business cost reduction strategy should reduce the **expenditure** on inputs, a differentiation strategy focuses on the **outputs** of business and aims for increased **sales turnover**. Sales turnover is dependent on the price, quality and serviceability of the product to potential and actual customers. Turnover can be increased when prices can be raised without demand falling, when sales volume is increased at the given price or when both of these situations occur.

Environmental differentiation strategies adopt an offensive approach. They directly address environmental problems of products offered in the market (Dyllick *et al.* 1997: 123). Resolution of environmental problems provides an opportunity to develop solutions and to market them as innovations. New business fields are established based on environmental claims of 'new' products, or existing business fields are more clearly defined as improved environmental performance becomes the standard for competitors to copy, or beat.

Environmental competitive advantages can be gained from potential, latent or current market opportunities. If organisations pursue an environmental differentiation strategy, they must try to position themselves as leaders in the market. Such leadership can be attained only through the use of 'green' marketing, product re-engineering and lateral thinking used in a creative way through basic research. According to Porter (1999a), both narrow (niche market) and broad (mass market) business fields can successfully adopt a differentiation strategy. In the past, an environmental orientation was connected with the theme 'small is beautiful'. However, as the following section indicates, 'think big' is an equally fitting slogan for business to adopt in this area. A brief summary should stimulate thinking about the role of **eco-niches**.

14.4 Environmentally oriented mass-market strategies

Since the 1980s and 1990s businesses have increasingly used environmental differentiation strategies in order to establish their place in market niches. Those with environmentally related claims that were given insufficient attention by mass producers located themselves in the range of bio-shops, in boutiques for natural textiles, in alternative weekly markets or in exclusive craft workshops. These niche groups are aimed at the intersection of those people with strong environmental preferences and those with above-average income and wealth, as the prices of niche suppliers are usually set well above the price of comparable, non-eco-friendly products. Apart from higher average **income**, people looking for environmentally sound products must spend **time** in finding out about purchasing opportunities in eco-niches. Knowledge about the market, quality and prices has also to be obtained—something that is not easy, given the large competing range of consumer information disclosed in the normal course of advertising.

Niche suppliers serve to satisfy elitist group goals through differentiation of their products. They create the option for purchasers to leave behind the mainstream. The environmental effect of such product and service innovations will remain limited as long as the mass market does not engage the niche activity. As pioneers, niche suppliers perform the function of producing innovations in latent competitive fields that can later be adopted by mass suppliers (see Fig. 14.1). Environmental quality and market share define the two dimensions of concern.

On the one hand, typical 'eco-pioneers' or 'ecopreneurs' (see Schaltegger and Petersen 2001; Schaltegger 2003; Schaper 2003) in niche markets (here, in reference to the biblical story of David and Goliath, called 'Davids') can try to expand their offerings to the mass market by a process of multiplying in number (multiplying 'Davids'). Also, several 'Davids' can be united through co-operative ventures in order to gain economies of scale to overcome cost disadvantages and to capitalise on their environmental competitive advantage together. On the other hand, large distributors (called 'Goliaths') can decide to expand their mass market to include products that have environmental qualitative advantages. According to Wüstenhagen (1998), this is the strategy of 'greening' 'Goliaths'.

The heuristic of 'David' and 'Goliath' has been used to make the description of the environmental market easier to understand. In reality, other actors exist between both extremes (Villiger *et al.* 2000: 22ff.). Among them, for example, are suppliers

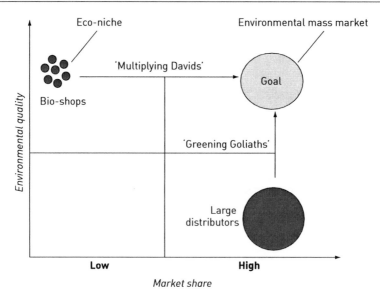

Note: 'Davids' are niche suppliers; 'Goliaths' are mass distributors.

Figure 14.1 **Paths to an environmental mass market**

Source: according to Wüstenhagen 1998

of integral cultivated food and textile manufacturers who follow the Eco-tex standard 100 for skin-friendly fashions (see www.hohenstein.de/englisch/leist0.htm and textileinfo.com). These enterprises try to increase the attraction of products by following a diagonal path in Figure 14.1 by improving environmental quality and volume of sales at the same time.

14.5 Environmentally oriented market development strategies

Often, the present starting position for environmentally oriented competitive strategies is that an environmental problem is recognised and its causes are investigated. Technological solutions for solving problems are constantly being developed. Wide conversion to environmental products is, however, as much a socioeconomic issue as it is a technological matter, because products cannot be offered at an attractive price or because the environmental characteristics of a product are not enough to establish an overall competitive advantage when all aspects of serviceability are considered by customers. Possibilities for differentiation are limited in the second case. The mass market remains unattainable. Innovations, although available, are restrained. Technologies remain unused (e.g. in some countries wind farms for generating 'green' electricity often produce expensive electricity and do not prosper without economic incentives being provided by government).

One way for businesses to overcome this situation without government help is to push to expand the market through development. Market development strategies aim to reduce barriers that limit the potential sales turnover of environmentally friendly goods in the business's sociocultural and legal spheres as well as in its sphere of political interests (Minsch *et al.* 1996; Schneidewind 1998). Development can address issues such as:

- Well-established life and consumption habits, reflecting lack of knowledge in a large part of the population

- Infrastructure barriers that, for example, obstruct the change to public transportation systems

- Absence of transparent, reliable and generally valid quality standards, product information and eco-labels

- Quality bottlenecks and financial adjustment hurdles facing raw material suppliers

- The unfavourable price relationship between politically determined cheap natural goods and labour, for which price has been adjusted upwards for political reasons

- The lack of competition because of monopolies in environmentally relevant activities such as rail transport

- Bureaucratic hindrance to environmentally oriented businesses in the service sector

- Differences between environmental and social standards as well as a lack of convergence between environmental regulations at the global level

- Public campaigns and lobbying by competitors who are less developed from an environmental point of view

Under these conditions, ecological market development strategies should improve the prospects for successful introduction of environmental innovations in the long term. Development strategies reach beyond the economic marketplace and influence the public and political spheres in an attempt to align legal frameworks with desired and desirable environmental solutions. Disputation with stakeholders who are defending the continuation of environmentally unsound products is to be expected. In contrast to the market support strategy, a development strategy looks for progressive expansion so that new fields of activity are introduced and environmental innovations are established in the marketplace. The stimulus involves potential and latent fields of competition. This requires entrepreneurial spirit and skills combined with a high priority being given to pursue environmental goals. Leading personalities and companies successful in combining these two aspects can be considered to be 'ecopreneurs' or 'sustainable entrepreneurs' (Schaltegger and Petersen 2001; Schaltegger 2003; Schaper 2003).

Single businesses are rarely in the position to change the market framework by themselves. The Body Shop (producing and selling cosmetics) and Interface carpets are two organisations that have succeeded in this, but examples are few and far between. Instead, market development strategies tend to be dependent on co-operation and on networks designed to focus market attention and investments on changing the 'rules of the game' (Minsch *et al.* 1996: 184ff.). This is clear, for example, when businesses co-operate to establish new eco-labels, carry out concentrated public relations campaigns or participate in the building of larger 'eco-department stores'. Environmental associations and proactive business associations often form coalitions, draw public attention to a plan and encourage the acceptance of progressive ideas.

The future is risky. With environmental market development, businesses face the risk that, in the end, those who have invested in the market do not profit and that later entrants adopt the new ideas without themselves having invested in development. Who benefits most will depend on the course of the game (Dyllick *et al.* 1997: 173). Businesses participate in the construction of new markets when they feel that their own competences provide an advantage. While they develop the market, they must closely monitor progress, observe possible competitor reaction and increase their competence levels in order to remain ahead through the promotion of environmentally sound products.

Questions for review

14.1 Why is competitive advantage important to business? Examine each of the four competitive strategies and consider their relevance to an organic coffee producer in Mexico and an organic coffee retailer in the USA. Are different strategies relevant to the two businesses? Explain.

14.2 Is there any link between environmentally oriented market development strategies and ecologically sustainable development?

Strategic environmental management
Risk management strategies

For the past 30 years the growing number of ecological catastrophes in production, transportation and storage has pushed the topic of environmental risk into the public arena. Public awareness of environmental risks has been increasing with each event: beginning with the Seveso catastrophe in 1976, where Icmesa, a related company of Hoffmann–La Roche, released large quantities of dioxin because of inappropriate storage and control systems (europa.eu.int/comm/environment/seveso); moving to Union Carbide's accident in Bhopal in 1984 (www.bhopal.net, www.bhopal.org, www.bhopal.com), where thousands were killed and injured; and including the meltdown of the Russian atomic power station in Chernobyl in 1986 (www.chernobyl.com, www.chernobyl.co.uk). Other environmental issues attracting attention have been the pollution of the River Rhine after the large fire in storage buildings of Sandoz Ltd in Schweizerhalle (www.gein.de/en/calDisasters.html, www.unece.org/env/documents/2000/teia/cp.teia.2000.14.e.pdf), the sinking of the oil tanker *Exxon Valdez* in 1989 (www.oilspill.state.ak.us), the catastrophic decimation of fish in the River Donau in 1999 as a result of heavy metal pollution, the breached dam in Spain in 2003 (www.antenna.nl/wise/uranium/mdaflf.html, www.antenna.nl/wise/uranium/mdaf.html) which ended up with the flooding of a huge area with highly toxic sewage at the Doñana World Heritage site, the Baia Mare cyanide spill in northern Romania (www.mineralresourcesforum.org/incidents/BaiaMare, www.zpok.hu/cyanide/baiamare, and the explosion of the Petrobras oil-drilling platform in Brazil in 2001 (eces.org/articles/static/98705160035629.shtml). The chain of accidents continues.

Although large, critical events may constitute the reason for a company to address environmental management issues, risk management deals mainly with the larger number of smaller risks. For example, apart from spectacular, periodic environmental oil spills, there are everyday occurrences of small oil leaks and spills (www.oilspill.state.ak.us). Accidents involving radioactivity are reported regularly, and toxic sewage is continually endangering life in rivers, lakes and in the seas and oceans. In statistical terms, these small environmental impacts are more important for environmental degradation than are the large accidents that catch the media headlines. Damage from a myriad of such small cases is reflected in legal cases, police investigations, neighbourhood complaints, liability suits and the detection of contaminated land and other environmental damages.

15.1 Relevant indicators for risk management

Apart from technical risks, market risk—such as the reduction of sales because of ecological scandals—is an important part of risk management. However, it often happens that compensation payments rather than environmental risks dominate discussions about environmental catastrophes.

15.1.1 Defining risk and assessment of risk

Risks can be formulated, in general, as being represented by the variance around a set goal or the possibility of a negative event preventing the achievement of a goal (Matten 1998: 149). Risks are caused by human activities, and the extent of damage can be assigned a likelihood:

$$\text{Risk} = (\text{extent of damage}) \times (\text{likelihood of the event occurring}) \qquad [15.1]$$

This interpretation means that risk can be statistically assessed. Matten (1998: 147ff.) warns against rapid quantification of a risk, especially in the environmental context where the extent of possible damage and the likelihood of the event occurring remain difficult to assess because of the complex links in ecological systems. These make reactions and effects in the causal chain very difficult to estimate. In addition, there is a high degree of uncertainty about the social reaction to, or social outrage resulting from, an environmental catastrophe. Media response (reflected in the attitude of journalists to the occurrence) ranges between moral accusation and social ignorance of the implications. Also, market reactions range between drastic reduction of sales turnover and apparent ignorance of environmental impacts.

15.1.2 Environmental risk is not the same as risk to the company

In spite of these difficulties, management must have some systematic approach to identifying and dealing with environmental risks. In this context, the difference between ecological risk and environmentally induced company risk is helpful (see Matten 1998: 152ff.). An environmental risk becomes a company risk only if the environmental damage has economic consequences for the business. Economic risks can result from direct physical contamination of land, property or equipment as well as from social risks and indirect market risks arising from stakeholder reactions to the environmental problem (see Fig. 15.1). If damage cannot be shown to be caused by a company or if the damage is not apparent to the stakeholders, then such damage does not constitute a high direct economic risk for the company. However,

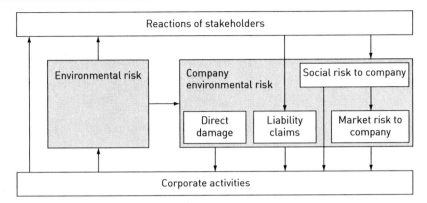

Note: Corporate activities create environmental risk and reactions of stakeholders. The stakeholder reactions in turn can materialise in a social risk and/or a market risk to the company or in liability claims. Environmental risks can also lead to direct damages (e.g. equipment failure) for the company.

Figure 15.1 **Direct and indirect effects, with environmental and economic consequences flowing from environmental risk**

social risks can also result from a lack of transparency if stakeholders think that there might be an environmental problem or risk, even if one does not exist, or if there is only a small potential impact on the environment (e.g. in the case of Love Canal, NY, where the social risk led to large compensation payments even when the evidence of technical risk was shown to be negligible [Tinker 1985; Whelan 1993]).

If legal consequences extend beyond the economic sphere (e.g. through the imposition of a term in prison for directors), then personal risk may become the driver of responses to environmental issues. Economic risks are mirrored best through liability claims, fines and compensation payments. Legal security obtained by complying with environmental laws and regulations is, therefore, one basis for risk management; however, it is not a sufficient basis. In addition a number of other considerations are important.

15.1.3 *From efficacy to efficiency and legitimacy in dealing with risks*

Risk management began by striving to obtain technical (efficacious) control of emissions from equipment and production processes (see Fig. 15.2). This involved the search for possible side-effects and time-lags in these effects. Risk control has achieved some good results in reducing a range of obvious and some less obvious technical risks in practice. However, some risks cannot be overcome by using this approach—this applies, in particular, to risks caused by human error. Furthermore, the risk of inappropriate human behaviour increases exponentially with increasing complexity of production processes and products. This is one reason why risk-free behaviour is not a possibility. There is no zero-risk world.

When it is recognised that there is a choice between different levels of risk, mathematical optimisation of risk prevention can be calculated on the basis of

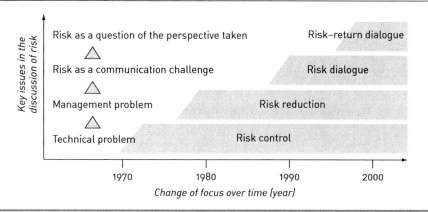

Figure 15.2 Changes in perception of the management of risks

Sources: based on Haller 1992, 2000

expected damage caused by environmental impacts. An optimal position is reached at the point just before the costs of risk prevention are greater than the expected reduction in environmental damage. With this management approach the marginal costs of risk prevention are compared with the expected risk based on statistical diagnostics gained from technical assessments. Risk prevention becomes an issue of efficiency, and the goal is to find out the optimal level of security and risk. Management choose whether and which risks should and can be insured, which risks should be reduced by technical and organisational means and which risks the company should continue to bear.

From the technical perspective and the cost perspective, risk prevention is concentrated on internal business issues. The public is mostly excluded from technological and financial risk evaluation. Although it is possible to include image and market risks, through public discussion of environmental damages, social acceptance by external stakeholders (the question of legitimacy) is not directly addressed under these approaches. Indeed, calculations by technical experts can be seen as being insensitive to human issues and can accentuate the problem of risk acceptance.

The idea of a risk dialogue, in contrast, can be used to address risk management by securing the legitimacy of the business. This insight has led to a change in the approach to risk. Risk has become more than an issue of optimisation and economic management.

The term 'risk dialogue', developed by Haller (1992), recognises that, with different communication platforms and approaches (virtual chatrooms, citizen forums, hotlines, e-mail, exhibitions and surveys), different kinds of information, preferences and opinions are exchanged. The main goal is to achieve a consensus or, if this cannot be achieved, to increase transparency and understanding of the reasons for the existence of contrary positions.

The assessment of environmental risks requires measurement and judgement by experts. However, calculations of probability and expected risk are not enough to create legitimacy. Beck (1986: 37) pointed out that 'behind all methods to factualise environmental problems' the question of acceptance repeatedly appears. Subjective perceptions about which risks are acceptable and which are not considered desirable are crucial. This is where risk dialogue between the various parties, stakeholders and media representatives becomes important (see Haller 1992: 338ff.). Dialogues require transparency and open discussion about the outcome from any exchange of opinions. Dialogues are very different from *ex post* public relations activities and must take place before decisions are taken. Only then can they improve or sustain credibility and provide a supportive atmosphere for the creation of solutions to risk management problems.

15.1.4 *The move to a risk–return dialogue*

Some authors feel that increased sensitivity of the public to environmental risk has created an overly strong concern with risk avoidance (e.g. Walter 1996). Throughout the world, following the terrorist attacks on the USA on 11 September 2001 such concern has multiplied. At the same time, grass-roots movements, 'green' politicians and environmental pressure groups are often called on to stop building up public fears about environmental risks because they reduce the freedom of business action and make business uncompetitive. An alternative to this negative response is for business to take up the environmental risk challenge and innovate.

Innovations are closely linked to returns and risks because they provoke changes with uncertain outcomes. The idea that 'only those who dare can win' uses discourse to contrast risk to returns. Returns and risks have to be discussed in parallel from an environmental perspective in order to contribute to assessments that lead to a consensus. The question changes to one concerning 'how much insecurity can be taken into account in order to realise the opportunities' (Haller 2000: 16) through monetary returns.

Biotechnology provides an example. The parallel consideration of opportunities and risks is well reflected in discussion about the possibilities for 'green' genetic engineering (Bonfadelli 2000). 'Green' biotechnology deals with the manipulation of plants for food production. 'Red' biotechnology deals with pharmaceutical and animal applications. On the one hand, the risks of 'green' genetic engineering, for example, include the potential spread of genetically manipulated plants into wilderness areas as well as the economic dependence of farmers on patented seeds. On the other hand, pesticide use can in the ideal case be reduced and the goal is that more food can be produced on a given area of agricultural land, thus reducing land use and feeding the world population without having to destroy wilderness areas. Dialogues can be used to help suppliers judge the acceptance of new products among consumers and farmers and can help management to decide on the kinds of project in which the business should invest and those that might not produce profitable results even though the environment is taken into account.

15.1.5 *Risk management as an iterative process*

Environmental risk management can be explained as an iterative process (see Fig. 15.3). Based on the **corporate goals** and a **SWOT analysis** (top of Fig. 15.3), it begins with the **survey** of opinions, expectations and issues that are being debated

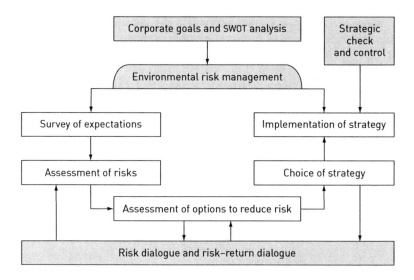

SWOT = strengths–weaknesses–opportunities–threats

Figure 15.3 **Process of risk management**

Source: based on Spiecker 1998: 12

in public. Some risks become apparent at this stage. Approaches such as scenario analysis add support to this stage. For businesses, uncertainty about the future lies at the centre of the business challenge. Scenarios enable a company to envisage the future, anticipate the implications for its operations and make informed decisions that help with risk management and reduce liabilities.[15]

The **assessment of risks** results from a combined consideration of the goals, strengths and weaknesses of the business and known threats to that business from the environment as well as from the survey results. In a next step, various options to reduce risks are to be evaluated on the basis of their effectiveness and cost. This builds the basis for **strategy choice** and **implementation** and can be fed into the risk–return dialogue. Strategic changes can result from actions taken directly by the company (action risks) or from changes in the external company environment (condition risks, such as environmental disasters and the introduction of new companies, new laws and new scientific developments). Factors faced by the business are forever changing, and its action risks fluctuate. Hence, risks are continually developing through a dynamic process of cause and effect (Haller 1992). The expected impact from any given risk, therefore, changes over time. The assessment of risks is not undertaken continuously, but only from time to time, although feedback about past risk-taking can be analysed on a regular periodic basis and included into the strategic check and control activity.

15 The World Business Council for Sustainable Development has drawn up three scenarios to help businesses in decision-making (see Box 10.5 on page 118; see also www.wbcsd. org/projects/tools_scenarios.htm).

15.1.6 Qualitative and quantitative assessment of risks

When assessing a risk, the first step is to describe all chains of environmental impacts in qualitative terms, from possible causes to final effects. Some causes are linked to a number of effects that in turn influence the causes in an interactive way. In other cases, a combination of causal factors can directly produce an undesired effect. A network of causes and effects can be identified and recorded (Probst 1992), thereby identifying weaknesses in the organisation and encouraging the development of risk reduction measures. If risks are characterised by technical issues, then a quantitative analysis of likelihood and effect often seems logical (Haller 1992: 331ff.). A risk or risk–return dialogue can add further information and knowledge to the process of risk assessment and allow business to give early consideration to project risks.

15.1.7 Choice of suitable options

Options for risk strategies are summarised in Figure 15.4 in a hierarchical order from top to bottom.

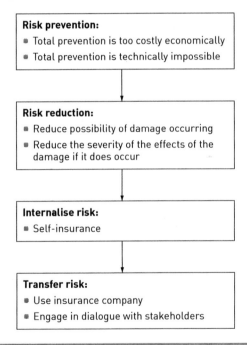

Risk prevention:
- Total prevention is too costly economically
- Total prevention is technically impossible

Risk reduction:
- Reduce possibility of damage occurring
- Reduce the severity of the effects of the damage if it does occur

Internalise risk:
- Self-insurance

Transfer risk:
- Use insurance company
- Engage in dialogue with stakeholders

Figure 15.4 Hierarchy of strategic options for dealing with environmental risks

15.1.7.1 Prevention and reduction of risk

One possibility is the substantial reduction of technical risks. However, from an economic perspective, total reduction of risk is not an option as it is too costly; in addition, it is not technically possible to remove risk without stopping production. As a consequence, measures of risk reduction are the main focus of attention. In this context, reduction means reduction of the probability that an event will happen as well as reduction of the extent of damage if the event does occur.

15.1.7.2 Insurance and self-insurance as complements to risk prevention and reduction

If risks cannot be reduced without unacceptable cost, then they have to be borne by the business, or production has to be stopped. However, the capacity to bear risk is limited, as environmental risks are not restricted to the business's production sites, and sometimes the risks can be greater than the financial resources of the business. Where the environmental damage is small and can be estimated, provisions can be made, from period to period, to serve as insurance. Some environmental risks can be insured by an insurance company. However, insurance strategies are not a substitute for risk prevention and risk reduction but act as a complementary part of an overall strategy. An active risk prevention and reduction plan (e.g. through an environmental management accounting system) can increase the credibility of the business to insurance companies and decrease the insurance rates to be paid. Some risks, such as the meltdown of an atomic power station, cannot be insured against and, in the end, become social costs if they exceed the financial capacity of the business to pay. The costs are then borne by stakeholder groups such as creditors, taxpayers, neighbours, employees and the public.

15.1.7.3 Aggressive and defensive risk and the risk–return dialogue

To secure social acceptance, assessment of environmental safety and risk options should be discussed with the stakeholders affected. The strategic decision should be communicated to stakeholders after the first open part of the dialogue but will remain as an evolving part of future dialogue. The decision can be forcefully communicated if environmental risk can be reduced as a result of the dialogue. If risks are to be transferred to stakeholders, then managers are in a defensive position. However, in such a case, the returns from the proposed course of action need to be compared with its risk and compensation options. Real issues of legitimation only arise where the benefits to business or society cannot exceed the environmental risk, or if preventable or reducible risks are not prevented or reduced.

15.1.8 Environmental risk standards

To reiterate the situation. Risks are made up of two elements: the likelihood of something happening and the magnitude of the consequences if it does. The world's first risk management standard was produced in Australia and New Zealand. Standards Australia and Standards New Zealand combined to publish *Risk Management* (SA/SNZ 1999). Guidance through HB 203-2000, *Environmental Risk Management* (SA/SNZ 2000), specifically addresses the principles and processes of environmental risk management. The aim of the standard is to help management manage environmental risks in the best way possible, because many stakeholders are averse to risk.

By following well-defined steps, better decision-making is supported through greater insight into environmental risks and their impacts. Risk management is seen as being as much about identifying opportunities for higher returns as it is about avoiding losses. There are many benefits from implementing risk management procedures, including:

- More effective strategic planning

- Better cost control

- Enhanced shareholder value through the minimisation of losses and the maximisation of opportunities

- Increased knowledge and understanding of exposure to risk

- A systematic, well-informed and thorough method of decision-making

- Increased preparedness for outside review

- Minimised disruptions

- Better utilisation of resources

- A strengthened culture for continued improvement

Questions for review

15.1 'Large environmental disasters receive much media attention, but management of small environmental risks are of major importance to future generations.' Comment.

15.2 'Technical risk can be statistically assessed. It is simply a question of natural scientists deciding on the threshold of risk that is acceptable.' Examine the various statistical methods available for assessing technical environmental risk.

15.3 Describe the events of the Love Canal environmental incident. Why was social risk more important than technical risk in this incident?

15.4 Is social legitimacy of concern in technical or social environmental risk management? Is business legitimacy an issue only when the environmental risks of business activity exceed the benefits to society? How can this situation be detected. That is, is there a performance measure that would indicate when business legitimacy in the context of its environmental impacts should be a concern?

15.5 'Environmental risk and return can be traded off by business, and an optimal position can be reached where the costs of risk prevention are equal to the expected reduction in environmental damage.' Provide a critical discussion of this view of the environmental risk–return relationship.

15.6 Scenario analysis and SWOT analysis are two methods for assessing the environmental risks of business. Illustrate the relationship between these two methods of analysis in the context of one instance of risk management that you are able to identify. Does SWOT analysis follow or precede the definition of business basic strategies?

15.7 Risk strategies include prevention, reduction, internalisation and risk transfer (either through insurance or passing the risk on to society or other stakeholders). Are any of these strategies linked to a risk–return trade off? Explain.

15.8 Is it realistic for business to claim that risk management is as much about identifying opportunities for higher returns as it is about avoiding losses? Would an environmental non-governmental organisaton hold a similar view? Explain the reasons for your answer.

Part 4
Concepts and tools of corporate environmental management

Part 1
Overview

Part 2
Success factors and fields of action

Part 3
Strategic environmental management

Part 4
Concepts and tools of corporate environmental management

To be effective, environmental management has to be operationalised, and the implementation has to be supported with specific management tools. Part 4 addresses three central concepts and tools of corporate environmental management:

- Chapter 16 deals with eco-marketing, which is directly related to strategic environmental management.

- Chapter 17 discusses environmental accounting, the most important approach to environmental information management in a business.

- Chapter 18 examines environmental management systems (EMSs) and standards and eco-control, a concept that attempts to guide and co-ordinate a company's diverse environmental management activities.

Thus, whereas the previous parts focused on available strategies for corporate environmental management and on what a business should do to address environmental management issues in different situations, this part focuses on operative approaches to corporate environmental management. It begins with eco-marketing because this often acts as a bridge between strategic environmental management (and thus business strategies) and operational measures and information management activities focused more on the short term.

16

Concepts and tools of corporate environmental management

Eco-marketing

Marketing contains all the market ideas and measures that can be introduced to increase the attractiveness of products to consumers (Section 16.1). Eco-marketing expands the customer orientation to include the product's environmental aspects. Section 16.2 illustrates the way in which this is undertaken. The starting point for understanding eco-marketing is through analysis of consumer behaviour (Section 16.3). Strategic decisions (Section 16.4) form the foundation for eco-marketing. Strategic decisions are transformed into operational marketing through ideas associated with the marketing mix (Section 16.5).

16.1 Management and the concept of marketing

The concept of marketing is in common use throughout the world. One of the main purposes of business is to create a customer for goods and services produced (Drucker 1974: 61). Marketing is concerned with creating customers. Customer creation is a specific function of management. It used to be referred to as the 'sales function' of business but is now thought of in much broader terms. The concept has a long history, but in industrial times one of the first people to see marketing clearly as a unique and central function of management was Cyrus H. McCormick (1809–84).[16] He invented some of the tools of modern marketing—market research and market analysis (Drucker 1974: 62)—and used advertising to sell his agricultural harvesting products. However, marketing itself was invented much earlier, in 1650 in Japan by the Mitsui family, who began the department store concept, promoting favourable conditions for customers (e.g. offering a variety of goods and a money-back guarantee and taking customer wishes into account in product design; see Drucker 1974: 62).

16   For a biography, see www.vaes.vt.edu/steeles/mccormick/bio.html.

If goods are produced and not sold, then realisation of value created by a business is delayed or does not occur at all. The emphasis of marketing is to make sure that this potential bottleneck on obtaining value from goods produced for sale is kept to the minimum. As more goods and services are produced or provided, markets get closer to saturation point and marketing tools are needed to try to expand either the total market or the market share of individual businesses (see Kotler and Bliemel 1999; Meffert and Bruhn 1996; for a critical analysis, see Hansen and Stauss 1995: 83). Customer management through marketing plays a vital function in the commercial success of business. Encouragement of customer satisfaction, customer engagement and customer competence are important goals for any business that wishes to remain legitimate in the market.

Although marketing is directed towards improving quality of life, criticism of the concept of marketing has built up and been constant since the 1960s (Aaker and Day 1982; Nader 1979; Packard 1966). Marketing is said to encourage excessive consumption and be concerned with powerful companies arousing the desires of potential customers in order to increase business sales and profits rather than to improve the quality of individual lives. Excessive consumption is itself criticised as leading to the waste of resources and overproduction relative to social ideals (see Reisch 1998; Scherhorn 1995; Wunderwald 1979). Such accusations make environmental issues—where reduction of waste and efficient use of resources are critical—a challenge for marketing (Becker 1998; Bruhn 1995; Kotler and Bliemel 1999; Meffert 1998). The concept of **eco-marketing** addresses the critique of conventional marketing. It has to discover how to deal with increased consumption and increased turnover of business products and services while resolving environmental problems caused by ever-increasing demand by business for material goods.

16.2 Eco-marketing: changing consumer expectations

The main aim of eco-marketing is to change the conditioning of customers (see also Maunders and Burritt 1991). In an ideal world, eco-marketing attempts to 'defrost' the 'frozen' customer expectations about what they consume, to educate them about environmental problems and to 'refreeze' their expectations so that they take environmental considerations into account in their purchase decisions. However, eco-marketing cannot simply be seen as 'the marketing of more environmentally friendly products'. Other elements of management are involved as well. The integration of responsibility for the avoidance or reduction of environmental pollution during the product life-cycle (Meffert and Kirchgeorg 1998) is important. Responsibility has two components—responsibility for actions and responsibility to account for those actions, in this case responsibility for marketing environmentally harmful products and services. One responsibility of eco-marketing is that it has to provide information about the qualities, use, maintenance, disposal and repair of products so that customers can make informed decisions. Although eco-marketing remains concerned with servicing the needs of customers, attention is directed towards maintaining a long-term credible relationship with the customer and recognition that production of environmentally unfriendly goods and services over the long run is not sustainable, given tightening environmental laws and penalties. Of course, eco-marketing portrays the advantage to consumers of purchasing 'green' products, an advantage that can translate into a price premium for 'greener' products and services (e.g. use of renewable fuels for electricity). This gives businesses an additional means of differentiating their products from those of their competitors and of receiving a competitive advantage (Porter 1987). At the same time, change in consumer behaviour is crucial if environmental problems are going to be reduced (e.g. Duchin and Lange 1994).

Marketing processes begin with market research, which examines consumer behaviour (see Fig. 16.1). Possible parameters associated with a specific change in purchase and consumption preferences are brought to the fore through market research. These issues are considered in the next section by looking at why consumers choose particular products and why they often give up a considerable part of their leisure time to obtain and consider information about different consumption alternatives.

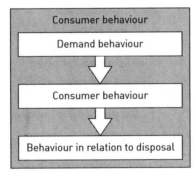

Figure 16.1 Consumer behaviour processes

16.3 Consumer behaviour in environmental terms

Consumer behaviour is expressed through the effective demand for goods (see Table 16.1). Effective demand is demand that is backed up with purchasing power. Decisions about purchases are, on the one hand, based on emotional, value-laden impulses and, on the other hand, on logical consideration of the serviceability of products. In combination, such emotional and cognitive processes create consumer involvement. **Involvement** is defined as: 'a person's perceived relevance of the object based on inherent needs, values and interests' (Zaichkowsky, quoted in Kroeber-Riel and Weinberg 1996: 360).

In general, four situations can be distinguished according to the depth of the emotional and the cognitive involvement (see Table 16.1). Low cognitive and emotional involvement lead to **habitual** decision-making. These are the things we buy out of

Emotional involvement	Cognitive involvement	
	Low	High
Low	Habitual	Limited
High	Impulsive	Extensive

Table 16.1 Basic forms of demand behaviour

habit, without much thought. This category includes most of the things put into the basket at the retail store or local market, the places for eating lunch (e.g. the local McDonald's) and the places for obtaining office supplies (see www.adcracker.com/involvement).

Extensive demand results from deliberative reflection about one's own needs and high emotional involvement in any final choice. Involvement is very high, with either the emotional or the cognitive involvement dominating the choice process. Business purchases that fall into this category might include such things as office design, advertising and the hiring of certain employees.

With **limited** purchases the demand for goods is defined in advance. Selection of the thing searched for takes place by comparing alternatives based on rational criteria. In this category are expensive business purchases: for example, anything relating to the technological infrastructure, office location and lease as well as the company health insurance plan.

Impulsive purchases are spontaneous or planned in such a way that the consumer is determined beforehand to give in to situational influences during a shopping expedition, depending on the customer's mood at the time (see Kroeber-Riel and Weinberg 1996: 399). The gratification we get from these products is emotional, sensual and short-lived. Little time is spent thinking about the purchase; examples might include a visit to the cinema, desserts at a restaurant or the purchase of an entertaining magazine or birthday card.

On the basis of this classification an empirical examination can be made of which of the four decision forms dominates the behaviour of demand of certain types of buyer or the demand for certain kinds of goods. Generally, higher-quality products, such as quality furniture or house appliances, generate a higher involvement than do everyday products from the supermarket. However, the decision form also varies depending on the atmosphere in the shop or the circumstances surrounding the purchase. Meffert (1998) interprets involvement as being a function that combines the meaning (cognitive) and novelty (emotional) of a product to the consumer. The allocation of products, consumers or purchasing situations to one of the four fields cannot, therefore, be determined in advance but is influenced by the strategic (or long-run) behaviour of the business. Such behaviour involves 'a strategic move ... that influences the other person's choice, in a manner favourable to one's self, by affecting the other person's expectations on how one's self will behave' (Schelling 1960: 160). Hence, the construction of a reliable **trademark** or **brand name** for everyday products is a stimulus to habitual choice whereby the consumer does not have to give too much thought to the purchase.

16.3.1 Involvement from an environmental point of view

Innovation is a second way of creating business customers, and it acts in a complementary way to marketing (Drucker 1974: 61). Environmentally benign products and services provide an avenue for business innovation. Environmental innovations can be successfully brought to the market only when marketing campaigns bring about customer involvement with the development and introduction of the new product or service. Recognition of the innovation, of its environmental merits and also the readiness of customers for new models of behaviour presuppose that the attention of the consumers has been aroused. Customers are asked to change their purchasing and consumption habits. Information is provided about the benefits of the new products to the environment and to the customer. Habitual and impulsive forms of behaviour provide marketing with an opportunity to change consumer habits or to encourage 'green' purchases based on emotive factors that raise new and other concerns:

- Extensive decision processes. Only in the case of an extensive decision is the consumer ready to reflect on needs, to refine his or her lifestyle and to test the acquisition of innovative goods on that lifestyle. Since extensive decisions involve mostly the purchase of high-quality goods, a critical comparison of costs and benefits normally precedes any change in purchases. Although energy-saving features, prolonged product life or health-promoting effects can be introduced in parallel to demonstrable improvements in environmental impacts, any additional costs of acquiring environmental product qualities act to constrain consumer choice when individual benefits appear somewhat diffuse.

- Limited decision processes. In the case of limited choice, consumers concentrate on a restricted number of alternatives on offer. Criteria for choice include a narrow spectrum of trademarks, prices and clearly defined quality advantages associated with the goods on offer. Therefore, the presentation of simplified **key information** that affects decisions at the margin is particularly important for the sale of such goods. For example, when the consumer can identify a desirable eco-label, environmental arguments can be included in the purchase decision.

- Impulsive decision processes. Impulsive decisions presuppose that the prospect of environmentally oriented consumption causes pleasure and is seen as a means of status, vitality, innovation or social recognition. Generation of feelings of fear, unethical behaviour or antipathy are less suitable drivers of impulsive consumer behaviour (see Lichtl 1999). Advertisements based on fear are successful only when the good on offer provides a direct way of evading a specific personal threat (e.g. accident insurance). In an environmental context, marketing based on information about fear, crisis or environmental doom acts to deter the impulsive purchase of environmentally benign goods. It is seen as manipulative and thereby reduces the credibility of suppliers (Trommsdorff 1998: 122).

- Habitual decision processes. Habitual consumption can be enriched environmentally only when consumer behaviour is 'unfrozen'. In contrast to the extensive form of behaviour, the consumer is to be seen as a reactive participant. Hence, involvement of habitual consumers can take place only through the introduction of strong **incentives**. These incentives encourage impulsive transfers to the new product or the short-term adoption of alternatives that appear more attractive. Once the behaviour has changed towards acceptance of the environmentally favoured goods, habitual behaviour is reinstated through a 'refreezing' process. Habitual purchases are a double-edged sword. Habitual faithfulness to a product or brand represents both an obstruction to competition and an opportunity for the permanent acceptance of a market in environmental innovations whereby the consumer continually converts to the preferred article. With the correct incentives for business manipulated through eco-marketing, its products can continually be made more environmentally benign.

In summary, it is emphasised here that consumer demand for environmentally benign goods and services depends on consumer involvement. Involvement can be based on a rational calculation of costs and benefits or on emotive factors that affect purchasing decisions. Both work together to influence the behaviour of consumers, and market research needs to be undertaken to establish which behaviour and types of involvement dominate when 'green' considerations are introduced for any particular product or service.

Since the late 20th century the proportion of goods purchased based on high emotional involvement has steadily increased. Positive consumer experiences arise from product aesthetics as well as from social recognition and empathy (see Kuckartz 1998: 73). This means that a larger number of problems arise when false environmental marketing claims promote consumer purchases based on emotive involvement. Likewise, there is an accompanying growth in the development of controls over false environmental marketing claims.[17]

16.3.2 Aspects of consumer behaviour

Further analysis of the behaviour of demand involves the partition of decision-making into separate decisions. According to Pepels (1996), the behaviour of demand is linked to six separate decisions (see Fig. 16.2): how much is available to spend on the product; how much time should be spend on obtaining information about goods; the product group and brands about which information is sought; and the volume of and places for purchase (e.g. whether discount, speciality shops or the Internet are preferred).

In an environmental context an additional, seventh, decision about disposal is also important, concerning which form of product disposal the consumer wishes to encourage or practice. Does the consumer wish to obtain the right of disposal, through ownership, or is use all that is required, through leasing or sharing, where the rights relating to disposal are not acquired? This decision has a bearing on whether consumer demand can be met through the provision of material goods or

17 See the US Federal Trade Commission Guides for the Use of Environmental Marketing Claims, at www.ftc.gov/bcp/grnrule/guides980427.htm#260.7.

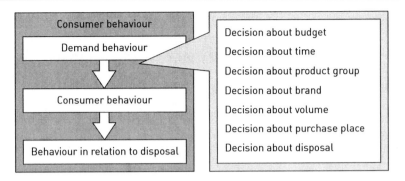

Figure 16.2 **Facets of demand behaviour**

Source: Pepels 1996

by means of services.[18] In principle, use of consumer goods can be improved through leasing, sharing and the provision of services; however, private property tends to be treated with greater care than is borrowed, shared or common property—a situation referred to as the 'tragedy of the commons' (see Beder 1996: 89).

Questions about methods of payment, about market and volume preferences and about consumer purchase habits provide the basis for empirical marketing research. According to Meffert (1998: 89ff.), **marketing research** can be distinguished from **market research** by its focus on markets as well as on supplementary analysis of the effects of further marketing activities (e.g. advertising). Isolated observations of current demand are an insufficient basis for marketing research because consumers relate their demand to experiences gained over time. Satisfaction obtained from consumption is another factor to be considered in marketing, as this is linked to customer service, faithfulness to brands and informal consumer opinion passed on to others.

16.3.3 *Customer satisfaction, quality of goods and consuming competence*

Marketing starts out with the customers, their demographics, their perceptions of reality, their needs and their values. It asks what the customer wishes to buy, not what the business wants to sell. It seeks to provide the satisfaction the customers are looking for, in accordance with their values and needs. **Satisfaction** originates from the fulfilment of the personal needs of customers. **Needs** are non-specific and latent (Brock 1995: 27). They are consolidated into **motives** and turn into urgent **wishes** that drive consumer purchasing behaviour. The phrase 'I have a longing' represents an uncertain need, whereas 'I have wanderlust' outlines the longing, yet it is only in the expression of beginning a trip to a specific country, say, that the need refers to an object and therefore can be addressed in market terms.

18   For example, in the USA Interface offers the leasing rather than ownership of carpets; see www.peopleandplanet.net.

Whether consumption provides a positive experience and leads to further purchases depends not only on the quality of goods provided but also on the customer's total consumption experience and the competence of that consumer (see Henning-Thurau 1999), including possible after-sales disappointments. Disappointment or dissonance following a market purchase and positive experiences influence the final satisfaction obtained from the purchase of the good or service. In order to satisfy their needs, competent consumers must be able to answer three questions (see Schulze 1996):

- What do I really want?
- Which good matches my desires?
- Am I technically and emotionally able to bring about the desired result or experience through the good acquired?

The first and most important form of consumer competence is the ability to identify different needs and to deduce desires from them. In order to avoid unsuccessful purchases, after-purchase dissonances and unnecessary waste there is a need for consumer competence to be enhanced in environmental terms by marketing (see Fig. 16.3). The distinction between the consumer's competence and the quality of product is often not drawn by the consumers themselves as this protects their own feeling of competence. Hence, failure to obtain satisfaction from purchases tends to be conceived of in terms of external causes such as lack of functionality rather than lack of consumer competence. Marketing has to take this situation into account and any offers made to customers need to address the lack of competency by creating the subjective perception of competence such that repeat purchases are more likely to occur. From a technical point of view, clearly written operating instructions handed out with the product, back-up instructions accessible through the Internet and telephone hotlines and call centres can be introduced to enhance the customer's level of competence in relation to purchases made. Hence, a lack of technical competence can be addressed by providing simple operating instructions and back-up technical services.

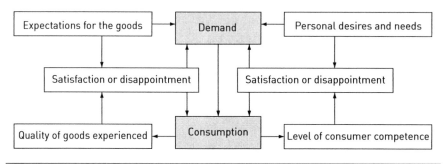

Figure 16.3 **Influence of satisfaction on demand and consumption**

The success of consumption is not always measured in technical terms on the basis of the external results of purchasing the goods (e.g. purchase of a chemical that cleans the carpet). It may also be based on emotional involvement—on the customer's personal experiences. In these circumstances, the consumer faces the risk of disappointment, which can be influenced by the supplier only indirectly. The supplier cannot guarantee enjoyment from the consumption of goods sold. Instead, the supplier can provide advice based on empathy with the consumer and can make emotive suggestions as to how consumers can best achieve their desires (see Schulze 1996: 439ff.).

The possibility of building in continuous satisfaction for customers can diminish the appeal of acquiring new consumer items. If the duration of consumption benefits is prolonged, a strategic conflict between the customer and new product sales can arise. Sales from competitors may be locked out, but the strategy also locks out new and repeat sales from the same business. Such conflict can be resolved by following a two-stage strategy: first, ensure that customers obtain high satisfaction directly after purchase; second, once purchase is complete, encourage emotional detachment from the product. In this way the customer is encouraged to seek out the positive experiences associated with the direct after-purchase phase, through a strategy essentially designed to provide only brief but intense fulfilment of desires. Such a marketing strategy is clearly in conflict with environmental goals. Resolution of this conflict is possible by offering services (e.g. reappraisal, repair, leasing, take-back and recycling) related to products previously purchased. These services will increase monetary gains without actually increasing product sales. Making consumers aware of the dangers of after-purchase dissonance can also be employed as an argument for the sale of environmentally benign services (e.g. Stahel 1997).

16.3.4 Eco-marketing: a broader perspective on marketing

Introduction of environmental considerations places the focus on both consumption and disposal behaviour, which means that the marketing perspective becomes broader (see Fig. 16.1). Packaging of products is an important issue to be addressed. Most consumers are affected by packaging (see Spiller 1999: 16ff.). For example, collection and separation of packaging for disposal or recycling is carried out by 90% of German households (Meffert and Kirchgeorg 1998: 382ff.), and in Australia the National Packaging Covenant encourages business to reduce and recycle packaging materials (ANZECC 1999).

Environmental appeals by business and public institutions have helped to encourage better behaviour in relation to disposal of products and product parts. Practices such as the separation of waste, availability of unpackaged products and the introduction of environmentally benign cleaning products provide consumers with the opportunity to contribute to the protection of the environment at a small cost. Therefore, environmental protection through improved product disposal processes does not essentially affect the **comfort**, **status**, **budget** or **leisure time** of consumers (see Diekmann and Preisendörfer 1992). Moreover, the benefit of waste avoidance is directly evident to the layperson. If eco-marketing wants to attract broader customer groups, it must facilitate the evaluation of personal advantages and the desire for consumers to receive simple instructions about environmentally benign treatment. The readiness of consumers to accept 'costs' associated with a change in behaviour solely for the benefit of the environment is limited, even when people are already environmentally aware (Balderjahn 1986; Dröge 1997). Eco-marketing gains greater acceptance when some personal benefit is combined with consumption of environmentally preferred goods. If net savings, improved health protection, prolonged product maintenance or increased status can be demonstrated in economic terms, environmentally benign behaviour will result even without explicit recognition of associated pro-environment arguments (see Kuckartz 1998: 2). Such arguments will intensify the case in favour of the product concerned but they are unnecessary to change behaviour. Moreover, in many cases, previous knowledge reduces the use of comments on environmental friendliness to symbolic allusions (e.g. sunflowers, water drops, green pastures). So, for instance, the environmental advantage of an electric car is as self-evident as the advantage of avoiding rapid acceleration and abrupt braking in heavy traffic.

The example of the electric car illustrates two possibilities for business to reduce environmental impact added by consumers during consumption:

● First, business can offer technical solutions that reduce pollution without consumers having consciously to change their behaviour (e.g. consumers can use an electric car for short journeys just as they would with a conventional car).[19]

● Second, business can, through advertising and provision of advice, add open or hidden appeals to consumers to change their everyday habits (e.g. consumers of the electric car can be encouraged to further reduce their environmental impact by walking or cycling where possible).[20]

16.3.5 The influence of environmental consciousness

Apart from situational influences, values, attitudes and personality characteristics foster different types of consumption. Environmental consciousness is a factor to be considered here. Public environmental consciousness is of the type encouraged by Rachael Carson (1962). In *Silent Spring* Carson argued that humankind was fatally tampering with nature by its reckless misuse of chemical pesticides, particularly the ubiquitous new wonder chemical DDT (dichlorodiphenyltrichloroethane). Writing in a language that everyone could understand and using the public's knowledge of atomic fallout as a reference point, Carson described how chlorinated hydrocarbons and organic phosphorus insecticides silently altered the cellular processes of plants, animals and possibly humans. In chapters on the contamination of soil, water, vegetation, birds and wildlife, Carson suggested that the long-term effects of these

---

19 Further examples include the introduction of electrical appliances that have a lower energy consumption or the reduction of toxic or otherwise harmful additives in products. For instance, business can produce refrigerators that consume less electricity or that do not contain substances that deplete the ozone layer (such as CFCs), or it may produce lights that are sensitive to movement (and hence do not remain lit once the user has left the room). Electricity consumption can also be reduced by encouraging consumers to purchase long-life light bulbs or even by giving such bulbs to customers.

20 Lufthansa AG, for example, advertises combined air and rail journeys, and the automobile manufacturer Ford invites customers to practice more economical driving styles (Lichtl 1999: 40ff.).

chemicals were detrimental to the continuation of life; the publication of her book thus led to an awakening of public environmental consciousness. Environmental consciousness is insight into the human impacts on the foundations of life, linked to a readiness to take remedial action.

Public environmental consciousness has also spread throughout the world following the results of different studies, emulating Carson's concerns. The strength of concern over environmental issues has had its ups and downs; for example, in Europe interest declined in the early 1990s but is now on the rise again (BMU 2000), whereas in Australia it increased in the early 1990s and fell back at the end of that decade. It is only recently that business environmental consciousness about positive opportunities has been awakened (GEMI 2001). Concern initially was with ways in which business could protect the environment while simultaneously reducing operating costs, increasing resource efficiency and streamlining the time to market—all bottom-line considerations. However, the latest report of the Global Environment Management Initiative (GEMI 2001) moves the environment to the top line, with eco-marketing as a key component in discussions of environmentally friendly ways to increase revenues or sales, to increase market share, to boost share price and to enhance branding. Business and consumer environmental consciousness highlight a range of environmentally benign behaviour styles and provide an extensive market potential for environmental products that provide solutions to environmental problems.

The top-line framework offers two sets of variables by which companies can characterise themselves in order to select the best strategy for employing environmental considerations to enhance top-line value (Baue 2001: 1). In the first brace of variables, a company's core strength tends to lean toward either product innovation or customer intimacy (Table 16.2). In the second set of variables, companies find that one of two strategies tends to suit them best: either a revenue-driven solution or a brand-driven tactic. Since these four variables can combine in four different ways, the top-line framework allows a company to tailor its environmental solutions to its own strengths. A revenue-driven strategy for product innovation yields a customer-oriented environmental solution, whereas a brand-driven tactic for product innovation leads to environmentally responsible products. A revenue-driven strategy for fostering customer relationships points to environmental services,

Business focus, by variable set 1	*Business strategy, by variable set 2*	
	Revenue-driven	**Brand-driven**
Product innovation	Provision of customer-oriented solutions	Production of environmentally responsible products
Customer intimacy	Provision of environmental services	Brand enhancement

Table 16.2 **Environmental business solutions, as suggested by the top-line framework**

Source: according to Baue 2001: 1

whereas a brand-driven tactic for fostering customer intimacy centres on enhancing the brand.

In spite of this recognition of the importance of environmental consciousness to business strategies in relation to the environment, it must be also be recognised that there is a difference between higher environmental consciousness and possible changes in environmental behaviour. For example, the discrepancy between the environmental consciousness expressed in Germany and the consumer behaviour of German people has been noted for many years (see e.g. De Haan and Kuckartz 1996). Studies by Dröge (1997) and Balderjahn (1986) verify that there is a relatively low correlation between attitude to environmental values and the demand for products and services that exhibit improved environmental performance. Similar observations are made elsewhere. There is clear evidence from a variety of sources that Australians are concerned about environmental degradation and that such concern will remain high (Castles 1992; DASET 1992). However, the clear change in the community's attitudes to the environment has been reflected only in a modest change in behaviour (DASET 1992; Davis 1989). Furthermore, differences in environmental consciousness and behaviour are seen to depend on gender and socioeconomic class (Hampel *et al.* 1995).

General surveys about consumer environmental consciousness can therefore be used only as a guide in the assessment of environmental market potential. Complexity behind the factors involved in determining consumer behaviour cannot be stressed too much. In Wimmer's (1998: 239ff.) words: 'The reasons, especially the motives, for buying a specific environmentally friendly product are very complex . . . At the time of the purchase of an environmentally friendly product many other values, motives and attitudes may have an influence'.

Environmentally benign consumer behaviour cannot be attributed solely to environmental consciousness. A range of social and individual motives lead to different options being followed and to different barriers to 'green' purchasing (see Lantermann 1999). Many consumers focus on a single environmental issue; for example, a consumer may love animals and buy only free-range eggs rather than battery-chicken eggs. Such individuals may not care a jot about the greenhouse effect. In addition, purchasing behaviour that is fair to the environment often only results from the combination of concern for the environment and other drivers of behaviour, such as the search for emotive experiences or the desire to be fit and healthy. Self-service and convenience are other factors to consider. Consumers look for relief from mundane everyday tasks.

The trend in industrialised countries towards single occupancy of homes, an ageing population and more flexible working hours in the 'new economy' provide additional starting points for the organisation of eco-marketing. Sometimes environmental consciousness and other preferences will be in harmony, and sometimes they will be in conflict. The balance between these complex factors will determine specific consumer behaviour from day to day and situation to situation. From an environmental perspective, conflicts are at their greatest when environmental problems are thought to be severe but the costs of alleviating poor environmental performance of products or services are also very high. Therefore, for eco-marketing the idealised picture of the 'green consumer' is set in the context of different lifestyles, socioeconomic classes and gender issues that can be directly opposed to environmental goals. Thus, the first criticism of environmental consciousness is that complex contextual factors are easy to ignore that relate to tendencies that do not support environmentally benign motives and behaviour.

The second criticism of environmental consciousness is that it generally draws on negative feelings associated with consternation, fear and indignation (see Preuss 1991). Some of Carson's (1962) examples of the types of statement from which environmental consciousness develops are as follows:

> Every human being is now subjected to contact with dangerous chemicals from the moment of conception until death . . . These chemicals are now stored in the bodies of the vast majority of human beings, regardless of age. They occur in the mother's milk, and probably in the tissues of the unborn child (1962: 31).

> The new environmental health problems are multiple . . . created by radiation, the never ending stream of chemicals and pesticides . . . their presence casts a shadow that is no less ominous because it is simply impossible to predict the effects of lifetime exposure to chemicals that should not be part of the biological experience of man (1962: 168).

Others demonstrate the same line of argument (BMU 1998: 24; see also www. umweltbundesamt.de):

> If we go on acting the way we have done so far, we are heading for an environmental catastrophe.

> When I read newspaper reports about environmental problems or watch TV programmes, I often feel indignant and furious.

> It always happens that politicians do very little for the environment.

Marketing experts point out that with few exceptions the environment is considered by consumers to be associated with negative impacts. Thus, when advertising, the environment has to be treated cautiously (Kroeber-Riel and Weinberg 1996: 674; Lichtl 1999: 84). Weakness in the correlation between environmental consciousness and consumer behaviour can be explained partly by the picture of negativity that environmental issues generate as groups of the population least involved in environmental protection are those who are afraid of environmental consequences (Ecolog-Institut 1999: 17). The same groups also complain about the lack of objective information about environmental issues—hence they suffer because of the subjectivity of their perceived fears. Involvement with environmental protection increases when environmental consciousness is accompanied by a high belief that the individual has control over environmental outcomes. If individuals feel that they cannot control or influence events and situations in their life, then environmental consciousness will not translate into environmental protection (Gierl and Stumpp 1999). Eco-marketing is therefore likely to be more effective if it targets people having a conviction that they can control events and outcomes and if it illustrates the possible contribution that every consumer decision can make to environmental protection.

16.3.6 *The meaning of environmental knowledge*

Evaluation of possible courses of action presupposes knowledge about environmental issues. Environmental knowledge is complex, as demonstrated by ongoing debates about whether global warming exists (compare Lomborg 2001 and replies at www.au.dk/~cesamat/debate.html). Results of empirical research turn out to be very different depending on the subjects interrogated (see Meffert and Kirchgeorg 1998; Monhemius 1993; Spiller 1999). In fact, even where there appears to be agreement about environmental facts, market-related knowledge about behaviour is rudimentary, as seen in answers to the following questions examined by Spiller (1999):

- What solutions to environmental problems are available?

- How is environmental performance enhanced by products and services on offer?

- Where can I find environmental products and services?

- How much do environmental products and services cost?

- How can I recognise environmental products and services?

Answers to this combination of questions are decisive if the potential turnover of environmental products and services is to be established. Communication of information is essential before knowledge about consumer behaviour can be established. Consumers need easy-to-understand basic information in plain language through advertisements that reach new consumers in the competitive 'jungle of advertisements'. Advertisements require funding to establish new products and services, or trademarks. With such funding, eco-marketing has the potential to become a successful key strategy that develops consumer knowledge about economically promising and environmentally important products and services and which integrates this strategy with the various marketing mix tools.

16.4 The process of strategic eco-marketing

The strategic marketing process, like any administrative practice, is far simpler to conceptualise than to operationalise within an organisation. In the strategic marketing process management has the task of recognising, analysing and influencing opportunities for and threats to the business associated with its environmental claims (Charter and Polonsky 1999). The cyclical strategic marketing process is implemented by applying the steps illustrated in Figure 16.4.

Marketing begins with the generation of ideas. Management examines which of these ideas are suitable in business terms by comparing market opportunities and threats with the strengths and weaknesses of the business (SWOT [strengths–weaknesses–opportunities–threats] analysis; see Section 12.2). Analyses of marketing opportunities determine the choice of market goals. Market goals establish the

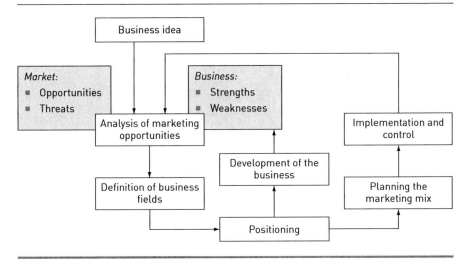

Figure 16.4 The circular process of strategic eco-marketing

foundation for defining the fields of business in which the goods or services are to be offered or positioned in such a way that they appear attractive to the potential consumer. Next, marketing plans can be drawn up and implemented with use of tools from the marketing mix (Section 16.5). In parallel to these steps, measures for development of the business are introduced, so that the profile of the organisation's strengths and employee competences are brought into harmony with the positioning that is sought.

Regular checking is required to confirm that the marketing analysis is correct and that the application of the marketing instruments proceeds as planned. Through customer queries, conversations with customers, product and service turnover statistics and actual observation of consumer demand, any special preferences and changes in customer predilections can be recorded as a base for continual planning. Furthermore, it has to be recognised that the business's strengths and weaknesses change over time, as personnel gain experience of the strategic and operational aspects of eco-marketing and generate new knowledge about the processes involved. The strategic marketing process cycle continues by looping through the steps outlined above and by either reconfirming prior assessment of the different steps or reassessing prior outcomes from each step as part of the planning and control process that works towards continual improvement.

16.4.1 Analysis of marketing opportunities

Unbounded market opportunities exist, such as those arising from possible demand for energy savings or experiences involving nature such as eco-tourism. However, marketing opportunities are relevant to eco-marketing. Such opportunities emerge from the combination of specific business strengths with gaps discovered in the product or services market. A marketing opportunity is available when the business considers that it is highly likely to achieve a competitive advantage by combining its available core competences and capital (see Kotler and Bliemel 1999). In order to recognise environmental marketing opportunities, detailed knowledge is required about the preferences of market participants. Therefore, the starting point for the analysis of opportunities is marketing research, including the knowledge and experience that are derived from personal contact with customers (see Simon 1996: 84ff.).

Analysis of eco-marketing opportunities requires that the following questions be addressed:

- Who is expected to ask for the environmentally improved performance from products and services?

- Which features and quality characteristics should the performance programme adopt for customers?

- In what ways do customers seek to obtain improved performance?

- How and where can customer attention be captured and preference for improved performance be encouraged?

- How much and in what form are customers willing to pay for improved performance?

In order to meet the need for information in an efficient and effective way, decisions about data sources take precedence (see Fig. 16.5). Normally, primary investigations are more expensive and more time-consuming than is reference to secondary data sources. However, the advantage of primary sources lies in their relevance to the current situation and in the direct reference to the idea being investigated. This means that the acquisition of qualitative information about the 'how' and 'why' of the consumer preference being examined can be the direct focus of attention. One such method is conjoint analysis.

16.4.1.1 Conjoint analysis

Conjoint analysis is one of the terms used to describe a broad range of techniques for estimating the value people place on the attributes or features that define products and services. Discrete choice, choice modelling, hierarchical choice, card sorts, trade-off matrices, and preference-based conjoint and pair-wise comparisons are some of the names used for various forms of conjoint analysis. The goal of any conjoint survey is to assign specific values to the range of options buyers consider when making a purchase decision. Armed with this knowledge, marketers can focus on the most important features of products or services and design messages most probable to strike a chord with target buyers.

Depending on the type of conjoint survey conducted, statistical methods such as ordinary least squares regression, weighted least squares regression and logit analysis are used to translate respondents' answers into importance values or utilities. Regardless of the statistical methodologies used, conjoint analysis results have withstood intense scrutiny from academics and professional researchers during the past 25 years.

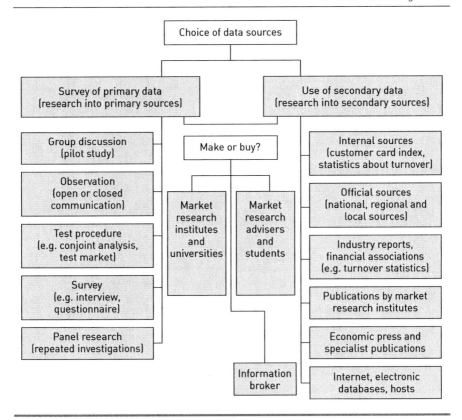

Figure 16.5 Choice of data sources and research methods

Traditional surveys on environmental consumer preferences lead to distorted results. Traditional survey approaches ask respondents to estimate how much value they place on each attribute. This is a very difficult task for any person to complete, much less someone who does not spend every waking moment thinking about the most important features of products such as toothpaste or wood preservatives. Conjoint analysis, however, attempts to break the task into a series of choices or ratings. These choices or ratings, when taken together, allow us to compute the relative importance of each of the attributes studied. Instead of 'stated importance', conjoint analysis uses 'derived importance' values for each attribute or feature (see www.dssresearch.com/library/conjoint/conjoint.asp.).

The main problem with assessing environmental aspects of consumer preferences is that environmental protection is, in principle, considered desirable by all consumers. Experimental subjects tend to provide exemplary answers from an ethical viewpoint (e.g. when answering the question as to the additional price they are willing to pay for environmentally fairer product alternatives and the additional habits they would consider adopting in order to obtain the item). Unfortunately, real buying behaviour reveals the difference between words and actions. Conjoint analysis takes this problem into account (see Meffert 1998: 385ff.; for the seven steps of conjoint analysis, see Box 16.1).

The are several basic steps to be taken by a marketer interested in applying conjoint analysis:

■ **Step 1.** Determine which product or service attributes or features (colour, form, durability or price) are most important to the consumer. In eco-marketing the grade of environmental protection provided could also be included (e.g. in relation to food, grading could be classified into 'conventional' and 'organic', based on local or international standards). Next, draw up prototypes with different combinations of the product features to be tested, to provide a choice to customers.

■ **Step 2.** Determine which data-collection method will be used to recruit respondents and how the data will be captured (e.g. by post, telephone, e-mail or the Internet).

■ **Step 3.** Determine which conjoint method will best fit the research problem; choice-based conjoint and preference-based conjoint methods are the most common methods used today.

■ **Step 4.** create an experimental design that will allow the calculation of the main effects and key interactions between the attributes being studied. Many conjoint studies focus only on the main effects or direct utilities for each attribute. However, when attributes such as environmental characteristics, price or brand name are used, potential interactions between attributes should also be considered.

■ **Step 5.** Collect the data. After pre-testing the attribute list and survey instrument, begin collecting data from the target market. Subjects are required to look closely at the different prototypes and to choose the product they prefer.

■ **Step 6.** From the choices made, derive statistics to represent how strong the real preference for environmentally friendly goods is, depending on the characteristics of other products and prices charged. Calculate the utilities for each respondent or for groups of respondents.

■ **Step 7.** Create a market simulation model. This allows prediction of the impact on the market of changes to existing products and the introduction of new products.

Box 16.1 Special use of conjoint analysis for eco-marketing

16.4.1.2 Market research institutes

Apart from choice of the appropriate source of data to use, the information to be investigated and the extent to which external parties should be consulted must also be determined. Investigation of primary data is often undertaken in market research institutes or universities. Market research is the collection and analysis of data for the purpose of decision-making and is used to describe existing market conditions, explain certain types of market behaviour and predict how consumers might respond to new products and changes in marketing mixes. The more important the decision or decisions to be made, the greater the value of market research to help guide those decisions. Market research can be invaluable (see www.dssresearch.com/library/general/when_mr.asp):

- When the costs of making a wrong decision far outweigh the costs of using market research to confirm or dispel managers' beliefs

- When the industry or market is highly competitive

- When the last product or marketing plan failed for some unknown reason

- When support is needed for a new idea or marketing plan before taking it to top management

- When long-term customers are being lost faster than new customers are being gained

- When the total quality management (TQM) programme has not proven successful with customers

- When the aim is to become 'customer-focused' but there is no knowledge of exactly what customers really want

Market research institutes can provide free, accessible secondary sources of information about consumer research in certain industries as well as conduct primary research at a cost to their clients. Members of the Association of European Market Research Institutes (AEMRI, www.aemri.org) comply with standards for undertaking best-practice market research, including high-quality project design, a clear statement of research objectives, information to be collected, the method to be used (and the reason for that choice, if relevant), the source of the sample, fieldwork control (including relevant quality checks), respondent types and quotas, analysis and data processing details, project timings and fee (with details of any applicable taxes). Organisations in different countries echo these professional aspects (see www.esomar.nl/mr_associations.html).

In addition, market research advisers can support management in its search for suitable research institutes, and information brokers who specialise in searching for appropriate information through the Internet and other online media sources can be employed (e.g. www.informationsbroker.org).

After the investigated data has been evaluated and interpreted, the research results are presented, making a clear distinction between what the data shows and any interpretation of the data by the institute. Market research organisations survive on the notion that accurate, relevant information used intelligently can make the difference between success and failure of their clients. Information about environmental consciousness and behaviour can be a critical part of this service.

16.4.2 Definition of business fields

As it is not possible to realise all available market opportunities, it is necessary for the business to focus on specific target markets. The market needs to be subdivided in such a way that products and services offered to consumers correspond to specific, identifiable needs. Segmentation of the market aims to divide it into homogeneous sub-markets, each distinguished from the other by its own specific consumer demand preferences and assumptions about what is on offer (for an example regarding the market for detergents, see Box 16.2).

Consumer preferences have an important impact on how markets are segmented. Market segments for the desired outcome of 'clean washing' include single households, family households and social establishments (hospitals, homes for the elderly and so on). Given the general desire for 'cleanliness', market research supplies empirical research results about each segment by identifying the importance of different characteristics to different segments (see Table 16.3). If the characteristic 'environmentally fair' is examined, some customers in all three groups are likely to consider environmental protection to be a suitable characteristic.

	Very important to:		
Preference	Single-person households?	Family households?	Social establishments?
Easy to use	Yes	Yes	No
Economical	No	Yes	Yes
Quick	Yes	No	No
Germ-free and hygienic	No	No	Yes

Table 16.3 The importance of various characteristics of detergent, by market segment: single-person household, family household and social establishment

Next a finer segmentation is called for, to discover what makes these customers different. Various possibilities are examined. In the family household segment, families with young children and the presence of highly educated parents may wash their clothes in a particularly environmentally conscious way. Hence, it could be decided to create a strategic business field with a market goal of supplying environmentally conscious family households in Asia, Europe and the USA with a specific focus on the largest potential source of market demand.

Box 16.2 Segmentation of the market for detergents

Within each segment business endeavours to obtain a high correlation between market performance and customer needs (Pepels 1996). For example, the market can be divided according to region, sales channel, age and income group, gender, family situation or lifestyle. Segments reflect the expectations of the different customer groups for certain types of performance. Results from marketing research are used to provide support for the choice of target markets in relation to each segment (Kotler and Bliemel 1999: 425ff.).

Apart from consumer preferences, eco-marketing has to address a second question: namely, the extent to which environmental differentiation in the target market is already used by competitors. Whether a market segment is attractive also depends on how well competitors address environmental preferences, are technically capable of capturing competitive advantages, are in a position to imitate and beat the competition in a credible way through use of environmental characteristics.

When target markets are chosen, it still remains an open question as to whether they will turn into successful fields of business activity. According to Ansoff (1966), different business fields arise from a combination of the product and target markets in which the product is to be positioned—that is, a combination of existing or new markets and existing or new products. According to Ansoff, the company's response to this combination falls into one of four categories: do nothing, undertake product development, carry out market development or follow diversification strategies. For environmental management this classification falls short because the usefulness of existing products in existing markets is not analysed in any depth.

In practice, specific functions can be achieved by use of different products and through the use of different techniques. For example, the function 'irrigation of a field' can occur above or below the ground, through open channels or enclosed pipes, by use of irrigation sprays or helicopters and by using spring water, groundwater, water from rivers or rainwater. In addition, the amount of water needed can be reduced through the use of suitable local plant varieties, genetic engineering, inter- and under-planting, the use of berms, etc. Each combination of ways in which the function is provided causes other costs and environmental effects. Abell (1980) identifies three factors that limit business fields (see Fig. 16.6):

- Customer groups: the group of potential customers

- Customer functions: the functions, or benefits, offered by the product to the customer

- Alternative technologies: technologies employed and technical know-how used to provide the function, or benefits, demanded by the customer groups

The three-dimensional chart avoids placing restrictions on existing (material) products and presents the range of underlying functions that the product fulfils. In eco-marketing, market opportunities have to be linked to provision of chosen function(s) and choice of an attractive customer group as well as choice of an eco-efficient technology. Only when customer groups, technology and the desired function match can an appropriate market segment successfully be developed. Success will depend on the business's own strengths and the threats that it faces from competition.

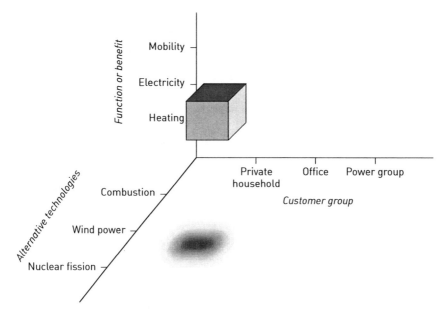

Note: The business field can be defined in the intersection of the three axes: technology, function and customer group. In this example, the company positions itself as a provider of wind-power facilities generating electricity for private households.

Figure 16.6 **Definition of the business field for the manufacturer of wind power facilities**

Source: Abell 1980

The breadth and depth of business fields can also be developed (see Fig. 16.7). These are normally developed over time. Initially, a small business may offer only one element (e.g. dishwashers for large commercial industries, e.g. hospitals) in the range illustrated in Figure 16.7. With a deepening strategy, the business differentiates its products—branching out into provision of facilities for the treatment of water, then also supplying washing-up liquid and accessories and, finally, offering washing services—thereby preventing the risks associated with excessive specialisation (Simon 1996: 58ff.). A broadening in strategy—in this case, the development of dishwashers designed specifically for single-person households and for family households—may be encouraged by, for example, the development of new technologies (an example in a different sector is the development of the personal computer as a replacement for the typewriter), by the appearance of new competitors (e.g. by an overseas competitor in a global market) or by a drop in sales turnover in certain target markets.

16.4.3 Positioning

Price and differentiation characteristics of a product turn into a competitive advantage only when they are noticed by the customer. Positioning is the process that

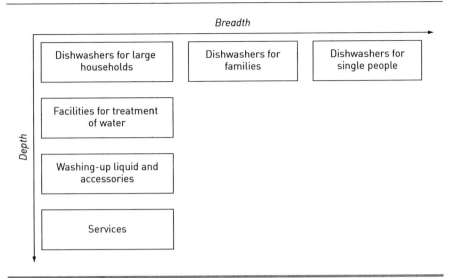

Figure 16.7 **Breadth and depth of business fields: an example of a company supplying dishwashing products and services**

Source: Simon 1996: 53

brings price and differentiation characteristics to the potential customer's attention. It is the part of strategic action that addresses customer perception. On the one hand, customers identify certain characteristics that affect their decision to make a purchase from the different products offered in the market. A product that is seen as the most serviceable is the one that is purchased. It may be especially good value, the design could be particularly attractive, after-sales service could be especially helpful or information available about products might appear especially credible. On the other hand, suppliers endeavour to differentiate their product in the target customer's consciousness by suggesting something special is being provided (Kotler and Bliemel 1999). In its positioning strategy the supplier defines how it wants to present itself relative to the competition. It plans the profile of its product and the orientation of that product in comparison with competitive products.

Businesses face the choice of either positioning their product characteristics close to those of existing suppliers or searching for a field that has not yet been entered (see Fig. 16.8). Positioning a product close to the products of existing suppliers (crosses near offers A and B in Fig. 16.8) directly affects those suppliers. By taking such a strategy the business presupposes that its strengths are greater than those of the competition, perhaps by providing additional environmental benefits or greater quality (than offer B) or a lower price (than offer A) than that provided by the competition. Positioning products in proximity to existing products of competitors makes it easier for target customers to benchmark the product, but such a strategy is liable to provoke the competitors. If, on the other hand, a new field or segment is chosen (offer C; e.g. by basing the product on new environmental technologies), this represents positioning for market expansion and is seen as less of a threat by competitors. However, in this case the need to provide information designed to add

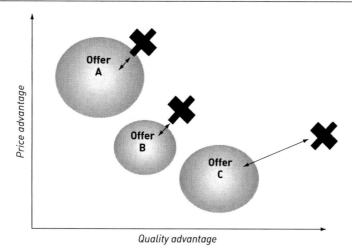

Quality advantage

Note: Product positioning is represented by a cross; proximity (positioning close to an existing market) is shown as a short double-headed arrow; product differentiation (positioning for market expansion) is shown by a long arrow; the size of the circles represents turnover of the existing product of a competitor.

Figure 16.8 **Positioning of a new product (cross) relative to competitors' products (circles)**

Source: Petersen and Schaltegger 2000: 178

to consumer knowledge and to influence customer perceptions assumes greater importance and, in addition, technical, economic or institutional constraints may have to be overcome.

16.5 Operationalising eco-marketing with the marketing mix

When the positioning strategy to be adopted has been made clear, it is then important to identify the set of product characteristics necessary to secure sales. In order to offer the targeted customer group the desirable product quality in the right place, at the right time and with an appropriate price, four groups of marketing instruments are available:

- Product: product profile
- Place: distribution of the product
- Price: price of the product
- Promotion: communication

Together, the 'four Ps' form the marketing mix. The purpose of marketing plans is to explain operative goals, budgets and the employment of instruments in the marketing mix in detail (Kotler and Bliemel 1999: 144ff.).

16.5.1 *Product: product policy*

Characteristics of products being offered for sale extend beyond the physical products themselves. There is equal concern for packaging (Section 16.5.1.2), branding strategy (Section 16.5.1.3) and the services that accompany products (Section 16.5.1.4). First, however, let us look at product characteristics.

16.5.1.1 The product

Before products can be environmentally improved it is necessary to examine and evaluate the environmental impact added by their production, marketing, sale, consumption and disposal. Products affect the environment in a number of ways, at each stage of their life-cycle—research and development (R&D), design, production, distribution, transportation and disposal. Benefits to the consumer may be added at each stage as well, but business does not realise that benefit until a sale is made. Sales may be made through business-to-business (B2B) transactions, direct marketing to customers and retail marketing.

Environmental impact added accompanies customer benefits (and value added) at every stage. To evaluate the environmental quality of a product, first, the environmental impact added during all the phases of a product's life has to be included. This requires a decision over the beginning and end points of activities related to the product. Second, environmental product quality must be evaluated relative to the potential harm caused by comparable alternatives.

Approaches to evaluating product environmental performance
No products are completely without impact on the environment, but some have a lower impact than others. Consequently, a comparison of relative environmental performance presupposes that environmental impact added and value created (benefit established) can be compared with each other at each stage of the life-cycle. A number of **tools** are available to help with this process of comparison:

- Product ecobalances or life-cycle assessments (Heijungs *et al.* 1992; Nisius and Scholl 1998; Schaltegger and Burritt 2000)

- Product line analysis (Rubik and Teichert 1997)

- ABC classifications and XYZ classifications (Hallay and Pfriem 1992; Rubik and Teichert 1997)

- Quality spinning or eco-compass (Fussler 1999)

Product ecobalance and life-cycle assessment
Product ecobalance assessment provides a basis for a management strategy of continual improvement in line with ISO 14001 environmental management system principles. Ecobalance calculations, popular in German-speaking countries, are

based on the assessment of inputs, outputs and waste of material and energy flows and are known as life-cycle assessment (LCA) if they cover each stage of the product life-cycle. The evaluation of environmental and other benefits and impact added leads to identification of areas for improvement. These have to be evaluated and plans for improvement drawn up. Ecobalance studies have been undertaken in a range of industries, such as those involved in canning, logging, packaging and building materials. In 1990, the first Austrian life-cycle assessment and ecobalance project compared biodegradable packaging material with polyvinyl chloride (PVC), styrofoam and polished wood and old paper packaging. The ecobalance assessment concluded that the BIOPAC product is a sensible packaging alternative in environmental terms. A recommendation was made that it should replace synthetic products and polished wood and old paper packaging that is made dirty by food residues (see www.ioew.at/ioew). The ecobalance process, as shown in Figure 16.9 and as proposed by the federal ministry for the environment (Bundesumweltministerium, BMU) and the environmental federal office (Umweltbundesamt, UBA) in Germany, has four steps:

- Defining and scoping

- Materials and energy balance

- Ecobalance and ecoprofile

- Evaluation

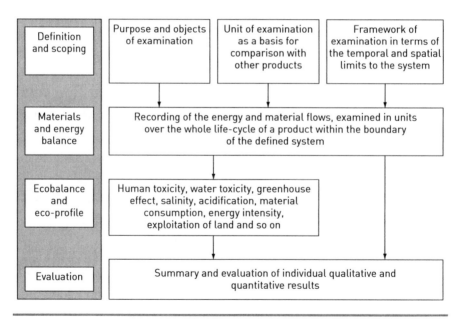

Figure 16.9 Working steps in the process of calculating product ecobalances

Source: BMU and UBA 1995

Product line analysis

According to the Eco-Institute of Freiburg, product line analysis expands the framework for examining products to include social and economic aspects by analysing the correlation between products, their social functions and the underlying economic needs (Rubik and Teichert 1997). For example, this technique has been used for the sustainable modernisation of existing buildings to provide an integrated approach to an economically viable, socially integrative and environmentally sound modernisation of public housing estates. This technique broke new ground both from an eco-constructional point of view as well as with regard to economic and social design in Germany (www.isoe.de/english/projects/nasa/descript.htm).

ABC classifications

In contrast to the above techniques, ABC classifications limit analysis to a few key relevant factors, using a simple evaluation yardstick for making decisions. ABC analysis (also known as the 80/20 rule or Pareto analysis) distinguishes between environmental problems that are thought to be particularly urgent (class A problems), problems that need to be addressed in the medium term (class B problems) and less-relevant environmental impacts (class C problems) in the product life-cycle.

Quality spinning or eco-compass

Quality spinning highlights the comparison of what the best environmental product should be and what the product actually is. If a specific function and use can be identified and a single recommendation is possible, analysis merely has to rank the options and select the best one from these (e.g. the use of biodegradable packaging material in a specific case). The comparison becomes more difficult when different products have different environmental impacts as well as slightly different functions and uses. In these cases comparison along a number of dimensions is needed. For example, comparison of the environmental impacts of non-returnable products with re-usable products (e.g. nappies, towels, packaging) is complicated by the fact that the environmental effects of different cleaning methods and forms of transportation can be linked to production and waste in only a qualitative way.

Likewise, comparison between environmental risks and the consumption of resources causes special problems. Assessment of the environmental credentials of atomic energy and fossil fuels, or the decision whether to try to reduce pesticide use through the introduction of genetically manipulated seed corn, cannot be determined solely through a scientific assessment of risk. Therefore, environmental products must provide environmental protection as well as avoid high-risk outcomes.

Information-gathering and principles for designing environmentally improved products

Usually, products consist of a bundle of functions, represented by aesthetic and symbolic values. Possession of a car provides mobility, independence, a hobby, the experience of speed, status and substitution for a partner. These multiple functions are perceived in cultural and individual contexts (Bredemeier *et al.* 1997). Therefore, comparison of the environmental impact added by a car trip per kilometre of distance travelled with the alternatives 'rail travel', 'car pooling', 'video conference' or 'virtual team meeting' presupposes that a common function exists, which is rare in practice. This means that the possibility of obtaining an environmental evaluation of alternative products is limited (Spiller 1996). It is also linked to information costs, which are often ignored in calculations.

Provision, by associations and research institutes, of 'base data' (also called 'basic inventory data') about average environmental effects from the use of raw materials is designed to reduce the cost of information-gathering. Such averaging of information reduces its quality—so much so that in many cases the loss in quality leads to incorrect comparative decisions being made (Pohl *et al.* 1996; Schaltegger and Burritt 2000). Hence, current ecobalance methods based on industry-average information are either to be avoided (Schaltegger 1997) or to be treated with considerable caution. However, a number of **principles** can help in the search **for environmentally improved product alternatives** that offer the opportunity for customers to 'unfreeze' their old views and 'refreeze' them after reconditioning (see Antes 1997; Fleig 1997; Hopfenbeck and Jasch 1995; Maunders and Burritt 1991; Stahel 1997):

- Product and material producer responsibility. This may involve
  - Avoiding use of materials that are harmful to health and the environment
  - Use of repurchase guarantees
  - The recycling or re-use of materials in new products
  - The use of 'material passports', monitored by a regulator, to trace environmental impacts generated along the value creation chain

- Life-cycle orientation. This may involve
  - The design of products that can be dismantled and recycled
  - The use of eco-labels for prefabricated parts and materials
  - The use of recyclable materials in production (e.g. the use of recycled glass in new glass production)
  - The reconditioning and re-use of product modules (e.g. toner cartridges) and products (e.g. photocopiers)

- Regionality and seasonality. This may involve
  - The purchase of inputs produced close to the main production facilities
  - The production of seasonal products

- Product durability. This may be achieved through
  - Use of robust processing
  - Use of replaceable modules
  - Design for cheap and effective repair and maintenance
  - The abandonment of rapid design changes make solely for cosmetic reasons

- Consistency. This may be achieved through
  - The harmonisation of industrial and natural metabolic processes
  - The use of materials that are easy to dismantle
  - 'Cold' utilisation of fossil materials (fuel cells)

- Dematerialisation. This may be achieved through
  - Increased resource productivity
  - Transportation of products in compact containers
  - A reduction in energy use

- Intensification of use. This may be achieved by
  - Reprocessing old products
  - Sharing and leasing products

- Sufficiency. This may involve
  - Rejection of certain product components that produce a minor benefit to the consumer but have a significant environmental impact (e.g. the use of clear plastic folders by banks, or the daily change of all towels in hotel rooms)
  - Sharing products with irregular use (e.g. car sharing, rental services)

16.5.1.2 Packaging

Packaging reduction and waste separation have been targeted in the past few years. For example, in 1988 the soft-drink industry in the USA used an average 453 g of packaging in the manufacture and distribution of each litre of soft drinks. By 1998, the amount of packaging used had been reduced to only 148 g per litre of drink, a reduction of 67% (see www.softdrink.ca/psreduen.htm). Some regions are aiming to achieve zero landfill waste by 2010 (e.g. the Australian Capital Territory, www.act. gov.au/nowaste/wastestrategy). Waste going to landfill has been reduced in the ACT from 78% in 1993/94 to 36% in 2001/02 (see www.act.gov.au/nowaste/2001-2002Progress.xls). However, because packaging is mixed with other waste at the collection point, a lack of accounting data means that the proportion of packaging in household waste is not separately derived. In Germany today, involvement in the dual system is the minimum requirement,[21] and even this—in international comparison—relatively progressive system is not thought to be enough by environmental associations and institutes if packaging reduction and recycling are to be encouraged. Meffert and Kirchgeorg (1998: 299) estimate that the packaging share in household waste was still 50% of total household garbage in Germany in 1998, and so the aim is commendable but will be difficult to achieve.

The same criteria for assessing the environmental impacts of packaging apply as for other aspects of products. Packaging provides protection for the product it contains (e.g. by absorbing impacts and vibrations in distribution) and for humans (e.g. through features that indicate if products have been tampered with). It provides communication through symbols that are read only by machines (e.g. barcodes) and intensive communication through vibrant colours and many printed messages that help sell the product and inform users and consumers of the attributes of the product it contains. Packaging provides consumers and users with enormous convenience. For example, products can be found in many different sizes and at various locations—something that would be nearly impossible without packaging.

21 For more information on the 'dual system', see www.gruener-punkt.de.

The trend towards the encouragement of product use by means of building convenience and practical benefit into the packaging (e.g. toothpaste tubes that stand up on end, or packets that contain complete meals for one person) means that, more and more, packaging is seen as part of the core product (Kotler and Bliemel 1999: 711ff.). Such multi-dimensional functionality draws attention to the situation that care must be taken to highlight trade-offs in customer benefits when environmental issues are taken into consideration. For example, the removal of plastic wrap around meat products may reduce the use of plastics but may be unhygienic and lead to health problems. Strategies for the reduction of packaging and multiple usage can therefore be successful only when they do not cut out the functional variety provided by packaging and instead interpret it in an environmentally benign way in relation to consumers.

16.5.1.3 Branding

As with packaging, the product brand is becoming increasingly important in shaping the product profile. The relationship between brand name and product are intertwined through the communication process (Bergmann 1996). Branding uses names, symbols, labels and layout to guarantee that a product is recognisable and distinct from competitive products in the market. The brand signals both the origin of the product and supplier responsibility for the product. Brand names create trust and are particularly helpful for promoting the environmental qualities of products when these would otherwise not be apparent (Hansen and Kull 1995).

From the customer's point of view, brands are welcome because they reduce the demand for information during purchase decisions. They also provide status through the image they generate, recognition of the brand name and expected high quality. In short, brands create a mental picture that provides focus for the customer when choosing between several alternatives. Eco-labels in particular contain highly concentrated, simplified messages about the environmental quality of a product.

From the supplier's point of view, branding enhances the opportunity for initial sales and repeat buying. By differentiating a product from its rivals, branding provides some scope for pricing discretion, although the extent of discretion depends on the market structure (Meffert and Kirchgeorg 1998: 305). Businesses often ask which type of branding they should use. Three main types of branding are identified and analysed by Temporal (1999):

- Product branding

- Corporate branding (sometimes referred to as umbrella or monolithic branding)

- House branding (sometimes referred to as endorsement branding)

Product branding
Product branding communicates information about the product. Procter & Gamble made product branding famous with products such as Tide® washing powder, where each individual product has its own brand name. With this strategy, the company name is either totally or virtually absent. It gives each brand the opportunity

to have unique values, personality, identity and positioning. As a consequence, this approach implies that every new product the company brings on to the market is a new brand and can be positioned precisely for a specific market segment.

Product branding makes it easier for the company to evaluate brand performance and value and makes for better resource allocation decisions. Moreover, if the product is a flop or is involved in a marketing disaster, the bad news does not attach itself to the company name. Product branding is costly, though, as advertising and promotion costs cannot be shared with other company products and its success depends on the product itself having a sustainable competitive advantage and clear positioning in the marketplace.

Product branding can also go further to product range branding, where a number of products or services in a broad category are grouped together under one brand name and promoted with one basic identity. An example here would be Intel's Pentium®.

Corporate branding

Corporate branding is where the corporate name is the brand, and here the products tend to be described more in alpha-numeric or letter terms rather than having distinctive brand names. Such is the case with the vehicle manufacturer BMW. Corporate branding gives each product the strength of the corporate brand values and positioning and saves a great deal on advertising and promotional spending. It builds up the strength of the corporate brand and its financial value.

Corporate branding is very appropriate for those companies engaged in service industries, as their products are more intangible in nature. When consumers cannot see the product, the company brand name helps to give the consumer an assurance of quality, heritage and authenticity. Many Asian companies have taken this route because the commitment and longevity of the company are judged to be of great importance in their countries. One of the great proponents of corporate branding is Sony Corporation (www.brandingasia.com/columns/temporal2.htm).

House or endorsement branding

House or endorsement branding uses both of the above ideas, with the corporate name placed alongside the product brand name, as is the case with Nestlé's Milo®, Nestlé's Milky Bar® or Kellogg's Corn Flakes®. This allows the product brand not only to assume its own identity and positioning but also to draw strength from the values of the corporate brand, giving consumers the assurance—in many cases related to quality—of the corporate brand. There are a variety of ways in which this can be achieved, with the corporate brand having lesser or greater prominence.

House branding also provides some economies of scale in advertising and promotion and helps with the introduction of new products, where it can be very difficult to break into mature markets without the endorsement of a strong and credible corporate parental brand name. One possible disadvantage is where the product is not favourably received and causes damage to the parental brand name.

In 1998 Nestlé paid £2.5 billion for Rowntree, best known for its fruit pastilles, Kit Kat® and other global brands—a company whose net assets were valued at only £300 million. In the same year, tobacco giant Philip Morris paid four times the net asset worth of Kraft to take over the company best known for its dairy products.

Brand names can turn into an essential component of the enterprise's value. Hence, brand construction justifies large investments for formation, testing, advertising, guarantees and brand maintenance.

Eco-branding

Similar considerations apply to the development of an eco-brand. Concern for eco-efficiency will encourage business to stimulate favourable eco-brand recognition in the most important market segments.

- Corporate eco-branding is exemplified by The Body Shop, with its mission statement (www.thebodyshop.com.au/infopage.cfm?pageid=53) which commits the company to the pursuit of social and ecological change as a constant reminder of its responsibilities to act in order to protect the environment, both globally and locally, and to strive for continuous improvements in its performance. Greenline Paper provides a second example. In this case the company provides 'green' office supplies.

- Product eco-brands include Juice®—a source of 'green' energy supply, produced by npower and Greenpeace in the United Kingdom, but without corporate branding.[22]

- House branding is represented by the Amazon EcoMall bookstore (see www.ecomall.com/biz/book.htm). This combines the strength of the corporate brand with an environmental product.

Eco-labels can be applied to each of these types of brand. The European Eco-label Internet site (europa.eu.int/comm/environment/ecolabel) lists products and manufacturers that have received their Flower eco-label, thereby providing information for any consumer who is familiar with product, company or house branding.

Businesses can also:

- Build on the credibility of their traditional brand (e.g. Kellogg's, Nestlé)

- Compose their own eco-label (e.g. Amazon EcoMall)

- Adopt the label of:
  - A neutral institution (e.g. the Forest Stewardship Council)
  - State or regional institution (e.g. the Blue Angel, Flower or Green Choice eco-labels)
  - A non-governmental organisation (e.g. Greenpeace, WWF [i.e. through its Panda label])
  - Manufacturing association (e.g. Bioland, Sustainable Forestry Initiative of the American Forestry and Paper Association)

A comprehensive list of these options is available at the website of Ecolabels.org (www.eco-labels.org/search_guide.cfm), searchable by label and by product.

---

22 See the comments made at www.npower.com/html/juiceandwindpower_4467.htm; for example: 'The really good news is that you can have it supplied to your home today, and at absolutely no extra cost compared to your existing supply. We're working to lower your bills and we're providing you with a clean, green choice!'

From the above observations some conclusions can be drawn regarding eco-marketing: trust and credibility are important. To obtain trust in eco-brands and eco-labels requires investment of time and other resources, or market power. Unknown brands are not trusted and will not be trusted unless they are publicised. Credibility is correlated to name recognition—corporate or product—and also to advertising budget. Verification of compliance with the criteria established for eco-labels is also an important source of credibility. Also, ownership and use of the eco-label can be separated to great effect, as a non-compliant label user can be excluded from use. Such a situation will strengthen consumer perceptions of the value of a user acquiring the label.

Some organisations generate an eco-label that is seen as exclusive to the business—to capture the maximum amount of product differentiation. Evidence suggests that eco-labels based on exclusiveness do not usually achieve the strong reputation associated with labels of neutral organisations (see Bodenstein and Spiller 1995; Hansen and Kull 1995). Environmental brands and labels of neutral organisations have the additional advantage of being able to externalise the costs of creating a brand or label.

16.5.1.4 Services accompanying products

Environmental services accompanying products can make it possible for the business to obtain and secure a competitive advantage (Simon 1996: 51ff.). In the environmental context, customer service fulfils the following key functions (Meffert and Kirchgeorg 1998: 314; Hansen and Jeschke 1995):

- It offers advice at the time of purchase in order to make transparent the environmental advantages of the product, to help avoid inappropriate purchases by customers and to provide tips about use of the product in an environmentally friendly way.

- It provides service instructions and installation in order to help the consumer use the product in an environmentally benign way and to help guarantee a long product life.

- It manages complaints and offers advice on problems when the expected environmental advantages do not materialise; this function includes the provision of information about consumer associations and ombudsmen.

- It provides cleaning, maintenance and repair services, designed to prolong product usage.

- It offers the repurchase of product and disposal services, to facilitate re-use and recycling.

Can business charge for these services in order to make it a profitable part of business? Ideally, each service offered can be transformed from a free additional service that supports sales of core products into a core service with its own market adding value for customers (Homburg and Garbe 1996). In practice, support services helpful to the environment are better developed in the industrial goods (B2B) sector than in consumer goods markets. Services that preserve product values (e.g. professional reconditioning, repair and maintenance of worn or defect parts) still do not appear as attractive as they should in consumer goods markets because of their perceived cost in comparison with the cost of a new product. Lack of taxation incentives for prolonging product life does not help the situation.

16.5.2 Place: distribution of the product

Distribution decisions are related to the whole life-cycle of a product from the supply of inputs, through manufacturing, to the final buyer and product disposal. Distribution is sometimes referred to as **logistics**. The aim is the preparation and removal of a product in the **time** that suits the customer, in the right **place** and in the **volume** demanded. Distribution channels are normally arranged through other businesses, such as wholesalers, retailers, warehouses, transport businesses and waste disposal specialists. The physical flow of goods is paralleled by a flow of information in the opposite direction, relating, for example, to the obligation of a manufacturer to take back used packaging, deal with orders for spare parts or respond to complaints made by customers (Kotler and Bliemel 1999: 821).

The first environmental tasks are related to resource-saving logistics; for instance, by using different transportation means, such as rail or ship, by using inventory control to reduce deliveries and by bundling products together (Meffert and Kirchgeorg 1998: 346ff.). Logistic decisions involve the employment of packaging for transportation (e.g. the use of re-usable containers) as well as systems for returning goods and the use of decentralised locations for production in order to reduce long haulage. Internet, telephone and faxed purchasing for B2B (business-to business) and final-consumer transactions reduce the need for customers to be transported to the purchasing site themselves. New communication devices also encourage the creation of virtual warehouses that can economise on inventories in store as well as achieve an efficient bundling of products for delivery. Hence, there is a trade-off between the environmental aspects of transportation and communication when considering environmentally sustainable futures (Janelle 1997: 39).

Furthermore, on the one hand, globalisation of markets encourages growth in environmental problems associated with transportation, because of the additional distances covered and the increased volume of pollutants generated. On the other hand, calls for tighter security, caused by uncertainty over potential terrorist threats, encourage local sourcing of products, because, for example, staff of transportation companies are better known and problems with security delays at customs can be avoided. Development of just-in-time (JIT) purchasing systems has also increased the number of deliveries in recent years (Janelle 1997: 39).

Factors such as these show that the reduction of environmental impacts associated with transportation are influenced by a complex web of issues, many of which are at present dominated by other considerations (e.g. lower labour costs in overseas countries). The challenge is how to make environmental issues more relevant in an eco-marketing strategy to gain competitive advantage while businesses consider their own position in relation to the following questions:

- Will smaller consignments associated with JIT deliveries continue to be encouraged by the introduction of more advanced, cheaper, information technologies and control technologies?

- What are the environmental costs of JIT systems and how should they be taken into account?

- Could use of Internet bulletin boards among transport companies facilitate the use of excess space, allowing greater capacity usage on road transport and improving competition with rail and air?

- Will new information systems and communications tools be used to reduce trips by managers and administrators, also reducing costs and environmental impacts (e.g. by use of virtual meetings and car pooling)?

16.5.3 The price

Product price is important, but in many industries—for example, in oligopolies, where there are a few large businesses acting as price leaders and a fringe of smaller players—competition and marketing tend to emphasise product differentiation. Environmental products will be affected by the price of goods on offer in comparison with other goods, but other factors affect overall success. Examined below are different agreement terms, guarantees and arrangements for payment. Prices and associated trading conditions vary over each product life-cycle—from development, through introduction to the market, to the establishment of the branding strategy and then possible saturation of the market and replacement with a new product.

16.5.3.1 The market price

From a competitive market perspective, production costs are only of secondary importance when determining the price of the product on offer. Businesses are price-takers. If they charge too much, they make insufficient sales to stay in business. If they do not charge enough, they cannot cover costs and they go out of business. In this respect, they live on a knife edge, unless they can differentiate their products through marketing. It is only when the costs per unit increase in the case of an increasing amount of production that the maximum profit lies in selling a quantity below the maximum amount of turnover. The ability of customers to pay—known as **effective demand**—is expressed through the **price elasticity of demand**. The price elasticity of demand measures the responsiveness of quantity demanded in relation to a change in price. With **elastic demand** there is no opportunity for price to be different from the amount determined in the market. With **inelastic demand** a business has some discretion over the sale price, because it has an advantage over the competition (e.g. a brand advantage). Hence, decisions about the product price policy depend on the ability to pay, the prices charged by competitors and life-cycle costs (Meffert 1998). Figure 16.10 illustrates that maximum turnover for a product is limited by price, all other things being equal, and is influenced by the price elasticity of demand.

Price elasticity is a function of the general ability and readiness of customers to pay and of existing prices being charged by competitors. For example, small products, such as a cake, have a relatively low price elasticity (i.e. they are characterised by inelastic demand). If the price of a cake is $1.00, then very few people would be willing to travel to the next cake shop in order to save 5 cents—that is to

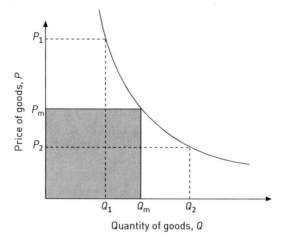

Quantity of goods, Q

Note: Price elasticity is proportional to the magnitude of the gradient of the curve; the point (Q_1, P_1) has the smallest price elasticity (inelastic demand with small change of quantity when price changes, such as for many transportation services) and the point (Q_2, P_2) has the largest price elasticity (already a small price change leads to a large change of quantity demanded, such as with many textiles); maximum turnover, Q_m, corresponds to price P_m and is defined by the price where the shaded area representing the proceeds (number of items sold multiplied by the price of each item) is maximised.

Figure 16.10 **Price elasticity of demand and maximum turnover**

say, 5%. In these circumstances, payment of 5 cents more for a bio-cake would be equally acceptable. If the purchase of technical goods is being considered, a 5% difference in price is important, as consumers shop around for the best price. If an eco-label is associated with products that cost more, then a high price elasticity will lead to lost demand. Usually, if the price is a small part of the consumer's budget, then demand is inelastic; also, if there are no substitutes, then price is inelastic.

In the long term, sales turnover also needs to account for the reaction of competitors and the ability of customers to find alternative sources of supply. Over time, price elasticity tends to increase. If the price is perceived as stable, it builds confidence and loyalty in the eyes of the customer. Environmental products do not have to be more expensive, but commercial pressure will tie eco-products back to the business's profitability goals. Profitability calculations presuppose that costs are covered, and so environmental cost calculation is an important part of the pricing process for eco-products (see Fichter *et al.* 1997; Schaltegger and Burritt 2000). Identification of the environmental costs of products helps people in business to avoid cross-subsidisation of conventional products. In fact, there may be a case for cross-subsidies in favour of environmental products as part of the investment process designed to establish a new eco-brand image. Environmental and economic **reasons** can be given in support **of such initial cross-subsidisation**:

- Environmental. Eco-products can provide a good image for business as well as favourable media coverage, and cross-subsidies can thus be justified. When these advantages disappear, eco-products must 'stand on their own two feet' or they will lose their popularity, and budgets will be restricted.[23] Subsidies can be used to establish eco-products at the beginning of their life-cycle but have to be withdrawn once the products are established.

● Economic. Growth of the market for eco-products will not occur without a sufficient return being available to business. Investment in continual eco-efficiency improvements will be necessary to establish the foundation for such growth and for the achievement of an acceptable economic return. Subsidies can be used to encourage the take-up of eco-efficiency projects.

Many eco-pioneers pursue a high-price strategy and accept that demand for eco-products will be restricted to niche markets. This means that, for example, the lower market share and small quantities (e.g. of organic processed cotton) lead to greater cost (see e.g. Box 10.11 on pages 133-34), and this extra cost is passed on to the customer. An absorption strategy, where the higher costs of eco-products are absorbed by other products, is rarely pursued but is appropriate where the mass market can be captured.

16.5.3.2 The terms of agreement

Whether or not an eco-product is acceptable to the buyer is not determined solely by the purchase price. Transaction costs also have a part to play, such as those associated with the terms of the agreement—including services offered, guarantees and payment arrangements. Leasing rather than transferring ownership has attracted close attention in the sale of eco-products. Leasing provides the flexibility for customers to keep up with technology when environmental standards are becoming tighter over time and when purchase for investment would require large amounts of capital. It provides better cost control and regular cash flow, which improves liquidity and tax advantages. An important advantage to the lessor (the business owning the product) is tax advantages that can be passed on to the lessee (the customer using the product). The financing of environmentally friendly products such as those listed by the US Environmental Protection Agency (EPA) on its website can all be undertaken through leasing (www.epa.gov/opptintr/epp).

For example, the US EPA makes the following observations about environmental problems with carpets:

> Environmental and health concerns associated with carpet include indoor air quality, toxic chemical emissions from manufacturing and disposal operations and solid waste impacts. A variety of volatile organic compounds (VOCs) can be emitted from carpet materials. For example, 4-phenylcyclohexene has a very low odour threshold and has been associated with indoor air quality complaints following the installation of new carpet. Other compounds emitted from carpet, such as formaldehyde and styrene, can present acute or chronic health concerns under certain exposure conditions. The manufacture and disposal by incineration of polyvinyl chloride, a common component of carpet backing, is a source of dioxin contamination in the environment. Dioxin is a potent carcinogen

---

23   This is referred to as the infant industry argument; infant industries need to be nurtured to start with, but eventually have to be self-supporting.

that is highly persistent in the environment and bioaccumulates through the food chain.

In addition, carpets, once used, tend to be disposed of at landfills. Avoiding these problems is a clear goal of eco-carpet production and sales. Interface, the largest commercial carpet manufacturer in the world (www.interfaceinc.com), addressed these issues and then introduced leasing of carpets rather than selling carpets, the idea being that at the end of the carpet's useful life, the company reclaims and recycles it (see footnote 18 on page 213).

16.5.4 Promotion: communication

The final part of the marketing mix refers to the process of informing consumers about the company's products. Marketing is synonymous with communicating; a marketer is a communicator. All aspects of the marketing process involve communication. Marketing promotion—mass-media advertising, public relations (PR) and publicity, sales promotion, events and personal selling—represent only one part of the marketing communication process. Aspects of product, price and place, as well as the nature and quality of research and service, also involve communication. As a marketer the comment that one 'cannot not communicate' (Watzlawick *et al.* 1990) emphasises that all the elements of the marketing mix can be seen as components of business communication. Product design provides messages about product functions. Whether products are sold in a discount or specialist shop is as revealing for the buyer as price signals. As already pointed out, eco-marketing aims at promoting credibility in the eyes of the potential consumer. In the narrower sense, a distinction can be made between marketing communication in the form of a monologue or a dialogue.

16.5.4.1 Instruments of monologue

A monologue involves one-way communication. In marketing this is where the marketer initiates the communication and controls the content and form of communication and where it is delivered all at the same time. Marketing communications verified or supported by third parties help to improve the credibility of monologues. These include eco-labels and endorsements by independent researchers, both designed to simplify messages in the face of limited consumer cognitive capacity at a time when so many messages are being projected in a short space of time by different communications media. In the context of 'green' products, advertising can build on accumulated factual knowledge about the environment.

A credibility problem occurs when environmentally unsound products are offered for sale in parallel to the environmental product line. For example, many eco-funds are offered to investors in parallel to investment funds that are constructed solely in terms of their economic returns. In these circumstances, it is important for business to seek continuous improvement in overall performance in relation to environmental goals. This should be part of the business's goals and would need to be communicated to outside parties: for example, by documentation of a continuous decrease in the average consumption of paint by an automobile producer, by publicity about the removal or substitution of dubious products from the trade range or by the rejection of advertisements for more harmful environmental product variants.

Unilateral communication aims to improve credibility through every form of advertisement and PR. The paradoxical result is that generation of a one-sided view of legitimacy or credibility with respect to environmental products is destined for disaster. Interactive communication holds the promise of considerable benefit in eco-marketing (Balderjahn 1986).

16.5.4.2 Instruments of dialogue

A dialogue is a conversation between two or more people. In the age of information technology, marketing communication can be customer-initiated, customer-controlled and ongoing between the business and the customer. Information dialogue through the Internet adds to the success of eco-marketing, as it is a customer-driven process for reducing possible asymmetries between the business and customers. It means that relationships, rather than transactions, are important.

Relational marketing involves all the marketing activities that are focused on getting to know customers and their needs better, cherishing, serving and including customers in consideration of the product life-cycle. Its purpose is the generation of trust and customer involvement with the product (Bruhn 1999; Kotler and Bliemel 1999: 75ff.).

Relational marketing is based on the observation that the acquisition of new customers is usually more expensive than the maintenance of existing relationships (Bruhn 1999). It creates better conditions for integrating customer views, desires and knowledge in product development. In short, it encourages customer involvement and commitment by facilitating exchange of views while maintaining customer privacy. With investment goods, solutions to specific marketing problems often develop in common. In the consumer goods sector, relational marketing uses standardised instruments such as the customer hotline or PO boxes for complaints (Hansen and Hennig 1995). If customer access goes beyond these, the possibility of enhancing consumer competence and influencing consumer behaviour improves.

The generation of trust also involves dialogue about customer needs, product shortcomings and a detailed assessment of specific products. The quality of the marketing relationship can then be measured by the course of the dialogue (Balderjahn 1996). Measures of dialogue include:

● The business interaction frequency plan. One of the most interesting Internet marketing plan decisions is the frequency of contact desired by the business. This includes:
  – Goals for user access frequency. How often does the business want users to visit its site, and what actions should the business take to make that happen?
  – Contact frequency guidelines. How frequent can the outgoing business communication be, and what factors govern this? The answer to this question determines the limit on direct outgoing communication methods.

● A trigger event matrix. Trigger events are customer activities that signal a dramatic change in the purchase probabilities for some group of products or services. Possible triggers include temporal factors (length of time since last visit), activity-based factors (shopping cart requested) or personal factors (such as birthdays) as evidenced in the user profile. A matrix combining triggers and actions is a powerful guide to system capabilities and data-collection needs.

● Responsiveness. One metric many companies find useful and challenging is very straightforward—the time to respond to an outgoing communication (e.g. to an e-mail, or an invitation to complete a questionnaire). Marketers may decide on average response times and on having special rules for critical customers (Hanson 2000).

Customer opinions become particularly relevant in the after-purchase phase. Complaints, suggestions for improvement or expressions of satisfaction create starting points for the further development and maintenance of a continuing, long-run relationship. Relational marketing is therefore closely associated with offering customers services associated with the product. There are potential problems, however. Customers are often in two minds about establishing relationships with business because these lead to implicit obligations and limit their freedom to choose. Many customers prefer anonymity and self-service in order to evade salespeople who appeal to customers to make a particular purchase. In addition, relational marketing produces costs for the supplier and the consumer. If personal contact is not preferred by the customer, anonymous relationship structures such as mail order through the various techniques available (e.g. e-mails or hotlines) connected with a well-known company or brand have to be established.

In summary, eco-marketing has to accomplish the task of communicating consistent information about the potential environmental benefits of the product to the user and about the associated promises regarding improvements to overall environmental quality. Business has to avoid making exaggerated promises or claims. For example, claims that consumption of environmentally friendly goods will lead to a more sustainable society as well as to heightened self-satisfaction for the consumer are costly to the business if these outcomes do not occur. If the products are customer-led, made specifically for the customer, based on lifetime pricing (i.e. including disposal costs), sold with the permission of the customer rather than based on persuasion, as befits a network-age marketing strategy, then the business is less likely to lose customers or to end up in court for having made false claims.

16.5.5 Megamarketing

Marketing is an individual concept that extends to any social unit consisting of individuals, groups, organisations, communities or nations of human beings. Shapiro (1985) demonstrates how a marketing programme must fit the needs of the marketplace, the skills of the business and the vagaries of the competition. The logical extension of this is to extend the marketing mix to the political, legal and sociocultural spheres, which establish the framework conditions for the market (see also

Chapter 7 and Table 7.1 on page 58). In other words, there is a need to fit the marketing programme with the legal sphere of influence, including the political environment and public opinion where these variables are important. This has been discussed under the term 'mega-marketing' by Kotler (1986), in the context of companies acting as agents changing regulatory and social market conditions (Schneidewind 1998), and more extensively under the term 'transitional marketing' (Belz 2001; Schneidewind 1998).

Regulations provide protection against unfair competition such as that resulting from misleading advertising about the environmental protection provided by products (Cordes 1994).

In the European Union (EU), eco-labels containing words such as 'bio' or 'eco' for vegetable products are strictly controlled. For example, the European Flower eco-label is controlled by Regulation (EC) 1980/2000, enacted on 17 July 2000 through the European Parliament and the European Council (europa.eu.int/comm/environment/ecolabel/background/pm_regulation.htm). The Flower scheme is part of a broader strategy aimed at promoting sustainable production and consumption. Being a market-based instrument, the primary function of the EU eco-label is to stimulate the supply and demand of those products having a reduced environmental impact. With respect to supply, the EU eco-label has a clear objective of encouraging businesses to market 'greener', officially licensed products. On the demand side, the European scheme gives consumers the means to make informed environmental purchasing choices. The Flower eco-label provides assurance of European 'green' authenticity.

The objective to 'provide guidance to consumers' has considerable implications for economic efficiency and the flow of information. In fact, the Flower eco-label will reduce costs for consumers, manufacturers and retailers by lowering the time and effort needed to obtain and provide reliable information on life-cycle considerations, 'green' products and specific European know-how.

Furthermore, it has a European rather than a single -country dimension. A manufacturer, retailer or service provider that meets the criteria for a product group and that applies for the award of the eco-label can market its eco-labelled product throughout the 15 member states of the EU. The Flower eco-label is also accepted and present in those counties that are signatories to the European Eco-label Agreement (Norway, Iceland and Liechtenstein) (europa.eu.int/comm/environment/ecolabel/description/scheme.htm). Links to candidate countries are being built up. The European approach avoids a company having to make an application in every country and thus avoids time-consuming and costly procedures. The same logo is used regardless of the product group in question, thereby eliminating confusion in the minds of consumers caused by the large number of self-proclaimed claims and 'green' logos in existence. In addition:

- It is selective. The label is awarded only to those products with the lowest environmental impact in a product range. Product categories are carefully defined so that all products that have direct 'equivalence of use', as seen through the eyes of the consumer, are included in the same product group.

- It is transparent. Transparency and widespread participation are further enhanced by the considerable input of representatives of industry, commerce, environmental and consumer organisations and trade unions. International observers are regularly invited and informed by the Commission and by the members of the European Union Eco-labelling Board.

● It uses multiple criteria. Eco-label criteria are not based on one single parameter but, rather, rest on studies that analyse the impact of the product or service on the environment throughout its life-cycle, starting from raw material extraction in the pre-production stage, and continuing through production, distribution and disposal of the product or service.

● It is voluntary. The scheme does not set ecological standards that all manufacturers must meet. It is for the producer, retailer or service provider to decide whether or not to apply.

At the same time, products eco-labelled in the EU scheme provide the guarantee that their compliance with established ecological criteria has been tested by independent third parties, the national and regional eco-label competent bodies. Information, as used by the scheme, is a key characteristic of EU market-based environmental policy. As such schemes are developing rapidly throughout the world, diffusion of information about the environmental effects of the product over its whole life-cycle is essential in order to support sustainable consumption patterns. This leads to consideration of the environmental accounting systems that are available and that are required in order to provide information as an input to such schemes. Such systems are the subject of the next chapter.

Questions for review

16.1 What are marketing and eco-marketing?

16.2 If a business increases its throughput, or turnover, does this mean that it must have an increasing demand for material goods that will eventually cause an environmental problem because these goods are scarce? In your answer, explain the meanings of Factor 4 and Factor 10.

16.3 Is there such a thing as an environmentally responsible consumer? Can eco-marketing help consumers to be more environmentally responsible? Give reasons for your views. Consider the importance of cognitive involvement in your answer. Can eco-marketing help producers to be more environmentally responsible?

16.4 Explain why differences between decision processes—extensive, limited, impulsive and habitual—are important when one is trying to involve consumers in 'green' purchasing. Would your answer be different for business-to-business purchasing instead of retail purchasing?

16.5 Why would a company seek to encourage emotional detachment by customers from the product once purchased? How does it affect the environment? How would 'green' businesses respond to this aspect of marketing?

16.6 What are the two strategies for business to adopt that help reduce environmental impacts caused by consumers during consumption? Can businesses be encouraged to reduce consumption of their own products in the interests of reducing environmental impact?

16.7 How does the top-line eco-marketing framework use environmental consciousness to promote sales of 'green' products? Are there any constraints on the use of environmental consciousness to promote 'green' consumption patterns?

16.8 Choose a product from one environmentally sensitive industry and examine steps in the process of strategic eco-marketing of that product.

16.9 Conjoint analysis can be applied to eco-marketing. What is conjoint analysis? How is it linked to the eco-marketing of a product?

16.10 Do marketing research and market research differ? Explain.

16.11 Examine the circumstances in which market research should be outsourced.

16.12 When adopting an eco-marketing strategy, does it matter to a business whether competitors already have a strategy, and what the strategy for eco-management is? Illustrate your answer with an example taken from the detergents market.

16.13 How do breadth and depth of business fields differ? Explain why the difference is important for:
  - Small businesses
  - Businesses emerging in a developing country

16.14 When will businesses position their environmental products close to the competition? In these circumstances, are there any predictable reactions from:
  - Customers?
  - Competitors?

16.15 Implementation of an eco-marketing strategy calls on four instruments: product, place, price and promotion. What is the collective name given to these four instruments? How does an eco-marketing plan bringing these four instruments together differ from a conventional marketing plan?

16.16 'A comparison of relative environmental performance presupposes that environmental impact added and value created (benefit established) can be compared with each other at each stage of the life-cycle.' A range of tools is available for such comparisons. Briefly outline the two tools that you consider to be the most important for this purpose, specifying the reasons for your choice.

16.17 Can packaging be unbundled from the products being sold by business in a market economy? Explain the reasons for your answer.

16.18 What is branding? What is an eco-label? Is an eco-label a brand? When answering this question:
  - Consider Temporal's views
  - Consider the Forest Stewardship Council or Marine Stewardship Council eco-labels

16.19 Who controls a brand? Who controls an eco-label? Does control matter? If credibility of a brand is associated with name recognition, who *should* pay for and who *does* pay for the development and maintenance of an eco-label developed by a 'neutral' institution? Provide an example.

16.20 Explain the relationship between just-in-time purchasing systems and the environmental impacts of business activity.

16.21 Why might cross-subsidisation be justifiable when introducing a new eco-brand on to the market?

16.22 Is eco-marketing synonymous with communicating? Justify your view. How does eco-marketing through the Internet differ from eco-marketing through a letter-drop? Is the Internet an instrument of monologue, dialogue or both?

16.23 Why might a business wish to measure the dialogue with its customers for communicating environmental information about:

  – The product?
  – The business?

What means for measuring dialogue are available?

Concepts and tools of corporate environmental management

Environmental accounting

Accountants gather data and provide purpose-oriented information for management as an aid to decision-making and as a basis for fulfilling accountability to internal and external stakeholders (Section 17.1). Good information can be an important foundation for improving a company's environmental record and contributing towards its sustainable development. The fundamental accounting process is outlined in Section 17.2. Environmental accounting provides monetary, physical and qualitative information to management about the environmental impacts of business and the financial consequences of environmentally relevant business activities—information that supports internal and external decision-making, reporting and accountability (Section 17.3).

17.1 Accounting and purpose-oriented information

Accounting fulfils a number of functions in an organisation. First, it provides **feedback to stakeholders about performance**. Some stakeholders, such as managers, can be thought of as being internal to the business, whereas others are seen as being external (see Fig. 17.1). Directors and managers are accountable to shareholders for the use of corporate resources. They have a position of stewardship over the resources entrusted to them. Accounting information provides feedback to internal (e.g. employees) and external (e.g. shareholders) stakeholders about stewardship of these resources. In practice, the distinction between internal and external stakeholders is blurred because, for example, managers may well own shares or share options, combining internal and external perspectives.

Second, it provides **information to managers to support the decisions** that they need to make. These include decisions such as determining the short-run price of their products, the mix of products and services to offer customers and the quality

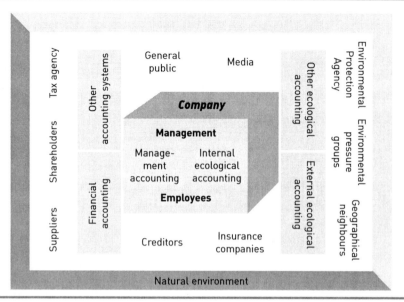

Figure 17.1 **Accounting systems and stakeholders**

Source: Schaltegger and Burritt 2000: 32

of their products. The making of long-run decisions (e.g. decisions about capital investment, about whether to enter a market or to close down a business or about a segment of a business) is also supported by accounting information.

Third, accounting acts as a **record, forming an organisational memory**. It stores knowledge about the organisation—knowledge that could be lost completely were it left to reside only in the minds of people employed by the business; knowledge that could be transferred to others in the business. Examples of such knowledge include that relating to past customers, knowledge about success in generating value for the business (or failure to do so) or knowledge about the development of processes within the business that can help conserve the environment while improving the financial bottom line (such as design for environment).

Last, accounting acts as an **instrument for path tracking and path finding** (or 'steersmanship'), showing where a business has been, where it is at present and, through extrapolation, where it plans to be in the future. It is, in effect, a performance measurement, a recording and reporting device, the product of which can be used by internal and external stakeholders.

Corporate managers make decisions and act in the present, usually guided by their experience and the information available to them about the past and present. The aim of their present decisions and actions is to achieve objectives that are established for the future of their organisations. Such objectives are usually complex, but for commercial corporations the pursuit of financial gain for shareholders is a high priority, as is satisfying the requirements of other stakeholders, particularly in terms of compliance with legal requirements (e.g. health and safety legislation). As the future is uncertain, managers need access to all the relevant information they can obtain at a reasonable cost about alternative courses of action available to them

(Chambers 1957: 3). In this context, information provides purpose-oriented data for users—that is, information about how a desired future state might be achieved. If the desired future state is sustainability, then accounting has a part to play.

17.2 The accounting process

The accounting process involves the recording of data in a logical, rigorous, meticulous way:

- Stage 1. The main accounts are identified and classified in a chart of accounts.

- Stage 2. Signs, signals or characteristics of transactions (e.g. the buying of raw materials, the hiring of labour or the takeover of a factory), transformations (e.g. the conversion of raw materials into a product) and external events (e.g. inflation) are recorded in chronological order, generally at the time they occur if a computer software package is used, or shortly afterwards if recorded by hand.

- Stage 3. The balances of each account are determined from period to period. The period may be a year, six months, a week, a day or some other time-period that is considered useful for those people responsible for making decisions and who are accountable for the stewardship of resources.

Much consideration is given to the 'account books' (such as journals and ledgers) in which records are kept and to how these are interrelated. However, as computer packages become available at lower and lower prices, less emphasis is placed on individual understanding of the inner structure of the accounts and more emphasis is given to the chart of accounts and to how many categories are included, as well as to interpreting statements that can be derived from account balances at stage 3 of the accounting process. An analogy would be the driving of a car. Drivers now need to know less about the mechanics of a car than they did, say, 50 years ago, as specialist mechanics are left to take care of these aspects of transportation; however, drivers now need to know more about putting in the right fuel and oil as well as about learning safe, economical and defensive driving skills than would have been the case 50 years ago.

The process of recording accounting data with use of computers is quite simple; however, the data gathered changes over time as information and knowledge about different issues are considered to be relevant. For example, accounting involves recording monetary information about the financial position and changes in financial position (the financial performance) of the business because the legal system requires such information to be collected and disclosed. However, it also records other styles of information. With the growing importance of environmental issues to business, considerable attention has recently been given to the need to record environmental information in the chart of accounts, and so some computer packages have been developed to accommodate this need. For example MYOB ('mind your own business') provides general accounting computer software for any business to use, including a module aimed specifically at the collection of environmental information. Also, the US Environmental Protection Agency (EPA) has developed specific pollution-prevention accounting software for conducting financial evaluations of current and potential investments (see www.emawebsite.org/library_detail.asp? record=109).

17.3 Conventional and environmental accounting

Today, a large number of companies in developed countries collect, use and distribute information related to the natural environment. This reflects a fundamental change compared with a decade ago (e.g. see Gray *et al.* 1996: 81; Schaltegger and Burritt 2000: 30). There is increasing pressure from stakeholders concerned about the impact of corporate activities on the environment, and the costs of environmental impacts have risen substantially—for example, through penalties established in new environmental legislation, and investments in environmentally benign processes and products encouraged by tighter environmental regulation. Such pressures have led to the emergence of various perceptions of the concept and practices of environmental accounting (e.g. Burritt *et al.* 2002; Gray *et al.* 1993, 1996; Parker 1999; Schaltegger 1996b; Schaltegger and Burritt 2000; Schaltegger and Stinson 1994; US EPA 1995c). These perceptions are considered in the following sections.

17.3.1 Conventional accounting

Conventional accounting provides separate information about monetary and physical aspects of the company's activities. Such systems, expressed in monetary units, include:

- Management accounting, which is designed to satisfy the internal needs of corporate decision-makers for short-term cost and revenue, long-term investment information and internal accountability

- Financial accounting, which, on a regular basis over specified periods of time, serves to provide external corporate stakeholders with information about the company's dated financial position and about changes in the financial position

- Other accounting systems, such as tax or bank regulatory accounting, intended to provide specific information, mostly for regulatory purposes

Conventional accounting systems also include information expressed in physical units such as production planning systems, inventory and material accounting systems and quality management systems.

17.3.1.1 Conventional management accounting

Management accounting provides the foundation for all the other accounting systems. The management accounting process involves 'the identification, measurement, accumulation, analysis, preparation and interpretation of information that assists executives in fulfilling organisational objectives' (Horngren and Foster 1987: 2). It thus focuses on internal accounting and reporting. It is only relatively recently that the specific importance of non-monetary information has been recognised (Horngren *et al.* 2000: 888): 'Management accounting . . . measures and reports financial and non-financial information that helps managers make decisions to fulfil the goals of an organisation.'

Conventional management accounting does not usually give explicit, separate recognition to company-related environmental impacts. Instead, it is designed mainly to satisfy the needs of managers seeking information about the economic performance of the company as a basis for decision-making (Burritt *et al.* 2002). Yet, from a pragmatic perspective, the critical test for any accounting system is whether it produces information, such as environmental information, that is useful to stakeholders (e.g. managers) for evaluating their own ends (Chambers 1966: 54; Schaltegger and Burritt 2000: 45). Hence, management accounting systems should be designed to satisfy the fact that different managers may require different information, including different information about the environment, as pressure mounts on managers to comply with tighter environmental legislation and to be aware of corporate environmental impacts on stakeholders (Schaltegger and Burritt 2000: 31). For example, on the one hand, top managers are interested in monetary information that shows material effects on shareholder value, including environmentally related impacts on the economic situation of companies. Corporate environment managers (see Parker 1999), on the other hand, are interested in various waste and pollution figures expressed in physical units and generally have no direct interest in whether the costs of pollution abatement or waste reduction measures are capitalised or considered as expenses in the monetary account.

The main stakeholders in management accounting hold different management positions (e.g. top, product and site managers). Because it is an internal information system, management accounting and accounts are subject to almost no external regulation. The USA is an exception, where a series of cost accounting standards have been introduced to guide, for example, ways of linking costs to transactions made between government and the private sector. The intention is to stop management loading up costs of conducting commercial business onto government contracts, especially in industries such as defence where contracts are for very large amounts of money. The United Nations Division for Sustainable Development (UNDSD) has launched an initiative to support governments in promoting environmental management accounting (Schaltegger *et al.* 2001a).

17.3.1.2 Conventional financial accounting

The International Accounting Standards Committee (now Board) (IASC 1998a: IAS 1) identifies that 'The objective of financial statements is to provide information about the financial position, performance and changes in the financial position of an enterprise that is useful to a wide range of users in making economic decisions'. Financial accounting is the branch of accounting that provides information to people outside the business (Horngren *et al.* 1997: 7). The purpose of financial accounting is to generate financial information about a company in order to provide a basis for transparency and accountability relationships with stakeholders, such as shareholders, creditors and non-governmental organisations (NGOs). Financial reporting is used by managers to communicate the dated financial information to external parties. In particular, information reported reflects the financial position and changes in financial position of a company's dated accrual-based information and additional information considered beneficial for stakeholders to receive (e.g. cash flows in and out of the business, and the cash balance). Accrual-based accounting is accounting that recognises and records the impact of a business transaction, transformation or event as it occurs, regardless of whether cash is affected (e.g. purchases on credit). One important aspect of accrual accounting is that it recognises assets and liabilities of the business, unlike cash-based accounting, which recognises only one asset—cash.

Financial accounts are reported to the public and hence there has been considerable discussion and pressure on the accounting profession and business for such information to be reported in a 'true and fair' way to complement the standardisation process that makes sure that similar transactions, transformations and events are treated in the same way. Financial accounting and reporting are strictly regulated and standardised. Investors (shareholders) and many other external stakeholders have an economic interest in receiving 'true and fair' information about the actual economic performance of a company. Uncertainty about the actual value of a company and of its shares increases the desire of shareholders to receive a 'true and fair view' of a company's financial position and performance. The reduction of these uncertainties to establish the situation would be extremely costly for an individual shareholder to undertake. One way of reducing these costs is for public, limited-liability companies to publish financial reports, thereby making their financial position and performance transparent to their shareholders and other stakeholders. However, the relationship between stakeholders and management is characterised by information asymmetry. Managers have control of the information shareholders require. Furthermore, managers have every incentive to present economic results in the way that most favours themselves. Hence, standard-setting bodies and regulatory agencies have been established to try to make sure that necessary information is supplied to stakeholders in an unbiased way.

Financial reporting systems use standardised conventions about how to treat (recognise, measure and disclose) specific items. The result of introducing standards and conventions is that the information that is compiled and disclosed should provide a 'true and fair' basis for stakeholder accountability and decision-making needs. Professional, independent financial auditors review company accounting books and financial reports on the basis of these standards and associated guidance notes and interpretations, thereby maintaining credibility of the reported information and the public reporting process.

Financial accounting and reporting standards have, therefore, a substantial influence on what type of information is collected, analysed and considered for disclosure by management (for a discussion of the role of standards in facilitating communication, see Blankart and Knieps 1993). This is one reason why it is so important for the monetary aspects of environmental issues to be adequately covered in financial accounting standards and conventions (see e.g. Achleitner 1995).

Figure 17.2 contrasts providers ('suppliers') of accounting frameworks with external users ('customers') of corporate financial reporting information. On the left-hand side of the figure, examples of prominent providers of regulations, standards, guidelines and recommendations for financial accounting are shown. Some of the main groups generating demand for financial report information are depicted on the right-hand side of Figure 17.2. These include shareholders, potential investors, financial analysts, banks, regulators, suppliers, the media and pressure groups (e.g. NGOs and local community organisations).

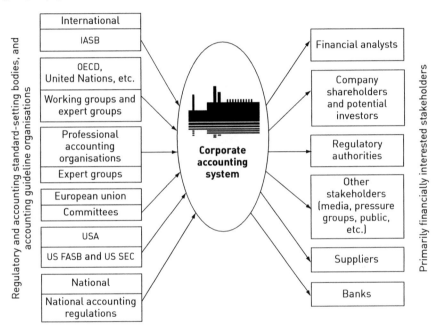

FASB = Federal Accounting Standards Board; IASB = International Accounting Standards Board; OECD = Organisation for Economic Co-operation and Development; SEC = Securities and Exchange Commission

Figure 17.2 **Different standard-setting bodies and stakeholders with financial interests in a company**

Source: Schaltegger and Burritt 2000: 164

17.3.1.3 Other accounting systems

Some accounting systems are specific to individual regulatory groups. The phrase 'other conventional accounting systems' refers to these additional, specific accounting systems, such as tax accounting and bank regulatory accounting. Tax accounting is mandatory for all regular businesses, as the government tax agencies require tax 'reports', whereas, for example, bank regulatory agencies have special accounting and reporting requirements only for banks. A range of environmental issues can be included in these systems.

17.3.2 Environmental accounting

The main difference between conventional and environmental accounting systems is that the latter separately identify, measure, analyse and interpret information about the environmental aspects of company activities. Within the conventional approach this distinction is somewhat unclear. Yet if, as suggested, environmental information is important, differences in the units of measurement, in the data quality and in its sources cannot simply be neglected if purpose-oriented information is to be provided for different managers. Hence, incorporation of environmental information in accounting systems leads to the need for development of comprehensive environmental accounting systems. These can be divided into three types:

- Environmental management accounting (EMA)

- External environmental accounting (EEA), both monetary and physical

- Other environmental accounting systems

Together these systems form environmental accounting and are examined in turn below.

17.3.2.1 Environmental management accounting

Framework and overview of environmental management accounting
EMA is an integrated system that includes monetary and non-monetary approaches to internal accounting (see e.g. Bennett and James 1998; Burritt et al. 2002; Bouma and Wolters 1996; IFAC 1998). EMA can be defined as a generic term that includes both monetary environmental management accounting (MEMA) and physical environmental management accounting (PEMA). This situation is illustrated in Table 17.1.

There is a wide consensus that there are two main groups of environmental impacts related to company activities (Schaltegger and Burritt 2000: 58):

- Environmentally related impacts on the economic situation of companies

- Company-related impacts on environmental systems

Environmentally related impacts on economic systems are reflected through monetary environmental information. Monetary environmental information addresses all corporate-related impacts on the past, present or future financial stocks and flows of that corporation and is expressed in monetary units (e.g. measures expressed in expenditure on cleaner production; cost of fines for breaching environmental laws; monetary values of environmental assets). Monetary environmental accounting systems can be considered as a broadening of the scope—or a further development or refinement of—conventional accounting in monetary units as they are based on the methods of conventional accounting systems.

Related impacts of corporate activities on environmental systems are reflected in physical environmental information. Thus, at the corporate level, physical environ-

Type of accounting	Units	
	Monetary	**Physical**
Internal	Monetary environmental management accounting (MEMA)	Physical environmental management accounting (PEMA)
	Environmental management accounting (EMA)	
External	Monetary external environmental accounting and reporting (MEEA)	Physical external environmental accounting and reporting (PEEA)
	Monetary environmental regulatory accounting and reporting	Physical environmental regulatory accounting and reporting
	External environmental accounting (EEA)	

Table 17.1 Environmental accounting systems

Source: based on Bartolomeo *et al.* 2000: 33

mental information includes all past, present and future material and energy amounts that have an impact on ecological systems. Physical environmental information is always expressed in physical units—such as kilograms, cubic metres or joules (e.g. information may be expressed in kilograms of material per customer served, or joules of energy used per unit of product).

Monetary environmental management accounting (MEMA) deals with environmental aspects of corporate activities expressed in monetary units and generates information for internal management use (e.g. costs of fines for breaking environmental laws; investment in capital projects that improve the environment). In terms of its methods MEMA is based on conventional management accounting extended and adapted to environmental aspects of company activities. It is a central, pervasive tool, providing, as it does, the basis for most internal management decisions as well as addressing the issue of how to track, trace and treat costs and revenues that are incurred because of the company's impact on the environment (Schaltegger and Burritt 2000: 59). MEMA contributes to strategic and operational planning, provides the main basis for decisions about how to achieve desired goals or targets and acts as a control and accountability device (Schaltegger and Burritt 2000: 90).

Physical environmental management accounting (PEMA) also serves as an information tool for internal management decisions. However, in contrast to MEMA it focuses on a company's impact on the natural environment, expressed in terms of physical units such as kilograms. PEMA tools are designed to collect information on environmental impact in physical units for internal use by management (Schaltegger and Burritt 2000: 61-63). PEMA as an internal environmental accounting approach serves as (Schaltegger and Burritt 2000: 261):

- An analytical tool designed to detect ecological strengths and weaknesses

- A decision-support technique concerned with highlighting relative environmental quality

- A measurement tool that is an integral part of other environmental measures, such as eco-efficiency

- A tool for direct and indirect control of environmental consequences

- An accountability tool providing a neutral and transparent base for internal and, indirectly, external communication

- A tool with a close and complementary fit to the set of tools being developed to help promote ecologically sustainable development

Table 17.2 categorises these environmental management accounting systems according to their monetary and physical dimensions and according to the timeframe on which they focus.

| Information type | Environmental management accounting (EMA) | | | |
| | Monetary: MEMA | | Physical: PEMA | |
	Short-term	Long-term	Short-term	Long-term
Past or present orientation				
Routinely generated	*Type 1:* Environmental cost accounting (e.g. variable, absorption and activity-based costing)	*Type 2:* Environmentally induced capital expenditure and revenues	*Type 9:* Material and energy flow accounting (short-term impacts on the environment at the product, site, division and company levels)	*Type 10:* Environmental (or natural) capital impact accounting
Ad hoc	*Type 3:* Ex post assessment of relevant environmental costing decisions	*Type 4:* Environmental life-cycle (and target) costing Post-investment assessment of individual projects	*Type 11:* Ex post assessment of short-term environmental impacts (e.g. of a site or product)	*Type 12:* Life-cycle inventories Post-investment appraisal of physical environmental investment

Note: The type numbers have been added to aid in the interpretation of Table 17.4. MEMA = monetary environmental management accounting; PEMA = physical environmental management accounting

Table 17.2 **Illustrative monetary and physical environmental management accounting tools, focusing on the short term and the long term** (continued opposite)

Source: Schaltegger *et al.* 2000

Information type	Environmental management accounting (EMA)			
	Monetary: MEMA		*Physical: PEMA*	
	Short-term	**Long-term**	**Short-term**	**Long-term**
Future orientation				
Routinely generated	*Type 5:* Monetary environmental operational budgeting (flows) Monetary environmental capital budgeting (stocks)	*Type 6:* Environmental long-term financial planning	*Type 13:* Physical environmental budgeting (flows and stocks; e.g. material and energy flow activity-based budgeting)	*Type 14:* Long-term physical environmental planning
Ad hoc	*Type 7:* Relevant environmental costing (e.g. special orders, product mix with capacity constraint)	*Type 8:* Monetary environmental project investment appraisal Environmental life-cycle budgeting and target pricing	*Type 15:* Tools designed to predict relevant environmental impacts (e.g. given short-run constraints on activities)	*Type 16:* Physical environmental investment appraisal Life-cycle assessment of specific projects

Table 17.2 (continued)

Different types of managers rely on and have their performance assessed by physical, monetary or both types of information. For example, managers in the corporate environmental department have various goals, including:

- Identifying environmental improvement opportunities

- Prioritising environmental actions and measures

- Environmental differentiation in product pricing, mix and development decisions

- Transparency regarding environmentally relevant corporate activities

- Meeting the claims and information demands of critical environmental stakeholders, to ensure resource provision and access

- Justifying environmental management division and environmental protection measures

PEMA information can be used to guide and advise these situations. A guide to the typical styles of information used by different managers is provided in Table 17.3.

Group	Examples of basic goals	Type of information desired
Top management	● Long-term profitability and survival of company ● The securing of legal compliance, at minimal cost to the corporation ● Realisation of all economically beneficial environmental protection measures ● Securing the provision of resources from critical stakeholders	● Highly aggregated financial and strategic (qualitative and quantitative) information on the business environment and the company's performance
Accounting and finance department	● Identifying and realising cost-saving potential ● Transparency regarding cost-relevant (environment-related) corporate activities ● Transparency regarding the impact of (environment-related) activities on the income statement and/or balance sheet ● Reduction of environmentally induced risks ● Compliance with accounting regulations ● Maximisation of shareholder value	● Financial measures of corporate activities (e.g. cost-related, income-related and balance-sheet-related issues, risk assessments, investment decisions, mergers and acquisitions) ● Financial information on the value and economic performance of the enterprise
Environmental department	● Identification of environmental improvement opportunities ● Prioritisation of environmental actions and measures ● Environmental differentiation of product pricing, mix and development decisions ● Transparency regarding environmentally relevant corporate activities ● To meet the claims and information demands of critical environmental stakeholders, to ensure resource provision and access	● Physical measures of material and energy flows and stocks and related processes and products, and their impacts on the environment

Table 17.3 Corporate environmental management accounting (EMA): generic aims and objectives of different management groups (continued opposite)

Sources: Schaltegger *et al.* 2001a; with reference also to Bennett and James 1998: 34ff.

Group	Examples of basic goals	Type of information desired
Environmental department *(continued)*	● Justification of the environmental management division and of environmental protection measures (Bennett and James 1998: 34ff.)	
Health and safety department	● Safeguarding the safety, health and welfare of employees at work from environmental accidents and disasters	● Physical measures of health and safety
Quality control department	● To meet the (environmental) product requirements of customers at a minimum cost for a given level of product quality	● Information on cost of quality ● Physical measures of technical product requirements
Human resources department	● To look after the job-related (including environmental) concerns of employees ● To remunerate employees, including rewards for good environmental performance ● To allocate jobs and monitor employee conditions	● Information on financial rewards ● Physical information on turnover, satisfaction and morale
Legal department	● To ensure (environmental) legal compliance by the company's operations	● Physical measures ● Qualitative compliance information
Research & development and design departments	● Development and design of marketable products and services ● Reduction of (environmental) risks of investments ● Development of improved production processes	● Strategic information about market demands ● Financial information about costs of new products and services ● Information on the technical feasibility and environmental impacts of newly designed products and services
Corporate marketing and public relations departments	● To meet the external information demands of critical stakeholders	● Information about stakeholder claims

Table 17.3 (from previous page; continued over)

Group	Examples of basic goals	Type of information desired
Corporate marketing and public relations departments (continued)	● To meet the claims and information demands of shareholders and other economic stakeholders (including those interested in environmental reports) ● To develop a 'green' image for the company and its products	● Physical and financial information on the company's environmental impacts and efforts regarding pollution reduction and prevention
Production management	● Task control over operations ● Optimisation of energy and material consumption ● Reduction of environmentally induced risks	● Information on material and energy flows and process records
Purchasing department	● Efficient procurement of inputs for corporate operations ● Establishing and securing favourable relationships with suppliers	● Information on quality and environmental properties of the goods purchased ● Financial information on prices
Logistics	● Efficient organisation of, collection, storage and physical distribution of goods and products	● Physical measures (e.g. on means of distribution and storage facilities and their related environmental impacts)
Marketing and sales department	● To increase sales and to attract and satisfy buyers ● To provide a means by which buyers can purchase the product ● To induce customers—by means of tools in the marketing mix (especially pricing, distribution and communication)—to buy the enterprise's products	● Information on operational market conditions (e.g. pricing, competitor activities) ● Information on customer demands
Disposal and recycling department	● Efficient disposal and recycling of wasted or used material ● Minimisation of waste to be treated, especially hazardous wastes	● Physical measures of the properties of disposable and recyclable goods ● Technical information on treatment and recycling options

Table 17.3 (continued)

All managers need qualitative information and so comment on this type of information is not separately detailed.

Three additional dimensions of environmental management accounting tools are important, especially for managers of small and medium-sized enterprises (SMEs):

● Time-frame. Is the time-frame being addressed by the tool the past, current or future?

● Length of time-frame. How long is the time-frame being addressed by the tool; for example, is it addressing the short term or does it have a focus on the long term?

● Routineness of information. How routinely is information gathered; for instance, is it gathered on an ad hoc basis or is there regular gathering of information?

Different managers have different time-frames and differing demands for routine or ad hoc information. For example, top managers tend to have a longer time-frame and need ad hoc information for critical decisions. A range of environmental accounting tools is available to different managers (e.g. environmental cost accounting). Each tool is likely to be of use to different managers, given their particular level in the business and their own specialisation. A group of tools is illustrated in Table 17.2. The suggested links between management level, decisions made, environmental information needed and main environmental accounting tools are listed in Table 17.4.

Group	Conventional rationale for link with tools	Main tools
Top management	● Main concern is with aggregate financial and strategic information about the company's overall investment and financial performance	● MEMA types 2, 4, 6 and 8 ● Regular and ad hoc information-gathering ● Long-term focus ● Past and future orientation
Divisional management	● Emphasis is on divisional financial and strategic information with a focus on short-term profitability measures such as return on capital employed, economic value added and residual income	● MEMA types 1, 3, 5 and 7 PEMA type 13 ● Regular and ad hoc information-gathering ● Long-term and short-term focus ● Past and future orientation

Note: Type numbers refer to those given in Table 17.2. MEMA = monetary environmental management accounting; PEMA = physical environmental management accounting

Table 17.4 Environmental management accounting: a comparison of the focus of different management groups, and illustrative accounting tools
(continued over)

Group	Conventional rationale for link with tools	Main tools
Accounting and finance department	▪ Focus is on short-term and long-term investment and financial performance measures of activities at the corporate, segmental and product levels (e.g. cost-related, income-related and balance-sheet-related issues, risk assessments, investment decisions, mergers and acquisitions); includes measures and estimates of costs of quality, health and safety and human resource management	▪ MEMA types 1–8 ▪ Regular and ad hoc information-gathering ▪ Long-term and short-term focus ▪ Past and future orientation
Environmental department	▪ Emphasis on physical measures of material and energy flows and stocks and related processes and products, and their impacts on the environment	▪ PEMA types 9–16 ▪ Regular and ad hoc information-gathering ▪ Long-term and short-term focus ▪ Future and past orientation
Health and safety department	▪ Physical information about health and safety (and concern about the impact of the environment on the health and safety of employees)	▪ PEMA types 9–16 ▪ Regular and ad hoc information-gathering ▪ Long-term and short-term focus
Quality control department	▪ Main focus is on physical information about technical product attributes and aspects of personnel and technology that provide the customer service or product	▪ PEMA types 9–16 ▪ Regular and ad hoc information-gathering ▪ Long-term and short-term focus ▪ Future and past orientation

Note: Type numbers refer to those given in Table 17.2. MEMA = monetary environmental management accounting; PEMA = physical environmental management accounting

Table 17.4 (from previous page; continued opposite)

Group	Conventional rationale for link with tools	Main tools
Human resources department	• Main emphasis is on short-term physical information about employee numbers and types, allocation of employees by business segment, turnover, employee satisfaction and morale and financial information about employee rewards	• MEMA types 1, 3, 5 and 7 PEMA types 9, 11, 13 and 15 • Regular and ad hoc information-gathering • Short-term focus • Past and future orientation
Legal department	• Main concern is with physical information about compliance with legislation and regulation and financial penalties for non-compliance	• PEMA types 9, 11, 13 and 15; some concern for MEMA types 1, 3, 5 and 7 • Regular and ad hoc information-gathering • Short-term focus • Past and future orientation
Research & development and design departments	• Focus on information about the technical feasibility and environmental impacts of newly designed products, services and operations	• PEMA type 16 • Ad hoc information-gathering • Long-term focus • Future orientation
Corporate marketing and public relations departments	• Information about stakeholder claims, and physical and financial information on the company's environmental impacts and efforts for pollution reduction and prevention	• MEMA types 2, 4, 6 and 8 PEMA types 10, 12, 14 and 16 • Regular and ad hoc information-gathering • Long-term focus • Past and future orientation
Production management	• Main concern is with short-term information about material and energy flows and production scheduling	• PEMA types 9, 11, 13 and 15 • Regular information-gathering • Short-term focus • Past and future orientation

Note: Type numbers refer to those given in Table 17.2. MEMA = monetary environmental management accounting; PEMA = physical environmental management accounting

Table 17.4 (from previous page; continued over)

Group	Conventional rationale for link with tools	Main tools
Purchasing department	▪ Focus is on information about the quality and environmental properties of the goods and services purchased and about prices	▪ MEMA types 1, 3, 5 and 7 PEMA types 9, 11, 13 and 15 ▪ Regular and ad hoc information-gathering ▪ Short-term focus ▪ Past and future orientation
Logistics department	▪ Focus on physical measures (e.g. on distribution means and storage facilities and their related environmental impacts)	▪ PEMA types 9–16 ▪ Regular and ad hoc information-gathering ▪ Long-term and short-term focus ▪ Past and future orientation
Marketing and sales department (and product managers)	▪ Information on operational market conditions (e.g. pricing, competitor activities) and customer demands	▪ MEMA types 1, 3, 5 and 7 PEMA types 9, 11, 13 and 15 ▪ Regular and ad hoc information-gathering ▪ Short-term focus ▪ Past and future orientation
Disposal and recycling department	▪ Emphasis on physical measures of the properties of disposable and recyclable goods, and technical information about treatment and recycling options	▪ PEMA types 9, 11, 13 and 15 ▪ Regular and ad hoc information-gathering ▪ Short-term focus ▪ Past and future orientation

Note: Type numbers refer to those given in Table 17.2. MEMA = monetary environmental management accounting; PEMA = physical environmental management accounting

Table 17.4 (continued)

Environmental management accounting tools

This section aims to give an overview of the major EMA tools presented in the EMA framework of Table 17.2. The type numbers in the following refer to the type numbers given in that table. These items span internal and external decisions and the accountability of business, illustrating also how EMA information interacts with internal as well as external uses.

Routine approaches
These include tools for MEMA as well as for PEMA that are applied on a regular basis, as EMA methods can be based either on monetary data or on physical data.

Type 1: environmental cost accounting. Environmental cost accounting as considered in the context of corporate management helps in the planning, management and control of operations (Seidel 1995). Cost accounting is past-oriented and has a short-term focus (Schaltegger *et al.* 2001a). Recently, a number of important conceptual developments have taken place in the field of environmental cost accounting (for an overview, see Bennett *et al.* 2002; Fichter *et al.* 1997). These include the use of variable costing, absorption costing and activity-based costing methods. Generally, the different approaches of environmental cost accounting can be classified based on the definition of environmental costs and the accounting method adopted (e.g. full-cost accounting, direct costing or process costing). A summary of different concepts can be found in Schaltegger and Burritt 2000: 109-18.

One possible system for addressing environmental cost accounting is the application of a form of process costing (see Schaltegger and Burritt 2000: 109ff.). Process costing is also often referred to as activity-based costing (ABC) or activity-based accounting.[24] ABC focuses on costing activities and then on allocating the cost of activities to products on the basis of the individual product's demand for those activities (Horvath and Mayer 1989; 1993; Parker 1999: 50). One specific variant of process costing is that of material flow-oriented ABC (see e.g. Schaltegger and Burritt 2000: 130-35) and material flow-oriented process costing, which has several sub-approaches. Examples of these are internal environmental accounting (Letmathe 1998), flow cost accounting (Strobel 2001), flow-oriented environmental accounting and environmentally oriented process cost accounting.

One of the main advantages of using ABC to assess environmental costs—apart from the advantages concerning environmental full-cost accounting—is the integration of environmental cost accounting into the strategic management process and its link to management objectives and activities.

Type 2: environmentally induced capital expenditure and revenue. Environmentally induced capital expenditure and revenues represent routinely generated information with a long-term focus which is past-oriented (Schaltegger *et al.* 2001a: 10). By definition environmentally induced capital expenditure and revenues are part of MEMA. Environmentally induced revenues can stem from the sale of recyclables or from the higher contribution margins of eco-products, whereas environmentally induced costs can be seen as the internal costs (including opportunity costs) of a business, the economic costs or all costs to society, including external costs (Schaltegger and Burritt 2000: 95-97). Environmental expenses are environmentally related costs that have provided a benefit that has now expired (Schaltegger and Burritt 2000: 175). Such expenses are matched against revenues in the profit-and-loss account (the income account or statement of financial performance). Despite

---

24 The term 'process costing' is generally used when the cost object is a specific technical process or process step, whereas the terms 'activity-based costing' or 'activity-based accounting' are generally used when the cost object tends to be the activity being undertaken by individual employees, groups of employees, machines or computers; however, the essential ideas behind these approaches are the same.

the magnitude of environmental expenses in many industries (see e.g. Fichter *et al.* 1997), no financial accounting standard requires their separate recognition, although company law does lay down some disclosure rules (e.g. S.299[1][f] Corporations Act 2001 in Australia [Burritt 2002c: 393]). Environmental issues are clearly part of the risk structure of a company and, where important, should be disclosed separately if environmentally induced financial risks are to be made transparent. Otherwise, investors will be unable to assess the risk of their investments.

Type 5: monetary environmental operational budgeting (flows) and monetary environmental capital budgeting (stocks).   Monetary environmental operational budgeting (flows) and monetary environmental capital budgeting (stocks) present another important approach of EMA. A budget can be defined as a 'quantitative expression of a proposed plan of action by management for a future time-period and is an aid to the co-ordination and implementation of the plan' (Horngren *et al.* 2000: 883). In practice, corporate budgets are used for a number of purposes, such as assisting in achieving a firm's business objectives, authorising managers to spend defined amounts of money in a specified period of time, forecasting events over which no control is exercised or making an attempt to affect factors that are open to influence and control. Monetary environmental operational budgeting (focusing on material and energy flows) and monetary environmental capital budgeting (concentrating on corresponding stocks of energy and materials) are two complementary instruments that 'encourage a proactive use of budgetary control that is based on a management philosophy designed to eliminate adverse corporate environmental effects' (Schaltegger and Burritt 2001b: 164). Both instruments are future-oriented (as they focus on future costs) and short-term (as they relate to defined time-horizons corresponding to the chosen budget period). Standard environmental costing, which complements operational budgeting in production, can be used to provide information for short-term planning.

Type 6: environmental long-term financial planning.   Environmental long-term financial planning is, by definition, long-term and therefore implicitly future-oriented. It is especially concerned with future environmental costs. Based on the general definition of environmental costs as being those costs intended to protect the environment, some authors propose that potential or future costs also be assessed (Schaltegger and Burritt 2000: 114). In principle, the assessment of future costs, especially when related to environmental issues, is very important indeed. Conventional accounting has been criticised for being far too oriented towards the past instead of towards present and future activities (see e.g. Johnson and Kaplan 1987a, 1987b). Since an important use of management accounting information is to assist planning for the future, extending these approaches to include budgeting is, therefore, another advantage of the full-cost, direct-cost and activity-based approaches because the future consequences for the environment are required to be taken into account if managers use these methods. Apart from the pros and cons mentioned above, anyone attempting to consider future costs faces quite substantial problems when trying to estimate those future costs. Estimation of the future costs of pollution prevention and environmental liabilities is particularly difficult as neither future technology nor future demands of stakeholder groups are known.

The introductory overview of the monetary approaches of EMA showed how much many of them depend on physical information of material, energy, waste and emission flows. This is one important reason for management to apply PEMA tools. Another reason to consider the use of PEMA is the many regulations requiring information on emissions and waste. Furthermore, the development of new products and production processes, and innovation in general, often depends on accurate physical information.

Type 9: material and energy flow accounting.   Material and energy flow accounting is part of conventional PEMA. It is past-oriented (i.e. it focuses on material and energy flows that took place in the past). It is also short-term in that it focuses on short-term impacts on the environment at the product, site, division and company levels (see e.g. Schaltegger and Burritt 2000: 145-46, 270). In its original sense, material and energy flow accounting is a routine activity, therefore generating regular information.

So far, a detailed and unambiguous definition of material flow accounting has not been established. The term 'material flow accounting' can refer to different objects of accounting. Material flow accounts can be defined in general as accounts in physical units (usually in terms of tonnes) corresponding to the extraction, production, transformation, consumption, recycling and disposal phases of materials as well as to a number of material flow accounting activities at the level of plants or businesses (Liedtke *et al.* 1994). Material flow accounting can help with attempts at sustainable development through:

- The derivation of environmental pressure indicators

- The development of integrated environmental and economic accounting

- The design and control of policy measures for sustainable development

The origins of material and energy flow accounting go back to the work of Müller-Wenk (1978). Müller-Wenk coined the term 'ecological book-keeping', which he defined as a measurement system that records the environmental impacts originating from a single company comprehensively, continuously and following established procedural guidelines (Müller-Wenk 1978: 17). As can be seen with this definition, the routineness of material and energy flow accounting is alluded to, as is the need for general guidelines for this type of accounting.

Type 10: environmental (or natural) capital impact accounting.   A complement to material and energy flow accounting is environmental (or natural) capital impact accounting. This is an instrument that has a long-term focus. However, it still is past-oriented and is based on physical measures (i.e. it remains part of physical environmental management accounting). It also generates information in a routine way, unlike other instruments that produce ad hoc information for decision-making. Environmental capital impact accounting assesses the damage to ecological capital, which is the reason for it being classified as long-term.

Type 13: physical environmental budgeting of flows and stocks.   Whereas materials and energy flow accounting as well as environmental capital impact accounting are instruments oriented towards the past, physical environmental budgeting of flows and stocks is a tool that is future-oriented. It is also a short-term instrument and is routinely applied to generate information. Physical environmental budgeting of flows and stocks is, in short, budgeting based on material and energy flow activity (Schaltegger and Burritt 2000: 117-18).

If (monetary) environmental budgeting is to consider the potential future costs of material and energy flows a future-oriented budgeting approach involving calculating future physical material flows from investments, production processes and business operations is needed to complement it. The focus of the activity-based approach to budgeting for potential future costs of all material and energy flows requires budgeting for all materials that are expected to be purchased in the next period, the cost of logistics for obtaining these materials, the wages of the staff who deal with these materials and the expected costs of related waste treatment. Such an approach may reveal an even greater potential for material flow savings compared with an analysis based on past and current operations. The main reason why a proactive approach may uncover greater material (and thus also cost) savings potentials is that measures introduced to reduce material and energy flows are often much cheaper than are measures for changing existing processes or installations. Therefore, proactive environmental management may be best reflected through a budgeting approach oriented towards material and energy flows.

Type 14: long-term physical environmental planning. Long-term physical environmental planning is, by definition, long-term in its orientation and based on physical estimates of environmental impacts (and therefore is part of PEMA). It provides routinely generated information and is future-oriented.

Ad hoc approaches
Ad hoc approaches include tools for MEMA as well as PEMA, applied in specific situations or cases.

Type 3: ex post *assessment of relevant environmental costing decisions.* Ex post assessment of relevant environmental costing decisions is a monetary calculation made in relation to environmental costs after they have been incurred. *Ex post* analysis is carried out after the production of goods or services. This allows management to make use of actual production costs. A post-calculation exercise also provides a valuable basis for calculations of future environmental costs for short-run decision-making. The carrying-out of *ex post* calculation exercises or product costing analyses focusing on environmental costs is mostly short-term in nature in order to assess the success of previous ad hoc decisions (e.g. relating to product mix and special orders and during short-term outsourcing costing exercises).

Type 4: environmental life-cycle costing and post-investment assessment of individual projects. Environmental life-cycle costing is a method in which all the costs of a product (or a process or activity) throughout its lifetime, from raw material acquisition to disposal, are identified (Schaltegger and Burritt 2000: 112; see also Spitzer *et al.* 1993: 6). Life-cycle costing can focus on internal costs or it can attempt to consider the internal and external costs of a business. In both cases, it attempts to measure in monetary terms the costs of a product during its lifetime.

Target costing was developed in the 1970s in Japan as a product-focused instrument for strategic target cost management and has been defined as a 'cost management tool for reducing the overall cost of a product over its entire life-cycle with the help of production, engineering, R&D, marketing and accounting departments' (Sakurai 1989: 40). The long-term product focus means that target costing reports on the actual costs of a product over its lifetime. It can be closely linked with target pricing (see type 8). Post-investment assessment of individual capital projects also links with the life-cycle notion.

Type 7: relevant environmental costing.   Relevant environmental costing is a monetary tool that focuses on the short term, is future-oriented and provides ad hoc information for decision-making. Examples for relevant environmental costing are special orders or the provision of support for product mix choices under capacity constraints. It differs from environmental cost accounting (see type 1), which is past-oriented and produces routinely generated information. Relevant environmental costing is oriented towards future activities expected to be carried out. This is a key reason why relevant environmental costing is usually carried out on an ad hoc basis, as and when need for decision-support arises. In contrast, environmental cost accounting is an ongoing process of assessing (past) environmental costs largely for control purposes (see e.g. Schaltegger and Burritt 2000: 109).

Type 8: monetary environmental project investment appraisal, environmental life-cycle budgeting and target pricing.   Monetary environmental project investment appraisal, environmental life-cycle budgeting and target pricing are three tools developed to address corporate environmental issues in a future-oriented manner and with a long-term focus. The basic idea of target pricing is to determine a target price for which effective demand exists in the market and then, on the basis of this, to find the acceptable maximum costs of the product. Applied to environmental costs, this means that the future acceptable price for a product is first established and then (after deducting an appropriate profit margin and other relevant costs) the maximum acceptable environmental costs are determined. Given the need for acceptable margins, new product development would then have to take account of this maximum cost level in the design, production and disposal of the product. That is, the product would have to be designed (e.g. by applying design for environment principles) and manufactured in a way that the maximum acceptable level of environmental costs would not be exceeded.

As with any investment appraisal, monetary environmental project investment appraisal has the basic goal of calculating the net effect of the costs and benefits of different investment alternatives. In doing so, it places a particular focus on environmental costs, including quantifiable environmental benefits arising from cost savings (Schaltegger and Burritt 2000: 139). Although calculation of direct costs forms a necessary part of any method of investment appraisal, environmentally related costs are sometimes hidden in the general overhead costs of a business and therefore may not be separately considered. Nevertheless, these costs can significantly affect the cost structure and thus the profitability of an investment. Another aspect of monetary environmental project investment appraisal is to extend the time-horizon and use long-term financial indicators, since environmental investments often have longer payback periods than do other investments. Calculation of long-term financial indicators will help managers to consider future financial impacts induced by environmental impacts. Two main long-term financial indicators (and their calculation procedures) are applied in practice: net present value (NPV) and option value.

Type 11: ex post *assessment of short-term environmental impacts.* *Ex post* assessment of short-term environmental impacts is the physical equivalent of a monetary *ex post* calculation exercise (see type 3). It, by definition, is expressed in physical terms and is past-oriented, as it is carried out '*ex post*'. Also, by definition, it is short-term, as it focuses on short-term environmental impacts (e.g. of a site or a product).

Type 12: life-cycle inventories and post-investment appraisal of physical environmental investment appraisal. Life-cycle assessment (LCA) is a key tool for producing physical ad hoc information about projects. Where LCA is carried out '*ex post*' (e.g. after a product has already been introduced to the market), it is past-oriented. In this sense it is equivalent to monetary post-investment assessment (i.e. it is a form of 'physical' environmental post-investment appraisal). Even though it is applied '*ex post*', LCA is long-term in the sense that it addresses long-term environmental impacts rather than having an orientation towards short-term impacts.

Often, major environmental impacts occur outside the boundaries of a business. Giving recognition to these 'external effects' will not be accepted within conventional management and accounting philosophies as long as the costs of such environmental impacts need not be borne by the firm.

Type 15: tools designed to predict relevant physical environmental impacts. Tools designed to predict relevant physical environmental impacts are very similar to those used in *ex post* assessment of short-term environmental impacts of, for example, a site or a product (see type 11). Both are based on physical calculations and are therefore part of PEMA. Both have a short-term focus (e.g. they provide a projection or assessment of environmental impacts given short-run constraints on the company's activities). However, there is a crucial difference in scope. Whereas the assessment of short-term environmental impacts is '*ex post*', the assessment of relevant environmental impacts is '*ex ante*' (i.e. it is future-oriented). This means it focuses on the short-term environmental impacts of future activities of the business.

Type 16: physical environmental investment appraisal and life-cycle assessment of specific projects. The introduction of an effective environmental information system is a precondition for the success of any reform in this area, which is why several authors have called for a survey of all discharges over the whole life-cycle of products (Environment Canada 1995; Fava *et al.* 1991, 1992; Lave *et al.* 1995; NCM 1995; Ream and French 1993; SustainAbility *et al.* 1992). Life-cycle assessment (LCA) is considered to be one of the most promising tools for such a survey (see e.g. Pidgeon and Brown 1994; Töpfer 1993) since it takes a broad view of product life-cycles and largely corresponds to the philosophy of 'deep greens' (see e.g. Maunders and Burritt 1991). Basically, LCA calculates environmental impacts in physical terms, whereas life-cycle costing attempts to measure the (financial) costs of a product during its lifetime in monetary terms. The same tools (LCA and environmental investment appraisal) as for post-investment appraisal are used for the appraisal of long-term, future-oriented physical environmental investment. Future-oriented LCA, such as environmental investment appraisal, is carried out '*ex ante*' (e.g. during new product development, but before the product is introduced to the market). The fundamental objective for *ex ante* environmental investment appraisal is, of course, as for any *ex ante* investment appraisal, to provide financial information for, and thus to enable comparison between, different investment alternatives (Schaltegger and Burritt 2000: 138). In order to achieve this objective, a number of environmental considerations have been proposed for incorporation into *ex ante* environmental investment appraisal (see e.g. Schaltegger and Burritt 2000: 139), including expansion of the cost inventory, comprehensive allocation of costs, extension of the time-horizon and the use of long-term financial indicators.

Once managers have a clear picture of the classification of MEMA and PEMA tools, it will be more likely that they will consider adopting the appropriate tools in a particular decision-making or accountability setting in which environmental aspects play a part, such as:

- Product and production managers taking 'green' opportunities when these are available

- Eco-efficiency improvements that reduce the volume of environmentally harmful materials used

- Use of environmental performance indicators to appraise staff

- The extent of subsidies from government that are environmentally damaging and that may be removed in the future

- Potential corporate impacts of environmental taxes and tightened regulations designed to bring corporations closer to tracking the full cost of their activities

- Divisional impacts on environmental capital such as biodiversity, land, water and air quality

- Corporate impacts on the goal of sustainable society

These settings span internal and external decisions and the accountability of business and illustrate how EMA information interacts with internal as well as external uses.

17.3.2.2 External environmental accounting

Introduction

The main audience for external environmental accounting (EEA) disclosures is external parties. Table 17.1 on page 259 highlights that EEA mirrors EMA inasmuch as it too records information in monetary and physical terms—through monetary external environmental accounting (MEEA) and physical external environmental accounting (PEEA).

Until recently, monetary environmental impacts on business were considered to be adequately addressed under existing accounting and reporting standards and regulations. However, the increasing number of environmental issues has generated substantial financial consequences for companies. Therefore, various external 'customers' of financial statements have started to influence standard-setting bodies and regulators to get them to alter existing and to create new reporting standards, regulations and guidelines.

Also, the most important regulators, standard-setters, professional organisations and other key groups with a stake in financial reporting have begun to acknowledge that existing standards may have to be augmented and that new guidelines should be provided. Three main groups ('providers') directly influence how the managing bodies of companies address environmental issues in financial reports:

- Regulatory bodies (e.g. the US Securities and Exchange Commission [SEC]). The SEC was founded in 1934 in response to the Wall Street Crash. It supervises the US securities exchanges. The SEC's mission is to administer federal securities laws and to issue rules and regulations to provide protection for investors and to ensure that the securities markets are fair and honest. This is accomplished primarily by promoting adequate and effective disclosure of information to the investing public.

- Standard-setting bodies such as the International Accounting Standards Board (IASB) or the US Financial Accounting Standards Board (FASB). The IASB was formed in 1973 to harmonise and improve financial reporting (NZZ 1995). It does this primarily by developing and publishing International Accounting Standards (IASs). These standards are developed through an international process that involves national standard-setting bodies, the preparers and users of financial statements, and accountants all over the world (IASC 1995: 7). The FASB was founded in 1973 (FASB 1994). Since then, it has been responsible for the United States Generally Accepted Accounting Principles (US GAAP). It is a private organisation without legal status. The US government can, however, influence the GAAP through the SEC (Arthur Andersen and SVFV 1994: 39). IASs are currently being accepted by more and more countries looking for reliable standards in the wake of accounting problems associated with US standards, such as the Enron debacle (Stone 2002: 112).

- Other stakeholders (e.g. professional accounting organisations, industry associations, international organisations; see e.g. CICA 1992 and the Global Reporting Initiative [GRI], at www.globalreporting.org).

Compulsory or voluntary disclosure?

Regulators have the strongest direct influence on environmental disclosures as they create legally enforceable requirements. For example, in Australia there are a number of provisions relating to general environmental disclosure by different organisations. Section 299(1)(f) of the Corporations Act 2001 (Burritt 2002c) (amending a similar provision introduced in 1998) requires that, 'if the entity's [listed company's] operations are subject to any particular and significant environmental regulation under a law of the Commonwealth or of a State or Territory', then it must 'give details of the [its] performance in relation to the environmental regulation'. This requirement is vague and general, although it has led to an increase in disclosure form and content relating to environmental matters (Frost 2001). Commercial and other Commonwealth (national) public-sector bodies have more definitive requirements under Section 516 of Division 1 of the Environment Protection and Biodiversity Conservation Act 1999 (EPBC Act 1999). Their annual reports must:

- Include a report on how the activities of, and the administration (if any) of legislation by, the reporter during the period accorded with the principles of ecologically sustainable development

- Identify how the outcomes (if any) specified for the reporter in an Appropriations Act relating to the period contribute to ecologically sustainable development

- Document the effect of the reporter's activities on the environment

- Identify any measures the reporter is taking to minimise the impact of activities by the reporter on the environment

- Identify the mechanisms (if any) for reviewing and increasing the effectiveness of those measures

The Act is based on the following principles of ecologically sustainable development:

- Decision-making processes should effectively integrate long-term and short-term economic, environmental, social and equitable considerations.

- If there are threats of serious or irreversible environmental damage, lack of full scientific certainty should not be used as a reason for postponing measures to prevent environmental degradation.

- Intergenerational equity should be observed; that is, the present generation should ensure that the health, diversity and productivity of the environment is maintained or enhanced for the benefit of future generations.

- The conservation of biological diversity and ecological integrity should be a fundamental consideration in decision-making.

- Improved valuation, pricing and incentive mechanisms should be promoted.

Public-sector businesses must report in detail on these issues, although guidelines have only just been released in order to encourage some uniformity in interpretation.

Specific reporting requirements imposed by a regulator on business include the National Pollutant Inventory (NPI), an Internet database designed to provide the community, industry and government with information on the types and amounts of certain substances being emitted to the environment (see www.npi.gov.au/about/index.html). The NPI is based on a national environment protection measure promulgated by the National Environment Protection Council of Australia.

In contrast, a number of voluntary environmental reporting initiatives exist. Voluntary public environmental reporting (PER) is encouraged by a framework introduced by the government for business and public-sector entities:

> Public environmental reporting (PER) is the voluntary public presentation of information about an organisation's environmental performance over a

specified period, usually a financial year. An organisation's PER may be published as a stand-alone document, a website or as part of an annual report (CoA 2000: 2).

PER is based on three phases:

● Plan

● Measure

● Report and review

The information to be reported is listed in Box 17.1 and exhibits great similarity to the information required in the GRI.

Another example of a voluntary EEA system relates to the Greenhouse Challenge (see Burritt 2002a). Business can sign up to the challenge set down by government to reduce greenhouse emissions. Once committed, businesses are required periodically to report their progress to the environment authority. If it is considered beneficial to do so, they may then report similar information to other stakeholders.

Monetary external environmental accounting

A number of issues of conventional financial accounting carry over to MEEA when it is based on the same conventions and principles. These include the decision whether to capitalise costs as assets and the treatment of indirect environmental costs.

Capitalise or write off as expenses?

Whether to capitalise monetary environmental costs or to treat them as expenses is an ongoing controversial issue that is driven by the accountant's choice of cost, rather than taking the market value, as the way to record transactions, transformations and events. In principle, the difference is clear:

> An **asset** is a resource controlled by the enterprise as a result of past events and from which future economic benefits are expected to flow to the enterprise (IASC 1995: 54, IAS F49).

whereas:

> **expenses** are decreases in economic benefits during the accounting period in the form of outflows or depletion of assets or occurrences of liabilities that result in decreases in equity, other than those relating to distributions to equity participants (IASC 1995: 60, IAS F70).

Like many debates in accounting, there is no definitive answer to the question of whether to capitalise environmental costs as assets, or whether to write them off against profits in the year in which they are incurred. The Canadian Institute of Chartered Accountants (CICA) identifies two approaches to the question of when to capitalise environmental costs (see CICA 1993; Holmark *et al.* 1995):

● The increased future benefits (IFB) approach, in which the disbursement has to result in an increase in expected future economic benefits from the asset

- Top management's commitment to PER
- Organisational profile
- The wider environment
- The latest environmental policy
- Management policies and systems
- The scope of the report, management systems and programmes, compliance requirements, external recognition and activities, suppliers, monetary information and communication with stakeholders
- Input indicators, such as:
  - Energy and water consumption
  - Land use
  - Biodiversity
  - Materials
  - Other resources used
- Non-product output indicators, such as:
  - Emissions to air
  - Greenhouse gas production
  - Waste-water emissions
  - Noise
  - Odour
  - Other emissions
  - Solid waste generation and disposal
  - Hazardous waste generation treatment and disposal
  - Site contamination
- Product or service stewardship
- Product design
- Packaging
- Sustainability reporting (for the triple bottom line)
- Social reporting
- Documentation of environmental accounting
- Data completeness, site data and site accuracy verification

PER = public environmental reporting

Box 17.1 **Information that can be reported in public environmental reports in Australia**

Source: CoA 2000

* The additional cost of future benefits (ACOFB) approach, in which environmental costs can be capitalised if they are considered to be a cost of the expected future benefits from the asset, regardless of whether there is any increase in economic benefits

Financial statements are prepared to report the financial performance of a company and should not be distorted with issues that are not material in financial terms. From a strict economic perspective, capitalisation of costs should be allowed only if these costs contribute to additional future economic benefits beyond those originally assessed (incremental future benefits, as in the IFB approach). However, in special cases, the costs of clean-up or pollution prevention may qualify as assets if they are absolutely necessary for the company to stay in business, even though they do not affect expected future cash flows. In this case, expenditure is seen as securing the value of future assets, a value that would fall, perhaps to a 'forced-sale' value, if the expenditure were not made. Less clear is the treatment that should be given to other costs that may enhance reputation but that are not directly attributable to a specific economic benefit or investment.

A further issue relates to a movement from end-of-pipe improvement to precautionary investment in environmental improvement. If a firm is using old-style end-of-pipe technology, it tends to be much easier to isolate the costs of environmental compliance. This is because the costs can usually be more readily identified and fairly clearly attributed to environmental compliance purposes. Hence, identification of an asset value is relatively easy in this case. However, the more a firm adopts cleaner production approaches, the more difficult it becomes to identify its environmental compliance costs. If environmental management decisions are built into the whole production process and produce environmental improvements and cost savings, then it is not easy to separate environmental management costs from expenditure designed to return a commercial profit (A'Hearn 1996).

From an environmental point of view, capitalisation in the accounts (and therefore the ACOFB approach) should be favoured if pollution prevention creates future environmental benefits. Furthermore, capitalisation facilitates amortisation over a number of years and, therefore, enhances long-term thinking (Williams and Phillips 1994). Nevertheless, it could also be argued that most environmental protection activities are expenses because they reflect a repayment of debt to society and nature. From this perspective, the costs associated with environmental clean-up should be considered as ordinary expenses because they are necessitated by government environmental policy. The purpose of the cost is to use the land properly and protect the public rather than to create a more valuable commercial asset. In this case, pollution is seen as an increase in the liabilities of a company (liabilities to nature). The costs of reducing liabilities should be expensed and not recognised as investments. Also, the payment of liabilities that were not recognised when they occurred should not be regarded as investments.

The ACOFB approach may be favoured if the rapid emergence of new environmental issues is considered to be unforeseeable and likely to cause unexpected future liabilities. In this case, prudent economic management would require those costs of environmental protection that impede possible future economic problems to be considered as assets.

The IASB has chosen the IFB approach (IASC 1995: IAS 16), whereas the Fédération des Expertes Comptables Européens (FEE) and the Emerging Issues Task Force (EITF) of the FASB have adopted the ACOFB approach. In the short run, such contradictory positions do little to enhance development of a 'global financial architecture' and the emergence of a truly global standard-setter within a global marketplace. This issue reveals to environmental managers one of many problems that is associated with applying conventional accounting to environmental issues.

Indirect environmental costs

Indirect environmental costs cannot be traced to products and can be linked to products only through the use of an allocation base. The allocation of costs to units of output is another controversial area in conventional accounting. The conventional view of assets is that they represent unexpired costs. Hence, the argument is that business expenditure represents costs that, if they are not related to benefits acquired in the present period, should provide some monetary benefit in future periods. If expenditure is made on environmental equipment such as scrubbers for a factory emission stack, it will become part of the infrastructure and will continue to be used to clean emissions from the stack—perhaps for many years. These future benefits to the business are seen as an asset, provided that other conditions also hold. These other conditions include the need to be able to measure the cost reliably, something that can be a problem when commercial expenditure is made and environmental benefits are integrated with the technology or equipment purchased. In these circumstances a rule of thumb is developed by accountants to try to cost the environmental component of expenditure—and of the asset cost. This is far from satisfactory as it increases the ability to manipulate the figures.

If an environmental asset has its cost reduced—called 'depreciation' (meaning a reduction in price)—then the accounting process recognises that unexpired costs become expired costs and are written off against revenues for the period, thereby reducing both the asset cost and the financial performance for the period. End-of pipe technologies present less of a problem for accounting based on recording the historical cost of transactions, as there is no doubt that these are environmental assets. However, proactive management will wish to convey to external parties the message that environmental risks are being reduced and that money is being spent on cleaner production technologies that are also more profitable. Development of such integrated technologies are to be encouraged, but the accounting problems associated with arbitrary allocation are increased at the same time.

Environmental assets

Unexpired cost expended on environmental capital is considered to represent a depreciable environmental asset under environmental accounting. Controversy about the valuation of environmental assets originates in the recommendation of accounting standards to record environmental assets at their net market value at each reporting date (e.g. as applies in Australia [AASB 1999]). Increments or decrements in net market value between one dated statement of financial position and another are to be included in the computation of income. Such increments and decrements may be unrealised. However, where there is no market the question arises over whether an asset can be recognised and over what measure can be used if an asset is to be recognised. Cost is suggested as one substitute; net present value (NPV) is another. Cost is often out of date for the user of the information, whereas NPV relies too heavily on subjective assessments of future cash inflows and outflows, discount rates and the economic life of the asset being depreciated.

Environmental liabilities

In the past, environmental issues were not a high priority for management until they showed up as liabilities in the books of account. Yet some environmental liabilities have exceeded even the worst-case scenarios of management. Among the major disasters in the 1980s were those of Bhopal (Union Carbide), Schweizerhalle (Sandoz), and Prince William Sound (Exxon), all of which had substantial financial consequences for the companies involved. However, although related to environmental disasters in the USA, legislation has had a greater influence on environmental liabilities than have some of these well-known accidents (Brüggemann 1994: 71). The 1980 Comprehensive Environmental Response, Compensation and Liability Act (CERCLA) aims at cleaning up abandoned waste sites (Superfund sites). The liability is regarded as joint and retrospective for all costs incurred in the clean-up. All parties involved can be held liable for the total costs of remediating the landfill. The liability exists even if the activity that caused the environmental problem was legal and the Superfund legislation did not exist at the time. The US Environmental Protection Agency (EPA) can require any person or company involved to bear the total of all remedial costs, no matter how much of these the respective party has actually caused (i.e. there is joint and several environmental liability). This shows that environmental liabilities are one way of internalising external costs. Even banks that have given mortgages or managed closed properties can be held liable as mortgagees in possession (Ernst & Young 1992; Skellenger 1992).

The main questions regarding the treatment of the environmental liabilities of a company are:

- What are (contingent) environmental liabilities?

- Should they be recognised and, if so, when?

- How can they be measured?

- Should they be disclosed and, if so, when?

Detailed discussion of these issues can be found in Schaltegger and Burritt (2000: 182). The Commission of the European Communities (CEC 2001a) has made a recommendation about accounting for environmental liabilities in the annual reports of companies.

An environmental liability is an obligation to make future expenditure to remedy environmental damage that has occurred because of past events or transactions or to compensate a third party that has suffered from that damage. A contingent environmental liability is an obligation to remedy environmental damage dependent on the occurrence or non-occurrence of one or more uncertain future events, or to compensate a third party who would suffer from such damage. Examples of (contingent) environmental liabilities that can emerge from corporate activities include:

- Energy emissions (e.g. heat, radioactivity, electromagnetic emissions, noise)

- Visual impact (e.g. as a result of the construction or demolition of buildings)

- Soil contamination (e.g. from underground storage or spills)

- Groundwater contamination (e.g. from contaminated surface water or soil contamination)

- Surface water contamination (e.g. from point sources such as industrial processes)

- Air emissions (e.g. from fugitive emissions and transportation activities as well as sound, noise and light)

The CEC comments on recognition, measurement and disclosure of environmental liabilities are summarised in Table 17.5.

As a rule, environmental liabilities should be recognised in financial statements if they are material and if the liabilities or the events leading to the liabilities are probable and can be reliably measured (or reasonably estimated). Management has substantial discretionary latitude in deciding when to recognise a liability even if it is likely to occur. First, interpretation is required about whether liabilities are part of normal business risk, because liabilities must not be separately recognised if they are part of the normal business risk. Second, legal obligations can take many years to finalise and be crucial for a company's survival.

Even more difficult than the definition of 'probability' is the formulation of criteria for when an environmental liability or contingent liability is 'reasonably estimable'. Thus, the main problem with environmental liabilities is the measurement or estimation of their amount.

A liability must be measured or reliably estimated in order to qualify for recognition in the main body of a financial statement. Key factors that can be considered when estimating environmental liabilities are (see Holmark *et al.* 1995; Roberts 1994b; Surma and Vondra 1992; US SEC 1993):

- Current laws and regulations

- The extent of regulatory involvement

- The number and viability of the parties involved

- Prior legal, economic, political and scientific experience

- The complexity of the problem, existing technologies and available technological experience

The CEC Recommendation places a focus on monetary information and also accepts discounted cash flow and NPV as an appropriate measure of long-term environmental liabilities—something of a controversial issue in accounting, as noted above (Burritt and Lodhia 2001). Liabilities may be recognised even if they cannot be reliably measured. This is usually accomplished by making reserves, provisions or charges to income.

Criteria	Details
(a) Recognition	
Environmental liabilities	* Environmental liabilities should be based on a clearly defined legal or contractual obligation or on a constructive obligation committed to by the enterprise. * Recognition occurs when a reliable estimate of the costs derived from the obligation can be made.
Provisions	* If there is a clearly defined obligation but at the balance date the amount or date of the outflow of resources is uncertain, a provision, rather than an environmental liability, should be recognised.
Contingent environmental liabilities	* Contingent environmental liabilities are not recognised in the balance sheet but should appear as a note in the accounts 'if there is a possibility that is less than probable' that the environmental damage has to be rectified in the future and an uncertain event has not occurred.
Offsets	* Environmental liabilities and expected recoveries should be recognised when reimbursement is 'virtually certain'. * Offsets are not allowed (unless there is a legal entitlement to do so) and should be shown separately as assets.
Environmental expenditure	* Environmental expenditure should be recognised as an expense unless it meets the criteria to be recognised as an asset set down in paragraphs 12–18. Such assets are to be amortised over their useful economic lives. * Rights, such as pollution permits, or emission rights, if they have been acquired for consideration and meet the criteria to be recognised as assets, are to be capitalised and amortised over their expected useful lives. * If an existing fixed asset is impaired (e.g. if land is contaminated), an adjustment should be made to the income account where the recoverable amount has fallen below the carrying amount.
(b) Measurement	
Environmental liability	* The measure used should be the best estimate of the expenditure required to settle the present obligation as at the balance date, taking probable future technical and legal developments into account. * If a reliable estimate is unavailable (cited as an 'extremely rare' situation), a contingent liability should be recorded.

Table 17.5 **Criteria set down by the Commission of the European Communities for environmental liabilities: (a) recognition, (b) measurement and (c) disclosure** (continued opposite)

Source: Burritt and Lodhia 2002 based on CEC 2001a

Criteria	Details
Environmental liability *(continued)*	● Measurement should include the incremental direct costs of remediation, the cost of employee compensation and the benefits to employees that directly spend 'significant' time on the restoration effort, the costs of post-remedial monitoring and the costs of implementing advances in technology that will probably be approved by the government. ● Measurement of environmental liabilities at present value is allowed where the liabilities will not be settled in the near future but where the amount and timing of payments are fixed or can be reliably determined. Measurement at current cost is also acceptable. The measurement method chosen should appear as a note in the accounts. ● If discounting is used, it should be consistently applied.
Provisions for site restoration and dismantling costs	● Estimated expenditure recognised as a liability is to be capitalised and then depreciated.

(c) Disclosure

Criteria	Details
Materiality	● Environmental issues should be disclosed only if they materially affect the financial performance or financial position of the entity.
Document of disclosure	● Disclosures may appear in the annual and consolidated annual report or in notes to the accounts of annual and consolidated accounts.
Purpose of disclosure	● The purpose is to provide a fair review of the development of the undertaking's business and position to the extent that environmental issues can directly affect it.

Type of disclosure	● Disclosure may take the following forms:
	    – Environmental policy and programmes in relation to environmental protection measures
	    – Improvements made in key areas of environmental protection
	    – The extent to which improvements have been or are being implemented
	    – Physical information on the environmental performance of the business—where appropriate using relative measures (e.g. eco-efficiency measures), absolute measures (e.g. total waste emitted) and comparative information with a link to monetary information on the balance sheet or income statement
	    – Cross-references to an environmental report should one be issued, especially whether the report has been subject to external verification

Table 17.5 (continued)

Disclosure of environmental liabilities is required in order to assess the monetary environmental risks facing the business. Disclosure is the process of incorporating elements of financial accounting (assets, liabilities, equity, expenses and income) into the statement of financial position (the balance sheet), the statement of financial performance (the income statement) or separate sections of the annual report, such as in notes to the accounts. All recognised items must be disclosed in the balance sheet. The monetary representation of the disclosed amounts depends on how the liabilities are measured. As can be seen from the CEC Recommendation, discretion is available to management about whether and how environmental liabilities are disclosed.

Tradable emission allowances
In certain circumstances businesses are provided with government permission to pollute the environment. The total amount of pollution is strictly limited through the total number of pollution permits issued and the amount of pollution permitted, usually calculated by natural scientists based on the perceived carrying capacity of environmental media. Often, a process of **grandfathering** is used to issue initial allowances—that is, existing polluters are provided with the permits first. From a monetary perspective, the importance of emission permits is that they can often be sold in the market to other parties seeking the right to pollute. These permits will be reflected in the financial accounts, and questions arise as to:

- Whether emission allowances are assets or expenses
- Whether they should be recognised
- How they should be measured
- How they should be disclosed

Similar considerations need to be given to emissions allowances as are given to environmental liabilities (see the subsection above on environmental liabilities; for more detail on emissions allowances, see Schaltegger and Burritt 2000). There are, however, some additional aspects to consider relating to the fact that assets can be classified in different ways. For example, emission allowances can be seen as inventories of the business that are held for sale in the ordinary course of business (i.e. as part of the production and sale process). If so, then monetary measurement by taking the lower of cost or market value will be used. However, if the allowances are classified as marketable securities that are held with the intention of selling them in the short run, then they are valued at net market value. Hence, depending on the purpose determined by management, different monetary amounts will be attributed to the emission allowances.

Final comment
As noted above for emission allowances, before the process of putting monetary measures on environmental assets and liabilities can be undertaken, some physical assessment of the emissions or environmental media is required. PEEA addresses this issue.

Physical external environmental accounting

Environmental information has become part of marketing and public relations (PR) for many companies. Dubious claims and an improper use of information by some businesses in the past, especially in relation to the publication of positive environmental information and the neglect of negative environmental disclosure, have reduced the incentives for other companies to improve their own environmental record (Schaltegger 1998). Introduction of a basic standard for PEEA is needed in order to secure disclosure of a minimum standard of information quality.

The international form of environmental accounting and reporting has been led by FEE (see Adams *et al.* 1999), the United Nations Intergovernmental Working Group of Experts on International Standards of Accounting and Reporting (ISAR) and the Coalition of Environmentally Responsible Economies (CERES), responsible for the GRI on sustainability (see www.globalreporting.org). PEEA standards are slowly being developed, and harmonisation is occurring. However, general reporting of PEEA information is tending to gain strength only in large companies rather than in small and medium-sized enterprises (SMEs). There is some confusion between macro PEEA indicators and business-level performance indicators, as promoted by the GRI (see below). Macro indicators are being developed by statistical organisations such as EUROSTAT (2001) and the Australian Bureau of Statistics (see www.abs.gov.au) in accordance with the suggestions of Chapter 40 of Agenda 21 (UNCED 1992), which encourages the development of indicators for sustainable development at the local, provincial, national and international levels. Business indicators are being developed by industry associations and international business groups with the purposes of business in mind. A closer examination of the GRI now follows.

The Global Reporting Initiative

The GRI bases its recommendations on a number of principles common to the preparation of accounts in business:

- Reporting entity
- Reporting scope
- Reporting period
- Going concern
- Conservatism
- Materiality

The reporting entity principle. The report will clearly define the boundary of the organisation adopted for the report (e.g. equity share, management control, site, company, group). As a result, the reporting consequences of strategic business decisions, such as subcontracting or joint venture arrangements, will be transparent. The GRI asks that reporters clearly and explicitly define the boundary conditions used in the report for the reporting organisation.

Financial accounting and reporting standards currently exist to define boundaries for different forms of corporate control (e.g. joint ventures, associates, subsidiaries).

Such standards do not yet exist to define boundaries for GRI reports. Until such standards are developed, GRI reporters may choose to use the traditional financial accounting and reporting boundary definitions as a starting point. However, it is important for a GRI reporter to define the organisation's boundaries in a way that assures readers that the originator of, or contributor to, the material impacts of its activities is included within those boundaries. To do otherwise would open the reporting organisation to accusations of producing a misleading report. Of course, a reporting organisation may wish to expand its boundaries in subsequent GRI reports to capture upstream and downstream effects of its products or services.

Organisations that form part of a supply chain face an important challenge with GRI reporting. In some cases, comprehensive reporting may require the total life-cycle impact of the product or service from resource extraction to its end of life to be addressed in some way. As a minimum, every GRI reporter is asked to include reference to the more significant supply-chain issues. Reporters are also encouraged to provide more detailed supply-chain information where feasible.

The reporting scope principle. The report will make clear the scope of activities reported (e.g. economic, environmental and social issues, or only environmental issues) and provide explanations for any restriction in reporting scope. The GRI Guidelines (www.globalreporting.com) address each of the individual elements of a full GRI report. The Guidelines also encourage reporters to work towards an integration of the economic, environmental and social elements. The GRI recognises, however, that some organisations may wish to progress incrementally towards a complete GRI report, using some of the individual elements of the Guidelines (e.g. the environmental elements) rather than the whole package. The GRI allows incremental adoption of the Guidelines provided there is full disclosure of such incremental adoption. Organisations choosing incremental adoption are asked to disclose the following items:

- The fact that, and the extent to which, they have used the GRI Guidelines as the basis for their reporting

- The reasons for incremental adoption (e.g. expense, availability of information, stakeholder needs)

- Their intentions regarding the future production of a complete GRI report

The reporting period principle. As far as possible, reportable impacts, events and activities will be presented in the reporting period in which they occur. The GRI asks that impacts, events and activities be reported in the reporting cycle in which they occur or are identified. Although a single reporting cycle is too short to capture many important economic, environmental and social impacts (such as changes in employee social conditions or environmental contamination), many economic, environmental and social indicators are likely to flow from management information systems that operate on a regular cycle. Further, as management's concern to integrate economic, environmental and social issues into overall corporate strategy increases, the more likely it will be that economic, environmental and social management systems will become aligned with conventional systems of financial management and control.

The going concern principle.   The published data will reflect the assumption that the reporting organisation is expected to continue operations into the foreseeable future. An organisation categorised as a 'going concern' for financial reporting purposes is generally expected to be financially viable and to be able to continue operations for the foreseeable future (note that the 'foreseeable future' in financial reporting terms is rarely longer than 18 months after the balance sheet date). The GRI asks that reporting organisations pay close attention to the broader implications of the 'going concern' concept. Thus, for example, organisations should consider reporting the following items in the appropriate section of their reports:

- Any 'going concern' qualifications contained in the financial audit report

- Any qualifications regarding the organisation's ability to fund necessary remediation activities; the extent to which significant internal and external operational, financial, compliance and other risks[25] are identified and assessed on an ongoing basis

- The likely impact of prospective legislation (e.g. related to products, the environment, fiscal matters or employees)

- Management's assessment of the consequences (including the economic and social consequences) of moving towards modes of production and/or service delivery compatible with sustainability

The conservatism principle.   GRI reports will claim credit only for those achievements that can be directly attributed to the reporting organisation. They will also be cautious in reporting expected future outcomes of current programmes. The GRI encourages reporting organisations to adopt a life-cycle approach and to report comprehensively on the upstream and downstream (indirect) effects of operations and activities. At the same time, the GRI asks reporting organisations to be cautious when reporting on effects that occur once the product or service has been delivered (i.e. effects 'outside the factory gates'). Reporters are asked to present a balanced picture, containing positive and negative effects of their activities.

The materiality principle.   Materiality in economic, environmental and social reporting depends on what is relevant to the reporting organisation or to its stakeholders. The reporting organisation is asked to determine what to report on the basis of applicable laws and the process of stakeholder dialogue and engagement. The economic, social and integrated indicators are presented for testing and experimentation by all reporting organisations. At this time, social indicators are less developed than environmental indicators. The application of the materiality concept to economic, environmental and social reporting is more complex than it is in financial reporting. In contrast to financial reporting, percentage-based or other precise quantitative materiality yardsticks will seldom be appropriate for determining materiality for GRI reporting purposes. Instead, materiality is heavily dependent on the nature and circumstances of an item or event as well as its scale or magnitude. For example, in environmental terms, the carrying capacity of the receiving

25   Significant risks may, for example, include those related to market, credit, liquidity, technological, legal, health, safety, environmental and reputational issues.

environment (such as a watershed or airshed) will be just one among several factors in the materiality of the release of one tonne or one kilogram of waste, air emissions or effluent. Similarly, health and safety information is likely to be of considerable interest to GRI report users despite its typical insignificance in traditional financial accounting terms.

In addition, different stakeholders may not agree on what is material. For the reporting organisation, the results of research into user needs, as well as continuing interaction with stakeholders, is necessary for determining materiality. The GRI recognises that an organisation's decisions about the materiality of specific aspects of performance might affect the form of the report itself. For example, an organisation that decides to report on conditions at individual operating sites may wish to support its primary GRI report with separate detailed material, perhaps via the reporter's website.

At the moment GRI is not designed to tell the reader of a report what the actual situation is as far as the environment is concerned. The notion of the precautionary principle is used to suggest that where scientific evidence about environmental impacts is unavailable then preservation of the environment should dominate decision-making—erring on the side of caution as far as the environment is concerned. It would be far better, for reasons of transparency, to report matters as they are and then let policy-makers decide whether the environmental concerns outweigh economic considerations. To do otherwise is to invite manipulation of information rather than to 'tell it like it is'. Being cautious about upstream and downstream impacts and about life-cycle analysis would simply destroy the main purpose of these tools.

Summary

The principles guiding the form of environmental accounting and reporting are thus to be treated with great caution as they encourage manipulation of reported information. Debate about the principles of environmental accounting and reporting continues and is, as yet, unresolved.

The physical environmental accounting information reported externally has been much analysed and criticised because of the underlying fear that the environment is still being degraded, that natural resources are dwindling and that all the time society is inching further away from sustainability (e.g. Maunders and Burritt 1991). Many empirical studies have been undertaken recently confirming that larger corporations are engaging with environmental issues and are looking to reduce their relative impact on the environment, though growth in business means that absolute environmental impacts may get worse (e.g. carbon dioxide emissions, which are thought to lead to global warming, may increase). Potential advantages suggested for those businesses reporting environmental information include:

- Improved public relations and corporate legitimacy

- The ability to meet the demands of shareholders

- The ability to anticipate the tightening of legal requirements for disclosure

- A competitive advantage

- Improved relationships with customers and environmental interest groups

At the moment, much improvement in reporting practice and standardisation is still necessary to create the 'true and fair view' in corporate environmental reports (e.g. Schaltegger and Burritt 2000: 332).

17.3.3 The importance of environmental accounting

Environment-related issues are becoming of increasing importance for the financial position of many companies. Thus, to support the economic basis of decision-making, companies with environmentally sensitive businesses should explicitly disclose in their conventional financial reports monetary amounts induced by environmental impacts. Management still has a large element of discretion in deciding which environmental issues to recognise, how to measure these and what to disclose. During the 1990s environmental management started to become an important issue in financial markets, hitherto a very conservative sector of the economy as far as environmental issues were concerned. Growth in the socially responsible investment (SRI) sector has added to this movement.

The importance of environmental accounting for other stakeholders cannot be played down either. Management, NGOs, shareholders, governments and other groups all are seeking information about the environmental risks and returns from business—information that environmental accounting systems are designed to capture, track and report.

Questions for review

17.1 Accounting has a number of functions. Consider whether the distinction between internal and external stakeholders is important for the provision of accounting information.

17.2 What is a chart of accounts? If anything is missing from a chart of accounts does this mean that it will not be accounted for? Why is the chart of accounts important in relation to the environmental impacts of a business?

17.3 Explain the difference between the financial position and the financial performance of a business. Is there a matching environmental position and environmental performance?

17.4 From an environmental perspective, how do cash and accrual accounting differ? What is the implication of this difference for environmental management?

17.5 How do conventional accounting and environmental accounting differ?

17.6 What are the main differences between the following types of accounting:
- Monetary environmental management accounting?
- Physical environmental management accounting?
- Monetary external environmental accounting?
- Physical external environmental accounting?

Which of these is most relevant to:
- A site manager?
- An environmental manager?
- A shareholder?
- A non-governmental organisation?

17.7 Select one stage of the value chain. What is the main type of environmental accounting information that the manager of this stage needs in order to make important decisions? Why has accounting for the recycling and disposal stage of the value chain been receiving greater attention in recent years?

17.8 Select one tool in the environmental management accounting matrix shown in Table 17.1 on page 58. Examine the application of this tool in one environmentally sensitive business with which you are familiar. Give reasons for the selection of the tool and business chosen by you.

17.9 How might external environmental accounting (monetary and physical) affect the environmental management of business? Does environmental management also affect external environmental accounting?

17.10 Identify one problem in applying conventional financial accounting standards to environmental issues. From the perspective of an environmental manager, are such problems important?

17.11 Provide one example of an environmental asset and one of an environmental liability. For most businesses, is one of these categories likely to be more important than the other? Why?

17.12 Explain what is meant by the term 'tradable emission allowance'. How can a business come to own or be entitled to such an allowance? Does conventional accounting have a set way of accounting for such allowances? Explain your answer.

17.13 A number of principles form the basis for the Global Reporting Initiative. Briefly describe each principle. Is any one of these more important than the others for environmental reporting? Give a reason for your answer.

17.14 Explain in your own terms the reasons why environmental accounting is important.

17.15 How is environmental accounting related to the various spheres of influence on a business?

*Concepts and tools of corporate
environmental management*

Environmental management
systems and eco-control

Management of environmental issues in business has been high on the agenda in
many countries for over 30 years. For example, Kast and Rosenzweig (1970: 151)
commented that they saw the need 'for the social role of an "environmental adminis-
trator" who will integrate the activities of various organisations and individuals with
an emphasis on environmental protection and improvement'. In the same year, Ways
(1970: 98) suggested that:

> US society is going to need tens of thousands of 'integrators' . . . who can
> handle environmental material from several natural sciences in combina-
> tion with material from several of the social sciences . . . The universities
> that produced the specialists who taught us how to take the world apart
> will now have to train the [people] who will take the lead in putting it
> together again.

Eco-control is about learning to manage issues in their totality, even though we have
organised our society and businesses to deal with problems in isolation from each
other.

Control is one of the fundamental functions of management and external
regulation. On the one hand, it embodies planning, action, measurement, comparison between plans and actual outcomes, feedback and revision of expectations for
future periods. These are all characteristics of a systems approach to management.
On the other hand, it may reflect the use of central power to dictate the actions that
an organisation must make if it is to retain its social legitimacy and continue to
operate. The former type of control is internal and co-ordinated by management,
whereas the latter type of control is implemented and monitored by governments
through 'command-and-control' regulation. Hence, the notion of control is not well
defined and has different meanings in different contexts and from different perspectives. Eco-control draws on the spectrum of possible controls available to keep an
organisation on track towards achieving its environmental and economic objectives.

For a large number of companies, eco-control provides the basis of comprehensive environmental management systems (EMSs). External regulation of such control systems combines with management control. Such systems as the European Union (EU) regulations relating to the Eco-management and Audit Scheme (EMAS) and eco-labels, British Standard (BS) 7750 and the ISO 14000 series from the International Organisation for Standardisation (ISO) have been introduced on a voluntary basis, with standards providing a basis for comparison between systems. Section 18.1 presents an overview of the most important regulations and standards relating to corporate EMSs. After providing a brief review of important methods of corporate environmental management (Section 18.2), Section 18.3 goes on to discuss the approach to eco-control, noting environmental accounting provides a core element in any EMS and in eco-control. A summary of this chapter is provided in Section 18.4.

18.1 Standardised environmental management systems and product certification

18.1.1 Overview and classification

For the past five years standards have strongly influenced corporate environmental management at the operational level. Various stakeholders defining standards of good environmental management practice have influenced corporate strategies for environmental management and environmental information management (Gray *et al.* 1996: 45; Schaltegger and Burritt 2000: 31). The growing importance of environmental management is reflected by a number of regulations and standards in force or being prepared, all with the aim of harmonising environmental management practices and procedures.

Standards can be technical, related to performance or be process-based, and they provide the foundation for continual improvement in relation to established benchmarks. Environmental management standards and certification systems can be classified according to their institutional background as well as according to their focus on the company or products (Table 18.1). From an institutional perspective, public and private standards can be distinguished depending on which institution issues the standard. For instance, EMAS is issued by the EU whereas ISO is an industry-based standardisation organisation. Standards issued by private industry associations or non-governmental organisations (NGOs) are based on the voluntary agreement of various involved stakeholders (industry, NGOs, public agencies, etc.). They describe rules that have proven to be helpful in corporate practice.

Standard-setting organisations such as ISO, the British Standards Institution (BSI), Deutsche Industrie Norm (DIN) or Standards Australia (SA), as well as other national standardisation organisations, have formulated standards against which environmental management can be audited. These standardisation organisations are private institutions financed by industry. Their markets (i.e. sales) depend on the price of auditing and certification services as well as on the reputation of the organi-

	Organisation	*Product-related*
Public	EMAS[a]	Euro Flower eco-label[b] German Blue Angel[c]
Private	ISO 14001[d] SA 8000[e]	FSC[f] MSC[g] Rugmark[h] Eco-tex standard[i]

EMAS = Eco-management and Audit Scheme; ISO = International Organisation for Standardisation; FSC = Forest Stewardship Council; MSC = Marine Stewardship Council; SA = Social Accountability
[a] See CEC 1993b, 2001b
[b] See europa.eu.int/comm/environment/ecolabel
[c] The Blue Angel; see www.blauer-engel.de
[d] See ISO 1994a
[e] See Social Accountability International, www.cepaa.org
[f] See Forest Stewardship Council, www.fscoax.org
[g] See Marine Stewardship Council, www.msc.org
[h] See Rugmark Foundation, www.rugmark.org
[i] See www.bttg.co.uk/Services/ShirleyTech/oekotex.htm

Table 18.1 Classification of certification systems: some examples

sation for ensuring that the material to be audited is of a high quality. The quality of these auditing services is, in turn, checked by regulators, who verify corporate environmental audits.

Environmental management standards issued by public institutions, such as EMAS or the EU eco-label standard (the Flower eco-label) are voluntary, too. One main difference between standards provided by private and public institutions is that public agencies and regulators institute regulatory rather than voluntary systems.

The second dimension in Table 18.1 deals with the object of certification, which can either be the organisation (company, site, association, etc.) or a product.

Among the most significant standards for EMSs are EMAS (CEC 1993b, 2001b; UBA 1998) and the ISO 14000 series (ISO 14001 for companies seeking certification, and ISO 14004 for companies not seeking certification; see ISO 1994a, 1999a). A company can participate in both standard systems at the same time. The additional costs of double certification are low if the differences in the standards are considered early enough.

ISO 14001, which is now being adopted widely, is a process standard. ISO is currently developing a family of EMSs that addresses management systems and the environmental aspects of products:

- ISO 14031, for the evaluation of environmental performance of a company (ISO 1999b)

- ISO 14020ff. as well as the Flower eco-label, as the EU standard for eco-labelling of products

- ISO 14040ff., for life-cycle assessment (LCA) of products

ISO 14031 relates to the evaluation of environmental performance of a company. In addition, to promote the inclusion of social aspects into management, social audits are increasingly being conducted by business. With Social Accountability (SA) 8000 and AccountAbility Standard (AA) 1000, two standards are available for the social audit of an organisation. Similarly, EMAS, ISO 14001 and SA 8000 aim at the certification of the company. However, other standards focus on the certification of products to allow them to carry eco-labels. ISO 14020ff. provides criteria for assessment of organisations issuing product certifications. LCA, being a core method of product assessment, can be organised according to ISO standard 14040ff.

The product-related ISO standards lead to certification according to the German Blue Angel (www.blauer-engel.de), or other labels such as 'TransFair' (www.transfair.org). The core question for corporate environmental management is which label to adopt. In addition to these product-based certification systems, there are sector-specific labels such as: the 'Eco-tex' standard for the textile industry; the EU regulation on organic farming (CEC 1991), which defines exact and strict criteria for food products that can be labelled as 'organic', 'bio' or 'eco'; and the scheme of the Forest Stewardship Council (FSC), which deals with the certification of wood products.

18.1.2 Environmental management standards: the Eco-management and Audit Scheme and the ISO 14000 series

An EMS is a set of management processes and procedures that allow an organisation to analyse, control and reduce the environmental impact of its operations and services to achieve cost savings, greater efficiency and oversight, and streamlined regulatory compliance—hence, it is closely linked with the notion of eco-efficiency.

Apart from early national initiatives such as BS 7750 (BSI 1992), which were important for the development of EMS standards in general but have not been applied widely, EMAS was the first important EMS standard. BS 7750, released as a draft standard in 1992 (the actual standard being released in 1994), was the first standard for corporate EMSs. It has substantially influenced ISO 14001, which was published as a draft version in 1994 and as a final document in 1996 (Hillary 1995: 294; Sheldon 1997; Tibor and Feldman 1996). Although ISO 14001 encompasses the general elements of BS 7750, it allows greater flexibility in application.

A major motivation for companies to establish EMSs comes from the introduction by the Commission of the European Communities (CEC) of the voluntary Eco-management and Audit Scheme (EMAS) for production sites and companies (CEC 1993b, 2001b). The term 'audit' could be misleading here, because EMAS covers much more than a traditional legal compliance audit. EMAS enables companies to have their sites audited according to criteria for 'good environmental management practices' (Pariser and Neidermeyer 1991). The first version, published in 1993, is based on 'Directive (EEC) Number 1836/93 of the Council of 28 June 1993 on the Voluntary Participation of Commercial Companies in a System for Environmental Management and Company Inspection' (CEC 1993a). The title of that publication, being too bureaucratic, was quickly exchanged in practice for the acronym EMAS.

With the revision of EMAS (so-called EMAS II) in 2001, the term received official status, although the official title remained similar: 'Directive (EG) Number 761/2001 of the European Parliament of 19 March 2001 on the Voluntary Participation of Organisations in a System for Environmental Management and Company Inspection' (CEC 2001b).

The central aim of the Directive is the continuous improvement of participating firms' environmental performance. Furthermore, the goal of EMAS is described in terms of creating and applying EMSs in organisations, the systematic and periodic assessment of those systems, the provision of information to the public and interested stakeholders about the measures taken as well as the integration of employees into the environmental management process. The last element has been added as a new goal in EMAS II.

With its revision, EMAS was expanded to include companies in the service sector, resulting in a more prominent role for the (often indirect) environmental impacts of services and products, which may be more significant in the service sector than they are in the manufacturing sector. Participation in EMAS is now open to any kind of organisation (company, public agency, clubs, universities, etc.). The scope of certification has to be precisely defined. Also, as part of the EMAS revision, the ISO 14001 standard has been included as an appendix to the revised EMAS Directive, enabling 'fast-track' EMAS registration of sites already certified in accordance with ISO 14001. A major reason for this inclusion is that in some countries (particularly in Germany, which has the highest number of EMAS-registered sites) EMAS has become a 'quasi-standard', which operates equally alongside ISO 14001.

An important part of EMAS focuses on the process of ensuring that an EMS is in place and functioning (Altham and Guerin 1999; Fichter 1995; Hilary 1993; Würth 1993; see also Fig. 18.1).

To comply with the provisions of EMAS, a company has to have implemented an EMS that helps to:

● Formulate an environmental policy and goals for corporate environmental protection

● Secure efficient environmental accounting (or information management)

● Evaluate environmental performance (and to support decision-making)

● Plan and steer company activities

● Implement the respective plans

● Build up an effective and efficient organisation

● Communicate with internal and external stakeholders (i.e. through environmental reporting)

In addition, the existence and functioning of the corporate EMS has to be verified by external auditors. Companies that comply with these requirements are free to display an EMAS logo in their letterhead. As part of its conditions, EMAS requires regular publication of an environmental statement, including an assessment of all significant environmental issues of relevance to the company's activities and a summary of figures on pollutant emissions, waste generation, consumption of raw mate-

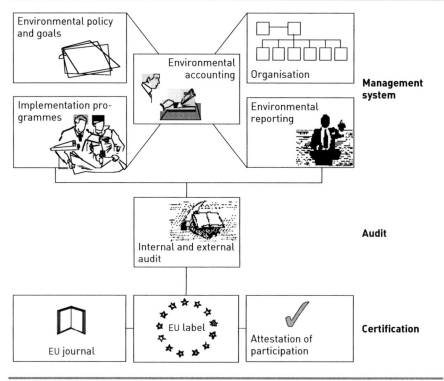

Figure 18.1 Core components of the European Union (EU) Eco-management and Audit Scheme (EMAS)

Source: Schaltegger and Burritt 2000: 376

rials, energy and water, noise emissions and other significant environmental aspects of relevance to the company's activities (Skillius and Wennberg 1998). This requirement also means that EMAS classifies environmental performance data according to environmental protection areas (e.g. energy, transport, emissions, waste, packaging, production, stock-keeping and water management) and not according to life-cycle assessment (LCA) categories such as greenhouse effect, nutrification, acidification, eco-toxicological effects and so on (Guinée and Heijungs 1993; Heijungs *et al.* 1992).

Part of the requirements for the EMAS environmental statement is to report on key environmental performance areas. Although EMAS does not prescribe precise environmental performance indicators or metrics, the information it requires to be disclosed within the statement constitutes an implicit prescription of such indicators (Table 18.2).

The result of the auditing process is that the environmental statement is validated. The environmental statement is then sent to the official registration office and registered (see europa.eu.int/comm/environment/emas). At registration the organisation receives a registration number and is allowed to publish the environmental statement. At the same time, permission is given for the new EMAS logo to be used in company reporting and communication (Fig. 18.2). The purpose of the new

Indicator or data to be recorded	Absolute dimension	Relative dimension
Production output	units of production output (e.g. kg)	not applicable
Raw material consumption	kg	kilograms per unit of production output
Energy consumption	kWh	kilowatt-hours per unit of production output
Water consumption	m^3	cubic metres per unit of production output
Total waste	kg	kilograms per unit of production output
Waste recycling rate	various units	percentage
Waste-water	m^3	cubic metres per unit of production output
Emissions to air*	kg	kilograms per unit of production output

* For example, carbon dioxide, nitrogen oxides and particulates.

Table 18.2 **Set of environmental indicators in accordance with the European Union Eco-management and Audit Scheme (EMAS): examples of units of measurement**

Source: BMU and UBA 1995

EMAS logo is to enable companies to demonstrate their environmental activities in public. The logo can be used:

- On the environmental statement
- On the letterheads of the company
- On any kind of promotional material where the organisation provides information about its activities with EMAS
- In the context of any kind of information taken from the environmental statement

The logo must not be used:

- On products or packaging
- To compare products or services
- In any kind of marketing of products or services

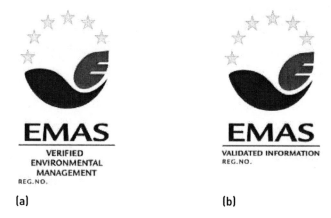

(a)   (b)

Note: The logos feature yellow stars (to mirror the flag of the European Union) over a green 'E' and a blue wave.

Figure 18.2 EMAS (Eco-management and Audit Scheme) logo for (a) an audited environmental management system and (b) for the information audited.

The EMAS logo has been launched to improve marketing and reporting possibilities. The EU explicitly asks the member countries to promote EMAS and to use the EMAS logo.

Figure 18.3 illustrates the idea behind ISO 14001. The main requirements for this EMS are similar to those of EMAS. The company has to establish:

- An environmental policy

- An environmental accounting or monitoring system

- Implementation plans

- Plans for correction

- An effective and efficient organisation

As with EMAS in 1998, when the scheme was extended to non-industrial companies, external revision of the ISO corporate EMS is necessary. One defect requiring attention is that, in contrast to EMAS, ISO 14001 does not require companies to adopt environmental reporting.

Initially, EMAS (until 1998) and ISO were both site-oriented. However, ISO 14001 does not exclude the application of its environmental management standard to products. As with quality standard ISO 9000 (ISO 2000e), strong pressure was expected to be exerted on companies to get their production sites certified. First results show that in some business-to-business relationships, adherence to an environmental management standard is becoming a requirement for suppliers (see e.g. Fichter 1995).

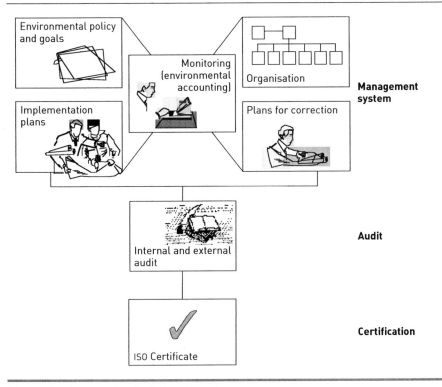

Figure 18.3 Core parts of ISO standard 14001

EMAS and ISO 14001 define requirements for corporate EMSs. However, none of these standards specifies how the requirements should be met, nor do they provide an indication of what goals corporate environmental management should strive to achieve (for a strong critique of the ISO 14000 series, see Krut and Gleckman 1998; for the importance of parallel changes to corporate culture, structure and systems, see Epstein and Roy 1997; for a discussion of the value of ISO 14000, see Begley 1997). All standards emphasise the need for environmental management control as well as the need for environmental, and particularly physical environmental, accounting as an important part of corporate environmental management. Nonetheless, the standards do not provide any methods for the management or implementation of decision-making processes (i.e. through incentive systems). Such freedom of action is designed to encourage development of efficient tools for effective environmental management. Company management should, therefore, establish an EMS that is flexible enough to be adapted to new developments (this will be discussed further in Section 18.3, on eco-control). Furthermore, to make sure that management efforts are environmentally and economically rewarding, clear objectives and goals, such as improvement in eco-efficiency, have to be identified and an environmental accounting system has to be established (see Chapter 17).

18.1.3 The main benefits of certification within an environmental management system: the Eco-management and Audit Scheme and ISO 14001

Expectations of an EMS and its certification can vary considerably depending on the organisation, the industry and the attitude of management towards the specific project and environmental management in general. Actual benefits from implementing an EMS also lead to widely differing results. Expectation, attitude and success may not correlate. The main benefits of introducing an EMS and receiving certification include the following (see UBA 1998):

- Minimisation of environmentally related economic and legal risks for the company and for management is the main issue for many organisations. Appropriate organisational structures, responsibilities for problematic activities and good documentation can help to reduce such risk.

- In many cases, reduction of environmental costs is achieved by companies participating in EMAS and ISO 14001. With improved documentation of the EMS, opportunities for lower purchasing costs, reduced waste from production and reduced disposal costs can be detected more easily and measures for cost reduction can be identified.

- The improvement of organisational procedures and structures is valued as a core benefit by most organisations. The links between health, safety and EMSs and the adoption of EMS procedures often lead to the identification of potential improvements to general operational processes of the company.

- Improvement in relations with government is mentioned as a motivational factor that encourages management to establish an EMS. Although certification itself may not be crucial in this context, contact with regulators, environmental protection agencies and industry associations during the process of introducing and establishing the EMS provides an important benefit.

To summarise, overall, experience with EMS standards is positive. Companies very rarely communicate that the project benefit has not exceeded its costs. However, there are a number of common reasons for unsuccessful certification to ISO 14001 (Hillary 2001: 34):

- A lack of understanding of environmental impacts and aspects

- A failure to address all activities (e.g. offices are often overlooked, disposal of information technology may be ignored, etc.)

- A failure to recognise indirect aspects (e.g. suppliers, canteens, disposal of products and so on)

- A failure to recognise services or activities that are not completely within the scope of the EMS (e.g. common site effluent treatment plants)

- A tendency to overlook site-wide issues as methodologies address only specific activities

- A tendency to overlook abnormal and emergency situations relating to high-risk activities

The next section discusses current developments of EMS standards and compares EMAS with ISO 14001.

18.1.4 Current development of standards for environmental management systems and a comparison of the Eco-management and Audit Scheme and ISO 14001

The current development of EMS standards and their application in practice is characterised by:

- Cost issues

- Disagreement about public disclosure and about the market effects of logos

- Membership development

- Eco-efficacy

For the average company, the application of EMAS or ISO 14001 leads to substantial cost savings. ISO, for example, reveals that 'more than 80% of 500 companies surveyed on their experiences with implementation of [ISO] environmental management systems (EMS) found them to be cost effective, with over 60% quoting payback periods on their investment of less than 12 months' (ISO 1999a). The economic effects of EMAS have been analysed by the independent working group of entrepreneurs, Arbeitsgemeinschaft Selbständiger Unternehmer (ASU) for Germany. Based on a survey and questionnaire with close to 800 companies, it found that the costs of implementing an EMAS-conforming EMS was on average around US$100,000. A third of the companies surveyed reduced costs by up to US$80,000 per year; a further third of the companies reduced their costs by more than this, by up to US$320,000 per year; whereas the remaining companies did not report any cost reductions. For the nearly 800 companies surveyed, the average payback period on investments in the EMS and on environmental protection measures was only 1.5 years (ASU and UNI 1997).

In relation to public disclosure of environmental impacts the expected market effect of ISO 14001 and EMAS logos present some problems. In particular, Europe and the USA have slightly different philosophies about disclosure. In the USA there is concern over the links between public disclosure and private litigation, which has discouraged a requirement for public environmental reporting about management systems. Consequently, the emphasis of ISO 14001 on compliance with processes rather than improved environmental performance makes it more appealing to some companies, but at the expense of credibility, feedback to stakeholders and external accountability. EMAS also appears to be stricter than ISO 14001, not just because it requires public disclosure but also because specific disclosures are required about activities, environmental issues raised, pollution emissions (including emission reductions and targets for continual improvement) and waste generation as well as comments about overall environmental performance, and these must be verified by an independent party. However, ISO 14001 is an internationally recognised standard that can be applied by all companies—small, medium and large—and identifies only a small set of core issues to be addressed. In this sense, it is a good, internationally acknowledged starting point for any company wishing to institute an EMS.

Companies that comply with EMAS and/or the ISO 14001 standard requirements are free to display the respective logo in their letterhead, something that it was hoped would become a mark of environmental excellence. It was expected that market pressure, especially in intercorporate business relationships, would encourage companies to participate in EMAS and ISO 14001 (see e.g. Fouhy 1995: 49; Heuvels 1993). However, as an economic analysis of the incentives provided by EMAS (Karl 1992, 1993) and experience show, this reason for participation may have been overestimated in the past (see e.g. Dyllick and Hamschmidt 2001; Janke 1995; Lindlar 1995; Sietz 1996). Competition continues between EMAS and ISO 14001 as alternative environmental management standards. Frequent reports are made on the relative take-up of these rival schemes (see e.g. ENDS 1998a) and emphasis is put on the development of membership.

Although since its revision EMAS has moved closer to ISO 14001, some differences remain. These differences between the standards are small—apart from the fact that ISO 14001 does not require the public disclosure of environmental impacts. Table 18.3 summarises the main differences and similarities between EMAS and ISO 14001. In general, EMAS can be considered to be a more compact standard whereas ISO 14000 is a widely spread family of standards of which ISO 14001 is a core standard. EMAS II adopts ISO 14001, including it word by word. Apart from a few additional considerations, the requirements of both standards are now the same.

As a rule the certification organisations and the certifiers have publicly accessible lists of the organisations that they audit. However, there is no general register of all ISO-certified organisations. With EMAS, in contrast, the organisation's environmental statement is sent to the official registration office and a publicly accessible list of registered organisations is available.

Once the EMS standard is introduced, practically no differences exist between EMAS and ISO 14001. In both cases a contract exists for three years. In the first year the validation or certification audit takes place. During the years that follow only a much easier, faster and cheaper check (ISO) or validation (EMAS) is needed to ensure that the EMS is still in line with requirements. In EMAS II, small organisations with fewer then 50 employees and with a turnover of less than €7 million can seek an easier and faster procedure. Small organisations need an update of the environmental statement only every three years. After three years, revalidation is due. This consists of all elements required for the first audit and validation or certification. Nevertheless, the three-year audit and revalidation process can be achieved with less effort than that required for the first audit and validation.

The interplay between politics and market pressure (the political and economic spheres) will determine which standard will prevail in the years to come. However, ISO is a clear favourite. First, ISO 14001 is an international standard applied widely

EMAS II	ISO 14001
An initial environmental check is required in order to identify and assess relevant environmental aspects.	A suggestion is made that organisations proceed first with an environmental check.
An EMS must be established according to ISO 14001 criteria, supplemented by: • Proof of legal compliance • An assessment of environmental aspects with the help of defined, auditable criteria • Integration of employee participation • Communication with external stakeholders	An EMS must be established according to ISO 14001 criteria.
Periodic checks must be made of EMS and company performance (looking at performance aspects as well as EMS aspects).	Periodical internal and external audits of the EMS must be undertaken, according to ISO 14010, 14011 and 14012.
Publication of an environmental statement is required.	No publication of an environmental statement is required.
An officially approved environmental certifier must check the external environmental audit, the internal environmental audit procedure, the EMS and the environmental statement.	An auditor from the ISO certification organisation, or from its national equivalent, must check the external audit of the EMS.
The certifier will sign the environmental statement to validate the environmental statement.	The certifier and certification organisation issue a certificate.
The environmental statement must be sent to an officially designated organisation (industry association) and the organisation is listed in the official EU register for EMAS.	No statement has to be issued.
The environmental statement and the EMAS logo may be used for marketing (but not for product marketing).	The certificate may be used for marketing (but not for product marketing). There is no specific ISO 14001 logo, and ISO will not allow its logo to be used in connection with conformity assessment activities (www.iso.ch/iso/en/xsite/namelogo.html).

EMS = environmental management system; EU = European Union; ISO = International Organisation for Standardisation

Table 18.3 **Comparison of the revised Eco-management and Audit Scheme (EMAS II) and ISO 14001**

(e.g. in the USA, Japan and South-East Asia) whereas EMAS covers only the member countries in the EU. Second, ISO and its national standardisation organisations are private organisations that already have established commercial relationships with many companies (e.g. with ISO 9000 on quality management). Third, thorough study and comparison of the two standards indicates that ISO 14001 leads to a smaller administrative workload for those companies involved.

In the next section ISO 14031, the ISO standard on environmental performance evaluation that can be combined with either of the international EMS standards, is discussed.

18.1.5 Environmental performance evaluation: ISO 14031

ISO 14031 is a standard on environmental performance evaluation in relation to environmental management (ISO 1999b). It has been approved in a number of countries and regions. For example, in November 1999 the European Committee for Standardisation (CEN, Comité Européen de Normalisation) approved the EN ISO 14031 standard. The standard for environmental performance evaluation assists companies that are interested in improving their environmental performance. The concept can be applied as part of a certified EMS but is independent of ISO 14001 or EMAS. ISO 14001 and EMAS are based on the idea of continuously improving the EMS in order to achieve improvements in the overall environmental performance of an organisation. Under ISO 14031, the environmental management Technical Committee, ISO/TC 207, aims to provide guidance towards the design and the use of measurement systems based largely on industry perspectives. It proposes that *three* types of indicators be used in environmental performance evaluation (EPE) (ISO 1999b; see also Fig. 18.4):

⬛ Operational performance indicators (covering environmental aspects), also called environmental performance indicators

⬛ Management performance indicators (evaluating management systems), also called environmental management indicators

⬛ Environmental condition indicators (covering environmental impacts)

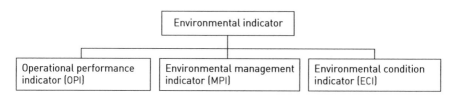

Figure 18.4 **The structure of environmental indicators, according to ISO 14031**

Source: ISO 1999b

Only operational and management performance indicators (OPIs and MPIs) are categorised by ISO 14031 as indicators of a company's environmental performance (ISO 1999b). According to ISO 14031 (ISO 1999b), in order to determine significant environmental aspects, as a basis for indicator development and performance evaluation, a business without a certified EMS should consider the following aspects of its operations:

- The scale and nature of material and energy use (i.e. the business's primary operations)
- Emissions
- Risks
- The condition of the environment
- The possibility of incidents
- Legal, regulatory and other requirements to which the organisation subscribes

Given that, in ISO 14031 terminology, only operational performance indicators refer to actual physical environmental performance, only these indicators are considered in greater depth in this section. In relation to the selection of operational performance indicators, ISO 14031 suggests that they should relate to (ISO 1999b):

- Inputs (materials, energy and services)
- Supply of inputs to the organisation's operations
- Design, installation and operation of facilities or plant and equipment
- Output (products, services, waste and emissions)
- Delivery of outputs

Annex A.4.3 of ISO 14031 develops operational performance indicators and provides examples of such indicators (ISO 1999b: 24). The method used to analyse or structure the organisation's operations is based on an input–output approach and is similar to an ecobalance analysis. Although the categories are different from those used in an ecobalance analysis, they cover the same set of stocks and flows (inputs and outputs)—only the level of detail is different.

The strength of ISO 14031 is its flexibility and broad applicability (Table 18.4). Flexibility is evident because it is possible to use the standard with or without a certified EMS being in place. Likewise, the broad guidelines for the development of environmental performance indicators allow applicability of the standard across a range of organisational types. Major weaknesses of ISO 14031 are the limited emphasis on standardisation and implementation, the large number of different indicators (which could hinder effective benchmarking) and the weak linkage between ISO 14031 and aspects of sustainability (Bennett and James 1999: 9). These main weaknesses need to be addressed (e.g. through a process similar to the EMAS revision procedure) if the standard is to reach its potential.

ISO 14031 is based on a circular process, with continuous collection and analysis of data, assessment of information, reporting and communication—in a manner

Opportunities	*Limitations*
It provides interesting ways to measure environmental performance and can be used as a source of ideas.	Certification is not offered.
It proposes the introduction of a dialogue with interested parties, which can be helpful in the designing of suitable performance indicators.	The indicators given as examples cannot be applied directly but have to be adapted to organisation-specific situations.

Table 18.4 Opportunities and limitations of ISO 14031

similar to a management control system. The process of environmental performance evaluation is regularly checked and improved. There is no certification involved with ISO 14031 and so no certifiers exist for this standard.

18.1.6 The Social Accountability 8000 Standard

SA 8000 was the first international standard to deal with the audit of the basic rights of employees (SAI 2001). The procedure is based on the conventions of the International Labour Office (ILO) (SAI 2001: 4), the UN Human Rights Convention and the UN Convention on the Rights of Children. SA 8000 deals with nine areas. It states (see also Quote 18.1):

1. There should be no child labour.

2. There should be no forced labour.

3. Health and safety in the workplace should be guaranteed.

‘1.1 The company shall not engage in or support the use of child labour . . .

2.1 The company shall not engage in or support the use of forced labour, nor shall personnel be required to lodge 'deposits' or identity papers on commencing employment with the company.

4.1 The company shall respect the right of all personnel to form and join trade unions of their choice and to bargain collectively.

5.1 The company shall not engage in or support discrimination in hiring, compensation, access to training, promotion, termination or retirement based on race, caste, national origin, religion, disability, gender, sexual orientation, union membership or political affiliation.

6.1 The company shall not engage in or support the use of corporal punishment, mental or physical coercion or verbal abuse.’

Quote 18.1 Aspects of the Social Accountability 8000 standard

Source: CEP 1997

4. Workers should have the right to join labour unions.

5. Workers should not be subject to discrimination.

6. There should be no corporal punishment, coercion or any other insult to employees.

7. A maximum number of working hours should be observed (to a maximum of 48 hours per working week).

8. A minimum wage should be set.

9. Management systems should be established to ensure the eight rights outlined above are observed.

For every type and size of business, the standard is audited by external auditors that are certified by the Accreditation Agency of the Council on Economic Priorities (CEPAA). GS Société Générale de Surveillance SA (SGS-ICS) was the first certification organisation to conduct external audits in accordance with SA 8000. On its website SGS-ICS describes the four steps (or stages) to achieving an SA 8000 certificate (Quote 18.2). Organisations that are audited are registered by the auditors.[26] The registration is valid for three years. Registered organisations are allowed to use the certificate for marketing purposes.

Standard SA 8000 requires compliance with minimum social standards. This differentiates it from ISO 14001, which allows an organisation to introduce a management system and establish a process for continuous improvement without complying with minimum environmental standards. Nevertheless, SA 8000 describes (in point 9) core aspects of a management system needed to secure compliance with the standard. Some parallels between SA 8000 and ISO 14001 and EMAS are clear. Important similarities are:

- The formulation, documentation and public availability of a detailed company policy (for working conditions and social accountability in the case of SA 8000)

- The periodic check of company policy in relation to appropriateness, suitability and effectiveness

- The naming of a representative with responsibility for compliance with laws and regulations

- Knowledge, understanding and implementation of the standard throughout the whole organisation

- The requirement to encourage adoption of the standard by suppliers and to check that the standards are adopted

- External reporting of social standards (as with EMAS)

SA 8000 sets requirements for eight areas plus the establishment of a management system in order to demonstrate that a minimum of social standards are achieved.

26   The list of all certified auditors and registered organisations can be found at www.cepaa. org.

❛❜ Stage 1: Plan. The standard is publicly available from the Council on Economic Priorities (CEP), SGS-ICS (GS Société Générale de Surveillance SA) or any other member of the CEP board. Within your organisation someone must be nominated to take responsibility for the process and obtain top management commitment. If possible, this person should be familiar with management systems auditing. The more skilled they are in this, the more you save in using outside help. This person will conduct an initial self-assessment to identify what needs to be done based on the standard and its accompanying guidance document. You may then need to appoint someone, a local non-governmental organisation (NGO), a consultant or specialist to help you. They will work with you to set up systems and processes to help you comply with SA 8000 and will advise you on how each section of the standard will be judged. It is up to you, the company, to demonstrate to the auditors that you comply with SA 8000.

❜ Stage 2: Do. You need to implement the SA 8000 management requirements to enable you to comply with SA 8000. Records are essential to provide evidence for the audits and ensure ongoing compliance.

❜ Stage 3: Check. At this stage you can request a pre-audit, which will not count towards the final audit but will show whether you are likely to comply with SA 8000 requirements and what needs to be done to become certified. In most cases you might opt directly for the main audit: If your system is in compliance with the standard's requirements, you will receive from SGS-ICS an SA 8000 certificate valid for three years. If you are not in compliance with the standard, SGS-ICS would request a clear demonstration of what corrective actions you are taking to achieve compliance. And only when all aspects of the standard have been complied with will you be awarded the certificate.

❜ Stage 4: Act. SGS-ICS will then undertake periodic surveillance audits (every six months to one year) to monitor your SA 8000 system and ensure it is maintained. However, management systems are based on the 'continuous improvement' approach, aimed at enhancing the organisation toward more global and more efficient compliance against the standard.❜

Quote 18.2 **Four steps to an SA 8000 certificate**

Source: www.sgsgroup.com

With this, some control activities of local labour unions and government agencies are replaced within the supply chain. Important opportunities and limitations of SA 8000 are summarised in Table 18.5.

18.1.7 Labelling and declaration: ISO 14020ff. and the European Flower eco-label

ISO 14020ff. deals with the content and procedures of product eco-labels and environmental declarations. Product labels are to be developed to be easily understandable. Environmental declarations and labels can only be used for marketing purposes when they are justified by real environmental benefits. By considering the whole life-cycle of a product, ISO intends to prevent any displacement effects shifting environmental impacts from one stage of the value chain to another.

Opportunities	Limitations
Companies can be certified as meeting the social standards of SA 8000.	The certification of a supplier does not ensure that the product supplied has been produced by the supplier (it may be a traded product) and thus it is not guaranteed that it has been produced according to SA 8000 standards.
Companies can ask their suppliers to comply with the same standards.	The requirements of SA 8000 focus on global minimum standards and are not progressive enough to meet the corporate social responsibility goals in the most developed countries.

Table 18.5 Opportunities and limitations of SA 8000

Environmental labels serve the purpose of declaring products to be environmentally friendly and of distinguishing them from conventional products. In the past 20 years many labels have been introduced. Some are well known and have a good reputation and high credibility whereas others are less well known and less credible (Fig. 18.5).

Eco-labels compete with each other, and only some will survive. Important aspects of eco-label survival include (Scholl and Hinterding 1995: 14ff.):

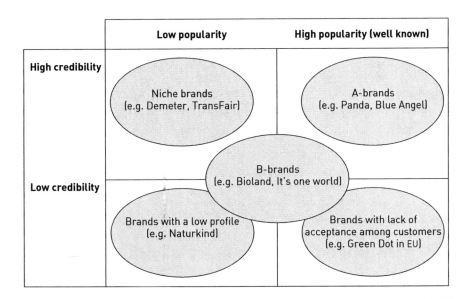

Figure 18.5 Typology of environmental labels

Sources: Schaltegger and Petersen 2002: 78; Spiller 1999

- Independence. There are limited possibilities for influence or control by the organisations applying for the label.

- Possibility of checks. There are clearly specified criteria and checks are made on the quality of the process that decides which companies or products qualify to use the labels.

- Understandability. Criteria are clear and are determined by the relevant environmental and social aspects of the product.

- Transparency. There is complete documentation of the process relating to how the labels are assigned.

The ISO 14020ff. family of standards is relatively young and adopts these general criteria as the basis for successful eco-labelling. The first publication of these standards was in 1998, for ISO 14020 (ISO 2000a), which addresses environmental labelling and declarations in very general terms. In contrast, ISO 14021 (ISO 1999c), ISO 14024 (ISO 1999d) and ISO 14025 (ISO 2000d) are relatively large, detailed documents. Detailed lists are available of aspects to be considered when management intends to make product-specific declarations or to develop a label for a specified product.

ISO 14021 deals with the role of various environmental attributes of products. In relation to supplier communication in environmental labelling and declarations, definitions of various common environmental expressions are defined in this standard, such as 'recycled content', 'reduced resource use', 'recovered energy', 'waste reduction' and 'reduced energy consumption'. The standard explains when these expressions can be applied.

ISO 14024 considers eco-labels. It provides the principles and protocols for third-party labelling when developing environmental criteria for a particular product.

ISO 14025 addresses the communication of quantitative environmental declarations and deals with the quantitative indicators that can be used for marketing purposes. Examples include the use of energy, water or resources and the release of emissions per unit of benefit. Like ISO 14024, this standard is also mainly relevant to labelling organisations.

A regulatory development in the area of product labelling that has not yet been very widely accepted is the European environmental label, the Flower eco-label, introduced in 1992 (Fig. 18.6).

EU plans are that in the long run all national environmental labels in Europe will merge with this label. However, to date, the Flower eco-label has not received the necessary degree of acceptance or level of popularity to compete with other labels. Nevertheless, it continues to be applied. At present, 15 groups of products are eligible to receive this EU product label. The plan is for 30 groups of products to be covered by the end of 2003.[27]

---

27 Further information is available on the Internet homepage of the European environmental label, at europe.eu.int/ecolabel.

Note: The label features a ring of blue stars (reflecting the flag of the European Union) surrounding a green 'E' above a green stem and leaves.

Figure 18.6 The European Flower eco-label

18.1.8 Life-cycle assessment according to ISO 14040

Product LCAs attempt to measure the environmental impacts of a product and—in the ideal case—consider the entire life-cycle of a product 'from cradle to grave'. LCAs create a basis for the environmental assessment, comparison and improvement of products. Since the 1980s LCAs have become established as a well-known tool of environmental product management.

ISO 14040 (ISO 1997) is concerned with environmental management, LCA principles and other general requirements. It forms the basis for the ISO 14041 (1998) standard on data inventory, the ISO 14042 (2000b) standard on impact assessment and the ISO 14043 (2000c) standard on the interpretation of LCAs. With this family of standards, ISO provides a framework for LCA in four stages:

1. Definition of goals and scope

2. Inventory

3. Impact assessment

4. Interpretation

According to ISO 14041, the first stage in LCA is the definition of the goals and scope of the analysis (i.e. the boundaries of the analysed system, data-quality requirements and so on). These definitions determine the following steps of the investigation. Goals and scope can focus on the improvement of a single product (e.g. a car) or on a comparison of two or more products (e.g. two different cars). A clear definition of the functional unit (e.g. a van) is indispensable if a comparison between products is intended. The rule is that the functions of the products being compared have to be comparable (e.g. vans should not be compared with trucks).

In this first step measurement of the functional unit (e.g. kilometres per person) is defined to facilitate quantification and comparison and to provide a basic reference point for measuring environmental impact added.

In practice, time, data and financial resources are constrained, so only a part of the total material and energy flows in a life-cycle can be investigated. There are some steps in the life-cycle that must be considered in all cases:

* Extraction and production of raw materials

* Production of important auxiliary materials

* Transportation of goods and materials

* Generation and use of energy, heat and electricity

* Production and use of products

* Disposal and recycling of production materials and products

Also, the categories of environmental impact to be considered should be defined during this early stage of LCA in order to provide the necessary basis for data collection. The categories of impact need to reflect adequately the environmental impacts of the product.

Establishing an inventory is the second stage of an LCA. The inventory, as described in ISO 14041, includes the collection and calculation of data for the whole life-cycle of a product. Inputs taken from the natural environment and outputs released into the environment are recorded. The goal is to compile an inventory of data that is related to the goals and scope of the LCA defined in the first stage.

In practice, direct input–output relationships are rare in a product life-cycle so that procedures are necessary to allocate indirect material and energy flows to the product(s) being examined. Such allocation procedures relate to flows for transportation, multi-purpose production processes, recycling and disposal. A range of allocation procedures is available; however, no 'best' allocation procedure has been developed so far. The main rules for allocation have been defined in environmental accounting literature; their advantages and disadvantages are mentioned in Chapter 17.

In impact assessment, according to ISO 14042, inventory data is aggregated, classified and assessed according to potential environmental impacts such as greenhouse effect, eutrophication, nutrification, etc. The contribution to each impact or classification group (e.g. greenhouse effect, depletion of ozone layer) is measured by an indicator (e.g. greenhouse warmth potential, ozone-depletion potential—explained in Burritt 1995). The standard distinguishes between compulsory and optional aspects of impact assessment (Fig. 18.7).

The starting point for impact assessment is the choice of impact categories, impact indicators and impact models. This step is to a large extent determined by goal definition and scoping. However, as greater knowledge about the product life-cycle becomes available, the choice of impact categories may have to be adjusted. The impact categories describe environmental problems that are scientifically accepted and discussed in public. Some impact categories are listed in Table 18.6. ISO 14042 has not defined the link between impact categories because this step is still not well developed by science.

Compulsory aspects

Choice of impact categories, impact indicators and impact models

Classification of inventory data to impact categories

Aggregation of impact results (i.e. characterisation)

Creation of an impact (environmental) profile

Optional aspects

Normalisation (relation of impact indicator relative to a reference)

Ranking (ordinal ranking)

Valuation (aggregation to one index value for environmental impact added)

Figure 18.7 **Steps in life-cycle impact assessment according to ISO 14042**

The final stage in an ISO 14043 LCA is interpretation. In this stage, results of the earlier steps of the LCA are interpreted and recommendations are made. The results of the LCA are to be communicated in an understandable way to make sure that the decision-makers receive a clear picture of the environmental impacts. Three steps are distinguished:

- Identification of significant parameters
- Evaluation of the quality of the LCA according to its completeness, the stability of the result and the consistency of assumptions and methods
- Recommendations and reporting

18.2 Methods of corporate environmental management

This is not the place to discuss specific environmental management tools in depth; rather, the aim is to show the link between the main tools of corporate environmental management with environmental accounting and EMSs. Table 18.7 indicates that contemporary methods of corporate environmental management are not particularly new and that they rely on well-known traditional management tools (for a detailed overview, see BMU *et al.* 2002 [downloadable in English at www.uni-lueneburg.de/csm]).

Impact category	Substances or emissions that contribute to the impact (examples)
Depletion of resources	Renewable and non-renewable resources (e.g. oil, coal, minerals, wood)
Greenhouse effect	CO_2, CH_4, NO_x
Depletion of the ozone layer	CFCs, halons
Human toxicity	Heavy metals (e.g. cadmium, mercury, lead), VOCs, dust (PM10), benzole, SO_2, NO_x, CO, soot
Terrestrial eco-toxicity	SO_2, NO_x, CFCs
Aquatic eco-toxicity	Lead, cadmium, copper, mercury, zinc, chrome, AOX,
Photochemical smog	NO_x, VOCs
Acidification of water	SO_2, NO_x, NH_3, HCl, HF
Acidification of soil	SO_2, NO_x, NH_3, HCl, HF
Eutrophication of water	NO_3^-, NH_4^+, COD, phosphorus
Eutrophication of soil	NO_x, NH_3
Land use	Resources extracted (e.g. coal, minerals, ores) Reduction of ecological quality

Abbreviations:
AOX = adsorbable organic halogens; CFC = chlorofluorocarbon; COD = chemical oxygen demand; PM10 = particulates less than 10 μm in diameter; VOC = volatile organic compound

Chemical compounds
CH_4 = methane; CO = carbon monoxide; CO_2 = carbon dioxide; HCl = hydrochloric acid; HF = hydrofluoric acid; NH_3 = ammonia; NH_4^+ = ammonium ion; NO_3^- = nitrate ion; NO_x = nitrogen oxides; SO_2 = sulphur dioxide

Table 18.6 **Examples of impact categories for use in ISO 14042**

Conventional management tool	Environmental management tool
Calculation and costing	Life-cycle assessment
Accounting	Environmental accounting
Auditing	Environmental auditing
Reporting	Environmental reporting
Total quality management	Total quality environmental management
Control	Eco-control

Table 18.7 **Methods of environmental management derived from methods of conventional economic management**

Source: Schaltegger 1994a

Environmental accounting, auditing and reporting, eco-control and total quality environmental management (TQEM) are all based on conventional accounting notions of: auditing, reporting, control and total quality management (TQM; see Dobyns and Crawford-Mason 1991; Greenberg and Unger 1991; Petrauskas 1992). Life-cycle assessment and costing is a special case of environmental accounting and simply corresponds to calculation (costing). It represents a single-time ecological calculation (ecological costing) with its scope extended to cover the entire life-cycle of a product.

No matter what standard of environmental management is adopted—BS 7750, EMAS, the EU regulation for a product eco-label or ISO 14001—all address some of the following key functions of 'good environmental management':

- Goal-setting

- Information management

- Support for decision-making, organisation or planning of environmental management programmes

- Steering, implementation and control

- Communication

- Internal and external auditing and review

Figure 18.8 provides an overview of various well-known environmental management methods and shows which tools support the key functions of environmental management as defined by EMAS and ISO 14001 (see also UNEP 1995). Other tools of environmental management such as environmental business re-engineering are not explicitly shown as they are usually derivatives of the previously mentioned set of tools. These tools support different corporate environmental management functions and are discussed briefly below.

- Life-cycle assessment. The main focus of LCA is on data management (single calculations for individual products) and assessment. LCA also addresses some aspects of goal-setting (strategy and planning) and decision support. However, other functions of corporate environmental management, such as steering and communication, are not, or are only partially, supported by LCA.

- Environmental accounting and reporting. Traditionally, accounting is the main corporate information management tool (see e.g. DTTI *et al.* 1993). All management activities rely on or are at least influenced by accounting information. Environmental accounting, as shown in Chapter 17, is the application of established tools of accounting (i.e. tools of information management, analysis and communication) to environmental management. However, environmental accounting is a management tool and must be comprehensively incorporated into the environmental management process. Only then can environmental information be integrated into goal-setting, steering, implementation and communication.

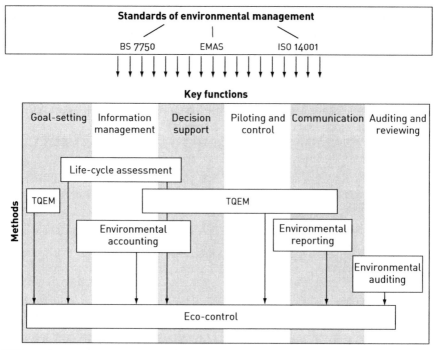

TQEM = total quality environmental management

Figure 18.8 **Functions and tools of corporate environmental management**

Source: Schaltegger 1996b

● Total quality environmental management. TQEM is the application of the principles of TQM (Deming 1982, 1993; Walton 1986) to environmental management. In this connection, the term 'quality' is expanded to include environmental quality. TQEM is based on statistical tools to achieve quality control: namely, various charts for data analysis, steering and internal communication (PCEQ 1991). In addition, TQEM is based on a statistical and engineering philosophy and supports goal-setting, with an emphasis on the continuous improvement of quality. In its original form, TQEM does not integrate measures of economic performance with measures of quality or, rather, environmental quality. Apart from an emphasis on statistical quality control and on continuous improvement (a notion central to environmental management standards), TQEM is holistic; that is, it looks at each part of environmental management as an integrated whole—a system in which all elements have to work together (including the environmental element) if goals are to be achieved.

● Environmental auditing. The main use of environmental auditing is as a checklist. In the USA, environmental auditing is understood as being a check of compliance with regulations (Friedman 1992; Hall and Case 1992), whereas in Europe it is interpreted as a management control system (see e.g. Fichter 1995; Paasikivi 1994; UNEP 1995: 4; Vinten 1991) which also checks compliance with company policies and regulatory requirements. The European interpretation is formally expressed in the voluntary regulation, EMAS. Internal company audits often help prepare a company for independent external audits by certified professionals.

● Eco-control. Traditionally, control is the key function of corporate management (see e.g. Emmanuel *et al.* 1990; Horngren *et al.* 2000; Horvath 1990). Control is achieved through a set of management controls. The control process is based on accounting information (see e.g. Merchant 2000; Neumann-Szyszka 1994). Eco-control is the application of controls to environmental management. The basic idea of applying control to environmental management was probably Seidel's (1988). The concept was designed with the purpose of integrating and co-ordinating other environmental management tools. Apart from its role in developing a company's environmental management, eco-control is also an important tool for the management of production site environmental performance in accordance with EMAS, ISO 14001 or BS 7750 (see e.g. Fichter 1995). Eco-control ensures that environmental issues are dealt with through a continuous, company-wide process, by focusing on incentives for making congruent decisions (decisions where individual and company goals are the same): that is, through use of internal taxes to achieve the desired behaviour.

Table 18.7 shows that environmental accounting and reporting, LCA, TQEM and environmental auditing are tools that are particularly strong in supporting specific functions of environmental management. It is also clear that every environmental management method aimed at supporting real improvement in performance will have to rely on some kind of environmental accounting. Environmental accounting supports information management: that is, compilation, analysis and decisions based on environmentally induced financial and environmental impact added data.

However, information is not a substitute for action but is simply necessary for informed action. To improve a company's environmental record in an effective and efficient way, the environmental information that has been collected and analysed has to be channelled into an environmental management feedback process. In conventional financial management, accounting information is used as the main input for control and decision-making. Eco-control, by analogy, is the systematic process and anchor for corporate environmental management.

In the next section eco-control is examined in further detail, as it is the only approach that relies on environmental accounting and was designed as a co-ordination and integration device for other tools of corporate environmental management.

18.3 Management eco-control

18.3.1 The basic concept

The concept of eco-control is the creation of a permanent, institutionalised, internal management process based on environmental accounting and reporting. The concept of eco-control, in contrast with financial and strategic control, is concerned with the environmental and related financial impacts of a company. Eco-control can be divided into five procedures (see also Fig. 18.9):

- Formulation of goals and policies (Section 18.3.2)

- Information management (e.g. environmental accounting and reporting; Section 18.3.3)

- Decision support systems (Section 18.3.4)

- Steering and implementation (Section 18.3.5)

- Communication (internal and external; Section 18.3.6)

All EMSs, including EMAS and ISO 14001, require an environmental policy as well as clear and measurable annual environmental protection goals. With a focus on the aim of improving corporate eco-efficiency, the economic and ecological aspects of operational goals should be considered (see also Section 8.1).

Information management is at the core of any EMS. In practice, it is often the case that only what is measured is managed. The establishment of an environmental

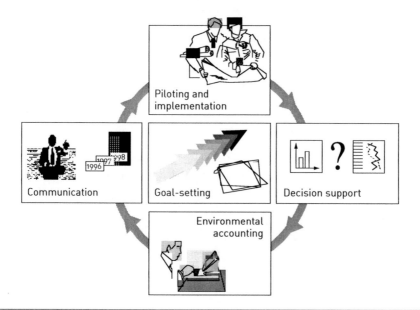

Figure 18.9 The concept of integrated eco-control

Source: based on Schaltegger and Sturm 1998

accounting system is one way of increasing the efficiency of information management.

Managers frequently suffer from excessively detailed information that hampers efficient selection and use of relevant data. Any information concerning environmental interventions must therefore be assessed according to its relevance. Furthermore, integration of economic and environmental aspects is necessary. Effective environmental management requires incentive systems to steer and implement corporate plans in the most efficient manner. Internal communications play a central role in efficient implementation. However, communications with external stakeholders are also supported by internal processes and this increases the gains from sound internal environmental management.

Although it is important to establish a clear structure and plan for all procedures, steps do not necessarily have to be completed in sequence. Nevertheless, below, Sections 18.3.2–18.3.6 present the five procedures in logical order.

Specific 'guiding' instruments are needed in order to implement the eco-control process. The process provides management with a detailed analysis of the place, cause, extent and timing of environmental impacts. In addition, the total corporate environmental impact caused should be kept in mind when dealing with individual problems. This will avoid ineffective and inefficient developments (e.g. spending more and more on scrubbers to reduce smaller and smaller amounts of sulphur dioxide [SO_2] instead of reducing far worse environmental impacts from nitrogen oxides [NO_x]).

The importance of each eco-control procedure depends on the environmental issues faced by the company and on their effect on commercial success factors. However, companies should carefully consider whether they have given every procedure enough thought. Too often, environmental management tools are introduced without any clear understanding of the corporate environmental strategy being followed.

18.3.2 Formulation of goals and policies

Unfortunately, the formulation of clear goals and policies as the first and most important step of environmental management is often neglected. Many top managers feel the pressure to do something to reduce the environmental impacts of their companies and they embark on 'environmental activism' that contains many isolated activities but has no clear direction. For a company to be a good and efficient environmental performer and to reap the benefits of being an environmental leader in its markets, the reason for investing in an EMS has to be very clear. It is essential that the top managers define the purpose of environmental management activities and are involved in the process of goal-setting in order to ensure organisational commitment to the environmental strategy once it is formulated.

On a general level, improvement of corporate eco-efficiency is an attractive goal as this encourages integration of economic and environmental goals. However, to be effective, this broad objective has to be subdivided with a focus on the needs, interests and activities of specific internal and external company segments and stakeholders.

Assessing and ranking exposure to and the importance of different environmental issues for overall company performance is one of the first steps in moving towards a situation that is under eco-control. Depending on this initial analysis, the operational goals of eco-control and the perspective taken will differ. Analysis should be conducted from a company stakeholder point of view. One should ask which aspects of eco-efficiency and thus which eco-efficiency indicators are relevant to the different stakeholder groups (see Section 8.1). The potential degree of exposure to different environmental issues should guide the company in its implementation of eco-control. Here, environmental science has to play its part by providing management with an idea of what, from a scientific point of view, the most dominant environmental issues are and how they apply to the company. Knowledge of the main issues is important because such issues are likely to influence company success sooner or later, whether through new legislation, through public or consumer perception and behaviour or otherwise.

Figure 18.10 provides an example of an exposure portfolio. The expected exposure of the company to different environmental problems (e.g. the greenhouse

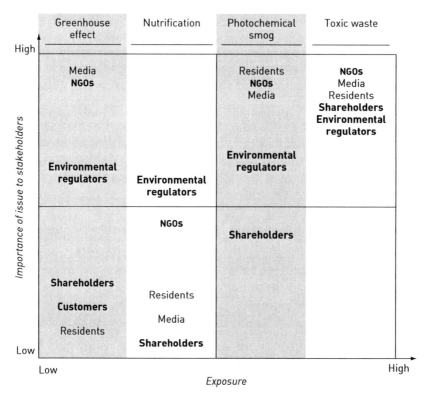

NGO = non-governmental organisation

Figure 18.10 **Key environmental issues and environmental exposure of a company: an example**

Source: Schaltegger and Sturm 1998

effect or the depletion of the ozone layer) increases from left to right along the horizontal axis. The importance assigned to these environmental issues by various stakeholders increases up the vertical axis. Those stakeholders that are most important economically for the company are printed in bold. For most companies, governmental stakeholders such as environmental protection agencies, customers, NGOs and investors are among the most powerful and are usually treated as the most important stakeholders where environmental issues are concerned.

The relative importance that different stakeholders assign to environmental problems can be measured by surveys or discussed in company working groups guided by learning-circle kits[28] that highlight the main issues as a basis for discussion, whereas company exposure to different environmental problems is revealed by environmental audit and ecological accounting (UNEP and SustainAbility 1996). The relative economic importance of different stakeholders depends on the amount and exchangeability of resources provided as well as the possibility of substituting one specific stakeholder group for another. Companies tend to negotiate with stakeholders in sequence, because of limited or 'bounded' rationality (Simon 1957; Cyert and March 1963), unless there is a critical incident when instant communication with all stakeholders is needed.

In the example shown in Figure 18.10, stakeholders who are concerned about the environment—shareholders, customers, NGOs and environmental regulators—are seen to have the strongest influence on the economic success of the company. However, only shareholders (looking at the economic consequences of toxic waste) and environmental regulators (seeking legal compliance with regulations concerning photochemical smog and toxic waste) are deeply concerned about the environmental problems to which the company is strongly exposed.

In the beginning, this first procedure is mainly a task for top management to tackle. However, to cover the whole range of corporate activities, it is recommended that representatives of different departments be involved from the beginning. In a second step, lower down the organisational hierarchy, line and staff managers who investigate and formulate opinions on topics of special importance in their field of competence should be involved in the formulation of the strategy by contributing to working groups.

Analysis of a company's expected exposure to different environmental problems, the weight given to these problems by various stakeholders and the economic importance of the stakeholder groups to be taken into account enable management to focus on high-priority environmental issues (those stakeholders printed in bold in the upper right-hand quadrant of Figure 18.10). However, the upper left-hand quadrant and the lower right-hand quadrant in Figure 18.10 should also be scrutinised, albeit less intensively, by management. Regarding the lower right-hand quadrant, issues of low public priority to which the company is a significant contributor may become important if a problem triggers a change in stakeholder perceptions. In short, the position of stakeholders on any issue noted in Figure 18.10 can change over time and, furthermore, company exposure can change as its process and production mixes change through natural adaptation, mergers, takeovers, joint ventures and franchises.

28 See Learning Circles Australia, www.learningcircles.org.au.

Also, in relation to the upper left-hand quadrant of Figure 18.10, environmental management requires managers to recognise that the risks associated with corporate environmental impacts and stakeholder perception of those risks can be substantially different. Hence, there is a need to manage scientific assessments of environmental hazards and the 'outrage' that may accompany an environmental intervention, even if in technical terms it is not a high-risk issue (Sandman 1986). People perceive things as being less risky if they are controllable rather than uncontrollable, voluntary rather than involuntary, familiar rather than unfamiliar, natural rather than artificial and chronic rather than acute (Sandman 1986).

After this first eco-control procedure is complete and priorities have become apparent, more detailed eco-efficiency information is gathered by using information from the environmental accounting system. This may lead to a reassessment of priorities and the revision of operational goals.

18.3.3 Information management

The recording of information about environmental intervention and environmentally induced financial information is necessary in order to build a basis for decisions based on an eco-efficiency criterion (see Section 8.1). Therefore, efficient environmental management requires well-designed systems of environmentally differentiated accounting and ecological accounting.

Recording begins after having established an environmental accounting system for the company. Identification of potential sources of data is the first step in compiling data in the environmental accounts. Special attention has to be paid to existing sources of environmentally relevant data, such as management accounting for materials and the amount of energy used, site permits for some pollutants, production statistics and the technical specifications of production machines.

From an economic perspective, because the costs of data collection may be high, it does not make sense to aim to provide a comprehensive inventory of all mass and energy flows—quite apart from the fact that this goal cannot be achieved anyway because of scientific limitations on data measurement and availability. Usually, the process of data compilation will need to be spread over several years, digging deeper each year until one arrives at the margin where the benefit from more detailed data is equal to the cost of obtaining that data.

Management accounting and ecological (physical) accounting employ similar terminology and methods. This ensures that the managers and staff compiling the data and the people who are to use that data have a gentle learning curve to ascend, and the approach is easy to understand. Management accounting benefits from having an inventory of environmental data in which environmentally induced costs (such as energy costs, pollution abatement costs or the costs of material flows) can be traced or allocated to appropriate cost centres and cost objects. Although a focus on selected relevant environmental interventions does not provide the same breadth of information for pollution-prevention strategies as does a fuller consideration of interventions, it requires fewer resources for the compilation of data, and one can still achieve a sound basis for improvement of corporate eco-efficiency through eco-control.

Contrary to common belief, measurement of economic performance has also gone through a rapid phase of redevelopment in recent years with increases in shareholder value being promoted as the benchmark for economic success. Management should therefore be aware of the effects of corporate environmental management on a company's shareholder value.

18.3.4 Decision-support system

The goal of the third procedure for achieving eco-control is to provide decision-makers with a logical and transparent method for taking environmentally and economically sound decisions in accordance with the data obtained from the second procedure (see Fig. 18.11).

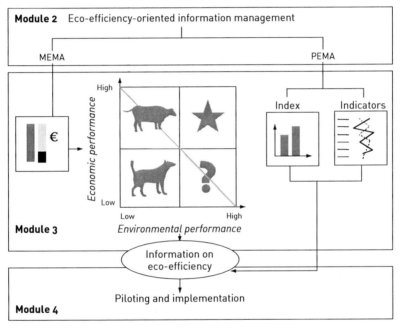

MEMA = monetary environmental management accounting
PEMA = physical environmental management accounting

Figure 18.11 **Decision-support system**

Source: based on Schaltegger and Sturm 1998

The reason for collecting information on corporate environmental impacts as well as on environmentally induced financial impacts is the calculation of eco-efficiency. Further measures, such as environmental impact added indicators for specific environmental problems (e.g. the greenhouse effect), are necessary to improve analysis of the different facets of environmental impacts and to identify alternatives for their cost-efficient prevention and reduction.

An effective way to visualise eco-efficiency is through an eco-efficiency portfolio (see Ilinitch and Schaltegger 1995; Schaltegger and Sturm 1994). At a conceptual level, this matrix-oriented tool can help companies evaluate the environmental and economic impacts of specific products, strategic business units and industry mixes (for diversified companies). Additionally, this tool supports: strategic decisions involving divestiture, acquisition, product development and marketing; communication with external stakeholders; and negotiation with environmental compliance groups and regulators.

Portfolio approaches have been used for several decades to help diversified companies analyse their business mix (for the Boston Consulting Group Matrix, see Hedley 1977; Hill and Jones 1992; Hofer and Schendel 1978; for other matrices, see Hill and Jones 1992; Pearce and Robinson 1991). Although the dimensions of the models and their corresponding matrices vary, each dimension addresses only the economic aspects of the corporate portfolio. Although most managers would agree that environmental decisions affect economic success, the environmental dimension has only recently been explicitly incorporated into strategic portfolio analysis.

Figure 18.12 illustrates an eco-efficiency portfolio matrix. The eco-efficiency portfolio involves quantification of the environmental impact added of business activities and the comparison of this with the business's economic performance. The vertical axis of Figure 18.12 relates to economic performance, and the horizontal axis relates to the environmental impact added. This general approach is applicable to any company or product group and can be employed with as many or as few details as are relevant to a manager. Terminology used is similar to that used in the Boston Consulting Group Matrix (see Hedley 1977: 10). However, the matrix combines different dimensions so that the conclusions cannot be interpreted in exactly the same way.

The optimum position on the eco-efficiency matrix is in the upper right-hand quadrant, marked 'green star', with its high economic impact and low environmental

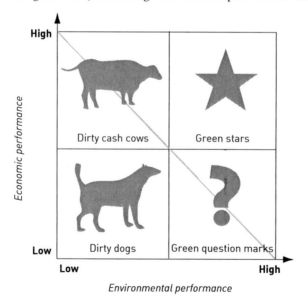

Figure 18.12 **Eco-efficiency portfolio matrix**

Sources: Schaltegger and Sturm 1995, 1998

harm (i.e. high environmental performance). An example of this sort of product might be a high-market-share, recyclable white paper produced by an energy-efficient mill that uses a non-chlorine bleaching process. Non-plastic coated paper and greetings cards made from recycled paper tend to be products with high contribution margins for which the demand is relatively large but which also have a relatively low environmental impact if produced in this way.

The opposite matrix cell (lower left-hand quadrant), the 'dirty dog' position, is to be avoided, although it may result from a combination of management decisions, the history of the company, imposition of tighter standards, increased industrial risk and newly emerging environmental issues. An example of a 'dirty dog' product might be bleached pulp produced by a smaller, older, energy-intensive mill that uses a chlorine-based bleaching process. Such mills cannot achieve the economies of scale needed to gain high market shares in their commodity markets. From an integrated ecological–economic perspective, many products manufactured with such generic methods cause environmental harm without producing significant economic benefits.

Many intermediate positions exist between these two extremes. 'Dirty cash cows' (upper left-hand quadrant) tend to possess high market shares in mature or declining 'dirty' industries. An example of a 'dirty cash cow' might be plastic-coated, white paper from a relatively large and efficient pulp mill that uses chlorine-bleaching technologies and which benefits from the paper industry lobbying for low emission standards or high pollution quotas. Such businesses can, in the short run, be highly profitable for companies and the communities in which they operate, so that there is an economic incentive to continue production. This position is very weak and risky in the long run, however, because of the increasing possibility that a potential loss of reputation, as well as liability for a potential environmental disaster, could turn into actual costs for the company. Increasingly, stakeholders and 'watch-dog groups' are searching for ways to establish financial and also criminal penalties for such actions.

A counterpoint to the 'dirty cash cow' might be the 'green question mark'. A 'green question mark' is in a weak position because of its low financial contribution, even though it is an environmentally attractive business. Examples of products in this position are high-priced, biodegradable paper products. Such products may have experienced either limited success or failure in their markets, depending on their cost structure, their technology and their ability to convince a growing number of consumers that paying premium prices for environmentally sound products is worthwhile. Products that may be 'green question marks' in an economic recession may have the long-term potential to become 'green stars' in a stronger economic climate. The strategic challenge for 'green question marks' is to become financially viable. This can be achieved by reallocation of environmentally induced costs (see Burritt 1998). In other cases, a market may have to be created for the products and/or the producer may have to capture market share. If consumer values and behaviour can be changed, or if production costs can be lowered, 'green question marks' may be profitable at some future date.

Strategies that move 'dirty cash cow' companies towards being 'greener cash cows' should enable these companies to improve eco-efficiency or even achieve sustainable development. Likewise, the cost of operating in the 'dirty cash cow'

328 An Introduction to Corporate Environmental Management

quadrant is increasing over time. If 'dirty cash cow' companies are unable or unwilling to develop environmentally sensitive products and invest in clean technologies, they may rapidly fall into the 'dirty dog' corner. Late efforts to improve the environmental record of entrenched 'dirty cash cows' may lead to an increase in costs without a similar increase in revenue. As a consequence, they may shift to the 'green question mark' position. For 'dirty cash cows', environmental costs have to be supervised and closely tracked. As they begin to rise, either a major clean-up effort or a quick divestiture is recommended.

Although companies with 'dirty cash cow' and 'dirty dog' cultures may not be inclined towards 'green' solutions, there need not be a conflict or trade-off between environmental and financial goals. Proactive, innovative pollution and risk-prevention strategies and the introduction of environmentally benign inputs may improve the company's environmental position. Such actions may also increase the contribution margin and net present value through lower input and production costs or through increasing sales, and therefore may even move 'dirty dogs' into the 'green star' quadrant.

Depending on the purpose of analysis, a three-dimensional eco-efficiency portfolio matrix with one environmental and two economic performance indicators (e.g. market growth and profitability) can be drawn. The advantage of a three-dimensional portfolio matrix is that more measures can be integrated and illustrated. However, the portfolios and their interpretation become quite complicated.

Economically or environmentally proactive strategies lead to better environmental and/or economic performance through innovation. Environmentally and economically reactive strategies, in contrast, are characterised by being second-best imitations performed with a time-lag. The result of poorly enforced or defensive strategies may be no movement at all through the eco-efficiency matrix.

As general recommendations are always dangerous, it is very important to analyse all opportunities available to convert 'dirty dogs' into 'green stars'. In practice, the following different approaches to improve the 'greenness' of products, business units and companies can be observed:

- The repair approach. Here the focus is on a specific product, such that the environmental intervention that causes most units of environmental impact added is investigated (e.g. a scrubber may be added to clean up the production step that creates an environmental intervention).

- The exchange approach. Here the focus is on inputs that cause hazardous environmental interventions to see if they may be replaced by other, less harmful inputs (e.g. hydrochlorofluorocarbons [HCFCs] may replace halons).

- The quick strategic approach. In this case, for example, the product with the greatest environmental impact added per dollar yield is eliminated.

- The functional approach. Here, management tries, for instance, to find entirely new and 'greener' ways to fulfil a certain function (e.g. to meet the wishes of buyers). This can be achieved by replacing a product by a service.

It is clear that in many cases only a functional approach will lead to an overall improvement in the economic and ecological results. However, sunk costs related to investments in production processes often limit this strategy. The functional approach is, therefore, often a long-term strategic choice rather than an operational option. Furthermore, as will be discussed in the next section, any decision taken on the basis of information processed and created has to be implemented effectively if it is actually going to lead to an improvement in corporate eco-efficiency.

18.3.5 *Steering and implementation*

Many environmental management tools fail to consider the importance of the implementation process. On the strategic management level, the sustainability balanced scorecard is emerging as a core strategy implementation and information tool (see Figge *et al.* 2002; Schaltegger and Dyllick 2002). It is, furthermore, crucial to design the organisation carefully for environmental management. Being a large and complex matter in itself, this issue can only be touched on here (for a more detailed overview, see Birke and Schwarz 1997; Pfriem 1991). In the eco-control approach the focus is at the operational management level. In this context, an important consideration is that environmental protection should not be delegated to a separate supporting team composed of specialised staff. If corporate environmental management is to be effective, responsibilities have to remain with line managers, even though they may have specialist staff to support their decision-making. New organisational forms provide additional reinforcement for this view. For example, network-form organisations are designed with line managers as the entrepreneurs, strategists and decision-makers; with middle managers as horizontal integrators, building competences across the company; and with top management challenging the status quo rather than allocating resources (Hope and Fraser 1997).

Eco-control addresses different levels within the organisation and combines the very different tasks of shop-floor environmental data compilation and strategic environmental management. To use the language of managers, it helps lower the barriers to implementation. In addition, it bridges the gaps between different users of environmental management information.

Given a divisional form of organisation, information has to be collected by production managers and passed on to middle-management controllers. The controllers have to consolidate data and prepare it for the top management so that these managers can make strategic decisions. Line managers need access to data in order to meet their responsibilities, be it for the marketing of a product, the appraisal of a new investment in production equipment or the control of operational or even strategic performance at a particular site.

Implementation is crucial to eco-control. More and more companies have developed sophisticated systems of performance evaluation to remunerate their employees. One way of ensuring the successful integration of eco-control is to link the remuneration package of managers to defined eco-efficiency targets. As with eco-efficiency indicators in general, the range of possible performance indicators is, in principle, unlimited. However, just as with payments linked to financial performance, incentive structures have to be chosen with great care and linked to the measures that are under a manager's control and that are linked to activities for which a manager is accountable. Nothing creates more frustration than targets that cannot be achieved because of factors beyond the control of the manager or employee being evaluated.

Eco-efficiency performance indicators always have an economic and an environmental dimension. Conventionally, upper-management performance indicators have a strategic dimension (e.g. 10% annual reduction of company contribution to the greenhouse effect per dollar of shareholder value). For lower management levels these performance indicators have to be more detailed and divided into economic and environmental indicators (e.g. if it is assumed that coal usage is mainly responsible for the contribution to the greenhouse effect, the environmental performance indicator can be defined as coal usage per unit of product manufactured). Another aspect of implementation is that it is important for people whose performance is being measured to be involved in the definition of the indicator.

If a decision-support system shows that a company's environmental problems are linked to only a few clearly defined substances an internal tax system can be established (see the arguments put forward in Burritt 1998). Internal taxation works in the same way as external taxation through the macroeconomic fiscal system by adding costs to the most harmful substances and undesirable practices. As an internal system, the taxes can be revenue-neutral for a company but can create a strong incentive for the various levels of management (e.g. product managers and divisional managers) to find environmentally benign and, therefore, internally 'untaxed' solutions for their products across the whole life-cycle. Implementation tools should also take careful account of the corporate culture, existing management tools and the importance of environmental accounting and internal reporting for maintaining accountability linkages.

18.3.6 Communication

Internal and external communication are of major and growing importance for the successful management of a company and thus form an integral part of the eco-control process. Internally, the link between environmental strategy and corporate success has to be explained, and progress towards established targets or benchmarks needs to be documented (Walleck et al. 1991; Watson 1993). Managers should be familiar with the environmental issues in their area of responsibility and of how the company is dealing, or plans to deal, with them. Managers should also have a clear idea of how they can use the information derived for eco-control to help improve corporate competitiveness.

The main focus of this text is on site-related, division-related and company-related information management. Thus, environmental accounting and eco-control place the emphasis of environmental management on company processes. They do not include environmental impact over the life-cycle of a company's products. However, this may produce insufficient relevant information for companies that have negligible emissions from their sites but produce highly scrutinised products with environmental problems. In such cases, an LCA of products based on site-specific information is to be recommended. If this approach is not applied, management should use screening and early detection methods (for an overview, see Liebl 1996; Steger and Winter 1996). Furthermore, consumer perceptions and buying patterns are also important. This implies that market-oriented information about consumer behaviour is important (see e.g. Meffert and Bruhn 1996; Monhemius 1993). Moreover, the role of eco-marketing and the communication of environmental issues in consumer markets will also have to be considered.

At the site and the company levels, the increasing importance of external communication about environmental issues is apparent because of the fast-growing number of environmental reports. Although many of these reports still read very much like public relations brochures, more and more of them are exhibiting a clear environmental strategy and they report in some detail about company targets, progress towards these targets and the actions and environmental management tools used to reach them. Although there are as yet no clear generally accepted standards for environmental accounting and reporting, stakeholder interest in these reports is growing. Contents of the report should reflect a company's specific situation and should address the information needed by each stakeholder group. A balance between local, site-oriented reporting and consolidated figures for the whole company has to be achieved. Site-specific data will be important to people living in the neighbourhood of plants and factories, to local authorities with responsibilities for planning and zoning and to employees working at a specific site. If necessary, detailed site-specific data can be computed and disclosed. Such data should be assessed in accordance with its relevance to the specific plant or factory environment. Consolidated, company-wide data is more relevant to shareholders, customers and top management who are trying to position the company relative to their competition. For multinational companies, only environmental interventions that have a global impact should be consolidated. Environmental interventions with local impacts do not have to be aggregated but need to be shown separately for different sites.

18.3.7 On achieving eco-control

If the concept of eco-control is to be widely adopted by companies of all sizes, in all industries throughout the world in their attempts to improve environmental management practice and environmental performance, three practical issues need to be addressed relating to the conversion of existing accounting and reporting systems to environmental accounting:

- First, a contemporary assessment of the characteristics of the current accounting and reporting system needs to be undertaken.

- Second, support needs to be given to the operators and users of existing accounting and reporting systems during the transition towards a revised system of environmental accounting and reporting.

- Last, the existing accounting and reporting systems need to be redesigned and, once redesigned, need to be implemented.

Maunders and Burritt (1991: 16) refer to these issues as being part of the process of 'deconditioning' and 'reconditioning' in relation to values and beliefs as well as the learning of new skills by information producers and users. Accountants have a natural advantage when it comes to the redesign of accounting and reporting systems. They are the gatekeepers of existing external and internal accounting systems that serve management decision-making, planning and control functions, including external communication. Their expertise in audit and independent verification provide credibility to the product of their labour and, as noted in this chapter and in Chapter 17, the implementation and communication principles 'albeit focused on a different vector of objectives' (Maunders and Burritt 1991: 17) are unlikely to be radically different from those that accountants currently practise.

Any systematic move towards the introduction of a new accounting and reporting system that is based on the importance of economic outcomes and also embodies the philosophy that 'green is good'—yet recognising that there are limits to 'greenness', just as there are limits to financial gain in a period (would companies really want to operate with zero wages, free material inputs and all costs being borne by others?)—will have to address a number of questions in order to implement some of the suggestions made in this book. These questions relate to examination of the current accounting and reporting system, support services for stakeholders during the transition to environmental accounting and the redesign for and implementation of eco-control (see Box 18.1).

Contemporary assessment of the characteristics of the current environmental and sustainability accounting and reporting system

Overview

1 How has the existing accounting and reporting system developed?

2 Why are reports required? Is it to enable integrated decision-making, for accountability purposes or as a guide to government policy-making?

3 Are reports tied to financial benefits?

4 Who is reporting at present?
   a What are the organisations' names, sectors and types?
   b Are they large, medium-sized or small?
   c Are there any allies and partners?
   d What are the industry associations?
   e Are there any multinational or domestic connections?

5 Who is supposed to be reporting?

6 When are reports expected?

7 Are reports being submitted speedily?

Recipients of reports

1 To whom are organisations reporting (to which stakeholders)?
   a Is accounting information reported to external parties (e.g. regulators, the financial community, media, local communities, non-governmental organisations, customers)?
   b Is the information reported internally (e.g. to employees)?

Box 18.1 Questions relating to the implementation of environmental and sustainability accounting and eco-control (continued opposite)

2 Is feedback from any of the stakeholders being received about the contents of reports?
  a If yes, is any of this feedback critical?
  b Has feedback helped improve performance or credibility?

Content of report

1 What is the typical content of an accounting report?
  a Analyse the content.
  b Look at the length of reports.
  c Are forecasts and actual data included, and is a comparison between forecast and actual data made?
  d Is base data included?
  e Is benchmark information included?

2 Are there exception reports for managers?

3 How much and what type of information (e.g. qualitative or quantified) is disclosed to the public?

4 Are there any 'commercial in-confidence' issues?

Frequency of reports

1 Are reports being made annually?

2 How many reports are being made and from which sites, divisions and product centres?

3 When are reports received?

4 Are any new reports expected in the immediate future?

5 How are reports submitted: as hard copy or in electronic form (e.g. on the Internet)?

Use of information

1 Is the reported information used by stakeholders (internal or external)?

2 How is the information used?

3 Is the information linked to established goals?

Support system

1 What types of support are being given to reporters by the company?

2 Is there internal and/or external support?

Provision of support services to stakeholders during the transition from the current accounting and reporting system to the new system

Overview

1 What support services can be offered to help participants with problems in drawing up or understanding their reports?

2 What staff, services, tools, manuals and documentation can be offered as help?
  a Are there tools to provide support direct to stakeholders?
  b Are there tools to help industry advisers and associations with the transition phase?

Box 18.1 (from previous page; continued over)

3 Are there any constraints on the introduction of a new system?
   a Is there a lack of participant time or expertise?
   b Is there a lack of financial resources?

4 How will support be offered to overcome any problems?

Advice to stakeholders

1 What advice can be provided to stakeholders?

2 Will it be reactive?
   a Will they receive assistance in understanding technical aspects?
   b Will an industry association or mentor examine the draft reports prior to publication?
   c Will verbal advice or feedback be received on draft reports?
   d Will written comments be received on draft reports?

3 Will it be proactive?
   a Are any problems anticipated (e.g. with the interdisciplinary nature of reported information)?
   b What support would be offered to overcome any problems?

4 Will the chief executive officer, environmental staff, technical accounting staff and industry advisers meet to explain changes?

5 What is the best way to provide information about the materiality of data reported?

6 What accuracy levels are expected?

7 What level of comprehensiveness is expected?

Information needs

1 What information will help stakeholders?

2 Who is to be able to understand the contents of manuals (e.g. internal stakeholders)?

3 Are there any technical problems with environmental and accounting calculations?

4 In what format are reports to be presented?

5 Will there be a helpline (e.g. for external stakeholders)?

Redesign and implementation of the accounting and reporting system to facilitate eco-control

1 What can be learned from eco-control accounting and reporting mechanisms in other countries or companies (see Schaltegger and Burritt 2000)?

2 What incentives (e.g. cost allocation) are to be used to encourage rapid take-up of the new accounting and reporting system?

3 What is the potential for synergies and linkages with other accounting and reporting requirements?

4 Why should environmental accounting and reporting be carried out? Consider:
   a Improvements in accountability
   b Maintenance of credibility (social acceptance)

Box 18.1 (from previous page; continued opposite)

    c The building of eco-efficiency capacities
    d The encouragement of training and familiarisation with problems
    e The relative position of the company as a good or bad performer and as a leader or laggard

5 Which centres should report? Consider:
    a Sites (sensitive and less sensitive)
    b Products and product lines

6 Are the reports to be responsibility-based?

7 To whom should centres report?

8 Who are seen as being the critical stakeholders?

9 Is reported information to be made available to all critical stakeholders?

10 What is the ideal content of a report?

11 Has reconfirmation of support been received from top management?

12 Are there links between reported information and an organisation's environmental policy, strategies and management systems?

13 Regarding accuracy, what should be the threshold for materiality for reporting?

14 What financial information is to be included?
    a Should the cost of compliance be reported?
    b Are capital and operating costs of actions to be reported, and, if so, are they to be reported separately?

15 Are there to be measures of effectiveness (absolute and normalised)?

16 Are there to be measures of efficiency (absolute and normalised)?

17 What minimum information should be required in order to meet the goals of the report?

18 What is the minimum of information to be reported to the public?

19 Does the report complement other reporting systems?

20 Should the requirements of reporting be differentiated based on size or industry type?

21 What level of assurance should be offered to stakeholders for the redesigned accounting and reporting system prior to implementation?

22 What environmental management tools should be developed and integrated?

23 Is there to be any testing of any new accounting and reporting tools (e.g. through a online reporting system or hotline)?

24 Is there to be development and testing of pro forma accounting systems and reports in term of form and content?

25 Are there to be any workshops and training programmes on the new accounting and reporting system?

Box 18.1 (continued)

18.4 **Summary**

No serviceable environmental management is possible without appropriate eco-control and environmental accounting information. Environmentally differentiated and ecological accounting provide necessary information for decision-making, steering, implementation and communication (reporting). However, the mere compilation and analysis of data will not improve a company's environmental track record. The value of environmental accounting and the economic and environmental information it provides depend on how well accounting information is incorporated into environmental management.

So far, the most comprehensive approach to environmental management is the eco-control procedural framework. This facilitates the integration of all the important corporate environmental management tools: environmental accounting supports information management and decision-making; the tools of TQEM and environmental auditing help managers to improve implementation, steering and control; and physical external environmental accounting forms a critical part of the stakeholder communication and accountability process.

Eco-control is designed to co-ordinate all tools supporting environmental management. Eco-control places the focus of environmental management squarely on in-house processes. It does not attempt to include environmental impacts over the life-cycle of a company's products. Instead, this management concept can be adjusted to the specific production site and specific company. A chemical company handling thousands of toxic substances will need to employ a more sophisticated concept of eco-control and will need to pursue different goals from, for example, a furniture manufacturer or a service company. It has been shown for many small, medium-sized and large companies that eco-control has enabled companies to manage and improve their eco-efficiency, their environmental performance and the environmentally induced financial impacts of a company and its production sites (see Schaltegger and Sturm 1998).

More and more companies are claiming that the achievement of sustainable development is one of their main goals. There is broad agreement that sustainable development has three dimensions: economic, environmental and social. Today, implementation of tools to help movement towards sustainable development are becoming increasingly important for those companies wishing to ensure their long-term success. Tools for assessing a company's social performance are still in the very early stages of development. There is far less consensus over the social aspects of sustainability than there is regarding the other two dimensions—economic and environmental—and these have formed the main thrust of this chapter on eco-control. However, eco-control by its very nature is concerned with influence, and with power relationships as well as with economic and environmental issues. Although the social dimension is not taken into account, eco-control as a notion is rapidly growing into a core management tool available to *all* companies, going through similar stages of development to those followed by financial control. The next step is to integrate developments in management control with eco-control as a foundation for sustainable development.

Questions for review

18.1 What is the ISO 14000 series of environmental management standards? Why do other environmental management standards exist as well? Are there any differences between EMAS and ISO 14001?

18.2 Do EMAS and ISO 14001 have a logo? Why would a company be attracted by a logo for its environmental management system? Does the logo directly help to sell more environmentally benign products?

18.3 EMAS II has a closer link with ISO 14001 than did the unrevised version of EMAS. Why was it considered necessary to revise EMAS? Which of the two systems (EMAS II and ISO 14001) do you feel will dominate the other? Give reasons for your answer.

18.4 'Environmental performance evaluation is, sadly, not a requirement of ISO 14001.' Do you agree with this statement? How does ISO 14031 complement the intent of ISO 14001? Explain.

18.5 Outline three standards (other than EMAS, EMAS II and ISO 14001) that are relevant to environmental management.

18.6 'Environmental accounting provides a core element in any environmental management system and in eco-control.' Examine the nature of this link.

18.7 Do environmental management systems specify which environmental goals a company should try to achieve? Do they support the objective of achieving greater eco-efficiency? Comment on your answers.

18.8 Good environmental management has a number of functions. List these and provide an illustration of bad environmental management, stating which functions have not been properly addressed by the business.

18.9 Eco-control is said to be 'a co-ordination and integration device for other tools of corporate environmental management'. It has five procedures. Outline these procedures. Are there any links between these procedures and systems thinking?

18.10 Is there a link between eco-control and improved corporate environmental performance?

18.11 To what extent are 'outrage' and limited cognitive capacity in decision-making of importance when a company is establishing eco-control goals and policies? Provide an illustration where each of these characteristics has influenced a company.

18.12 How can an eco-efficiency portfolio matrix provide decision support to a business?

18.13 Why might the management of small business adopt a repair approach to improving the 'greenness' of its products and processes rather than a functional approach? Consider incentives that might encourage small businesses to adopt a functional approach.

18.14 Is there a link between eco-control and each of the spheres of influence over business? Explain.

*Concepts and tools of corporate
environmental management*
Outlook and future of corporate environmental management

This book provides an overview of key corporate environmental management topics and shows that environmental management is characterised by various specific management problems, questions and approaches that do not form a part conventional corporate management but that are nevertheless crucial to business success. Part 2 of this book illustrated this point by revealing that environmental management emphasises the need for a substantially stronger understanding and normative analysis of influences from various sources, or spheres of influence. Socioeconomic, legal, political and technological considerations are recognised to play a greater part than is acknowledged in the conventional financial management of a business. As shown in Part 3, strategic management can be fundamentally influenced by specific environmental issues that require examination and thought about new aspects of competitiveness, new forms of co-operation and new strategic considerations that are captured by the concept of strategic environmental management. Strategy works through into operational practice and, in Part 4, eco-marketing, environmental accounting and eco-control were discussed as three core methods of corporate environmental management.

Corporate environmental management, as discussed in this book, is developing fast and brings business to the threshold of triple-bottom-line (environmental, social and economic) management and sustainability management. To make these leaps successfully, businesses face a number of challenges for which good environmental management establishes the groundwork (BMU *et al.* 2002):

■ **Environmental challenge.** This addresses the absolute impact on nature. Ecosystems have carrying capacities, and the reduction of biodiversity is occurring at an ever-faster rate. At present, most corporate environmental management activities in practice are focused on relative improvements, captured by eco-efficiency measures, but absolute improvements are becoming the core environmental challenge for business. Future environmental management has therefore to focus on increasing its eco-effectiveness—that is, on the reduction of its total impact on nature—and conducting itself in an eco-equitable way in its relations towards its various stakeholders.

● **Social challenge.** This is gaining increasing attention in the corporate world. The legitimacy of companies to operate is being challenged more frequently than it was in the past and at a growing number of locations around the world. To develop triple-bottom-line management and sustainability management, environmental management has to include activities that reduce the negative and increase the positive social impacts of business in the most effective way and to address dialogue and power imbalances with stakeholders. Triple-bottom-line management and sustainability management will therefore increase the socio-effectiveness of corporate activities in an equitable way.

● **Economic challenge.** This challenge to environmental protection and social impact is twofold. As profit-oriented companies have been established for economic reasons, and as they are acting in ever more competitive marketplaces, environment management is challenged to demonstrate how its environmental and social activities contribute to higher profitability and added value for all stakeholders. Triple-bottom-line management should therefore be able to increase eco-efficiency (the ratio between economic performance and environmental impact added) and socio-efficiency (the ratio between economic performance and social impacts) and lead to triple-win solutions. The goal is to increase value creation through business activities while reducing negative impacts and the ecological footprint of business.

● **Integration challenge.** This is one of the most difficult aspects of corporate environmental management. First, to work towards triple-bottom-line and sustainability management, all three dimensions and thus the first three challenges mentioned above have to be simultaneously addressed. Hence, contextual integration of sustainability aspects is a necessary condition. A second necessary condition is that environmental management itself has to be integrated into core business processes, tools, decision-making and accountability. Currently, environmental management often works through parallel systems (e.g. environmental management systems) and is dealt with by managers of environmentally oriented support departments that are constantly struggling with the issue of how to get line managers to consider environmental goals. For success within the context of the various spheres of influence and available fields of action identified in this book, environmental management must therefore become an integral part of conventional management processes and approaches. In addition, it will have to be integrated with even newer developments in triple-bottom-line management and sustainability management.

Appendix
Model environmental agreement

The following model agreement is edited from the agreement drawn up by the US Environmental Defense Office and the Pew Charitable Trust (the 'Alliance' referred to in the original document).[28] The aim of the agreement is, they state, to 'define the groundrules of a partnership and clarify expectations for all parties engaged in a project'. Items in square brackets indicate information specific to a particular project to be filled. Items in curly brackets offer alternative wording or approaches to particular language.

A.1 Terms of agreement

1. [Name of project], a project of [names of organisations and government departments] (the 'Alliance'), and [company name] (the 'Parties') hereby agree to work together to [short summary of project scope], as more specifically defined in the separate document {the attached} Scope of Work (the 'Project'). This Agreement sets out the terms on which the Alliance and [company name] will work together.

2. The Parties will prepare and distribute to the public a final report that describes the results of their work together. It is contemplated that the Parties will complete their work within [anticipated length of project] from the date of execution of this Agreement. On completion of the report, the Parties will determine what (if any) further activities to pursue.

3. The Project will be carried out by appropriate Alliance and [company name] staff, and will require priority effort and time commitment by each

28 The text of the agreement drawn up by the US Environmental Defense Office and the Pew Charitable Trust can be found at www.environmentaldefense.org/Alliance/ modelagreement.html.

of the Parties. The Parties will each bear all their own costs and expenses in working on the Project, and [company name] will not compensate the Alliance in any way for any such costs or expenses. Meeting locations and other Project activities will be chosen to equalise the expenses of the Parties.

4. The Project work will require substantial information. Where possible, the information needs of the Project will be met using expertise within or accessible to the Parties. Where outside expertise is needed, the Parties will jointly agree on and direct the work of the expert consultants. The cost of hiring outside experts or other substantial information-gathering activities as jointly agreed on will be {borne by (company name)} will be allocated in a manner to be determined at such time.

5. Each of the Parties has the right to terminate the Project at any time. In such an event, the Parties will be free to comment on the Project as they see fit.

6. The public report will be jointly released and published by the Parties after review and agreement by each. In the event that there is disagreement among the Parties about a portion of the report, separate statements reflecting the different perspectives may be included. Each Party will have the opportunity to review and offer non-binding comments on these statements. The report itself, and any executive summary or other mutually acceptable summary of the report, will not be released or disseminated by any of the Parties in other than its full form except by mutual agreement. Following publication, the Parties will otherwise be free to disseminate, use and comment on the report, and to comment on the Project, as they see fit.

7. In order for the Parties to work effectively, it will be necessary for [company name] to disclose certain confidential information to the Alliance. The Alliance agrees that all information identified by [company name] at the time of disclosure as confidential will remain confidential and will not be disclosed without the written permission of [company name] or used by the Alliance other than in connection with this Project, subject to the additional terms and conditions contained in Appendix 1. This confidentiality obligation shall remain in place until [company name] informs the Alliance in writing that the information is no longer confidential.

8. In order to maximise the environmental benefits from the Project, the Alliance and [company name] agree that information and innovations that arise from their work together should be made as widely available as possible. At the completion of their work, the Alliance and [company name] agree that both Parties are free to make publicly available information, tools and methods developed in the Project. This may be done through the public report or through other materials released by one or both Parties, providing that such disclosure is consistent with the other terms of this Agreement, including the terms in Paragraphs 6 and 7.

9. [Company name] shall not refer to the Alliance's work with [company name] in the Project, other than through dissemination of the report, in any advertising, marketing or point-of-sale material without the prior written approval of the Alliance {or [name of individual organisation in the Alliance]}. It is anticipated that once the Project is complete and implemented, [company name] may describe the Project's work in materials such as environmental press materials, an annual environmental report or other similar fact-based, non-advertising materials; for these purposes the Alliance will not unreasonably withhold written permission. Each Party may communicate with its directors, shareholders, members, employees and, for the Alliance, potential or existing funders about the Project, subject to any restrictions on confidential information.

10. The Parties agree that any subsidiaries, agents, vendors or consultants to [company name], or any other such parties used in connection with the Project, will be required to comply with Paragraphs 8 and 9 of this Agreement. For subsidiaries, agents, vendors or consultants to [company name], [company name] agrees to:

    (a) Provide these parties with a copy of this Agreement and advise them that they are required to comply with Paragraphs 8 and 9

    (b) Take commercially reasonable efforts to enforce such parties' compliance with these provisions

    (c) Promptly inform the Alliance if [company name] has reason to believe or becomes aware that any such party is not complying with these provisions

11. As the work of the Project proceeds, each Party may pursue their business and advocacy activities on environmental issues as they see fit.

12. This agreement shall become effective on the date of execution by the last executing Party.

Accepted and agreed to:

[Company name] by

    [Name]

    [Title]

    [Date]

and by

    [Name]

    [Title]

    [Date]

The [full name of the alliance], [name of first member of alliance] by

    [Name]

    [Title]

    [Date]

and by

    [Name]

    [Title]

    [Date]

A.2 Appendix 1 to the Agreement: additional terms and conditions regarding confidentiality

Pursuant to Paragraph 7 of the agreement, the Alliance's obligation to maintain the confidentiality of information identified by [company name] at the time of disclosure as confidential will not apply if such information: (a) is publicly known; (b) is provided to the Alliance by a third party; or (c) is discovered independently by the Alliance. If [company name]'s initial designation of information as confidential is provided in other than written form, [company name] agrees to provide the Alliance with a written designation of such information as confidential within a reasonable period, not to exceed one week; otherwise the Alliance will not be required to hold such information as confidential. The Alliance agrees to: (A) protect and prevent disclosures of the confidential information; (B) exercise at a minimum the same care its members would exercise to protect their own confidential information; and (C) not use, reproduce, distribute, disclose or otherwise disseminate the confidential information except as authorised by [company name] to perform the Project. In no event shall the Alliance exercise less than a reasonable standard of care to keep confidential the confidential information. This confidentiality obligation shall not apply to information that is required by law to be publicly disclosed, provided that the Alliance gives [company name] prompt notice of any such legal request so that [company name] may enter objections and/or defences to such disclosure.

Bibliography

Aaker, D.A., and G.S. Day (1982) *Consumerism: Search for the Consumer Interest* (New York: The Free Press, 4th edn).

AASB (Australian Accounting Standards Board) (1999) *AASB 1037: Self Generating and Regenerating Assets* (Sydney: Prentice Hall).

Abell, D.F. (1980) Defining the Business: The Starting Point of Strategic Planning (Englewood Cliffs, NJ: Prentice Hall).

ACCA (Association of Chartered Certified Accountants) (2001) *Environmental, Social and Sustainability Reporting on the World Wide Web: A Guide to Best Practice* (London: ACCA, October 2001).

Achard, F., H.D. Eva, A. Glinni, P. Mayaux, H.-J. Stibig and T. Richards (1998) *Identification of Deforestation Hot Spot Areas in the Humid Tropics* (TREES Publication Series B, Research Report 4, EUR 18079 EN; Luxembourg: Commission of the European Communities).

Achleitner, A. (1995) *Die Normierung der Rechnungslegung (The Standardisation of Accounting)* (Zürich: Treuhand-Kammer).

Adams, R., M. Houldin and S. Slomp (1999) 'Towards a Generally Accepted Framework for Environmental Reporting', in M. Bennett and P. James with L. Klinkers (eds.), *Sustainable Measures: Evaluation and Reporting of Environmental and Social Performance* (Sheffield, UK: Greenleaf Publishing): 314-29.

AEG (1997) *Grünbuch '97 (Greenbook '97)* (Nürnberg, Germany: AEG).

A'Hearn, T. (1996) 'Environmental Management and Industry Competitiveness', paper presented at the Environmental Policy and International Competitiveness, Economics Seminar Series, Department of Environment, Sports and Territories, Canberra, Australia, www.buseco.monash. edu.au/depts/mgt/research/working_papers/wp21-02.pdf.

Akerlof, G.A. (1970) 'The Market for "Lemons": Quality Uncertainty and the Market Mechanism', *Quarterly Journal of Economics* 84.3: 488-500.

Alijah, H. (ed.) (1995–2000) *Betriebliches Umweltmanagement (Corporate Environmental Management)* (Augsburg, Germany: WEKA Fachverlag für Technische Führungskräfte).

Altham, W.J., and T.F. Guerin (1999) 'Where Does ISO 14001 Fit into the Environmental Regulatory Framework?', *Australian Journal of Environmental Management* 6: 86-98.

Anheier, H.K. (1999) 'Das Stiftungswesen in Zahlen: Eine sozial-ökonomische Strukturbeschreibung deutscher Stiftungen' ('Foundations in Figures: A Socioeconomic Description of German Foundations'), in Bertelsmann Stiftung (ed.), *Handbuch Stiftungen: Ziele–Projekte–Management–Rechtliche Gestaltung (Handbook Foundations: Goals–Projects–Management–Legal Status)* (Wiesbaden, Germany: Bertelsmann Stiftung): 47-82.

Ansoff, H.I. (1966) *Management Strategie* (Munich: Verlag Moderne Industrie).

Antes, R. (1997) 'Ökologisch verträgliche Produktpolitik' ('Environmentally Acceptable Product Policy'), in T. Hehner and W. Knell (eds.), *Grüne Produkte—schwarze Zahlen: Markterfolge mit Ökologie* (*Green Products–Black Figures: Market Success with Ecology*) (Reinbek, Germany: Rowohlt): 183-220.

ANZECC (Australia and New Zealand Environment and Conservation Council) (1999) *The National Packaging Covenant: Final* (Canberra: ANZECC).

Apelt, M. (1999) *Vertrauen in der zwischenbetrieblichen Kooperation* (*Trust in Company-Internal Co-operation*) (Wiesbaden, Germany: Deutscher Universitäts-Verlag).

Arthur Andersen and SVFV (Schweizerische Vereinigung für Finanzanalyse und Vermögensverwaltung) (1994) *Transparente Rechnungslegung und Berichterstattung von Banken* (*Transparent Accounting and Reporting of Banks*) (Zürich: Arthur Andersen/SVFV)

ASU (Arbeitsgemeinschaft Selbständiger Unternehmer) and UNI (Unternehmerinstitut eV) (1997) *Öko-Audit in der mittelständischen Praxis: Evaluierung und Ansätze für eine Effizienzsteigerung von Umweltmanagementsystemen in der Praxis* (*Eco-Audit in the Practice of SMEs: Evaluation and Approaches for an Increase in Efficiency of Environmental Management Systems in Practice*) (Bonn: ASU).

Aucott, M. (1998) 'Bewertung der Umweltschutzleistung: Das Bindeglied zwischen Umweltmanagementsystemen und Realität' ('Assessment of Environmental Performance: The Link between Environmental Management Systems and Reality'), in K. Fichter and J. Clausen (eds.), *Schritte zum nachhaltigen Unternehmen: Zukunftsweisende Praxiskonzepte des Umweltmanagements* (*Steps to a Sustainable Company: Prospective Concepts of Environmental Management in Practice*) (Berlin: Springer): 79-98.

Aulinger, A. (1996) *Theorie der Unternehmung Band 4. (Ko-)Operation Ökologie: Kooperationen im Rahmen ökologischer Unternehmenspolitik* (*Theory of the Company. IV. [Co-]operation Environment: Co-operations as Part of an Corporate Environmental Policy*) (Marburg, Germany: Metropolis).

Avenarius, H. (1995) *Public Relations: Die Grundformen der gesellschaftlichen Kommunikation* (*Public Relations: The Basic Form of Social Communication*) (Darmstadt, Germany: Wissenschaftliche Buchgesellschaft).

Bachmann, R., and C. Lane (1999) 'Vertrauen und Macht in zwischenbetrieblichen Kooperationen: Zur Rolle von Wirtschaftsrecht und Wirtschaftsverbänden' ('Trust and Power in Co-operations between Companies: The Role of Economic Law and Associations'), in J. Sydow (ed.), *Management von Netzwerkorganisationen: Beiträge aus der 'Managementforschung'* (*Management of Networks: Contributions From 'Management Research'*) (Wiesbaden, Germany: Gabler): 75-106.

Backhaus, K. (1997) *Industriegütermarketing* (*Marketing of Industrial Goods*) (Munich: Vahlen, 5th edn).

Balderjahn, I. (1986) *Das umweltbewusste Konsumentenverhalten* (*The Environmentally Conscious Behaviour of Consumers*) (Berlin: Duncker & Humboldt).

—— (1996) 'Dialogchancen im ökologischen Marketing' ('Opportunities of Dialogue in Green Marketing'), in U. Hansen (ed.), *Marketing im gesellschaftlichen Dialog* (*Marketing in the Social Dialogue*) (Frankfurt/New York: Campus): 311-28.

Balling, R. (1998) *Kooperation: Strategische Allianzen, Netzwerke, Joint Ventures und andere Organisationsformen zwischenbetrieblicher Zusammenarbeit. Theorie und Praxis* (*Co-operations: Strategic Alliances, Networks, Joint Ventures and other Forms of Organisations of Co-operation between Companies. Theory and Practice*) (Frankfurt: Lang, 2nd edn)

Bartolomeo, M., M. Bennett, J. Bouma, P. Heydkamp, P. James and T. Wolters (2000) 'Environmental Management Accounting in Europe: Current Practice and Future Potential', *European Accounting* 1: 31-52.

Barton, A.D. (1999) 'A Trusteeship Theory of Accounting for Natural Capital Assets', *Abacus* 35.2: 207-22.

Baskin, G.W., and C.E. Aronoff (1988) *Public Relations: The Profession and the Practice* (Dubuque, IA: Brown).

Bassfeld, J. (1997) 'Aktive Mitarbeit an der Umgestaltung der Wirtschaft: Wirtschaftskooperationen beim Bund für Umwelt und Naturschutz (BUND)' ('Active Collaboration in Changing the Economy: Economic Co-operations at the Society for Environment and Nature Conservation'), *Ökologisches Wirtschaften* 2.97: 25-26.

Bates, G.M. (1995) *Environmental Law in Australia* (Sydney: Butterworth, 4th edn).

Baue, W. (2001) 'GEMI Elevates Environmental Consciousness from the Bottom to the Top Line', www.socialfunds.com/news/article.cgi?sfArticleId=725.

Baumol, W.J. (1959) *Business Behaviour, Value and Growth* (New York: Macmillan).

Bea, F.X., and E. Göbel (1999) *Organisation: Theorie und Gestaltung (Organisation: Theory and Shaping)* (Stuttgart: Lucius & Lucius).

Bebbington, J. (2001) 'Sustainable Development: A Review of the International Development, Business and Accounting Literature', *Accounting Forum* 25.2: 128-57.

Beck, U. (1986) *Risikogesellschaft: Auf dem Weg in eine andere Moderne (Risk Society: On the Path to another Modernity)* (Frankfurt: Suhrkamp).

Becker, G. (1983) 'A Theory of Competition among Pressure Groups for Political Influence', *Quarterly Journal of Economics* 68.3: 371-99.

Becker, H., and I. Langosch (1995) *Produktivität und Menschlichkeit: Organisationsentwicklung und ihre Anwendung in der Praxis (Productivity and Humanity: Organisational Development and its Implementation in Practice)* (Stuttgart: Enke, 4th edn).

Becker, J. (1998) *Marketing-Konzeption: Grundlagen des strategischen und operativen Marketing-Managements (Marketing Conception: Basics of Strategic and Operative Marketing Management)* (Munich: Vahlen).

Beder, S. (1996) *The Nature of Sustainable Development* (Newham, Australia: Scribe, 2nd edn).

Begley, R. (1997) 'Value of ISO 14000 Management Systems put to the Test', *Environmental Science and Technology/News* 31.8: 364-66.

Belz, F. (2001) *Integratives Öko-marketing: Erfolgreiche Vermarktung ökologischer Produkte und Leistungen (Integrative Eco-marketing: Successful Marketing of Ecological Products and Services)* (Wiesbaden, Germany: Gabler).

Bennett, M., and P. James (eds.) (1998) *The Green Bottom Line. Environmental Accounting for Management: Current Practice and Future Trends* (Sheffield, UK: Greenleaf Publishing).

—— with L. Klinkers (eds.) (1999) *Sustainable Measures: Evaluation and Reporting of Environmental and Social Performance* (Sheffield, UK: Greenleaf Publishing).

Bennett, M., J.J. Bouma and T. Wolters (eds.) (2002) *Environmental Management Accounting: Informational and Institutional Developments* (Dordrecht, Netherlands: Kluwer Academic).

Berekoven, L. (1995) *Erfolgreiches Einzelhandelsmarketing: Grundlagen und Entscheidungshilfen (Successful Retail Marketing: Basics and Decision Support)* (Munich: Beck).

Bergmann, G. (1996) *Zukunftsfähige Unternehmensentwicklung: Realistische Visionen einer anderen Betriebswirtschaft (Future-Enabling Company Development: Realistic Visions of a Different Business Administration)* (Munich: Vahlen).

Bick, H. (1998) *Grundzüge der Ökologie (Basics of Ecology)* (Stuttgart: Fischer, 3rd edn).

Bierhoff, H.W. (1995) 'Vertrauen in Führungs- und Kooperationsbeziehungen' ('Trust in Leadership and Co-operative Relationships'), in A. Kieser, G. Reber and R. Wunderer (eds.), *Handwörterbuch der Führung* (Stuttgart: Schäffer-Poeschel, 2nd edn): 2,148-58.

Biesecker, A. (1998) *Shareholder, Stakeholder and Beyond: Auf dem Weg zu einer Vorsorgenden Wirtschaftsweise (On the Way to a Caring Method of Economics)* (Bremer Diskussionspapiere zur Institutionellen Ökonomie und Sozialökonomie, 26; Bremen, Germany).

Birke, M., and M. Schwarz (1997) 'Ökologisierung als Mikropolitik' ('Ecologisation as Micropolitics'), in M. Birke, C. Burschel and M. Schwarz (eds.), *Handbuch Umweltschutz und Organisation (Handbook of Environmental Protection and Organisation)* (Munich/Vienna: Oldenbourg): 189-225.

Blankart, C.B., and G. Knieps (1993) 'State and Standards', *Public Choice* 1: 39-52.

BMU (Bundesministerium für Umwelt) (ed.) (1998) *Umweltbewusstsein in Deutschland 1998: Ergebnisse einer repräsentativen Bevölkerungsumfrage (Environmental Awareness in Germany 1998: Results of a Representative Survey)* (Berlin: BMU).

—— (ed.) (2000) *Umweltbewusstsein in Deutschland 2000: Ergebnisse einer repräsentativen Bevölkerungsumfrage (Environmental Awareness in Germany 2000: Results of a Representative Survey)* (Berlin: BMU).

BMU (Bundesumweltministerium) and UBA (Umweltbundesamt) (eds.) (1995) *Handbuch Umweltcontrolling (Handbook of Eco-control)* (Munich: BMU/UBA).

—— (eds.) (1997) *Leitfaden betriebliche Umweltkennzahlen* (*Guideline Corporate Environmental Performance Indications*) (Bonn/Berlin: BMU/UBA).

—— (eds.) (2000) *Handbuch Umweltcontrolling* (*Handbook of Eco-control*) (Munich: Vahlen).

BMU (Bundesministerium für Umwelt), BDI (Bundesverband der Deutschen Industrie), S. Schaltegger, O. Kleiber and J. Mueller with C. Herzig (2002) *Nachhaltigkeitsmanagement in Unternehmen: Konzepte und Instrumente zur nachhaltigen Unternehmensentwicklung* (*Sustainability Management in Business Enterprises: Concepts and Instruments for Sustainable Organisation Development*) (Bonn: BMU; Lüneburg: CSM, downloadable at www.uni-lueneburg.de/csm).

Bode, T. (2000) Die Regierung hat kein zukunftsweisendes Umweltkonzept: Greenpeace-Chef Thilo Bode im FAZ-Gespräch' ('The Government has no future-oriented environmental concept: Greenpeace CEO Thilo Bode in an Interview with the *Frankfurter Allgemeine*'), *Frankfurter Allgemeine Zeitung*, 31 August 2000: 19.

Bodenstein, G., and A. Spiller (1995) 'Das Informationsdilemma der umweltorientierten Kommunikationspolitik' ('The Information Dilemma of the Environmentally Oriented Communications Policy'), in W. Faix, R. Kurz and F. Wichert (eds.), *Innovation zwischen Ökonomie und Ökologie* (*Innovation between Economics and Ecology*) (Landsberg am Lech, Germany: Verlag Moderne Industrie): 192-230.

Bonfadelli, H. (2000) 'Popularisierung oder Frühwarnung: Gentechnik in den Medien' ('Popularisation or Early Warning: Gene Technique in Media'), in *Bulletin ETH Zürich* 277.S14–S17: 32-35.

Boos, F., A. Exner and B. Heitger (1994) 'Soziale Netzwerke sind anders' ('Social Networks are Different'), in B. Heitger and F. Boos (eds.), *Organisation als Erfolgsfaktor* (*The Organisation as a Factor of Success*) (Vienna: Service-Fachverlag): 119-36.

Bouma, J., and T. Wolters (1996) *Developing Eco-management Accounting* (ECOMAC [Eco-management Accounting] Project; Zoetemeer, Netherlands: EIM).

Braun, W., and G. Schreyögg (1989) 'Macht und Argumentation: Zu den wissenschaftstheoretischen Grundlagen des Machtbegriffs und zu seiner Verwendung in der Betriebswirtschaftlehre' ('Power and Argumentation: Scientific Foundations of the Concept of Power and its Use in Business Administration'), in G. Reber (ed.), *Macht in Organisationen* (*Power in Organisations*) (Stuttgart: Schäffer-Poeschel): 19-35.

Brealey, R., and S. Meyers (1991) *Principles of Corporate Finance: Application of Option Pricing Theory* (New York: McGraw–Hill).

Bredemeier, C., G. Brüggemann, H. Petersen and C. Schwarzer (1997) *Funktionsorientierung als Perspektive für innovative Unternehmensstrategien* (*Functional Orientation as a Perspective for Innovative Corporate Strategies*) (Schriftenreihe des Lehrstuhls für ABWL, Unternehmensführung und betriebliche Umweltpolitik [Papers of the Chair of Business Administration, Leadership and Corporate Environmental Policy]; Oldenburg, Germany: Carl von Ossietzky Universität Oldenburg).

Brickwedde, F. (1999) 'Umweltschutz als strategisches Handlungsfeld von Stiftungen' ('Environmental Protection as a Strategic Field of Action for Foundations'), in Bertelsmann Stiftung (eds.), *Handbuch Stiftungen: Ziele–Projekte–Management–Rechtliche Gestaltung* (*Handbook Foundations: Goals–Projects–Management–Legal Shaping*) (Wiesbaden, Germany: Gabler): 123-42.

Brock, B. (1995) 'Vergegenständlichungszwang: Zwischen Ethik und Logik der Aneignung' ('The Urge to Materialise: Between Ethics and the Logic of Possession'), in D. Steffen (ed.), *Welche Dinge braucht der Mensch? Hintergründe, Folgen und Perspektiven der heutigen Alltagskultur* (*What Things Does a Human Being Need? Background, Consequences and Perspectives of Today's Daily Culture*) (Frankfurt: Anabas).

Brockhaus, M. (1996) *Gesellschaftsorientierte Kooperationen im ökologischen Kontext: Perspektiven für ein dynamisches Umweltmanagement* (*Societal Co-operations in the Ecological Context: Perspectives for a Dynamic Environmental Management*) (Wiesbaden, Germany: Gabler).

Brüggemann, A. (1994) 'Umwelthaftung des Darlehensgebers' ('Environmental Liability of Creditors'), *Schweizerische Zeitschrift für Wirtschaft* 2.94: 71-82.

Brüggemann, G. (1998) *Funktionenorientierung in kulturellen Perspektiven: Dynamische Wirkungsgefüge von Produktkulturen als neue Basis funktionsorientierter Unternehmenspolitik* (*Functional Orientation in Cultural Perspectives: Dynamics of Production Cultures as a New Basis of Functional-Oriented Environmental Policy*) (PhD dissertation; Oldenburg, Germany: Carl von Ossietzky Universität Oldenburg).

Bruhn, M. (1990) *Sozio- und Umweltsponsoring: Engagements von Unternehmen für soziale und ökologische Aufgaben* (*Social and Environmental Sponsoring: The Engagement of Companies for Social and Environmental Jobs*) (Munich: Vahlen).

—— (1995) *Marketing: Grundlagen für Studium und Praxis* (*Marketing: Fundamentals for Study and Practice*) (Wiesbaden, Germany: Gabler).

—— (1998) *Sponsoring: Systematische Planung und integrativer Einsatz* (*Sponsoring: Systematic Planning and Integrative Implementation*) (Frankfurt/Wiesbaden: Gabler, 3rd edn).

—— (1999) 'Relationship-Marketing: Neustrukturierung der klassischen Marketinginstrumente durch eine Orientierung an Kundenbeziehungen' ('Relationship Marketing: Restructuring of Classical Marketing Instruments through Customer Orientation'), in R. Grünig and M. Pasquier (eds.), *Strategisches Management und Marketing: Festschrift für Prof. Dr. Richard Kühn zum 60. Geburtstag* (Bern): 189-218.

Brunnengräber, A., and H. Walk (1997) 'Die Erweiterung der Netzwerktheorie: Nicht-Regierungs-Organisationen verquickt mit Markt und Staat' ('The Enlargement of Network Theory: NGOs Linked with the Market and State'), in E. Altvater, A. Brunnengräber, M. Haake and H. Walk (eds.), *Vernetzt und verstrickt: Nicht-Regierungsorganisationen als gesellschaftliche Produktivkraft* (Münster, Germany: Westfälisches Dampfboot): 65-84.

BSI (British Standards Institution) (1992) *Specification for Environmental Management Systems* (BS 7750; London: BSI).

BUND (Bund für Umwelt und Naturschutz) and Misereor (eds.) (1996) *Zukunftsfähiges Deutschland: Ein Beitrag zu einer global nachhaltigen Entwicklung* (*Future-Oriented Sustainable Germany: A Contribution towards Global Sustainable Development*) (Studie des Wuppertaler Instituts für Klima, Umwelt, Energie; Basel/Boston, MA/Berlin: BUND).

Buner, R. (1996) 'Medienlogik', in R. Königswieser, M. Haller, P. Maas and H. Jarmai (eds.), *Risiko-Dialog: Zukunft ohne Harmonieformel* (*Risk Dialogue: A Future without a Formula for Harmony*) (Cologne: Deutscher Institutsverlag): 175-97.

Burgheim, W. (1996) 'Acht Lernpfade für das lernende Unternehmen' ('Eight Paths of Learning for a Learning Organisation'), *Harvard Business Manager* 3.96: 53-60.

Burritt, R.L. (1995) 'Accountants, Accountability and the "Ozone Regime" ', *Accounting Forum* 19.2–3: 219-43.

—— (1997) *Environmental Disclosures in Annual Reports of Australian Gold and Copper Mining Companies with Activities in Papua New Guinea and/or Indonesia* (Resource Management in Asia-Pacific Working Paper Series, WP-1997/13; Canberra: Australian National University).

—— (1998) 'Corporate Environmental Performance Indicators: Cost Allocation, Boon or Bane?', in M. Bennett and P. James (eds.), *The Green Bottom Line. Environmental Accounting for Management: Current Practice and Future Trends* (Sheffield, UK: Greenleaf Publishing): 152-61.

—— (2002a) 'Application of Effectiveness Analysis: The Case of Greenhouse Gas Emissions Reduction', in P. ten Brink (ed.), *Voluntary Environmental Agreements: Process, Practice and Future Use* (Sheffield, UK: Greenleaf Publishing): 280-96.

—— (2002b) 'Stopping Australia Killing the Environment: Getting the Reporting Edge', *Australian CPA*, April 2002: 70-73.

—— (2002c) 'Environmental Reporting in Australia: Current Practices and Issues for the Future', *Business Strategy and the Environment* 11: 391-405.

Burritt, R.L., and S. Lodhia (2001) 'Green-hand Economics', *Charter*, December 2001: 52-53.

—— (2002) 'The European Commission Initiative on Environmental Accounting: What Does it Mean for Members of the Australian Accountancy Profession?', *Journal of the Asia Pacific Centre for Environmental Accountability* 8.1: 17-20.

Burritt, R.L., T. Hahn and S. Schaltegger (2002) 'Towards a Comprehensive Framework for Environmental Management Accounting: Links between Business Actors and EMA Tools', *Australian Accounting Review* 12.2: 39-50.

Buser, H., and S. Schaltegger (1996) 'Belebung der Natur mit Öko-Controlling?' ('Revival of Nature through Eco-control?'), in S. Schaltegger and A. Sturm (eds.), *Öko-Effizienz durch Öko-Controlling* (*Eco-efficiency through Eco-control*) (Stuttgart/Zürich: Schäffer-Poeschel): 115-31.

Caldas, T. (1995) 'Challenging the Cotton–Pesticide Alliance', *Pesticide News* 28 (June 1995): 12-13.

Carson, R. (1962) *Silent Spring* (New York: Houghton Mifflin).

Castles, I. (1992) *Environmental Issues, People's Views and Practices* (Canberra: Australian Bureau of Statistics).

CEC (Commission of the European Communities) (1991) 'Council Regulation (EEC) No. 2092/91 of 24 June 1991 on Organic Production of Agricultural Products and Foodstuffs', *Official Journal of the European Communities* L198: 1-15.

—— (1993a) 'Directive (EEC) Number 1836/93 of the Council of 28 June 1993 on the Voluntary Participation of Commercial Companies in a System for Environmental Management and Company Inspection'.

—— (1993b) 'Council Regulation No. 1836/93 of June 1993 Allowing Voluntary Participation by Companies in the Industrial Sector in a Community Eco-management and Audit Scheme', *Official Journal of the European Communities* L168: 1-18.

—— (2001a) 'Commission Recommendation of 30 May 2001 on the Recognition, Measurement and Disclosure of Environmental Issues in the Annual Accounts and Annual Reports of Companies', *Official Journal of the European Communities* L156: 33-42.

—— (2001b) 'Corrigendum to Regulation (EC) No. 761/2001 of the European Parliament and of the Council of 19 March 2001 Allowing Voluntary Participation by Organisations in a Community Eco-management and Audit Scheme (EMAS), *Official Journal of the European Communities* L114, 24 April 2001.

CEP (Council on Economic Priorities) (1997) *Social Accountability 8000* (London: CEP Accreditation Agency).

CERCLA (Comprehensive Environmental Response, Compensation, and Liability Act) (1980) 42 USC (Washington, DC: US Government Printing Office).

Ceyp, M. (1996) *Ökologieorientierte Profilierung im vertikalen Marketing: Dargestellt am Beispiel der Elektrobranche (Ecologically Oriented Profiling in Vertical Marketing: Described Using the Example of the Electronics Sector)* (Frankfurt: Lang).

Chambers, R.J. (1957) *Accounting and Action* (Sydney: The Law Book Company of Australasia Pty Ltd).

—— (1966) *Accounting, Evaluation and Economic Behaviour* (Houston, TX: Scholars Book Company).

Charter, M., and M.J. Polonsky (eds.) (1999) *Greener Marketing: A Global Perspective on Greening Marketing Practice* (Sheffield, UK: Greenleaf Publishing, 2nd edn).

CICA (Canadian Institute of Chartered Accountants) (1992) *Environmental Accounting and the Role of the Accounting Profession* (Toronto: CICA).

—— (1993) *Environmental Costs and Liabilities: Accounting and Financial Reporting Issues* (research report; Toronto: CICA).

Clausen, J., and K. Fichter (1995) *Umweltbericht – Umwelterklärung: Praxis glaubwürdiger Kommunikation von Unternehmen (Environmental Report–Environmental Statement: The Practice of Credible Communication by Companies)* (Munich: Hanser).

Clausen, J., and M. Mathes (1998) 'Ziele für das nachhaltige Unternehmen' ('Goals for the Sustainable Company'), in K. Fichter and J. Clausen (eds.), *Schritte zum Nachhaltigen Unternehmen: Zukunftsweisende Praxiskonzepte des Umweltmanagements (Steps towards a Sustainable Company: Sustainable Practices of Environmental Management)* (Berlin/Heidelberg/New York: Springer): 27-44.

Clausen, J., and H. Wruk (2002) *Normenorientiertes Umweltmanagement (Standards-Oriented Environmental Management)* (Hagen, Germany: FernUniHagen; Lüneburg, Germany: Centre for Sustainability Management, University of Lüneburg).

CoA (Commonwealth of Australia) (1999) *Regulations and Guidelines under the Environment Protection and Biodiversity Conservation Act 1999* (consultation paper; Canberra: Australian Government Publishing Service).

—— (2000) *A Framework for Public Environmental Reporting: An Australian Approach* (Canberra: Environment Australia, March 2000).

—— (2001) *Inquiry into Development of High Technology Industries in Regional Australia based on Bioprospecting* (Canberra; Standing Committee on Primary Industries and Regional Services, House of Representatives, August 2001).

Copeland, T., T. Koller and J. Murrin (1993) *Valuation: Measuring and Managing the Value of Companies* (New York: John Wiley).

Cordes, C. (1994) *Umweltwerbung:Wettbewerbsrechtliche Grenzen derWerbung mit Umweltschutzargu-menten (Environmental Advertisements: Legal Competitive Limits of Advertising with Environmental Arguments)* (Cologne: Heymann).

Corporations Act (2001) Section 299(1)(f) (Canberra: Australian Government Publishing Service).

Cowe, R. (1994) 'Greenpeace campaign targets investors over PVC flotation', *The Guardian*, 22 October 1994.

Crozier, M., and E. Friedberg (1979) *Macht und Organisation: Die Zwänge kollektiven Handelns (Power and Organisation: The Pressures of Collective Action)* (Königstein im Taunus, Germany: Athenaeum).

Cyert, R.M., and J.G. March (1963) *A Behavioral Theory of the Firm* (Englewood Cliffs, NJ: Prentice Hall).

—— (1992) *A Behavioural Theory of the Firm* (Cambridge, MA/Oxford, UK: Blackwell Business, 2nd edn).

DASET (Department of the Arts, Sports, the Environment and Territories) (1992) *The Environment and the ESD Process:An Attitude Research Analysis* (Canberra: Commonwealth of Australia).

Davis, B. (1989) 'Green Begins to Pale', *Australian Business* 9.3: 4-6.

Dederichs, A.M. (1997) 'Vertrauen als affektive Handlungsdimension: Ein emotionssozialogischer Bericht' ('Trust as an Affective Dimension of Action: An Emotion–Sociological Report'), in M. Schweer (ed.), *Vertrauen und soziales Handeln: Facetten eines alltäglichen Phänomens (Trust and Social Action: Facets of a Daily Phenomenon)* (Neuwied, Germany: Luchterhand): 62-77

De Haan, G., and U. Kuckartz (1996) *Umweltbewusstsein: Denken und Handeln in Umweltkrisen (Environmental Awareness. Thinking and Action in Environmental Crises)* (Opladen, Germany: Westdeutscher Verlag).

Deming, E. (1982) *Out of the Crises* (Cambridge, MA: The MIT Press).

—— (1993) *The New Economics for Industry, Government, Education* (Cambridge, MA: The MIT Press).

Dettmer, M., and E. Niejahr (1995) 'Täuschung im Vorfeld: Als NGOs getarnte Anti-Öko-Gruppen unterwandern die Umweltbewegung' ('Deception First: Anti-Eco Groups Disguised as NGOs Infiltrate the Environmental Movement'), *Der Spiegel*, November 1995 (special issue on 'Die Macht der Mutigen: Politik von unten. Greenpeace, Amnesty and Co.' ['The Power of the Courageous: Politics from the Bottom. Greenpeace, Amnesty and Co.']): 141.

Diekmann, A., and P. Preisendörfer (1992) 'Persönliches Umweltverhalten' ('Personal Environmental Behaviour'), *Kölner Zeitschrift für Soziologie und Sozialpsychologie* 44.2: 226-51.

Dittmann, D. (1994) 'Kooperation BUND/Hertie', in S. Hellenbrandt and F. Rubik (eds.), *Produkt und Umwelt: Anforderungen, Instrumente und Ziele einer ökologischen Produktpolitik (Product and the Environment: Requirements, Tools and Goals of an Environmental Product Policy)* (Marburg, Germany: Metropolis): 211-20.

Dixit, A., and R. Pindyck (1993) *Investment under Uncertainty* (Princeton, NJ: Princeton University Press).

Dlugos, G. (1981) 'Von der Betriebswirtschaftspolitik zur betriebswirtschaftlichpolitologischen Unternehmungspolitik' ('From Business Policy to Business Politics'), in M. Geist and R. Köhler (eds.), *Die Führung des Betriebes (The Management of an Enterprise)* (Stuttgart: Poeschel): 53-70.

Dobyns, L., and C. Crawford-Mason (1991) *Quality or Else* (New York: Houghton Mifflin).

Donaldson, T., and L.E. Preston (1995) 'The Stakeholder Theory of the Corporation: Concepts, Evidence and Implications', *Academy of Management Review* 20.1: 65-91.

Dröge, R. (1997) *Werthaltungen und ökologierelevantes Kaufverhalten (Values and Environmentally Relevant Consumer Behaviour)* (Wiesbaden, Germany: Gabler).

Drosdowski, G. (1998) *Das Herkunftswörterbuch: Etymologie der deutschen Sprache. Band VII (The Book of Word Origins: The Etymology of the German Language. Vol. VII)* (Mannheim, Germany: Duden).

Drucker, P.F. (1973) *People and Performance: The Best of Peter Drucker on Management* (London: Heinemann).

—— (1974) *Management: Tasks, Responsibilities, Practices* (London: Heinemann).

Drucker, P.F., E. Dyson, C. Handy, P. Saffro and P.M. Senge (1997) 'Looking Ahead: Implications of the Present', *Harvard Business Review*, September/October 1997: 18-35.

DTTI (Deloitte Touche Tohmatsu International), IISD (International Institute for Sustainable Development) and SustainAbility (1993) *Coming Clean: Corporate Environmental Reporting: Opening up for Sustainable Development* (London: DTTI).

Duchin, F., and G. Lange (1994) *The Future of the Environment: Ecological Economics and Technological Change* (New York: Oxford University Press).

Dunphy, D., J. Benveniste, A. Griffiths and P. Sutton (2000) *Sustainability: The Corporate Challenge of the 21st Century* (Sydney: Allen & Unwin).

Dyllick, T., and J. Hamschmidt (2001) *Wirksamkeit und Leistung von Umweltmanagementsystemen: Eine Untersuchung von ISO 14001-zertifizierten Unternehmen in der Schweiz (Efficacy and Performance of Environmental Management Systems: An Analysis of ISO 14001-Certified Companies in Switzerland)* (Zürich: vdf, Hochschule an der ETH).

Dyllick, T., F. Belz and U. Schneidewind (1997) *Ökologie und Wettbewerbsfähigkeit (Ecology and Competitiveness)* (Munich: Hanser).

Ebers, M. (1999) *The Formation of Inter-organisational Networks* (Oxford, UK: Oxford University Press).

Ecolog-Institut (1999) *Wegweiser durch soziale Milieus und Lebensstile für Umweltbildung und Umweltberatung (Signals through Social Milieux and Lifestyles for Environmental Education and Consulting)* (Hannover: Ecolog-Institut).

Eichhorn, W. (1996) *Agenda-Setting-Prozesse: Eine theoretische Analyse individueller und gesellschaftlicher Themenstrukturierung (Agenda-Setting Processes: A Theoretical Analysis of Individual and Social Structuring of Themes)* (Kommunikationswissenschaftliche Studien, 16; Munich: Reinhard Fischer).

EIRIS (Ethical Investment Research Service) (1989) *The Financial Performance of Ethical Investments* (London: EIRIS).

Eisenhardt, K. (1989) 'Agency Theory: An Assessment and Review', *Academy of Management Review* 1: 57-74.

Ellringmann, H. (2000) *Geschäftsprozesse ganzheitlich managen (Managing Business Processes in a Holistic Way)* (Cologne: Verlag Deutscher Wirtschaftsdienst).

Emmanuel, C.R., and D.T. Otley (1985) *Accounting for Management Control* (Wokingham, UK: Van Nostrand Reinhold).

Emmanuel, C.R., D.T. Otley and K. Merchant (1990) *Accounting for Management Control* (London: Chapman & Hall, 2nd edn).

ENDS (Environmental Data Services) (1998a) 'EMAS uptake grows but ISO 14001 levels off', *ENDS Report* 282 (June 1998): 8.

—— (1998b) 'Meacher asks top firms to report on greenhouse gases', *ENDS Report* 285 (October 1998): 6.

Enquete Kommission (Enquete Kommission Schutz des Menschen und der Umwelt des 13 Deutschen Bundestages) (ed.) (1998) *Konzept Nachhaltigkeit: Vom Leitbild zur Umsetzung (The Concept of Sustainability: From Vision to Implementation)* (Bonn: Enquete Kommission).

Environment Canada (Environment Canada, Solid Waste Division) (1995) 'The Life Cycle Concept: Backgrounder', *Ecocycle* 1: 6.

Environment Protection Authority of Victoria (2003) *Environmental Management Accounting: An Introduction and Case Studies for Australia* (Sydney: Institute of Chartered Accountants in Australia).

EPBC Act (Environment Protection and Biodiversity Conservation Act) (1999) Section 516 of Division 1 (Canberra: Australian Government Publishing Service).

Epstein, M.J., and M.-J. Roy (1997) *Strategic Learning through Corporate Environmental Management: Implementing the ISO 14001 Standard* (WP-97/61/AC of the Centre for the Management of Environmental Resources [CMER]; Fontainebleau, France: Research and Development Department, INSEAD).

Ernst & Young (1992) *Lender Liability for Contaminated Sites: Issues for Lenders and Investors* (WP-3; Ottawa: National Round Table on the Environment and the Economy).

Esteva, G. (1992) *Fiesta: Jenseits von Entwicklung, Hilfe und Politik (Fiesta: Beyond Development, Help and Policy)* (Frankfurt: Brandes & Apsel/Suedwind).

EUROSTAT (2001) *Environmental Pressure Indicators for the EU* (Luxembourg: EUROSTAT).

Faltin, S., and P. Ohlendorf (1997) 'Ökokleidung ohne Aufpreis' ('Eco-clothes without Higher Prices'), *Globus*, July 1997, www.umwelt.de/magazin/globus/glb0797/kleider.html.

Faulstich, W. (1992) *Grundwissen Öffentlichkeitsarbeit: Kritische Einführung in Problemfelder der Public Relations* (*Basic Knowledge of Public Relations: A Critical Introduction to Problems of Public Relations*) (Bardowick, Germany: Wissenschaftlicher Verlag).

Fava, J., R. Denison, B. Jones, M. Curran, B. Vigon, S. Selke and J. Barnum (eds.) (1991) *A Technical Framework for Life-cycle Assessment* (Smugglers Notch, VT: Society of Environmental Toxicology and Chemistry).

Fava, J., A. Jensen, S. Pomper, B. DeSmet, J. Warren and B. Vignon (eds.) (1992) *Life-cycle Assessment Data Quality: A Conceptual Framework* (Wintergreen, VA: Wintergreen Society of Environmental Toxicology and Chemistry).

Feldman, S.J., P.A. Soyka and P. Ameer (1997) 'Does Improving a Firm's Environmental Management System and Environmental Performance Result in a Higher Stock Price?', *Journal of Investing* 6.4: 87-97.

Fichter, K. (1995) 'Der Ablauf des Gemeinschaftssystems' ('The Process of the Community System'), in K. Fichter (ed.), *Die EG-Öko-Audit-Verordnung: Mit Öko-Controlling zum zertifizierten Umweltmanagementsystem* (*The EC Eco-audit Regulation: Using Eco-control towards a Certified Environmental Management System*) (Munich: Hanser): 55-70.

—— (1998) *Umweltkommunikation und Wettbewerbsfähigkeit: Wettbewerbstheorien im Lichte empirischer Ergebnisse zur Umweltberichterstattung von Unternehmen* (*Environmental Communication and Competitiveness: Theories of Competitiveness in the Light of Empirical Results on Companies' Environmental Reporting*) (Theorie der Unternehmung, 7; Marburg, Germany: Metropolis).

Fichter, K., and J. Clausen (eds.) (1998) *Schritte zum Nachhaltigen Unternehmen: Zukunftsweisende Praxiskonzepte des Umweltmanagements* (*Steps towards the Sustainable Company: Future-Oriented Practices of Environmental Management*) (Berlin/Heidelberg/New York: Springer).

Fichter, K., T. Loew and E. Seidel (1997) *Betriebliche Umweltkostenrechnung: Methoden und praxisgerechte Weiterentwicklung* (*Company Environmental Cost Accounting: Methods and a Practice-Oriented Continued Development*) Berlin: Springer).

Figge, F. (2001) *Wertschaffendes Umweltmanagement: Keine Nachhaltigkeit ohne ökonomischen Erfolg; Kein ökonomischer Erfolg ohne Nachhaltigkeit* (*Value-Based Environmental Management: No Sustainability without Economic Success*) (Frankfurt: PricewaterhouseCoopers).

Figge, F., T. Hahn, S. Schaltegger and M. Wagner (2002) 'The Sustainability Balanced Scorecard: Linking Sustainability Management to Business Strategy', *Business Strategy and the Environment* 11.5: 269-84.

Fischer, D., B. Kühling, R. Pfriem and C. Schwarzer (1995) *Kommunikation zwischen Unternehmen und Gesellschaft: Voraussetzungen angemessener Umweltberichterstattung von Unternehmen* (*Communication between Companies and Society: Requirements for Adequate Environmental Reporting by Companies*) (Schriftenreihe des Lehrstuhls für Allgemeine Betriebswirtschaftslehre [ABWL], Unternehmensführung und betriebliche Umweltpolitik [Papers of the Chair of Business Administration, Leadership and Corporate Environmental Policy] Nr 4; Oldenburg, Germany: Carl von Ossietzky Universität Oldenburg, 2nd edn).

Fischer, H., C. Wucherer, B. Wagner and C. Burschel (1997) *Umweltkostenmanagement: Kosten senken durch praxiserprobtes Umweltcontrolling* (*Environmental Cost Management: Reducing Costs with Proven Methods of Environmental Control*) (Munich: Hanser).

Fleig, J. (1997) 'Neue Produktkonzepte in der Kreislaufwirtschaft: Zur Nutzungsintensivierung und Lebensdauerverlängerung von Produkten' ('New Product Concepts in the Recycling Economy: Intensifying Use and Increasing Product Durability'), *Umwelt Wirtschafts Forum*, December 1997: 11-17.

Fontanari, M.L. (1995) 'Voraussetzungen für den Kooperationserfolg: Eine empirische Analyse' ('Requirements for Successful Co-operation: An Empirical Analysis'), in W. Schertler (ed.), *Management von Unternehmenskooperationen. Branchenspezifische Analysen: neueste Forschungsergebnisse* (*Management of Company Co-operations. Sector-Specific Analysis: New Research Results*) (Vienna: Überreuter): 115-87.

Fouhy, K. (1995) 'New Payback for Environmental Commitment', *Chemical Engineering* 102.3 (March 1995): 49.

Fox, A. (1974) *Beyond Contract:Work, Power and Trust Relations* (London: Faber & Faber).

Freeman, E. (1984) *Strategic Management:A Stakeholder Approach* (Marshfield, MA: Pitman).

Freimann, J., and E. Hildebrandt (eds.) (1995) *Praxis der betrieblichen Umweltpolitik: Forschungsergebnisse und Perspektiven* (*The Practice of Corporate Environmental Policy: Research Results and Perspectives*) (Wiesbaden, Germany: Gabler).

French, J.R.P., and B. Raven (1959) 'The Bases of Social Power', in D. Cartwright (ed.), *Studies in Social Power* (Ann Arbor, MI: Institute for Social Research): 150-67.

Frey, B.S. (1997) *Markt und Motivation: Wie ökonomische Anreize die (Arbeits-) Moral verdrängen* (*Market and Motivation: How Economic Incentives Crowd Out (Work) Morale*) (Munich: Vahlen).

Frey, B.S., and G. Kirchgässner (1994) *Demokratische Wirtschaftspolitik* (*Democratic Economic Public Policy*) (Munich: Vahlen, 2nd edn).

Frey, R., E. Staehlin-Witt and H. Blöchliger (eds.) (1993) *Mit Ökonomie zur Ökologie* (*Using Economics for the Environment*) (Basel/Stuttgart: Helbing & Lichtenhahn, 2nd edn).

Friedman, B. (1992) *All about Environmental Auditing* (New York: Harper).

Fritsch, M.,T. Wein and H.-J. Ewers (1999) *Marktversagen und Wirtschaftspolitik: Mikroökonomische Grundlagen staatlichen Handelns* (*Market Failure and Economic Policy: Microeconomic Fundamentals of Public Action*) (Munich: Vahlen, 3rd edn).

Frooman, J. (1999) 'Stakeholder Influence Strategies', *Academy of Management Review* 24.2: 191-205.

Frost, G. (2001) 'An Investigation of the Introduction of Mandatory Environmental Reporting in Australia', paper presented at the Third Asian Pacific Interdisciplinary Research in Accounting Conference, Adelaide, 15–17 July 2001.

Fuderholz, J. (1998) *Kultur Virtueller Unternehmen: Arbeiten und Vertrauen in der Informationsgesellschaft* (*The Culture of Virtual Companies: Work and Trust in the Information Society*) (Berlin: Logos).

Fussler, C. (1999) *Die Öko-Innovation: Wie Unternehmen profitabel und umweltfreundlich sein können* (Stuttgart: Hirzel; English version: with P. James, *Driving Eco-Innovation: A Breakthrough Discipline for Innovation and Sustainability* [FT Prentice Hall, 1997]).

Future eV (ed.) (2000) *Nachhaltigkeit: Jetzt! Anregungen, Kriterien und Projekte für Unternehmen* (*Sustainability: Now! Ideas, Criteria and Projects for Companies*) (Munich: Future eV).

Galbraith, J.K. (1983) *The Anatomy of Power* (Boston, MA: Houghton Mifflin).

Gälweiler, A. (1990) *Strategische Unternehmensführung* (*Strategic Management*) (Frankfurt/New York: Campus).

GEMI (Global Environmental Management Initiative) (2001) *Environment: Value to the Top Line* (Washington, DC: GEMI).

Giddens, A. (1997) *Die Konstitution der Gesellschaft: Grundzüge einer Theorie der Strukturierung* (*The Constitution of Society: The Basics of a Theory of Structuration*) (Frankfurt/New York: Campus, 3rd edn).

Gierl, H., and S. Stumpp (1999) 'Der Einfluss von Kontrollüberzeugungen und globalen Einstellungen auf das umweltbewusste Konsumentenverhalten' ('The Influence of Control Beliefs and Global Views on Environmentally Oriented Consumer Behaviour'), *Marketing ZFP* 2.99: 121-29.

Göbel, E. (1995) 'Der Stakeholderansatz im Dienste der strategischen Früherkennung' ('The Stakeholder Approach Serving Strategic Early Warning'), *Zeitschrift für Planung* 6.95: 55-67.

Gorz, A. (1989) *Critique of Economic Reason* (London: Verso).

Götzelmann, F. (1992) *Umweltschutzinduzierte Kooperationen der Unternehmung: Anlässe, Typen und Gestaltungspotentiale* (*Environmental Protection-Driven Co-operations of the Company: Occasions, Types and Potentials for Design*) (Frankfurt: Lang).

Gowthorpe, C., and G. Flynn (2001) 'Corporate Reporting on the Internet: The UK Smaller Listed Company Viewpoint', paper presented at the Fifth Financial Reporting and Communications Conference, Cardiff, Wales, 5–6 July 2001.

Gray, R., J. Bebbington and D. Walters (1993) *Accounting for the Environment* (London: Chapman).

Gray, R., D. Owen and C. Adams (1996) *Accounting and Accountability: Changes and Challenges in Corporate Social and Environmental Reporting* (Hemel Hempstead, UK: Prentice Hall Europe).

Greenberg, R., and C. Unger (1991) 'Getting Started: Introducing Total Quality Management Measures into Environmental Programmes', *Corporate Quality and Environmental Management*: 35-39.

Gregory, R. (2000) *Environment*, June 2000.

Greve, C. (2001) 'New Avenues for Contracting Out and Implications for a Theoretical Framework', *Public Performance and Management Review* 24.3: 270-84.

GRI (Global Reporting Initiative) (2000) *Sustainability Reporting Guidelines on Economic, Environmental and Social Performance* (Boston, MA: GRI).

Gröner, S., and M. Zapf (1998) 'Unternehmen, Stakeholder und Umweltschutz' ('Companies, Stakeholders and Environmental Protection'), *UmweltWirtschaftsForum* 3: 52-57.

Guinée, J., and R. Heijungs (1993) 'A Proposal for the Classification of Toxic Substances within the Framework of Life-Cycle Assessment of Products', *Chemsphere* 26.10: 1,925-44.

Gunningham, N., and P. Grabosky (1998) *'Smart Regulation': Designing Environmental Policy* (Oxford, UK: Clarendon Press).

Günther, E., and B. Wagner (1993) 'Ökologieorientierung des Controlling' ('Environmental Orientation of Control'), *Die Betriebswirtschaft* 53.2: 143-66.

Hahn. R.W. (1989)' Economic Prescriptions for Environmental Problems: How the Patients Followed the Doctor's Orders', *Journal of Economic Perspectives* 3: 95-114.

Hall, R., and D. Case (1992) *All about Environmental Auditing* (Washington, DC: Federal Publications).

Hallay, H., and R. Pfriem (1992) *Öko-Controlling (Eco-control)* (Frankfurt: Campus).

Haller, M. (1992) 'Risiko-Management und Risiko-Dialog' ('Risk Management and Risk Dialogue'), in R. Königswieser and C. Lutz (eds.), *Das systemisch evolutionäre Management (Systemic Evolutionary Management)* (Vienna: Orac, 2nd edn): 321-40.

—— (2000) 'Verschiebung der Wahrnehmung und Überlagerung der Diskurse: Öffentlichkeit und Risiko' ('Change of Perception and Overlapping of Discourses: Publicity and Risk'), *Bulletin ETH Zürich* 277: 14-17.

Hampel, B., R. Holdsworth and J. Boldero (1995) 'Urban/Rural Differences in Environmental Consciousness among Adolescents', *Rural Society* 5.4: 13-27.

Hansen, U. (1995) 'Ökologisches Marketing im Handel' ('Ecological Marketing in Retail'), in U. Hansen (ed.), *Verbraucher- und Umweltorientiertes Marketing: Spurensuche einer dialogischen Marketingethik (Customer- and Environment-Oriented Marketing: Searching for Traces of Dialogue-Oriented Marketing Ethics)* (Stuttgart: Schäffer-Poeschel): 349-72.

Hansen, U., and S. Kull (1995) 'Öko-Label als umweltbezogenes Informationsinstrument: Begründungszusammenhänge und Interessen' ('The Eco-label as an Environmentally Oriented Information Tool'), in U. Hansen (ed.), *Verbraucher- und Umweltorientiertes Marketing: Spurensuche einer dialogischen Marketingethik (Customer- and Environment-Oriented Marketing: Searching for Traces of Dialogue-Oriented Marketing Ethics)* (Stuttgart: Schäffer-Poeschel): 405-21.

Hansen, U., and T. Hennig (1995) 'Der Co-Produzenten-Ansatz im Konsumgütermarketing: Darstellung und Implikationen einer Neuformulierung der Konsumentenrolle' ('The Co-Producer Approach in Consumer Goods Marketing: Description and Implications of a Reformulation of the Consumer's Role'), in U. Hansen (ed.), *Verbraucher- und Umweltorientiertes Marketing: Spurensuche einer dialogischen Marketingethik (Customer- and Environment-Oriented Marketing: Searching for Traces of Dialogue-Oriented Marketing Ethics)* (Stuttgart: Schäffer-Poeschel): 309-30.

Hansen, U., and K. Jeschke (1995) 'Beschwerdemanagement: Die Karriere eine kundenorientierten Unternehmensstrategie im Konsumgütersektor' ('Crisis Management: The Development of Customer-Oriented Business Strategy in the Consumer Goods Sector'), *Marketing* 17.2: 77-88.

Hansen, U., and B. Stauss (1995) 'Marketing als marktorientierte Unternehmenspolitik oder als deren integrativer Bestandteil?' ('Marketing as Market-Oriented Company Policy or its Integrative Part?'), in U. Hansen (ed.), *Verbraucher- und Umweltorientiertes Marketing: Spurensuche einer dialogischen Marketingethik (Customer- and Environment-Oriented Marketing: Searching for Traces of Dialogue-Oriented Marketing Ethics)* (Stuttgart: Schäffer-Poeschel): 10-21.

Hansen, U., U. Niedergesäss, B. Rettberg and I. Schoenheit (1995) 'Unternehmensdialoge als besondere Verfahren im Rahmen des Interessenausgleichs zwischen Unternehmen und Gesellschaft' ('Company Dialogues as Special Processes of Exchanging Interests between Companies and Society'), in U. Hansen (ed.), *Verbraucher- und Umweltorientiertes Marketing: Spurensuche einer dialogischen Marketingethik (Customer- and Environment-Oriented Marketing: Searching for Traces of Dialogue-Oriented Marketing Ethics)* (Stuttgart: Schäffer-Poeschel): 109-25.

Hanson, W. (2000) *Principles of Internet Marketing* (Cincinatti, OH: South Western).

Hecker, S. (1997) *Kommunikation in ökologischen Unternehmenskrisen: Der Fall Shell und Brent Spar* (*Communication in Environmental Crises: The Case of Shell and Brent Spar*) (Wiesbaden, Germany: Deutscher-Universitäts-Verlag).

Hedley, B. (1977) 'Strategy and the Business Portfolio', *Long Range Planning* 10: 3-15.

Heijungs, R., J. Guinée, G. Huppes, R.H. Lankreijer, U. de Haes and A. Sleeswijk (1992) *Environmental Life Cycle Assessment of Products: Guide and Backgrounds* (Leiden, Netherlands: CML [Centrum voor Milieukunde]).

Hellenbrandt, S., and F. Rubik (eds.) (1994) *Produkt und Umwelt* (*The Product and the Environment*) (Marburg, Germany: Metropolis).

Hellmer, F., C. Friese, H. Kollros and W. Krumbein (1999) *Mythos Netzwerk: Regionale Innovationsprozesse zwischen Kontinuität und Wandel* (*Myth Network: Regional Innovation Processes between Continuity and Change*) (Berlin: Sigma).

Henning-Thurau, T. (1999) 'Steigert die Vermittlung von Konsum-Kompetenz den Erfolg des Beziehungsmarketing? Das Beispiel Consumer Electronics' ('Does the Obtaining of Consumer Competence Increase the Success of Relationship Marketing? The Example of Consumer Electronics'), *Die Unternehmung*, January 1999: 21-38.

Hess Natur (1998) *Vision: Gemeinsam die Herausforderung annehmen* (*Vision: Accepting the Challenge Jointly*) (Butzbach, Germany: Hess Natur).

Heuvels, K. (1993) 'Die EG-Öko-Audit-Verordnung im Praxistest: Erfahrungen aus einem Pilot-Audit-Programm der Europäischen Gemeinschaften' ('The EC Eco-audit Regulation Tested in Practice: Experiences from a Pilot Audit Programme of the European Union'), *Umwelt-WirtschaftsForum* 3: 41-48.

Hill, C., and G. Jones (1992) *Strategic Management: An Integrated Approach* (Boston, MA: Houghton Mifflin).

Hill, W. (1985) 'Betriebswirtschaftslehre als Managementlehre' ('Business Administration as Management Discipline'), in R. Wunderer (ed.), *Betriebswirtschaftslehre als Management- und Führungslehre* (*Business Administration as Management and Leadership Discipline*) (Stuttgart: Poeschel): 111-46.

—— (1991) 'Basisperspektiven der Managementforschung' ('Fundamental Perspectives of Management Research'), *Die Unternehmung* 1.91: 2-15.

—— (1993) 'Unternehmenspolitik' ('Corporate Policy'), in W. Wittmann (ed.), *Handwörterbuch der Betriebswirtschaft. Teilband 5* (*Handbook of Business Administration. Part V*) (Stuttgart: Poeschel): 4,366-79.

Hillary, R. (1993) *The Eco-management and Audit Scheme: A Practical Guide* (London: Technical Communications).

—— (1995) 'Environmental Reporting Requirements under the EU Eco-management and Audit Scheme (EMAS)', *The Environmentalist* 15: 293-99.

—— (2001) 'The Impact of ISO 14001: ISO 14001 Case Studies: Beyond Rhetoric to Reality', *ISO Management Systems*, December 2001: 31-36.

Hofer, P., and D. Schendel (1978) *Strategy Formulation: Analytical Concepts* (St Paul, MN: West Publishing).

Holmark, D., P. Rikhardsson and H. Jørgensen (1995) *The Annual Environmental Report: Measuring and Reporting Environmental Performance* (Copenhagen: Price Waterhouse).

Holzbaur, U., M. Kolb and H. Rosswang (eds.) (1996) *Umwelttechnik und Umweltmanagement: Ein Wegweiser für Studium und Praxis* (*Environmental Technology and Environmental Management: A Guide for Study and Practice*) (Heidelberg, Germany: Spektrum).

Homburg, C.T., and B. Garbe (1996) 'Industrielle Dienstleistungen: Lukrativ aber schwer zu meistern' ('Industrial Services: Lucrative but Difficult to Handle'), *Harvard Business Manager*, January 1996: 68-75.

Hope, J., and R. Fraser (1997) 'Beyond Budgeting: Breaking through the Barrier to "the Third Wave" ', *Management Accounting*, December 1997: 20-23, www.cam-i.org/columns/budgeting.pdf.

Hopfenbeck, W., and C. Jasch (1995) *Öko-Design: Umweltorientierte Produktpolitik* (*Ecodesign: Environmentally Oriented Product Policy*) (Landsberg am Lech, Germany: Verlag Moderne Industrie).

Horngren, C., and G. Foster (1987) *Cost Accounting: A Managerial Emphasis* (Englewood Cliffs, NJ: Prentice Hall, 6th edn).

Horngren, C.T., G. Foster and S.M. Datar (2000) *Cost Accounting: A Managerial Emphasis* (Englewood Cliffs, NJ: Prentice Hall International).

Horngren, C.T., W.T. Harrison, Best, Frazer and Isan (1997) *Accounting* (Sydney: Prentice Hall, 2nd edn).

Horvath, P. (1990) *Controlling (Control)* (Munich: Vahlen, 3rd edn).

Horvath, P., and R. Mayer (1989) 'Prozesskostenrechnung: Der neue Weg zu mehr Kosten-transparenz und wirkungsvolleren Unternehmensstrategien' ('Process Costing: The New Approach for More Cost Transparency and More Effective Corporate Strategies'), *Controlling* 1.4: 214-19.

—— (1993) 'Prozesskostenrechnung: Konzeption und Entwicklungen' ('Process Costing: Concept and Developments'), *Kostenrechnungspraxis* 2: 15-28.

Huber, M. (1998) 'PVC im Kreuzfeuer der Kritik: Die publizistische Auseinandersetzung über den Werkstoff PVC nach dem Brand am Rhein-Ruhr-Flughafen' ('PVC in the Crossfire of Critique: The Journalistic Discussion of the Material PVC after the Fire in the Rhine–Ruhr Airport'), in G. Bentele and L. Rolke (eds.), *Konflikte, Krisen und Kommunikationschancen in der Medien-gesellschaft (Conflicts, Crises and Opportunities of Communication in a Media Society)* (Berlin: Vistas): 136-92.

Hummel, J. (1997) *Strategisches Öko-Controlling: Konzeption und Umsetzung in der textilen Kette (Strategic Eco-control: Concept and Implementation in the Textiles Chain)* (Wiesbaden, Germany: Deutscher Universitäts-Verlag).

IASC (International Accounting Standards Committee) (1995) *International Accounting Standards 1995* (London: IASC).

—— (1998a) *International Accounting Standard 1: Presentation of Financial Statements* (London: IASC).

—— (1998b) *International Accounting Standard 37: Provisions, Contingent Liabilities and Contingent Assets* (London: IASC).

IdU (Institut der Umweltgutachter und -berater in Deutschland eV) (1998) *Richtlinie zum Validier-ungsverfahren gemäss Verordnung (EWG) (Guideline for the Validation Process According to the Regulation)* (publication 1836/93; Bonn: IdU).

IFAC (International Federation of Accountants) (1998) *The Consideration of Environmental Matters in the Audit of Financial Statements* (New York: International Auditing Practices Committee, IFAC).

Ilinitch, A., and S. Schaltegger (1995) 'Developing a Green Business Portfolio', *Long Range Planning* 28: 2.

IMUG (Institut für Markt Umwelt Gesellschaft eV) (ed.) (1997) *Unternehmenstest: Neue Heraus-forderungen für das Management der sozialen und ökologischen Verantwortung (Company Test: New Challenges for the Management of Social and Environmental Responsibility)* (Munich: Franz Vahlen).

ISO (International Organisation for Standardisation) (1994a) *Environmental Management Systems: Specification with Guidance for Use* (Committee Draft ISO/CD 14001; London: ISO).

—— (1994b) *Life-cycle Impact Assessment* (draft, to be included in WG 1 document *Life-Cycle Assessment: General Principles and Procedures*; London: ISO).

—— (1994c) *ISO TC 207. Environmental Performance Evaluation Framework Document on Defini-tions, Principles and Methodology* (final draft; Toronto, Canada: Environmental Management Subcommittee 4, ISO).

—— (1997) *ISO 14040: 1997. Environmental Management. Life Cycle Assessment. Principles and Framework* (Geneva: ISO).

—— (1998) *ISO 14041: 1998. Environmental Management. Life Cycle Assessment. Goal and Scope Definition and Inventory Analysis* (Geneva: ISO).

—— (1999a) *Environmental Management and ISO 14000: Development Manual 10* (Geneva: ISO).

—— (1999b) *ISO 14031. Environmental Management. Environmental Performance Evaluation. Guidelines* (Geneva: ISO).

—— (1999c) *ISO 14021: 1999. Environmental Labels and Declarations. Type II Declaration Labels. Self-declared Environmental Claims* (Geneva: ISO).

—— (1999d) *ISO 14024: 1999. Environmental Labels and Declarations. Type I Environmental Labelling. Principles and Procedures* (Geneva: ISO).

—— (2000a) *ISO 14020: 2000. Environmental Labels and Declarations. General Principles* (Geneva: ISO).

—— (2000b) *ISO 14042: 2000. Environmental Management. Life Cycle Assessment. Life Cycle Impact Assessment* (Geneva: ISO).

—— (2000c) *ISO 14043: 2000. Environmental Management. Life Cycle Assessment. Life Cycle Interpretation* (Geneva: ISO).

—— (2000d) *ISO/TR 14025: 2000. Environmental Labels and Declarations. Type III Environmental Declarations* (Geneva: ISO).

—— (2000e) *ISO 9000: 2000 Quality Management Systems. Fundamentals and Vocabulary* (Geneva: ISO).

James, P. (1992) 'Quality and the Environment: From Total Quality Management to Sustainable Quality Management', *Greener Management International* 6 (April 1994): 62-70.

Janelle, D. (1997) 'Sustainable Transportation and Information Technology: Suggested Research Issues', *Journal of Transport Geography* 5.1: 39-40.

Jänicke, M. (1998) 'Umweltpolitik: Global am Ende oder am Ende global? Thesen zu ökologischen Determinanten des Weltmarktes' ('Environmental Public Policy: Globally Finished or Global in the End? Theses on the Ecological Criteria of the World Market'), in U. Beck (ed.), *Perspektiven der Weltgesellschaft (Perspectives for a World Society)* (Frankfurt: Suhrkamp): 332-43.

Jänicke, M., and H. Weidner (1997) 'Zum aktuellen Stand der Umweltpolitik im internationalen Vergleich: Tendenzen zu einer globalen Konvergenz?' ('The State of the Art of Environmental Public Policy in an International Comparison: Tendencies towards Global Convergence?'), *Aus Politik und Zeitgeschichte* B27.97: 15-24.

Jänicke, M., M. Stitzel and P. Kunig (1999) *Umweltpolitik (Environmental Public Policy)* (Bonn: Dietz).

Janisch, M. (1992) *Das strategische Anspruchsgruppenmanagement (Strategic Management of Stakeholders)* (Bamberg, Germany: Haupt).

Janke, G. (1995) *Öko-Auditing: Handbuch für die interne Revision des Umweltschutzes im Unternehmen (Eco-auditing: Handbook for the Internal Revision of Environmental Protection in Companies)* (Berlin: Schmidt).

Janzen, H. (1996) *Ökologisches Controlling im Dienste von Umwelt- und Risikomanagement (Ecological Control Serving Environmental and Risk Management)* (Stuttgart: Schäffer-Poeschel).

Johnson, H., and R. Kaplan (1987a) *Relevance Lost: The Rise and Fall of Management Accounting* (Boston, MA: Harvard Business School Press).

—— (1987b) 'The Rise and Fall of Management Accounting: Management Accounting Information is Too Late, Too Aggregated, and Too Distorted to be Relevant', *Management Accounting*, January 1987: 22-29.

Jones, T. (1995) 'Instrumental Stakeholder Theory', *Academy of Management Review* 20.2: 404-37.

Jost, P.-J. (2000) *Organisation und Koordination: Ein ökonomische Einführung (Organisation and Co-ordination: An Economic Introduction)* (Wiesbaden, Germany: Gabler).

Junge, K. (1998) 'Vertrauen und die Grundlagen der Sozialtheorie: Ein Kommentar zu James S. Coleman' ('Trust and Basics of Social Theory: A Comment on James S. Coleman'), in H.-P. Müller and M. Schmid (eds.), *Norm, Herrschaft und Vertrauen: Beiträge zu James S. Colemans Grundlagen der Sozialtheorie (Standard, Government and Trust: Contributions to James S. Coleman's Basics of Social Theory)* (Opladen, Germany: Westdeutscher Verlag): 26-63.

Kantner, R.M. (1994) *The Change Masters: Corporate Entrepreneurs at Work* (London: Routledge).

Kaplan, R., and D. Norton (1996) *The Balanced Scorecard: Translating Strategy into Action* (Boston, MA: Harvard Business School Press).

Karl, H. (1992) 'Mehr Umweltschutz durch Umwelt-Auditing? Audit-Konzeption der Europäischen Gemeinschaft' ('More Environmental Protection through Eco-auditing? The Audit Concept of the European Community'), *Zeitschrift für angewandte Umweltforschung* 5.3: 297-303.

—— (1993) 'Europäische Initiative für die Einführung von Umweltschutz-Audits: Kritische Würdigung aus ökonomischer Sicht' ('The European Initiative to Introduce Environmental Audits: A Critical Assessment from an Economic Viewpoint'), *List Forum für Wirtschaftspolitik* 19.3: 207-20.

Kast, F.E., and J.E. Rosenzweig (1970) *Organisation and Management. A Systems Approach* (Tokyo: McGraw–Hill Kogakusha, 2nd edn).

Keller, K.L. (1998) *Strategic Brand Management: Building, Measuring and Managing Brand Equity* (Upper Saddle River, NJ: Prentice Hall).

Kirchgeorg, M. (1998) *Unternehmensstrategische Gestaltungsprobleme von Stoffkreisläufen* (*Company Strategic Problems of Organising Material Flows*) (Wiesbaden, Germany: Gabler).

Kissler, L. (1984) *Recht und Gesellschaft: Einführung in die Rechtssoziologie* (*Law and Society: An Introduction to the Sociology of Law*) (Opladen, Germany: Leske & Budrich).

Klassen, R.D., and C.P. McLaughlin (1996) 'The Impact of Environmental Management on Firm Performance', *Management Science* 42.8: 1,199-214.

Klein, A. (1997) 'Die NGOs als Bestandteil der Zivilgesellschaft und Träger einer partizipativen und demokratischen Entwicklung' ('NGOs as a Component of Civil Society and as Carriers of Participatory and Democratic Development'), in E. Altvater, A. Brunnengräber, M. Haake and H. Walk (eds.), *Vernetzt und verstrickt: Nicht-Regierungsorganisationen als gesellschaftliche Produktivkraft* (Münster, Germany: Westfälisches Dampfboot): 308-32.

Klein, N. (1999) *No Logo: Taking Aim at the Brand Bullies* (New York: Picador).

Knaus, A., and O. Renn (1998) *Den Gipfel vor Augen: Unterwegs in eine nachhaltige Zukunft* (*The Peak in Sight: Towards a Sustainable Future*) (Marburg, Germany: Metropolis).

Knodel, H., and U. Kull (1981) *Ökologie und Umweltschutz* (*Ecology and Environmental Protection*) (Stuttgart: Metzler, 2nd edn).

Kotler, P. (1986) 'Megamarketing', *Harvard Business Review,* March/April 1986: 117-24.

Kotler, P., and F. Bliemel (1999) *Marketing-Management: Analyse, Planung, Umsetzung und Steuerung* (*Marketing Management: Analysis, Planning, Implementation and Control*) (Stuttgart: Schäffer-Poeschel, 9th edn).

Kottmann, H., T. Loew and J. Clausen (1999a) *Arbeitsmaterialien zur Einführung von Umweltkennzahlensystemen* (*Working Materials for the Introduction of Environmental Indicators*) (ed. Landesanstalt für Umweltschutz, Baden-Württemberg, and the Ministerium für Umwelt und Verkehr des Landes, Karlsruhe).

—— (1999b) 'Umweltkennzahlen für den betrieblichen Verbesserungsprozess' ('Environmental Indicators for a Company Internal Improvement Process'), *UmweltWirtschaftsForum* 7.1: 50-55.

—— (1999c) *Umweltmanagement mit Kennzahlen* (*Environmental Management with Indicators*) (Munich: Franz Vahlen).

Kreikebaum, H. (1993) *Strategische Unternehmensplanung* (*Strategic Corporate Planning*) (Stuttgart: Kohlhammer, 5th edn).

Kreitner, R., and A. Kinicki (1992) *Organizational Behaviour* (Boston, MA: Irwin, 2nd edn).

Kriener, M. (1999) 'Brennpunkt Umweltverbände: Fusion oder Kooperation' ('Focal Point Environmental Associations: Merger or Co-operation'), *Natur and Kosmos,* July 1999: 54-59.

Kritzmöller, M. (1999) 'Das Eins-Sein mit dem Objekt' ('Agreeing with the Object'), *Form* 3.99: 24-25.

Kroeber-Riel, W., and P. Weinberg (1996) *Konsumentenverhalten* (*Consumer Behaviour*) (Munich: Vahlen, 6th edn).

Krueger, A. (1974) 'The Political Economy of the Rent-Seeking Society', *American Economic Review* 64: 291-303.

Krüssel, P. (1997) 'Ökologische Entscheidungsfindung in Unternehmen aus machtpolitischer Perspektive' ('Environmental Decision-Making in Companies from a Political Perspective'), *UmweltWirtschaftsForum* 5: 72-77.

Krut, R., and H. Gleckman (1998) *ISO 14001: A Missed Opportunity for Sustainable Global Industrial Development* (London: Earthscan Publications).

Krystek, U. (1999) 'Vertrauen in Unternehmensnetzwerken' ('Trust in Corporate Networks'), in D. Fink (ed.), *Handbuch Telekommunikation und Wirtschaft* (*Handbook of Telecommunication and Economy*) (Munich: Vahlen): 437-55.

Krystek, U., and S. Zumbrock (1993) *Planung und Vertrauen: Die Bedeutung von Vertrauen und Misstrauen für die Qualität von Planungs- und Kontrollsystemen* (*Planning and Trust: The Importance of Trust and Mistrust in the Quality of Planning and Control Systems*) (Stuttgart: Schäffer-Poeschel).

Kuckartz, U. (1998) *Umweltbewusstsein und Umweltverhalten* (*Environmental Awareness and Environmental Behaviour*) (Berlin: Springer).

Kull, S. (1998) *Ökologieorientiertes Handelsmarketing: Grundlegungen, konzeptuale Ausformungen und empirische Einsichten* (*Environmentally Oriented Retail Marketing: Basics, Concepts and Empirical Insights*) (Markt und Konsum, 6; Frankfurt: Lang).

Lantermann, E.D. (1999) 'Zur Polytelie umweltschonenden Handelns' ('Polytelics of Environmentally Sound Activities'), in V. Linneweber and E. Kals (eds.), *Umweltgerechtes Handeln: Barrieren und Brücken* (*Environmentally Sound Activities: Obstacles and Bridges*) (Berlin: Springer): 7-20.

Lave, L.B., E. Cobas-Flores, C.T. Henderson and F.C. McMichael (1995) 'Life-cycle Assessment: Using Input–Output Analysis to Estimate Economy-Wide Discharges', *Environmental Science and Technology* 29.9: 420-26.

Leggett, J. (ed.) (1996) *Climate Change and the Financial Sector: The Emerging Threat; The Solar Solution* (Munich: Gerling-Akademie).

Lerch, A., and H. G. Nutzinger (1995) 'Perspektiven einer nachhaltigen Wirtschaftsweise' ('Perspectives of Sustainable Economics'), *Sparkasse* 7.95: 294-99.

Letmathe, P. (1998) *Umweltbezogene Kostenrechnung: Theoretische Grundlagen und praktische Konzepte* (*Environmentally Oriented Costing: Theory and Practical Concepts*) (Munich: Vahlen).

Li, Y., and B.J. McConomy (1999) 'An Empirical Examination of Factors Affecting the Timing of Environmental Accounting Standard Adoption and the Impact on Corporate Valuation', *Journal of Accounting, Auditing and Finance* 14.3: 279-319.

Lichtl, M. (1999) *Ecotainment: Der neue Weg im Umweltmarketing* (*Ecotainment: The New Route in Environmental Marketing*) (Vienna: Überreuter).

Liebl, F. (1996) *Strategische Frühaufklärung: Trends, Issues, Stakeholders* (*Strategic Early Warning: Trends, Issues, Stakeholders*) (Munich: Oldenbourg).

—— (1997) 'Zur Karriere des Stakeholder-Konzeptes' ('On the Development of the Stakeholder Concept'), *Technologie und Management* 46 (February 1997): 16-19.

—— (1999) 'Marketing für Bastler' ('Marketing for Handicrafts Makers'), *Econy*, April 1999: 132-33.

Liedtke, C., C. Manstein, H. Bellendorf and S. Kranendonk (1994) *Öko-Audit und Ressourcenmanagement: Erste Schritte in Richtung eines EU-weit harmonisierungsfähigen Umweltmanagementsystems* (*Eco-audit and Resource Management: First Steps towards an EC-Wide Harmonisable Environmental Management System*) (Wuppertal Paper, 18; Wuppertal, Germany: Wuppertal Institute, June 1994).

Lindblom, C.K. (1994) 'The Implications of Organizational Legitimacy for Corporate Social Performance and Disclosure', paper presented at the Conference on Critical Perspectives on Accounting, New York, 13–15 June 1994.

Lindlar, A. (1995) *Umwelt-Audits: Ein Leitfaden für Unternehmen über das EG-Gemeinschaftssystem für das Umweltmanagement und die Betriebsprüfung* (*Environmental Audits: A Guideline for Companies for the EC System for Environmental Management and Review*) (Bonn: Economica).

Logan, D. (1998) *Corporate Citizenship: Defining Terms and Scoping Key Issues* (London: The Corporate Citizenship Company).

Lomborg, B. (2001) *The Skeptical Environmentalist: Measuring the Real State of the World* (Cambridge, UK: Cambridge University Press).

Loose, A., and J. Sydow (1994) 'Vertrauen und Ökonomie in Netzwerkbeziehungen: Strukturationstheoretische Betrachtungen' ('Trust and the Economy in Network Relationships: A View from Structuration Theory'), in J. Sydow and A. Windeler (eds.), *Management interorganisationaler Beziehungen: Vertrauen, Kontrolle und Informationstechnik* (*Management of International Relationships: Trust, Control and Information Technology*) (Opladen, Germany: Westdeutscher Verlag): 160-93.

Lowi, T.J. (1967) 'Four Systems of Policy, Politics, and Choice', *Public Administration Review* 32: 298-310.

Luhmann, N. (1973) *Vertrauen: Ein Mechanismus der Reduktion sozialer Komplexität* (*Trust: A Mechanism for Reducing Social Complexity*) (Stuttgart: Enke, 2nd edn).

Mache, H.-M. (1997) *Umweltrecht, Reihe Fischer Heymanns: Ratgeber Recht* (*Environmental Law*) (Cologne/Frankfurt: Fischer).

McCombs, M., and D. Shaw (1972) 'The Agenda-Setting: Functions of Mass Media', *Public Opinion Quarterly* 36.2: 176-87.

McGuire, J., A. Sundgren and T. Schneeweis (1981) 'Corporate Social Responsibility and Firm Financial Performance', *Academy of Management Journal* 31.4: 854-72.

Marcus, A. (1998) 'Strategic Environmental Management: Introduction to the Compendium on Strategic Environmental Management', in *Compendium on Strategic Environmental Management* (Ann Arbor, MI: National Pollution Prevention Centre for Higher Education, University of Michigan, www.umich.edu/~nppcpub/resources/compendia/SEMpdfs/SEMintro.pdf): 11.

Marggraf, R., and S. Streb (1997) *Ökonomische Bewertung der natürlichen Umwelt: Theorie, politische Bedeutung, ethische Diskussion* (*Economic Assessment of the Natural Environment: Theory, Political Relevance, Ethical Discussion*) (Heidelberg/Berlin: Spektrum Akademie Verlag).

Matten, D. (1998) *Management ökologischer Unternehmensrisiken: Zur Umsetzung von Sustainable Development in der reflexiven Moderne* (*Management of Ecological Company Risks: Implementing Sustainable Development in Reflexive Modern Times*) (Stuttgart: M&P Verlag für Wissenschaft und Forschung).

Maunders, K.T., and R.L. Burritt (1991) 'Accounting and Ecological Crisis', *Accounting, Auditing and Accountability Journal* 4.3: 9-26.

MCA (Minerals Council of Australia) (2000) *Australian Minerals Industry Code for Environmental Management* (Canberra: MCA, February 2000).

Meffert, H. (1998) *Marketing: Grundlagen marktorientierter Unternehmensführung* (*Marketing: Fundamentals of Market-Oriented Management*) (Wiesbaden, Germany: Gabler).

Meffert, H., and M. Bruhn (1996) 'Das Umweltbewusstsein von Konsumenten' ('The Environmental Awareness of Consumers'), *Die Betriebswirtschaft* 56.5: 631-48.

Meffert, H., and M. Kirchgeorg (1998) *Marktorientiertes Umweltmanagement: Konzeption–Strategien–Implementierung mit Praxisfällen* (*Market-Oriented Environmental Management: Concept–Strategies–Implementation with Case Studies*) (Stuttgart: Schäffer-Poeschel, 3rd edn).

Meister, H.-P., and H. Banthien (1998) 'Die Rolle internationaler Industrieverbände für die Ermittlung und Implementierung einer Ethik: Das Responsible Care-Programm der Chemischen Industrie' ('The Role of International Industry Associations in Determining and Implementing Ethics: The Chemical Industry's Responsible Care Programme'), in H. Steinmann and G.R. Wagner (eds.), *Umwelt und Wirtschaftsethik* (*Environmental and Economic Ethics*) (Stuttgart: Schäffer-Poeschel): 107-29.

Merchant, K.A. (2000) *Modern Management Control Systems: Text and Cases* (Englewood Cliffs, NJ: Prentice Hall).

Minsch, J., A. Eberle, B. Meier and U. Schneidewind (1996) *Mut zum ökologischen Umbau: Innovationsstrategien für Unternehmen, Politik und Akteursnetze* (*Courage for the Ecological Restructuring: Innovation Strategies for Companies, Politics and Networks*) (Basel: Birkhäuser).

Mintzberg, H. (1973) *The Nature of Managerial Work* (New York: Harper).

Mintzberg, H., and J.B. Quinn (1996) *The Strategy Process* (Englewood Cliffs, NJ: Prentice Hall).

Mintzberg, H., B. Ahlstrand and J. Lampel (1999) *Strategy Safari: Eine Reise durch die Wildnis des strategischen Managements* (*Strategy Safari: A Journey through the Wilderness of Strategic Management*) (Vienna/Frankfurt: Überreuter).

Mitchell, W., and M. Munger (1991) 'Economic Models of Interest Groups', *American Economic Review* 35: 512-46.

Monhemius, K.C. (1993) *Umweltbewusstes Kaufverhalten von Konsumenten: Ein Beitrag zur Operationalisierung, Erklärung und Typologie des Verhaltens in der Kaufsituation* (*The Environmentally Conscious Purchasing Behaviour of Consumers: A Contribution to the Operationalisation, Explanation and Typology of Behaviour in Purchasing Situations*) (Frankfurt: Lang).

Morgan, G. (1986) *Images of Organisations* (Newbury Park/Beverly Hills, CA: Sage).

Müller-Wenk, R. (1978) *Die ökologische Buchhaltung* (*Ecological Book-keeping*) (Frankfurt: Campus).

Münchner Rückversicherung (1995) *Jahresbericht* (*Annual Report*) (Munich: Münchner Rückversicherung).

Muntwyler, M. (1994) *Die Bedeutung regionaler Akteursnetze für den ökologischen Strukturwandel in der Lebensmittelbranche* (*The Importance of Regional Networks for the Ecological Change of Structures in the Food Industry*) (DP-3; Bern, Switzerland: Geographisches Institut, Universität Bern).

Murphy, D.F., and J. Bendell (1997) *In the Company of Partners: Business, Environmental Groups and Sustainable Development Post-Rio* (Bristol, UK: Polity Press).

Mutz, M. (1995) 'Kommerz und Karitas: Der Wettlauf der Hilfsorganisationen um Spendengelder' ('Commerce and Charity: The Race of Charity Organisations for Donations'), *Der Spiegel*, November 1995 (special issue on 'Die Macht der Mutigen: Politik von unten Greenpeace, Amnesty and Co.'): 131-32.

Nader, R. (1979) 'Moderner Konsumentenschutz: Trends–Ideen–Postulate' ('The New Consumer: Trends–Ideas–Theories'), in R. Brun (ed.), *Der neue Konsument. Der Abschied von der Verschwendung: Die Wiederentdeckung des täglichen Bedarfs (The New Consumer. Goodbye to Waste: The Rediscovery of Daily Needs)* (Frankfurt: Fischer): 17-30.

Näsi, J. (1995) 'What is Stakeholder Thinking? A Snapshot of a Social Theory of the Firm', in J. Näsi (ed.), *Understanding Stakeholder Thinking* (Helsinki: LSR-Publications): 19-32.

NCM (Nordic Council of Ministers) (1995) *LCS Nordic Technical Reports* (Copenhagen: NCM).

Neuberger, O. (1994) *Führen und geführt werden (Leading and Being Led)* (Stuttgart: Enke, 4th edn).

Neumann-Szyszka, J. (1994) *Kostenrechnung und umweltorientiertes Controlling: Möglichkeiten und Grenzen des Einsatzes eines traditionellen Controllinginstruments im umweltorientierten Controlling (Costing and Environmental Control: Options and Limitations of Using the Traditional Control Tool in Environmental Control)* (Wiesbaden, Germany: Deutscher Universitätsverlag).

Nieder, P. (1997) *Erfolg durch Vertrauen: Abschied vom Management des Misstrauens (Success through Trust: Goodbye to the Management of Mistrust)* (Wiesbaden, Germany: Gabler).

Nisius, S., and G.U. Scholl (1998) 'Umweltentlastungen durch Produkt-Ökobilanzen?' ('Environmental Relief through LCA?'), in K. Fichter and J. Clausen (eds.), *Schritte zum nachhaltigen Unternehmen: Zukunftsweisende Praxiskonzepte des Umweltmanagements (Steps towards a Sustainable Company: Future-Oriented Practice Concepts of Environmental Management)* (Berlin: Springer): 169-82.

Nutzinger, H.G., and V. Radke (1995) 'Das Konzept der nachhaltigen Wirtschaftsweise: Historische, theoretische und politische Aspekte' ('The Concept of a Sustainable Economy: Historical, Theoretical and Political Aspects'), in H. G. Nutzinger (ed.), *Nachhaltige Wirtschaftsweise und Energieversorgung: Konzepte, Bedingungen, Ansatzpunkte (Sustainable Economics and Energy Supply: Concepts, Conditions, Starting Points)* (Marburg, Germany: Metropolis): 13-52.

NZZ (Neue Zürcher Zeitung) (1995) 'Wachsende Bedeutung der Rechnungslegung nach IAS' ('The Increasing Importance of Accounting According to IAS'), *NZZ* 60: 13.

O'Donovan, G. (1999) 'Managing Legitimacy through Increased Corporate Environmental Reporting: An Exploratory Study', *Interdisciplinary Environmental Review* 1.1: 63-99.

OECD (Organisation for Economic Co-operation and Development) (2000) *The Global Environment Goods and Service Industry* (Paris: OECD).

Oikos (ed.) (1994) *Kooperationen für die Umwelt: Im Dialog zum Handeln (Co-operations for the Environment: Using Dialogue towards Action)* (Zürich: Oikos).

Ortmann, G. (1998) 'Mikropolitik' ('Micropolitics'), in P. Heinrich and J. Schulz zur Wiesch (eds.), *Wörterbuch der Mikropolitik (Dictionary of Micropolitics)* (Opladen, Germany: Leske & Budrich): 1-5.

Osterloh, M., B.F. Frey and J. Frost (1999) 'Was kann das Unternehmen besser als der Markt?' ('What Can the Company Do Better than the Market?'), *Zeitschrift für Betriebswirtschaft* 69.H11: 1,245-62.

Paasikivi, R. (1994) 'Towards a European Standard', *Espace économique européen [EEE] Bulletin*, Winter 1994: 8-10.

Packard, V. (1966) *Die grosse Verschwendung* (Düsseldorf/Vienna: Econ, 3rd edn; originally published in 1960 as *The Waste Makers* [D. Mackay Co.]).

Pariser, D., and A. Neidermeyer (1991) 'Environmental Due Diligence: The Internal Auditor's Role', *Journal of Bank Accounting and Auditing*, Winter 1991: 22-30.

Parker, L. (1999) *Environmental Costing: An Exploratory Examination* (Melbourne: Australian Society of Certified Practising Accountants, February 1999).

PCEQ (President's Commission on Environmental Quality) (1991) *The Report of the President's Commission on Environmental Quality* (Washington, DC: PCEQ).

Pearce, D., and K. Turner (1990) *Economics of Natural Resources and the Environment* (New York: Harvester Wheatsheaf).

Pearce, J., and R. Robinson (1991) *Strategic Management: Formulation, Implementation and Control* (Homewood, IL: Irwin).

Pepels, W. (1996) *Kommunikations-Management: Marketing-Kommunikation vom Briefing bis zur Realisation* (*Communications Management: The Marketing Conception? From Briefing to Realisation*) (Stuttgart: Schäffer-Poeschel, 2nd edn).

Petersen, H., and S. Schaltegger (2000) 'Gütermarktorientiertes Umweltmanagement' ('Market-Oriented Environmental Management'), in S. Schaltegger (ed.), *Wirtschaftswissenschaften: Reihe Studium der Umweltwissenschaften* (*Economics: Studying Environmental Sciences and Studies*) (series editor E. Brandt; Berlin: Springer): 169-96.

Petrauskas, H. (1992) 'Manufacturing and the Environment: Implementing Quality Environmental Management', speech given at the University of Michigan, Ann Arbor, MI, 20 November 1992.

Pfeffer, J. (1992) *Managing with Power: Politics and Influence in Organisations* (Boston, MA: Harvard Business School Press).

Pfister, G., and O. Renn (1997) *Die Studie 'Zukunftsfähiges Deutschland' des Wuppertal-Instituts im Vergleich zum Nachhaltigkeitskonzept der Akademie für Technikfolgeabschätzung* (*The Report 'Sustainable Germany' by the Wuppertal Institute Compared with the Sustainability Concept of the Academy for Technology Assessment*) (WP-75 of the Akademie für Technikfolgeabschätzung, Baden-Württemberg; Stuttgart).

Pfriem, R. (1991) 'Öko-Controlling und Organisationsentwicklung von Unternehmen' ('Eco-control and Organisational Development of the Company'), *IÖW-Informationsdienst* 6.2: 1-14.

—— (1995) *Unternehmensführung in sozialökologischen Perspektiven: Theorie der Unternehmung. Band 1* (*Management in a Socio-ecological Perspective: The Theory of the Company. Vol. I*) (Marburg, Germany: Metropolis).

Pfriem, R., and C. Schwarzer (1996) 'Ökologiebezogenes organisationales Lernen' ('Environmentally Oriented Organisational Learning'), *UmweltWirtschaftsForum*, September 1996: 10-16.

Picot, A., R. Reichwald and R. T. Wigand (1998) *Die grenzenlose Unternehmung: Information, Organisation und Management* (*The Company without Boundaries: Information, Organisation and Management*) (Wiesbaden, Germany: Gabler, 3rd edn).

Pidgeon, S., and D. Brown (1994) 'The Role of Lifecycle Analysis in Environmental Management: A General Panacea or One of Several Useful Paradigms?', *Greener Management International* 7 (July 1994): 36-44.

Pohl, C., M. Ros, B. Waldeck and F. Dinkel (1996) 'Imprecision and Uncertainty in LCA', in S. Schaltegger (ed.), *Life Cycle Assessment: Quo Vadis?* (Basel: Birkhäuser).

Porter, M.E. (1987) 'From Competitive Advantage to Corporate Strategy', *Harvard Business Review*, May/June 1987: 43-59.

—— (1990) *The Competitive Advantage of Nations* (London: Macmillan).

—— (1999a) *Wettbewerbsstrategien: Methoden zur Analyse von Branchen und Konkurrenten* (Frankfurt: Campus, 10th edn; published in English as *Competitive Strategy* [New York: The Free Press]).

—— (1999b) *Wettbewerbsvorteile: Spitzenleistungen erreichen und behaupten* (Frankfurt: Campus, 5th edn; published in English as *Competitive Advantage* [New York: The Free Press]).

Preuss, S. (1991) *Umweltkatastrophe Mensch: Über unsere Grenzen und Möglichkeiten ökologisch bewusst zu handeln* (*Environmental Catastrophe Man: Limits and Opportunities for Acting Environmentally Consciously*) (Heidelberg, Germany: Ansanger).

Probst, G. (1992) 'Vernetztes Denken für komplexe strategische Probleme' ('Systemic Thinking for Complex Strategic Problems'), in R. Königswieser and C. Lutz (eds.), *Das systemisch evolutionäre Management* (*Systemic Evolutionary Management*) (Vienna: Orac): 22-40.

—— (1993) *Organisation: Strukturen, Lenkungsinstrumente, Entwicklungsperspektiven* (*Organisation: Structures, Control Tools and Perspectives of Development*) (Landsberg am Lech, Germany: Verlag Moderne Industrie).

Probst, G., S. Raub and K. Romhardt (1999) *Wissen managen: Wie Unternehmen ihre wertvollste Ressource nutzen* (*Managing Knowledge: How Companies Can Use their Most Valuable Resource*) (Frankfurt: Frankfurter Allgemeine Zeitung für Deutschland, 3rd edn).

Rappaport, A. (1986) *Creating Shareholder Value: The New Standards for Business Performance* (New York: The Free Press).

—— (1998) *Creating Shareholder Value: A Guide for Managers and Investors* (New York: Simon & Schuster, rev. edn).

Ream, T., and C. French (1993) *A Framework and Methods for Conducting a Life-cycle Impact Assessment* (Research Triangle Park, NC: US Environmental Protection Agency).

Reisch, L. (1998) 'Abschied vom "immer mehr"' ('Goodbye to "More and More"'), *Politische Ökologie Sonderheft* 11: 43-47.

Renn, O. (1995) *Ökologisch denken–sozial handeln: Die Realisierbarkeit einer nachhaltigen Entwicklung und die Rolle der Kultur- und Sozialwissenschaften* (*Thinking Ecologically–Acting Socially: The Feasibility of Sustainable Development and the Role of Cultural and Social Sciences*) (WP-45 of the Akademie für Technikfolgenabschätzung in Baden-Württemberg; Stuttgart).

Renn, O., and T. Webler (1994) 'Konfliktbewältigung durch Kooperation in der Umweltpolitik: Theoretische Grundlagen und Handlungsvorschläge' ('Solving Conflicts through Co-operation in Environmental Politics: Theory and Suggestions for Action'), in oikos (ed.), *Kooperationen für die Umwelt: Im Dialog zum Handeln* (*Co-operations for the Environment: Acting Using Dialogue*) (Chur/Zürich: oikos): 11-52.

Roberts, C. (1996) 'Intrapersonal Mastery', in P. Senge, A. Kleiner, C. Roberts, R. Ross and B. Smith (eds.), *Das Fieldbook zur Fünften Disziplin* (*The Fieldbook of the Fifth Discipline*) (Stuttgart: Klett-Cotta)

Roberts, R. (1994a) 'SAB 92 and the SEC's Environmental Liability', speech given at the 1994 Quinn, Ward and Kershaw Environmental Law Symposium, University of Maryland School of Law, Baltimore, MD, April 1994.

—— (1994b) 'Environmental Liability Disclosure Developments', speech given at the Corporate Environmental Management Workshop on Environmental Reporting and Accountability, Environmental Law Institute, Washington, DC, June 1994.

Rotter, J.B. (1980) 'Interpersonal Trust, Trustworthiness and Gullibility', *American Psychologist* 35: 1-7

Royston, M.G. (1982) 'Making Pollution Prevention Pay', in D. Huisingh and V. Bailey (eds.), *Making Pollution Prevention Pay: Ecology with Economy as Policy* (New York: Pergamon Press).

Rubik, F., and V. Teichert (1997) *Ökologische Produktpolitik* (*Ecological Product Policy*) (Stuttgart: Schäffer-Poeschel).

SA (Standards Australia) and SNZ (Standards New Zealand) (1999) *Risk Management* (SA/SNZ 4360; Canberra: SA).

—— (2000) *Environmental Risk Management: Principles and Process* (HB 203-2000; Sydney/Wellington: SA/SNZ).

SAI (Social Accountability International) (2001) *SA 8000* (New York: SAI).

Sakurai, M. (1989) 'Target Costing and How to Use It', *Journal of Cost Management*, Summer 1989: 39-50.

Sandman, P.M. (1986) *Explaining Environmental Risk* (Washington, DC: Office of Toxic Substances, US Environmental Protection Agency).

Saretzki, T. (1996) 'Wie unterscheiden sich Argumentieren und Verhandeln? Definitionsprobleme, funktionale Bezüge und strukturelle Differenzen von zwei verschiedenen Kommunikationsmodi' ('How Do Arguing and Negotiating Differ? Problem Definition, Functional Relationships and Structural Differences of Two Different Modes of Communication'), in V. von Prittwitz (ed.), *Verhandeln und Argumentieren: Dialog, Interessen und Macht in der Umweltpolitik* (*Negotiating and Arguing: Dialogue, Interests and Power In Environmental Politics*) (Opladen, Germany: Leske & Budrich): 19-40.

Schaltegger, S. (1994) 'Zeitgemässe Instrumente des betrieblichen Umweltschutzes' ('Contemporary Tools of Corporate Environmental Management'), *Die Unternehmung* 4: 117-31.

—— (ed.) (1996a) *Life Cycle Assessment: Quo vadis?* (Basel: Birkhäuser).

—— (1996b) *Corporate Environmental Accounting* (with contributions from K. Müller and H. Hindrichsen; London: John Wiley).

—— (1997) 'Economics of Life Cycle Assessment: Inefficiency of the Present Approach', *Business Strategy and the Environment* 6: 1-8.

—— (1998) 'Information Costs, Quality of Information and Stakeholder Involvement: The Necessity of International Standards of Ecological Accounting', *Eco-management and Auditing*, November 1997: 1-11.

—— (1999) 'Bildung und Durchsetzung von Interessen zwischen Stakeholder der Unternehmung: Eine politisch-ökonomische Perspektive' ('Development and Enforcement of Interests between Company Stakeholders: A Political–Economic Perspective'), *Die Unternehmung*, January 1999: 3-20.

—— (2000) *Studium der Umweltwissenschaften:Wirtschaftswissenschaften* (*Studying Interdisciplinary Environmental Studies: Economics*) (Berlin: Springer).

—— (2003) 'A Framework for Ecopreneurship: Leading Bioneers and Environmental Managers to Ecopreneurship', *Greener Management International* 38 (Summer 2002): 45-58.

Schaltegger, S., and R. Burritt (2000) *Contemporary Environmental Accounting: Issues, Concepts and Practice* (Sheffield, UK: Greenleaf Publishing).

—— (2001a) *Contemporary Environmental Accounting:Issues, Concepts and Practice. Solutions Manual* (Sheffield, UK: Greenleaf Publishing).

—— (2001b) 'Eco-efficiency in Corporate Budgeting', *Environmental Management and Health* 12.2: 158-74.

Schaltegger, S., and T. Dyllick (2002) *Nachhaltig managen mit der Balanced Scorecard: Konzept und Fallstudien* (*Managing in a Sustainable Manner with the Balanced Scorecard: Concept and Cases*) (Wiesbaden, Germany: Gabler).

Schaltegger, S., and F. Figge (1997) *Umwelt und Shareholder Value* (*Environment and Shareholder Value*) (Study 54; Basel: Wirtschaftswissenschaftliches Zentrum and Bank Sarasin, 1st edn).

—— (1998) *Environmental Shareholder Value* (Study 54; Basel: Wirtschaftswissenschaftliches Zentrum and Bank Sarasin, 5th edn, December 1998).

—— (1999a) 'Öko-Investment: Spagat zwischen Shareholder Value und Sustainable Development?' ('Green Investment: Splits between Shareholder Value and Sustainable Development?'), *UmweltWirtschaftsForum* 7.3: 4-8.

—— (1999b) 'Finanzmärkte: Treiber oder Bremser des betrieblichen Umweltmanagements?' ('Financial Markets: Driver or Brakeman of Corporate Environmental Management?'), in E. Seidel (ed.), *Betriebliches Umweltmanagement im 21. Jahrhundert:Aspekte,Aufgaben, Perspektiven* (*Corporate Environmental Management in the 21st Century:Aspects, Responsibilities, Perspectives*) (Berlin: Springer): 287-99.

Schaltegger, S., and S. Kempke (1996) 'Öko-Controlling: Überblick bisheriger Ansätze' ('Eco-control: An Overview of Current Approaches'), *Zeitschrift für Betriebswirtschaft* 2: 1-96.

Schaltegger, S., and H. Petersen (2001) *Ecopreneurship: Konzept und Typologie* (*Ecopreneurship: Concept and Typology*) (Lüneburg, Germany: Centre for Sustainability Management, University of Lüneburg; Luzern: Rio-Managementforum).

—— (2002) 'Ecopreneure: Nach der Dekade des Umweltmanagements das Jahrzehnt des nachhaltigen Unternehmertums?' ('Ecopreneurs: After the Decade of Environmental Management the Decade of Sustainable Entrepreneurship?'), *Politik und Zeitgeschichte*, 5 August 2002: 37-46.

Schaltegger, S., and C. Stinson (1994) *Issues and Research Opportunities in Environmental Accounting* (DP-9124; Basel: Wirtschaftswissenschaftliches Zentrum).

Schaltegger, S., and A. Sturm (1990) 'Ökologische Rationalität: Ansatzpunkte zur Ausgestaltung von ökologieorientierten Managementinstrumenten' ('Ecological Rationality: Points of Departure in Developing Environmentally Oriented Management Tools'), *Die Unternehmung* 4: 273-90.

—— (1992/1994/2000) *Ökologieorientierte Entscheidungen in Unternehmen. Ökologisches Rechnungswesen statt Ökobilanzierung: Notwendigkeit, Kriterien, Konzepte* (*Environmentally Oriented Decisions in Companies. Environmental Accounting instead of Ecobalancing: Necessity, Criteria, Concepts*) (Bern, Switzerland: Haupt, 1st/2nd/3rd edns; www.uni-lueneburg.de/csm).

—— (1995) *Öko-Effizienz durch Öko-Controlling* (*Eco-Efficiency through Eco-control*) (Stuttgart/Zürich: Schäffer-Poeschel).

—— (1996) 'Managerial Eco-Control in Manufacturing and Process Industries', *Greener Management International* 13 (January 1996): 78-91.

—— (1998) *Eco-efficiency through Eco-control* (Zürich: VDF).

Schaltegger, S., and T. Synnestvedt (2002) 'The Link Between "Green" and Economic Success: Environmental Management as the Crucial Trigger between Environmental and Economic Performance', *Journal of Environmental Management* 65.4: 339-46.

Schaltegger, S., K. Müller and H. Hindrichsen (1996) *Corporate Environmental Accounting* (Chichester, UK/New York/Tokyo: John Wiley).

Schaltegger, S.,T. Hahn and R. Burritt (2001a) *EMA: Links. Government, Management and Stakeholders:Improving Governments' Role in Promoting Environmental Management Accounting (EMA)*

(Workbook 2; Expert Working Group on Improving Government's Role in Environmental Management Accounting of the United Nations Division of Sustainable Development [UNDSD]; NewYork: UNDSD).

Schaltegger, S., T. Hahn and M. Wagner (2001b) *Umweltrechnungswesen und Umweltindikatoren: Studienband für den Bereich 'Betriebliches Umweltmanagement' (Betriebswirtschaftslehre) des Interdisziplinären Fernstudiums Umweltwissenschaften (infernum)* (*Environmental Accounting and Environmental Indicators: Course Book for Corporate Environmental Management for the Interdisciplinary Distance-Learning Programme Environmental Science [infernum]*) (Hagen, Germany: FernUniversität Hagen).

Schaltegger, S., R. Burritt and T. Hahn (2002) 'EMA-Links', in M. Bennett, J. Bouma and T. Wolters (eds.), *Environmental Management Accounting: Informational and Institutional Developments* (Dordrecht, Netherlands: Kluwer Academic Publishers): 21-35.

Schaper, M. (2003) 'The Essence of Ecopreneurship', *Greener Management International* 38 (Summer 2002): 26-30.

Schein, E.H. (1996) 'Three Cultures of Management: The Key to Organisational Learning', *Sloan Management Review*, Autumn 1996: 9-19.

Schelling, T. (1960) *The Strategy of Conflict* (Cambridge, MA: Harvard University Press).

Scherhorn, G. (1995) 'Der Zusatznutzen: Sinnbild des Mehrkonsums' ('The Additional Benefit: Interpretation of Additional Consumption'), in D. Steffen (ed.), *Welche Dinge braucht der Mensch? (What Things Does a Human Being Need?)* (Giessen, Germany: Anabas): 45-48.

Schmidheiny, S. (1992) *Kurswechsel* (Frankfurt: Artemis; published in English as *Changing Course: A Global Business Perspective on Development and the Environment* [Cambridge, MA: The MIT Press]).

Schmidheiny, S., and F. Zorraquín (1996) *Finanzierung des Kurswechsels: Die Finanzmärkte als Schrittmacher der Ökoeffizienz* (Munich: Best Business Books; published in English as *Financing Change: The Financial Community, Eco-efficiency, and Sustainable Development* [Cambridge, MA: The MIT Press]).

Schneidewind, U. (1995) 'Ökologisch orientierte Kooperationen aus betriebswirtschaftlicher Sicht' ('Ecologically Oriented Co-operations in a Business Administration Perspective'), *Umwelt-WirtschaftsForum*, December 1995: 16-21.

—— (1998) *Die Unternehmung als strukturpolitischer Akteur (The Corporation as a Structure-Political Actor)* (Marburg, Germany: Metropolis).

—— (2000) *Vorleistungsmärkte: Vom Supply Chain Management zum Substance Chain Management (Industrial Markets: From Supply-Chain Management to Substance-Chain Management)* (unpublished manuscript; Oldenburg, Germany: Carl von Ossietzky Universität Oldenbourg).

Schneidewind, U., and H. Petersen (1998) 'Changing the Rules: Business–NGO Partnerships and Structuration Theory', *Greener Management International* 24 (Winter 1998): 105-14.

—— (2000) 'Vorleistungsmärkte' ('Industrial Markets'), in S. Schaltegger and H. Petersen (eds.), *Marktorientiertes Umweltmanagement (Market-Oriented Environmental Management)* (Hagen, Germany: Fernstudienheft): 78-88.

Scholl, G., and A. Hinterding (1995) *Darstellung und Bewertung umwelt- und sozialbezogener Kennzeichen für Produkte und Dienstleistungen (Description and Assessment of Environmental and Social Labels for Products and Services)* (Heidelberg, Germany: Institut für Ökologische Wirtschaftsforschung Projektbericht, and IKEA-Stiftung).

Schulz, E., and W. Schulz (1993) *Umweltcontrolling in der Praxis: Ein Ratgeber für Betriebe (Environmental Control in Practice: A Guide for Enterprises)* (Munich: Vahlen).

Schulze, G. (1996) *Die Erlebnisgesellschaft: Kultursoziologie der Gegenwart (The Experience Society: Cultural Sociology at Present)* (Frankfurt/New York: Campus, 6th edn).

Seidel, E. (1988) 'Ökologisches Controlling' ('Eco-control'), in R. Wunderer (ed.), *Betriebswirtschaftslehre als Management- und Führungslehre (Business Administration as Management and Leadership Science)* (Stuttgart: Poeschel): 367-82.

—— (1995) 'Ökologisches Risikocontrolling' ('Environmental Risk Control'), in H. Schierenbeck and H. Moser (eds.), *Handbuch Bankcontrolling* (Wiesbaden, Germany: Gabler): 921-45.

—— (ed.) (1999) *Betriebliches Umweltmanagement im 21. Jahrhundert (Corporate Environmental Management in the 21st Century)* (Berlin/Heidelberg: Springer).

Seidel, E., J. Clausen and E. Seifert (eds.) (1998) *Umweltkennzahlen (Environmental Indicators)* (Munich: Franz Vahlen).

Selle, G. (1993) 'Produktkultur als Aneignungseregnis zwischen industrieller Matrix, sozialen Normen und individuellem Gebrauch' ('Product Culture as Owner Experience between Industrial Matrix, Social Norm and Individual Use'), in W. Ruppert (ed.), *Chiffren des Alltags* (*Ciphers of Daily Life*) (Marburg, Germany: Jonas Verlag): 23-48.

Senge, P. (1996) *Die Fünfte Disziplin: Kunst und Praxis der lernenden Organisation* (Stuttgart: Klett-Cotta, 3rd edn; published in English as *The Fifth Discipline: The Art and Practice of the Learning Organization* [New York: Doubleday]).

Senge, P., A. Kleiner, B. Smith, C. Roberts and R. Ross (1996) *Das Fieldbook zur Fünften Disziplin* (*The Fieldbook of the Fifth Discipline*) (Stuttgart: Schäffer-Poeschel).

Shapiro, B.P. (1985) 'Rejuvenating Marketing Mix', *Harvard Business Review* 63 (September/October 1985): 28-34.

Sheldon, C. (ed.) (1997) *ISO 14001 and Beyond: Environmental Management Systems in the Real World* (Sheffield, UK: Greenleaf Publishing).

Sietz, M. (ed.) (1996) *Umweltbetriebsprüfung und Öko-Auditing: Anwendungen und Praxisbeispiele* (*Environmental Review and Eco-audit: Application and Practice*) (Berlin: Springer, 2nd edn).

Simon, H. (1996) *Die heimlichen Gewinner: Die Erfolgsstrategien unbekannter Weltmarktführer* (*The Hidden Champions: The Success Strategies of Unknown World Market Leaders*) (Frankfurt/New York: Campus).

Simon, H.A. (1957) *Administrative Behaviour* (New York: Macmillan).

Skellenger, B. (1992) 'Limitation of Liability Clauses Gaining Popularity among Environmental Consultants', *Environline* 3 (Spring 1992): 4-5.

Skillius, Å., and U. Wennberg (1998) *Continuity, Credibility and Comparability: Key Challenges for Corporate Environmental Performance Measurement and Communication* (report prepared by the International Institute for Industrial Environmental Economics, Lund University; commissioned by the European Environment Agency: Brussels: European Environment Agency).

Smith, M. (1997) *Strategic Management Accounting. Issues and Cases* (Sydney: Butterworths, 2nd edn).

Sonntag, R. (1998) '. . . sei kein Frosch . . . in Future' ('. . . Don't Be a Frog . . . in Future'), *Das Hoechst Magazin* 2.98: 32-36.

Spicer, B. (1978) 'Investors, Corporate Social Performance and Informational Disclosure: An Empirical Study', *Accounting Review* 53: 94-111.

Spiecker, C. (1998) *Umweltschutzbezogenes Risikomanagement mit produktionsintegriertem Umweltschutzmassnahmen* (*Environmentally Related Risk Management with Integrated Environmental Protection Measures*) (Schriftenreihe des Lehrstuhls für Allgemeine Betriebswirtschaftslehre [ABWL], Produktionswirtschaft und Industriebetriebslehre, Universität Bremen, Bremen; Vol. 1, No. 1; Bremen, Germany: Lehrstuhl für Allgemeine Betriebswirtschaftslehre).

Spiller, A. (1996) *Ökologieorientierte Produktpolitik. Forschung, Medienberichte und Marktsignale: Theorie der Unternehmung. Band 3* (*Ecologically Oriented Product Policy: Research, Media Reports and Market Signals. Vol. III*) (Marburg, Germany: Metropolis).

—— (1999) *Umweltbezogenes Wissen der Verbraucher: Ergebnisse einer empirischen Studie und Schlussfolgerungen für das Marketing* (*Environmentally Related Knowledge of Consumers: Results of an Empirical Report and Conclusions for Marketing*) (Diskussionsbeiträge des Fachbereichs Wirtschaftswissenschaften der Gerhard-Mercator-Universität Duisburg; Duisburg, Germany: Universität Duisburg).

Spitzer, M. (1992) 'Calculating the Benefits of Pollution Prevention', *Pollution Engineering*, September 1992: 33-38.

Spitzer, M., R. Pojasek, F. Robertaccio and J. Nelson (1993) 'Accounting and Capital Budgeting for Pollution Prevention', paper presented at the Engineering Foundation Conference, San Diego, CA, January 1993.

Sprenger, R. (1995) *Das Prinzip Selbstverantwortung: Wege zur Motivation* (*The Principle of Self-Responsibility: Paths for Motivation*) (Frankfurt/New York: Campus).

Staehle, W. (1992) *Management: Eine verhaltenswissenschaftliche Perspektive* (*Management: A Behavioural Perspective*) (Munich: Vahlen, 6th edn).

Stafford, E.R., M.J. Polonsky and C.L. Hartman (1999) 'Environmental NGO–Business Collaboration and Strategic Bridging: A Case Analysis of the Greenpeace–Foron Alliance', *Business Strategy and the Environment* 9: 122-35.

Stahel, W.R. (1997) 'Umweltverträgliche Produktkonzepte' ('Environmentally Related Product Concepts'), *UmweltWirtschaftsForum*, December 1997: 4-10.

Staehlin-Witt, E. (1993), Bewertung von Umweltgütern' ('Assessment of Environmental Goods'), in R.L. Frey, E. Staehlin-Witt and H. Blöchliger (eds.), *Mit Ökonomie zur Ökologie (Using Economics for the Environment)* (Basel/Stuttgart: Helbing & Lichtenhahn).

Stahlmann, V., and J. Clausen (2000) *Umweltleistung von Unternehmen: Von der Öko-Effizienz zur Öko-Effektivität (Environmental Performance of Companies: From Eco-efficiency to Eco-efficacy)* (Wiesbaden, Germany: Gabler).

Steger, U. (1988) *Umweltmanagement (Environmental Management)* (Wiesbaden, Germany: Gabler).

Steger, U., and M. Winter (1996) 'Strategische Früherkennung zur Antizipation ökologisch motivierter Marktveränderungen' ('Strategic Early Warning for the Anticipation of Environmentally Motivated Market Changes'), *Die Betriebswirtschaft* 56.5: 607-29.

Steinmann, H., and G. Schreyögg (1997) *Management: Grundlagen der Unternehmensführung (Management: Fundamentals of Leading a Company)* (Wiesbaden, Germany: Gabler, 4th edn).

Stengel, M. (1998) 'Kooperation in virtueller Realität' ('Co-operation In Virtual Reality'), in E. Spiess (ed.), *Formen der Kooperation: Bedingungen und Perspektiven (Types of Co-operations: Requirements and Perspectives)* (Göttingen, Germany: University of Göttingen): 247-61.

Stone, E.J. (ed.) (2002) Special Issue: Enron, *Journal of Corporate Accounting and Finance*.

Streit, M.E. (1991) *Theorie der Wirtschaftspolitik (The Theory of Economic Public Policy)* (Düsseldorf: Werner, 4th edn).

Strobel, M. (2001) *Systematisches Flussmanagement (Systematic Flow Management)* (Augsburg, Germany: Institut für Management und Umwelt [IMU]).

Surma, J., and A. Vondra (1992) 'Accounting for Environmental Costs: A Hazardous Subject', *Journal of Accountancy*, March 1992: 51-55.

SustainAbility, Spold and Business in the Environment (eds.) (1992) *The LCA Sourcebook* (London: Spold/SustainAbility).

Sydow, J. (1993) *Strategische Netzwerke: Evolution und Organisation (Strategic Networks: Evolution and Organisation)* (Wiesbaden, Germany: Gabler).

Sydow, J., and B. van Well (1996) 'Wissensintensiv durch Netzwerkorganisation: Strukturationstheoretische Analysen eines wissensintensiven Netzwerkes' ('Intensive Information through Network Organisations: Structuration-Theory Analysis of a Information-Intensive Network'), in G. Schreyögg and P. Conrad (eds.), *Wissensmanagement (Information Management)* (Berlin/New York: De Gruyter): 191-234.

Temporal, P. (1999) *Branding in Asia: The Creation, Development and Management of Asian Brands for the Global Market* (Singapore: John Wiley, www.brandingasia.com/columns/temporal2.htm).

Tibor, T., and I. Feldman (1996) *ISO 14000: A Guide to the New Environmental Management Standards* (Chicago: Irwin Professional).

—— (1997) *Implementing ISO 14000: A Practical, Comprehensive Guide to the ISO 14000 Environmental Management Standards* (New York: McGraw–Hill).

Tietzel, M., and M. Weber (1991) 'Von Betrügern, Blendern und Opportunisten: Eine ökonomische Analyse' ('Of Swindlers, Phoneys and Opportunists: An Economic Analysis'), *Zeitschrift für Wirtschaftspolitik* 2.91: 109-37.

Tinker, T. (1985) *Paper Prophets: A Social Critique of Accounting* (London: Holt, Rinehart & Winston).

Tollison, R. (1982) 'Rent Seeking', *Kyklos* 35.4: 575-602.

Töpfer, K. (1993) 'Die Diskussion um die Ökobilanz wird nun erst richtig beginnen' ('The Discussion on Ecobalancing Will Start Right Now'), *Handelsblatt*, 28 September 1993: B1.

TransFair (1998) *Eine Idee hat Erfolg! Seit über fünf Jahren Produkte mit dem TransFair-Siegel im Ladenregal (An Idea Succeeds! Products with the TransFair Label Have Been on the Shelf for over Five Years)* (Cologne: TransFair, www.transfair.org).

Trommsdorff, V. (1998) *Konsumentenverhalten (Consumer Behaviour)* (Stuttgart: Kohlhammer, 3rd edn).

Tullock, G., R. Tollison and C. Rowley (eds.) (1988) *The Political Economy of Rent Seeking* (Boston, MA: Harvard University Press).

UBA (Umweltbundesamt) (1998) *EG-Umweltaudit in Deutschland: Erfahrungsbericht 1995 bis 1998* (*EC Environmental Audit in Germany: Report of Experiences 1995 to 1998*) (*EC Environmental Audit in Germany. A Report on the Experiences from 1995 to 1998*) (Berlin: UBA).

—— (1999) *EG-Umweltaudit in Deutschland: Erfahrungsbericht 1995 bis 1998* (Berlin: UBA).

Ulrich, H. (1968) 'Grundlagen der Unternehmenspolitik' ('Fundamentals of Corporate Policy'), *Die Unternehmung* 2.68: 77-86.

—— (1987) *Unternehmenspolitik* (*Corporate Policy*) (Bern/Stuttgart: Haupt, 2nd edn).

Ulrich, P. (1977) *Die Grossunternehmung als quasi-öffentliche Institution* (*Large Companies as Quasi-Public Institutions*) (Stuttgart: Poeschel).

UNCED (United Nations Conference on Environment and Development) (1992) *Agenda 21: Programme of Action for Sustainable Development*, Rio de Janeiro, Brazil, 3–14 June 1992.

UNEP (United Nations Environment Programme) (1995) 'Environmental Management Tools: Facts and Figures', *Industry and Environment* 18.2–3: 4-10.

UNEP (United Nations Environmental Programme) and SustainAbility (1996) *Engaging Stakeholders* (2 vols.; London: UNEP/SustainAbility).

Urbani, E., C. Rubin and M. Katzman (1994) *Transnational Environmental Law and its Impact on Corporate Behaviour* (Huntington, UK: Juris Publishing).

USDT (US Department of Transportation) (1996) *Public Involvement Techniques for Transportation Decision Making* (report prepared by Howard/Stein-Hudson Associates Inc., and Parsons Brinckerhoff Quade and Douglas, on behalf of the Federal Highway Administration and the Federal Transit Administration, www.fhwa.dot.gov/reports/pittd/cover. htm).

US EPA (US Environmental Protection Agency) (1995a) *TRI-Phase 3: Expansion of the EPA Community's Right-to-know Programme to Increase the Information Available to the Public on Chemical Use* (issues papers 2 and 3; Washington, DC: Office of Pollution Prevention and Toxics, US EPA).

—— (1995b) *Design for the Environment: EPA's Environmental Network for Managerial Accounting and Capital Budgeting* (Washington, DC: US EPA, March 1995).

—— (1995c) *Introduction to Environmental Accounting* (Washington, DC: US EPA).

—— (1995d) *Toxics Release Inventory: Public Data Release Report* (Washington, DC: Office of Pollution Prevention and Toxics, US EPA).

US FASB (US Financial Accounting Standards Board) (1994) *Accounting Standards: Current Text* (Norwalk, CT: US FASB).

US SEC (US Securities and Exchange Commission) (1993) *Staff Accounting Bulletin 92* (Washington, DC: US SEC).

van Dieren, W. (ed.) (1995) *Mit der Natur rechnen: Der neue Club-of-Rome-Bericht. Vom Bruttosozialprodukt zum Ökosozialprodukt* (*Calculating with Nature: The New Club of Rome Report. From Gross National Product to Eco-social Product*) (Basel: Birkhäuser).

Villiger, A., R. Wüstenhagen and A. Meyer (2000) *Jenseits der Öko-Nische* (*Beyond the Eco-niche*) (Basel: Birkhäuser).

Vinten, G. (1991) 'The Greening of Audit', *Internal Auditor*, October 1991: 30-36.

VNCI (Vereniging van de Nederlandse Chemische Industrie [Association of the Dutch Chemical Industry]) (ed.) (1991) *Integrated Substance Chain Management* (Leidschendam, Netherlands: VNCI).

Volkart, R. (1995) 'Shareholder Value Management: Kritische Überlegungen zur wertorientierten Führung' ('Shareholder Value Management: Critical Considerations on Value-Based Leadership'), *Der Schweizer Treuhänder* 12: 1,064-67.

von Hayek, F.A. (1986) *Recht, Gesetzgebung und Freiheit: Regeln und Ordnung* (*Law, Legislation and Freedom: Rules and Order*) (Landsberg am Lech, Germany: Verlag Moderne Industrie).

von Weizsäcker, E., A.B. Lovins and L.H. Lovins (1997) *Factor Four: Doubling Wealth, Halving Resource Use* (London: Earthscan Publications).

Wackernagel, M., and E. Rees (1996) *Our Ecological Footprint: Reducing Human Impact on the Earth* (Gabriola Island, BC: New Society Publishers).

Wagner, M., S. Schaltegger and W. Wehrmeyer (2002) 'The Relation between the Environmental and Economic Performance of Firms: What Does Theory Propose and What Does Empirical Evidence Tell Us?', *Greener Management International* 34 (Summer 2001): 95-108.

Walk, H. (1997) ' "Ein bisschen mehr schadet nie": Die Doppelstrategie von NGO-Netzwerken' ('A little more never does any harm: The Double Strategy of NGO Networks'), in E. Altvater, A. Brunnengräber, M. Haake and H. Walk (eds.), *Vernetzt und verstrickt: Nicht-Regierungsorganisationen als gesellschaftliche Produktivkraft* (*Linked and Enmeshed: Non-governmental Organisations as a Social Productivity Force*) (Münster, Germany: Westfälisches Dampfboot): 196-223.

Walleck, A., J.D. O'Halloran and C. Leader (1991) 'Benchmarking Worldclass Performance', *The McKinsey Quarterly* 1: 3-24.

Walter, W. (1996) 'Mehr Risiko!' ('More Risk!'), in R. Königswieser, M. Haller, P. Haas and H. Jarma (eds.), *Risiko-Dialog: Zukunft ohne Harmonieformel* (*Risk Dialogue: A Future Without a Formula for Harmony*) (Cologne: Deutscher Instituts-Verlag): 199-212.

Walton, M. (1986) *The Deming Management Method* (New York: Perigée).

Watson, G. (1993) *Strategic Benchmarking* (New York: John Wiley).

Watzlawick, P., J.H. Beavin and D.D. Jackson (1990) *Menschliche Kommunikation: Formen, Störungen, Paradoxien* (*Human Communication: Forms, Disturbances, Paradox*) (Bern: Haupt).

Ways, M. (1970) 'How to Think about the Environment', *Fortune*, February 1970: 98.

WBCSD (World Business Council for Sustainable Development) (1997a) *Exploring Sustainable Development: WBCSD Global Scenarios 2000–2050* (Geneva: WBCSD).

—— (1997b) *Environmental Performance and Shareholder Value* (Geneva: WBCSD).

—— (1999) *Eco-efficiency Indicators and Reporting: Report on the Status of the Project's Work in Progress and Guideline for Pilot Application* (Geneva: WBCSD, April 1999).

WCED (World Commission on Environment and Development) (1987) *Our Common Future* (The Brundtland Report; Oxford, UK: Oxford University Press).

Weber, M. (1980) *Wirtschaft und Gesellschaft: Grundriss der verstehenden Soziologie* (*Economy and Society: Fundamentals for Understanding Sociology*) (Tübingen, Germany: Mohr, 5th edn).

Westebbe, A., and D. Logan (1995) *Corporate Citizenship: Unternehmen im gesellschaftlichen Dialog* (*Corporate Citizenship: Business in an Organisational Dialogue*) (Wiesbaden, Germany: Gabler).

Whelan, E.M. (1993) *Toxic Terror: The Truth behind the Cancer Scares* (Buffalo, NY: Prometheus Books).

Wiener, N. (1948) *Cybernetics, or Control and Communication in the Animal and the Machine* (Cambridge, MA: The Technology Press; New York: John Wiley).

Williams, G., and T. Phillips (1994) 'Cleaning up Our Act: Accounting for Environmental Liabilities: Current Financial Reporting Doesn't Do the Job', *Management Accounting* 75: 30-33.

Williamson, E., and A. Boyle (2000) 'A New Structure for a New Millennium', *Management Services*, October 2000: 14-16.

Williamson, O.E. (1985) *The Economic Institution of Capitalism* (New York: The Free Press).

Wimmer, F. (1998) 'Environmental Aspects of Consumer Behaviour in Germany', in I. Balderjahn, C. Mennicken and E. Vernette (eds.), *New Developments and Approaches in Consumer Behaviour Research* (Stuttgart: Schäffer-Poeschel): 238-53.

Winter, G. (1998) *Das umweltbewusste Unternehmen* (*The Environmentally Conscious Company*) (Munich: Vahlen).

World Bank (2001) 'Business Partnerships', www.worldbank.org/business/03partnerships. html, accessed September 2001.

Wruk, H., and H. Ellringmann (eds.) (2002) *Praxishandbuch Umweltschutz-Management* (*A Practical Handbook for Environmental Management*) (Düsseldorf: Deutscher Verlag).

Wunderwald, J. (1979) 'Anmerkungen zum psychosozialen Aspekt des Konsums' ('Comments on the Psychological Aspect of Consumption'), in R. Brun (ed.), *Der neue Konsument. Der Abschied von der Verschwendung: Die Wiederentdeckung des täglichen Bedarfs* (*The New Consumer. Goodbye to Waste: The Rediscovery of Daily Needs*) (Frankfurt: Fischer): 47-52.

Wurche, S. (1994) *Strategische Kooperation: Theoretische Grundlagen und praktische Erfahrungen am Beispiel mittelständischer Pharmaunternehmen* (*Strategic Co-operations: Theoretical Foundations and Practical Experiences Using the Example of Small and Medium-sized Pharmaceutical Enterprises*) (Wiesbaden, Germany: Deutscher Universitäts-Verlag).

Würth, S. (1993) *Umwelt-Auditing: Die Revision im ökologischen Bereich als wirksames Überwachungsinstrument für die ökologiebewusste Unternehmung* (*Environmental Audit: The Revision in the Environmental Area as an Effective Tool to Control the Environmentally Conscious Company*) (Winterthur, Switzerland: Schellenberg).

Wüstenhagen, R. (1998) *Greening Goliaths versus Multiplying Davids: Pfade einer Coevolution ökologischer Massenmärkte und nachhaltiger Nischen* (*Greening Goliaths versus Multiplying Davids: Paths of a Co-evolution of Ecological Mass Markets and Sustainable Niches*) (DP-61, Institut für ökologische Wirtschaftsforschung; St Gallen, Switzerland: Universität St Gallen).

Zadek, S. (2000) *Doing Good and Doing Well: Making the Business Case for Corporate Citizenship* (New York: The Conference Board).

Zhang, M.H. (2001) 'Collaborative Partnerships on Forests', *UN Chronicle* 38.3: 49.

Zillessen, H. (1998) 'Mediation als kooperatives Konfliktmanagement' ('Mediation as Co-operative Management of Conflicts'), in H. Zillessen (ed.), *Mediation: Kooperatives Konfliktmanagement in der Umweltpolitik* (*Mediation: Co-operative Management of Conflicts in Environmental Public Policy*) (Opladen/Wiesbaden, Germany: Westdeutscher Verlag): 17-38

Abbreviations

AA	AccountAbility standard
AASB	Australian Accounting Standards Board
ABB	Asea Brown Boveri
ABC	activity-based costing
ACCA	Association of Chartered Certified Accountants
ACF	Australian Conservation Foundation
ACOFB	additional cost of future benefits
AEMRI	Association of European Market Research Institutes
ANZECC	Australia and New Zealand Environment and Conservation Council
AOX	adsorbable organic halogens
ASU	Arbeitsgemeinschaft Selbständiger Unternehmer (Germany)
B2B	business-to-business
BASD	Business Action for Sustainable Development
BAUM	Bundesdeutscher Arbeitskreis für umweltbewusstes Management (Germany)
BMU	Bundesumweltministerium (Germany)
BRBA	Buy Recycled Business Alliance
BS	British Standard
BSI	British Standards Institution
BUND	Bund für Umwelt und Naturschutz Deutschland
CEC	Commission of the European Communities
CEN	Comité Européen de Normalisation
CEP	Council on Economic Priorities
CEPAA	Accreditation Agency of the Council on Economic Priorities
CERCLA	Comprehensive Environmental Response, Compensation and Liability Act, 1980 (USA)
CERES	Coalition of Environmentally Responsible Economies
CFC	chlorofluorocarbon
CH_4	methane
CICA	Canadian Institute of Chartered Accountants
CO	carbon monoxide
CO_2	carbon dioxide
CoA	Commonwealth of Australia
COD	chemical oxygen demand

DASET	Department of the Arts, Sports, the Environment and Territories (Australia)
DDT	dichlorodiphenyltrichloroethane
DIN	Deutsche Industrie Norm
DTTI	Deloitte Touche Tohmatsu International
ECR	efficient consumer response
EDI	electronic data interchange
EDP	electronic data processing
EEA	external environmental accounting
EF!	Earth First!
EIRIS	Ethical Investment Research Service
EITF	Emerging Issues Task Force (FASB)
EMA	environmental management accounting
EMAS	Eco-management and Audit Scheme
EMS	environmental management system
ENDS	Environmental Data Services
EPA	Environmental Protection Agency (USA)
EPBC	Environment Protection and Biodiversity Conservation Act, 1999 (Australia)
EPE	environmental performance evaluation
EU	European Union
EUROSTAT	Statistical Office of the European Communities
FASB	Financial Accounting Standards Board (USA)
FEE	Fédération des Expertes Comptables Européens
FSC	Forest Stewardship Council
GAAP	Generally Accepted Accounting Principles (USA)
GCC	Global Climate Coalition
GEMI	Global Environmental Management Initiative
GM	genetically modified
GmbH	Gesellschaft mit beschränkter Haftung
GRI	Global Reporting Initiative
HCFC	hydrochlorofluorocarbon
HCl	hydrochloric acid
HF	hydrofluoric acid
IAS	International Accounting Standard
IASB	International Accounting Standards Board (formerly Committee)
IASC	International Accounting Standards Committee
IFAC	International Federation of Accountants
IFB	increased future benefits
ILO	International Labour Office
INEM	International Network for Environmental Management
ISAR	International Standards of Accounting and Reporting
ISO	International Organisation for Standardisation
JIT	just-in-time
LCA	life-cycle assessment
LPG	liquid petroleum gas
MCA	Minerals Council of Australia
MEEA	monetary external environmental accounting
MEMA	monetary environmental management accounting
MPI	management performance indicator
MSC	Marine Stewardship Council
MYOB	'mind your own business'
NABU	Naturschutzbund Deutschland
NCM	Nordic Council of Ministers
NGO	non-governmental organisation
NH$_3$	ammonia

NH_4^+	ammonium ion
NIMBY	'not in my back yard'
NO_3^-	nitrate ion
NO_x	nitrogen oxides
NPI	National Pollutant Inventory (Australia)
NPV	net present value
NZZ	*Neue Zürcher Zeitung*
OECD	Organisation for Economic Co-operation and Development
OPI	operational performance indicator
PCEQ	President's Commission on Environmental Quality (USA)
PEEA	physical external environmental accounting
PEMA	physical environmental management accounting
PER	public environmental reporting
PEST	political, economic, sociocultural and technological
PM10	particulate matter less than 10 μm in diameter
PR	public relations
PVC	polyvinyl chloride
R&D	research and development
RCP	recycled content product
SA	Social Accountability
SA	Standards Australia
SAI	Social Accountability International
SEC	Securities and Exchange Commission (USA)
SGS-ICS	GS Société Générale de Surveillance SA
SME	small or medium-sized enterprise
SNZ	Standards New Zealand
SO_2	sulphur dioxide
SRI	socially responsible investment
SVFV	Schweizerische Vereinigung für Finanzanalyse und Vermögensverwaltung
SWOT	strengths–weaknesses–opportunities–threats
TQEM	total quality environmental management
TQM	total quality management
TRI	Toxics Release Inventory
UBA	Umweltbundesamt (Germany)
UN	United Nations
UNCED	United Nations Conference on Environment and Development
UNDSD	United Nations Division for Sustainable Development
UNEP	United Nations Environment Programme
UNI	Unternehmerinstitut eV (Germany)
USDT	US Department of Transportation
VAT	value added tax
VNCI	Vereniging van de Nederlandse Chemische Industrie
VOC	volatile organic compound
WBCSD	World Business Council for Sustainable Development
WCED	World Commission on Environment and Development
WEF	World Economic Forum
WSSD	World Summit on Sustainable Development
WTO	World Trade Organisation
WWF	formerly the World Wildlife Fund and the World Wide Fund for Nature

Index